ISBN 978-1-332-31311-2
PIBN 10312676

For support please visit www.forgottenbooks.com

English
Français
Deutsche
Italiano
Español
Português

www.forgottenbooks.com

Mythology Photography **Fiction**
Fishing Christianity **Art** Cooking
Essays Buddhism Freemasonry
Medicine **Biology** Music **Ancient
Egypt** Evolution Carpentry Physics
Dance Geology **Mathematics** Fitness
Shakespeare **Folklore** Yoga Marketing
Confidence Immortality Biographies
Poetry **Psychology** Witchcraft
Electronics Chemistry History **Law**
Accounting **Philosophy** Anthropology
Alchemy Drama Quantum Mechanics
Atheism Sexual Health **Ancient History**
Entrepreneurship Languages Sport
Paleontology Needlework Islam
Metaphysics Investment Archaeology
Parenting Statistics Criminology
Motivational

THE
VICTORY AT SEA

BY REAR-ADMIRAL WILLIAM SOWDEN SIMS
U.S. NAVY

COMMANDER OF THE AMERICAN NAVAL FORCES OPERATING
IN EUROPEAN WATERS DURING THE GREAT WAR

IN COLLABORATION WITH
BURTON J. HENDRICK

WITH PORTRAIT AND PLANS

LONDON
JOHN MURRAY, ALBEMARLE STREET, W.
1920

Admiral William Sowden Sims
U.S. Navy

THE
VICTORY AT SEA

BY REAR-ADMIRAL WILLIAM SOWDEN SIMS
U.S. NAVY
COMMANDER OF THE AMERICAN NAVAL FORCES OPERATING
IN EUROPEAN WATERS DURING THE GREAT WAR

IN COLLABORATION WITH
BURTON J. HENDRICK

WITH PORTRAIT AND PLANS

LONDON
JOHN MURRAY, ALBEMARLE STREET, W.
1920

FIRST EDITION . . . *November* 1920
Reprinted . . . . *December* 1920

Printed by Hazell, Watson & Viney, Ld., London and Aylesbury, England.

TO

THE GALLANT OFFICERS AND MEN

WHOM I HAD THE HONOUR TO COMMAND

DURING THE GREAT WAR

IN

GRATEFUL RECOGNITION OF

A LOYAL DEVOTION TO THE CAUSE

THAT GREATLY LIGHTENED THE

RESPONSIBILITY

BORNE BY

" THE OLD MAN "

PREFACE

THIS is not in any sense a history of the operations of our naval forces in Europe during the Great War, much less a history of the naval operations as a whole. That would require not only many volumes, but prolonged and careful research by competent historians. When such a work is completed, our people will realize for the first time the admirable initiative with which the gallant personnel of our navy responded to the requirements of an unprecedented naval situation.

But in the meantime this story has been written in response to a demand for some account of the very generally misunderstood submarine campaign and, particularly, of the means by which it was defeated. The interest of the public in such a story is due to the fact that during the war the sea forces were compelled to take all possible precautions to keep the enemy from learning anything about the various devices and means used to oppose or destroy the underwater craft. This necessity for the utmost secrecy was owing to the peculiar nature of the sea warfare. When the armies first made use of airplane bombs, or poison gas, or tanks, or mobile railroad batteries, the existence of these weapons and the manner of their use were necessarily at once revealed to the enemy, and the press was permitted to publish full accounts of them and, to a certain extent, of their effect and the means used to oppose them. Moreover, all general movements of the contending armies that resulted in engagements were known with fair accuracy on both sides within a short time after they occurred and were promptly reported to an anxious public.

vessels, such as the battles of Jutland and of the Falkland Islands, the naval war was, for the most part, a succession of contests between single vessels or small groups of vessels. The enemy submarines sought to win the war by sinking the merchant shipping upon which depended the essential supplies of the allied populations and armies; and it was the effort of the Allies to prevent this, and to destroy submarines when possible, that constituted the vitally important naval activities of the war. By means of strategical and tactical dispositions, and various weapons and devices, now no longer secret, such as the depth charge, the mystery ship, hydrophones, mine-fields, explosive mine nets, special hunting submarines, and so forth, it was frequently possible either to destroy submarines with their entire crews, or to capture the few men who escaped when their boats were sunk, and thus keep from the German Admiralty all knowledge of the means by which their U-boats had met their fate. Thus the mystery ships, or decoy ships, as the Germans called them, destroyed a number of submarines before the enemy knew that such dangerous vessels existed. And even after they had acquired this knowledge, the mystery ships used various devices that enabled them to continue their successes until some unsuccessfully attacked submarine carried word of the new danger back to her home port.

Under such unprecedented conditions of warfare, it is apparent that the Allied navies could not safely tell the public just what they were doing or how they were doing it. All articles written for the press had to be carefully censored, and all of these interesting matters ruthlessly suppressed; but now that the ban has been removed, it is desirable to give the relatives and friends of the fine chaps who did the good work sufficient information to enable them to understand the difficulty of the problem that was presented to the anti-submarine forces of the Allies, the manner in which it was solved, and the various means invented and employed.

The subject is of course largely technical, but an effort has been made to present the story in such form that the layman can readily understand it. As it is difficult, if not quite impossible, for a naval officer to determine just which of the details that are a part of his daily life, and what incidents of sea experience would interest his civilian friends, the story has been written in collaboration with Mr. Burton J. Hendrick, to whom I am greatly indebted for invaluable assistance; and who, being an experienced hand at this writing business, deserves all the credit the reader may be disposed to accord him for both the form and such graces of descriptive style as he may be able to detect.

While opinions may differ to a certain extent as to the influence exerted upon the campaign by the various forms of tactics, the means and weapons employed, and the general strategy adopted, I have given what I believe to be a consensus of the best informed opinion upon these matters; and I have taken advantage of all of the information now available to insure accuracy in the account of the conditions that confronted the European naval forces, and in the description of the various operations that have been selected as typical examples of this very extraordinary warfare.

It is probably unnecessary to add that this book is published with the full approval of the Navy Department. My correspondence on this subject with the Secretary will be found in the Appendix.

W. S. S.

CONTENTS

CONTENTS

THE VICTORY AT SEA

CHAPTER I

WHEN GERMANY WAS WINNING THE WAR

I

In the latter part of March, 1917, a message from the Navy Department came to me at Newport, where I was stationed as president of the Naval War College, summoning me immediately to Washington. The international atmosphere at that time was extremely tense, and the form in which these instructions were cast showed that something extraordinary was impending. The orders directed me to make my visit as unostentatious as possible; to keep all my movements secret, and, on my arrival in Washington, not to appear at the Navy Department, but to telephone headquarters. I promptly complied with these orders; and, after I got in touch with the navy chiefs, it took but a few moments to explain the situation. It seemed inevitable, I was informed, that the United States would soon be at war with Germany. Ambassador Page had cabled that it would be desirable, under the existing circumstances, that the American navy be represented by an officer of higher rank than any of those who were stationed in London at that time. The Department therefore wished me to leave immediately for England, to get in touch with the British Admiralty, to study the naval situation and learn how we could best and most quickly co-operate in the naval war. At this moment we were still technically at peace with Germany. Mr. Daniels, the Secretary of the Navy, therefore thought it wise that there should be no publicity about my movements. I was to remain ostensibly as head of the War College,

2   1

and, in order that no suspicions should be aroused, my wife and family were still to occupy the official residence of its president.   I was directed to sail on a merchant vessel, to travel under an assumed name, to wear civilian clothes and to take no uniform.   On reaching the other side I was to get immediately in communication with the British Admiralty, and send to Washington detailed reports on prevailing conditions.

A few days after this interview in Washington two commonplace-looking gentlemen, dressed in civilian clothes, secretly boarded the American steamship *New York*.   They were entered upon the passenger list as V. J. Richardson and S. W. Davidson.   A day or two out an enterprising steward noticed that the initials on the pyjamas of one of these passengers differed from those of the name under which he was sailing and reported him to the captain as a suspicious character.   The captain had a quiet laugh over this discovery, for he knew that Mr. Davidson was Rear-Admiral Sims, of the United States Navy, and that his companion who possessed the two sets of conflicting initials was Commander J. V. Babcock, the Admiral's *aide*.   The voyage itself was an uneventful one, but a good deal of history was made in those few days that we spent upon the sea.   Our ship reached England on April 9th ; one week previously President Wilson had gone before Congress and asked for the declaration of a state of war with Germany.   We had a slight reminder that a war was under way as we neared Liverpool, for a mine struck our vessel as we approached the outer harbour.   The damage was not irreparable ;   the passengers were transferred to another steamer and we safely reached port, where I found a representative of the British Admiralty, Rear-Admiral Hope, waiting to receive me.   The Admiralty had also provided a special train, in which we left immediately for London.

Whenever I think of the naval situation as it existed in April, 1917, I always have before my mind two contrasting pictures—one that of the British public, as represented in their press and in their social gatherings in London, and the other that of British officialdom, as represented in my confidential meetings with British statesmen and British naval officers.   For the larger part the English newspapers were publishing optimistic statements about the German submarine campaign. In these they generally scouted the idea that this new form of piracy really threatened in any way the safety of the British Empire. They accompanied these rather cheerful outgivings by weekly statistics of submarine sinkings ; figures which, while not particularly reassuring, hardly indicated that any serious inroads had yet been made on the British mercantile marine. The Admiralty was publishing tables showing that four or five thousand ships were arriving at British ports and leaving them every week, while other tables disclosed the number of British ships of less than sixteen hundred tons and more than sixteen hundred tons that were going down every seven days. Thus the week of my arrival I learned from these figures that Great Britain had lost seventeen ships above that size, and two ships below ; that 2,406 vessels had arrived at British ports, that 2,367 had left, and that, in addition, seven fishing vessels had fallen victims to the German submarines. Such figures were worthless, for they did not include neutral ships and did not give the amount of tonnage sunk, details, of course, which it was necessary to keep from the enemy. The facts which the Government thus permitted to come to public knowledge did not indicate that the situation was particularly alarming. Indeed the newspapers all over the British Isles showed no signs of perturbation ; on the contrary, they were drawing favourable conclusions from these statistics. Here and there one of them may have sounded a more apprehensive note ; yet the generally prevailing feeling both in the press and in general discussions of the war seemed to be that the submarine campaign had already failed, that Germany's last desperate attempt to win the war had already broken down, and that peace would probably not be long delayed. The newspapers found considerable satisfaction in the fact that the " volume of British shipping was being maintained " ; they displayed such headlines as " improvement continues " ; they printed prominently the encouraging speeches of certain British statesmen, and in this way were apparently quieting popular apprehension concerning the outcome. This same atmosphere of cheerful ignorance I found everywhere in London society. The fear of German submarines was not disturbing the London season, which had now reached its height ; the theatres

the war from the beginning with the greatest inte
had read practically everything printed about i1
American and foreign press, and I had had access
official information as was available on our side
Atlantic. The result was that, when I sailed for]
in March, I felt little fear about the outcome.
fundamental facts in the case made it appear im
that the Germans could win the war. Sea powei
ently rested practically unchallenged in the hand
Allies ; and that in itself, according to the un
lessons of history, was an absolute assurance of \
victory. The statistics of shipping losses had bee
larly printed in the American press, and, whi
wanton destruction of life and property seemed ap
there was apparently nothing in these figures tl
likely to make any material change in the result.
it appeared to be altogether probable that the wa
end before the United States could exert any 1
influence upon the outcome. My conclusions were
by most American naval officers whom I knew, s
of warfare, who, like myself, had the utmost res
the British fleet and believed that it had the nava
tion well in hand.

Yet a few days spent in London clearly showed
this confidence in the defeat of the Germans rest
a misapprehension. The Germans, it now appear
not losing the war—they were winning it. The
Admiralty now placed before the American repres
facts and figures which it had not given to the
press. These documents disclosed the astound
that, unless the appalling destruction of merch;
nage which was then taking place could be m
checked, the unconditional surrender of the Britisl
would inevitably take place within a few months

On the day of my arrival in London I had
interview with Admiral Jellicoe, who was at that
First Sea Lord. Admiral Jellicoe and I needed 1
duction. I had known him for many years a1

considerable period we had been more or less regular correspondents. I had first made his acquaintance in China in 1901 ; at that time Jellicoe was a captain and was already recognized as one of the coming men of the British navy. He was an expert in ordnance and gunnery, a subject in which I was greatly interested ; and this fact had brought us together and made us friends. The admiration which I had then conceived for the Admiral's character and intelligence I have never lost. He was then, as he has been ever since, an indefatigable worker, and more than a worker, for he was a profound student of everything which pertained to ships and gunnery, and a man who joined to a splendid intellect the real ability of command. I had known him in his own home with his wife and babies, as well as on shipboard among his men, and had observed at close hand the gracious personality which had the power to draw everyone to him and make him the idol both of his own children and the officers and jackies of the British fleet. Simplicity and directness were his two most outstanding points ; though few men had risen so rapidly in the Royal Navy, success had made him only more quiet, soft spoken, and unostentatiously dignified ; there was nothing of the blustering seadog about the Admiral, but he was all courtesy, all brain, and, of all the men I have ever met, there have been none more approachable, more frank, and more open-minded.

Physically Admiral Jellicoe is a small man, but as powerful in frame as he is in mind, and there are few men in the navy who can match him in tennis. His smooth-shaven face, when I met him that morning in April, 1917, was, as usual, calm, smiling, and imperturbable. One could never divine his thoughts by any outward display of emotion. Neither did he give any signs that he was bearing a great burden, though it is not too much to say that at this moment the safety of the British Empire rested chiefly upon Admiral Jellicoe's shoulders. I find the absurd notion prevalent in this country that his change from Commander of the Grand Fleet to First Sea Lord was something in the nature of a demotion ; but nothing could be farther from the truth. As First Sea Lord, Jellicoe controlled the operations, not only of the Grand Fleet, but also of the entire British navy ; he had no superior officer, for the First Lord of the Admiralty, the position in England that corresponds to our Secretary of the Navy, has no power to give any order whatever to the fleet—a power which our Secretary possesses. Thus the defeat of the German submarines was a direct responsibility which Admiral Jellicoe could divide with no other official. Great as this duty was, and appalling as was the submarine situation at the time of this interview, there was nothing about the Admiral's bearing which betrayed any depression of spirits. He manifested great seriousness indeed, possibly some apprehension, but British stoicism and the usual British refusal to succumb to discouragement were qualities that were keeping him tenaciously at his job.

After the usual greetings, Admiral Jellicoe took a paper out of his drawer and handed it to me. It was a record of tonnage losses for the last few months. This showed that the total sinkings, British and neutral, had reached 536,000 tons in February and 603,000 in March; it further disclosed that sinkings were taking place in April which indicated the destruction of nearly 900,000 tons. These figures indicated that the losses were three and four times as large as those which were then being published in the press.[1]

It is expressing it mildly to say that I was surprised by this disclosure. I was fairly astounded; for I had never imagined anything so terrible. I expressed my consternation to Admiral Jellicoe.

" Yes," he said, as quietly as though he were discussing the weather and not the future of the British Empire. " It is impossible for us to go on with the war if losses like this continue."

" What are you doing about it ? " I asked.

" Everything that we can. We are increasing our anti-submarine forces in every possible way. We are using every possible craft we can find with which to fight submarines. We are building destroyers, trawlers, and other like craft as fast as we can. But the situation is very serious and we shall need all the assistance we can get."

[1] The statements published were not false, but they were inconclusive and intentionally so. They gave the number of British ships sunk, but not their tonnage, and not the total losses of British, Allied, and neutral tonnage.

" It looks as though the Germans were winning the war," I remarked.

" They will win, unless we can stop these losses—and stop them soon," the Admiral replied.

" Is there no solution for the problem ? " I asked.

" Absolutely none that we can see now," Jellicoe announced. He described the work of destroyers and other anti-submarine craft, but he showed no confidence that they would be able to control the depredations of the U-boats.

The newspapers for several months had been publishing stories that submarines in large numbers were being sunk ; and these stories I now found to be untrue. The Admiralty records showed that only fifty-four German submarines were positively known to have been sunk since the beginning of the war ; the German shipyards, I was now informed, were turning out new submarines at the rate of three a week. The newspapers had also published accounts of the voluntary surrender of German U-boats ; but not one such surrender, Admiral Jellicoe said, had ever taken place ; the stories had been circulated merely for the purpose of depreciating enemy *moral*. I even found that members of the Government, all of whom should have been better informed, and also British naval officers, believed that many captured German submarines had been carefully stowed away at the Portsmouth and Plymouth navy yards. Yet the disconcerting facts which faced the Allies were that the supplies and communications of the forces on all fronts were threatened ; that German submarines were constantly extending their operations farther and farther out into the Atlantic ; that German raiders were escaping into the open sea ; that three years' constant operations had seriously threatened the strength of the British navy, and that Great Britain's control of the sea was actually at stake. Nor did Admiral Jellicoe indulge in any false expectations concerning the future. Bad as the situation then was, he had every expectation that it would grow worse. The season which was now approaching would make easier the German operations, for the submarines would soon have the long daylight of the British summer and the more favourable weather. The next few months, indeed, both in the estimation of the Germans and the British, would witness the great crisis of the war; the basis of the ruthless campaign upon which the submarines had entered was that they could reach the decision before winter closed in. So far as I could learn there was a general belief in British naval circles that this plan would succeed. The losses were now approaching a million tons a month; it was thus a matter of very simple arithmetic to determine the length of time the Allies could stand such a strain. According to the authorities the limit of endurance would be reached about November 1, 1917; in other words, unless some method of successfully fighting submarines could be discovered almost immediately, Great Britain would have to lay down her arms before a victorious Germany.

"What we are facing is the defeat of Great Britain," said Ambassador Walter H. Page, after the situation had been explained to him.

In the next few weeks I had many interviews with Admiral Jellicoe and other members of the Admiralty. Sitting in conference with them every morning, I became, for all practical purposes, a member of their organization. There were no secrets of the British navy which were not disclosed to their new American ally. This policy was in accordance with the broad-minded attitude of the British Government; there was a general desire that the United States should understand the situation completely, and from the beginning matters were discussed with the utmost frankness. Everywhere was manifested a willingness to receive suggestions and to try any expedient that promised to be even remotely successful; yet the feeling prevailed that there was no quick and easy way to defeat the submarine, that anything even faintly resembling the much-sought "answer" had not yet appeared on the horizon. The prevailing impression that any new invention could control the submarine in time to be effective was deprecated. The American press was at that time constantly calling upon Edison and other great American inventors to solve this problem, and, in fact, inventors in every part of two hemispheres were turning out devices by the thousands. A regular department of the Admiralty which was headed by Admiral Fisher had charge of investigating their proposals; in a few months it had received and examined not far from 40,000 inventions, none of which answered the purpose, though many of them were exceedingly ingenious. British naval officers were not hostile to such projects ; they declared, however, that it would be absurd to depend upon new devices for defeating the German campaign. The overshadowing fact—a fact which I find that many naval men have not yet sufficiently grasped—is that time was the all-important element. It was necessary not only that a way be found of curbing the submarine, but of accomplishing this result at once. The salvation of the great cause in which we had engaged was a matter of only a few months. A mechanical device, or a new type of ship which might destroy this menace six months hence, would not have helped us, for by that time Germany would have won the war.

I discussed the situation also with members of the Cabinet, such as Mr. Balfour, Lord Robert Cecil, and Sir Edward Carson. Their attitude to me was very different from the attitude which they were taking publicly ; these men naturally would say nothing in the newspapers that would improve the enemy *moral*; but in explaining the situation to me they repeated practically everything that Jellicoe had said. It was the seriousness of this situation that soon afterward sent Mr. Balfour and the British Commission to the United States. The world does not yet understand what a dark moment that was in the history of the Allied cause. Not only were the German submarines sweeping British commerce from the seas, but the German armies were also defeating the British and French on the battlefields in France. It is only when we recall that the Germans were attaining the high peak of success with the U-boats at the very moment that General Nivelle's offensive had failed on the Western Front that we can get some idea of the real tragedy of the Allied situation in the spring of 1917.

" Things were dark when I took that trip to America," Mr. Balfour said to me afterward. " The submarines were constantly on my mind. I could think of nothing but the number of ships which they were sinking. At that time it certainly looked as though we were going to lose the war."

One of the men who most keenly realized the state of affairs was the King. I met His Majesty first in the vestibule of St. Paul's, on that memorable occasion in April, 1917, when the English people held a thanksgiving service to commemorate America's entrance into the war. Then, as at several subsequent meetings, the King impressed me as a simple, courteous, unaffected English gentleman. He was dressed in khaki, like any other English officer, and his manner was warm-hearted, sincere, and even democratic.

"It gives me great pleasure to meet you on an occasion like this," said His Majesty, referring to the great Anglo-American memorial service. "I am also glad to greet an American admiral on such a mission as yours. And I wish you all success."

On that occasion we naturally had little time to discuss the submarines, but a few days afterward I was invited to spend the night at Windsor Castle. The King in his own home proved to be even more cordial, if that were possible, than at our first meeting. After dinner we adjourned to a small room and there, over our cigars, we discussed the situation at considerable length. The King is a rapid and animated talker ; he was kept constantly informed on the submarine situation, and discussed it that night in all its details. I was at first surprised by his familiarity with all naval questions and the intimate touch which he was evidently maintaining with the British fleet. Yet this was not really surprising, for His Majesty himself is a sailor ; in his early youth he joined the navy, in which he worked up like any other British boy. He seemed almost as well informed about the American navy as about the British ; he displayed the utmost interest in our preparations on land and sea, and he was particularly solicitous that I, as the American representative, should have complete access to the Admiralty Office. About the submarine campaign, the King was just as outspoken as Jellicoe and the other members of the Admiralty. The thing must be stopped, or the Allies could never win the war.

Of all the influential men in British public life there was only one who at that time took an optimistic attitude. This was Mr. Lloyd George. I met the Prime Minister frequently at dinners, at his own country place and elsewhere, and the most lasting impression which I retain of this wonderful man was his irrepressible gaiety of spirits. I think of the Prime Minister of Great Britain as a great, big, exuberant boy, always laughing and joking, constantly indulging in repartee and by-play, and even in this crisis, perhaps the darkest one of British history, showing no signs of depression. His face, which was clear in its complexion as a girl's, never betrayed the slightest anxiety, and his eyes, which were always sparkling, never disclosed the faintest shadow. It was a picture which I shall never forget—that of this man, upon whose shoulders the destiny of the Empire chiefly rested, apparently refusing to admit, even to himself, the dangers that were seemingly overwhelming it, heroically devoting all his energies to uplifting the spirits of his countrymen, and, in his private intercourse with his associates, even in the most fateful moments, finding time to tell funny stories, to recall entertaining anecdotes of his own political career, to poke fun at the mistakes of his opponents, and to turn the general conversation a thousand miles away from the Western Front and the German submarines. It was the most inspiring instance of self-control that I have ever known; indeed only one other case in history can be compared with it; Lloyd George's attitude at this period constantly reminded me of Lincoln in the darkest hours of the Civil War, when, after receiving news of such calamities as Fredericksburg or Chancellorsville, he would entertain his cabinet by reading selections from Artemus Ward, interlarded with humorous sayings and anecdotes of his own. Perhaps Lloyd George's cheerfulness is explained by another trait which he likewise possessed in common with Lincoln; there is a Welsh mysticism in his nature which, I am told, sometimes takes the form of religious exaltation. Lloyd George's faith in God and in a divine ordering of history was evidently so profound that the idea of German victory probably never seized his mind as a reality; we all know that Lincoln's absolute confidence in the triumph of the North rested upon a similar basis. Certainly only some such deep-set conviction as this could explain Lloyd George's serenity and optimism in the face of the most frightful calamities. I attended a small dinner at which the Premier was present four days after the Germans had made their terrible attack in March, 1918. Even on this occasion he showed no evidences of strain; as usual his animated spirits held the upper hand; he was talking incessantly, but he never even mentioned the subject that was absorbing the thoughts of the rest of the world at that moment; instead he rattled along, touching upon the Irish question, discussing the impression which Irish conscription would make in America, and, now and then, pausing to pass some bantering remark to Mr. Balfour. This was the way that I always saw the head of the British Government; never did I meet him when he was fagged or discouraged, or when he saw any end to the war but a favourable one.

On several occasions I attempted to impress Mr. Lloyd George with the gravity of the situation; he always refused to acknowledge that it was grave.

" Oh, yes, things are bad," he would say with a smile and a sweep of his hand. " But we shall get the best of the submarines—never fear ! "

The cheerfulness of the Prime Minister, however, was exceptional; all his associates hardly concealed their apprehension. On the other hand, a wave of enthusiasm was at that time sweeping over Germany. Americans still have an idea that the German Government adopted the submarine campaign as the last despairing gambler's chance, and that they only half believed in its success themselves. There is an impression here that the Germans never would have staked their Empire on this desperate final throw had they foreseen that the United States would have mobilized against them all its men and resources. This conviction is entirely wrong. The Germans did not think that they were taking any chances when they announced their unrestricted campaign; the ultimate result seemed to them to be a certainty. They calculated the available shipping which the Allies and the neutral nations had afloat; they knew just how many ships their submarines could sink every month, and from these statistics they mathematically deduced, with real German precision, the moment when the war would end. They did not like the idea of adding the United States to their enemies, but this was because they were thinking of conditions after the war; for they would have preferred to have had American friendship in the period of readjustment. But they did not fear that we could do them much injury in the course of the war itself. This again was not because they really despised our fighting power; they knew that we would prove a formidable enemy on the battlefield ; but the obvious fact, to their eyes, was that our armies could never get to the front in time. The submarine campaign, they said, would finish the thing in three or four months ; and certainly in that period the unprepared United States could never summon any military power that could affect the result. Thus from a purely military standpoint the entrance of 100,000,000 Americans affected them about as much as would a declaration of war from the planet Mars.

We confirmed this point of view from the commanders of the occasionally captured submarines. These men would be brought to London and questioned ; they showed the utmost confidence in the result.

" Yes, you've got *us*," they would say, " but what difference does that make ? There are plenty more submarines coming out. You will get a few, but we can build a dozen for every one that you can capture or sink. Anyway, the war will all be over in two or three months and we shall be sent back home."

All these captives laughed at the merest suggestion of German defeat ; their attitude was not that of prisoners, but of conquerors. They also regarded themselves as heroes, and they gloried in the achievements of their submarine service. For the most part they exaggerated the sinkings and estimated that the war would end about the first of July or August. Similarly the Berlin Government exaggerated the extent of their success. This was not surprising, for one peculiarity of the submarine is that only the commander, stationed at the periscope, knows what is going on. He can report sinking a 5,000 ton ship and no one can contradict his statement, for the crew and the other officers do not see the surface of the water. Not unnaturally the commander does not depreciate his own achievements, and thus the amount of sunken tonnage reported in Berlin considerably exceeded the actual losses.

The speeches of German dignitaries resounded with the same confidence.

" In the impending decisive battle," said the Kaiser, " the task falls upon my navy of turning the English war method of starvation, with which our most hated and most obstinate enemy intends to overthrow the German people, against him and his allies by combating their sea traffic with all the means in our power. In this work the submarine will stand in the first rank. I expect that this weapon, technically developed with wise forethought at our admirable yards, in co-operation with all our other naval fighting weapons and supported by the spirit which, during the whole course of the war, has enabled us to perform brilliant deeds, will break our enemy's war will."

"In this life and death struggle by hunger," said Dr. Karl Helfferich, Imperial Secretary of the Interior, "England believed herself to be far beyond the reach of any anxiety about food. A year ago it was supposed that England would be able to use the acres of the whole world, bidding with them against the German acres. To-day England sees herself in a situation unparalleled in her history. Her acres across sea disappear as a result of the blockade which our submarines are daily making more effective around England. We have considered, we have dared. Certain of the result, we shall not allow it to be taken from us by anybody or anything."

These statements now read almost like ancient history, yet they were made in February, 1917. At that time, Americans and Englishmen read them with a smile ; they seemed to be the kind of German rodomontade with which the war had made us so familiar ; they seemed to be empty mouthings put out to bolster up the drooping German spirit. That the Kaiser and his advisers could really believe such rubbish was generally regarded as absurd. Yet not only did they believe what they were saying but, as already explained, they also had every reason for believing it. The Kaiser and his associates had figured that the war would end about July 1st or August 1st ; and English officials with whom I came in contact placed the date at November 1st—always provided, of course, that no method were found for checking the submarine.[1]

II

How, then, could we defeat the submarine ? Before approaching this subject, it is well to understand precisely what was taking place in the spring and summer of 1917 in

[1] See Appendices II and III for my cable and letter to the Navy Department, explaining the submarine situation in detail.

those waters surrounding the British Isles.   What was this strange new type of warfare that was bringing the Allied cause to its knees ?   Nothing like it had ever been known in recorded time ; nothing like it had been foreseen when, on August 4, 1914, the British Government threw all its resources and all its people against the great enemy of mankind.

Leaving entirely out of consideration international law and humanity, it must be admitted that strategically the German submarine campaign was well conceived.   Its purpose was to marshal on the German side that force which has always proved to be the determining one in great international conflicts—sea power.   The advantages which the control of the sea gives the nation which possesses it are apparent.   In the first place, it makes secure such a nation's communications with the outside world and its own allies, and, at the same time, it cuts the communications of its enemy.   It enables the nation dominant at sea to levy upon the resources of the entire world ; to obtain food for its civilian population, raw materials for its manufactures, munitions for its armies ; and, at the same time, to maintain that commerce upon which its very economic life may depend.   It enables such a power also to transport troops into any field of action where they may be required.   At the very time that sea power is heaping all these blessings upon the dominant nation, it enables such a nation to deny these same advantages to its enemy.   For the second great resource of sea power is the blockade.   If the enemy is agriculturally and industrially dependent upon the outside world, sea power can transform it into a beleaguered fortress and sooner or later compel its unconditional surrender.   Its operations are not spectacular, but they work with the inevitable remorselessness of death itself.

This fact is so familiar that I insist upon it here only for the purpose of inviting attention to another fact which is not so apparent.   Perhaps the greatest commonplace of the war, from the newspaper standpoint, was that the British fleet controlled the seas.   This mere circumstance, as I have already said, was the reason why all students of history were firm in their belief that Britain could never be defeated.   It was not until the spring of 1917 that we really awoke to the actual situation ; it was not until I had spent several days in England that I made the all-important discovery, which was this—that Britain did *not* control the seas. She still controlled the seas in the old Nelsonian sense; that is, her Grand Fleet successfully "contained" the German battle squadrons and kept them, for the greater part of the war, penned up in their German harbours. In the old days such a display of sea power would have easily won the war for the Allies. But that is not control of the seas in the modern sense; it is merely control of the *surface* of the seas. Under modern methods of naval warfare sea control means far more than controlling the top of the water. For there is another type of ship, which sails stealthily under the waves, revealing its presence only at certain intervals, and capable of shooting a terrible weapon which can sink the proudest surface ship in a few minutes. The existence of this new type of warship makes control of the seas to-day a very different thing from what it was in Nelson's time. As long as such a warship can operate under the water almost at will—and this was the case in a considerable area of the ocean in the early part of 1917—it is ridiculous to say that any navy controls the seas. For this subsurface vessel, when used as successfully as it was used by the Germans in 1917, deprives the surface navy of that advantage which has proved most decisive in other wars. That is, the surface navy can no longer completely protect communications as it could protect them in Nelson's and Farragut's times. It no longer guarantees a belligerent its food, its munitions, its raw materials of manufacture and commerce, or the free movement of its troops. It is obviously absurd to say that a belligerent which was losing 800,000 or 900,000 tons of shipping a month, as was the case with the Allies in the spring of 1917, was the undisputed mistress of the seas. Had the German submarine campaign continued to succeed at this rate, the United States could not have transported its army to France, and the food and materials which we were sending to Europe, and which were essential to winning the war, could never have crossed the ocean.

That is to say, complete control of the subsurface by Germany would have turned against England the blockade, the very power with which she had planned to reduce the German Empire. Instead of isolating Germany from the rest of the world, she would herself be isolated.

In due course I shall attempt to show the immediate connexion that exists between control of the surface and control of the subsurface ; this narrative will disclose, indeed, that the nation which possesses the first also potentially possesses the second. In the early spring of 1917, however, this principle was not effective, so far as merchant shipping was concerned.

Germany's purpose in adopting the ruthless submarine warfare was, of course, the one which I have indicated : to deprive the Allied armies in the field, and their civilian populations, of these supplies from overseas which were essential to victory. Nature had been kind to this German programme when she created the British Isles. Indeed this tight little kingdom and the waters which surround it provided an ideal field for operations of this character. For purposes of contrast, let us consider our own geographical situation. A glance at the map discloses that it would be almost impossible to blockade the United States with submarines. In the first place, the operation of submarines more than three thousand miles from their bases would present almost insuperable difficulties. That Germany could send an occasional submarine to our coasts she demonstrated in the war, but it would be hardly possible to maintain anything like a regular and persistent campaign. Even if she could have kept a force constantly engaged in our waters, other natural difficulties would have defeated their most determined efforts. The trade routes approach our Atlantic sea-coast in the shape of a fan, of which different sticks point to such ports as Boston, New York, Philadelphia, Norfolk, and the ports of the Gulf of Mexico. To destroy shipping to American ports it would be necessary for the enemy to cover all these routes with submarines, a project which is so vast that it is hardly worth the trial. In addition we have numerous Pacific ports to which we could divert shipping in case our enemy should attempt to blockade us on the Atlantic coast ; our splendid system of transcontinental railroads would make internal distribution not a particularly difficult matter. Above all such considerations, of course, is the fact that the United States is an industrial and agricultural entity, self-supporting and self-feeding, and, therefore, it could not be starved into surrender even though the enemy should surmount these practically insuperable

3

obstacles to a submarine blockade. But the situation of
the British Isles is entirely different. They obtain from
overseas the larger part of their food and a considerable
part of their raw materials, and in April of 1917, according
to reliable statements made at that time, England had
enough food on hand for only six weeks or two months.
The trade routes over which these supplies came made the
submarine blockade a comparatively simple matter. Instead of the sticks of a fan, the comparison which I have
suggested with our own coast, we now have to deal with the
neck of a bottle. The trade routes to our Atlantic coast
spread out, as they approach our ports ; on the other hand,
the trade routes to Great Britain converge almost to a
point. The far-flung steamship lanes which bring Britain
her food and raw materials from half a dozen continents
focus in the Irish Sea and the English Channel. To cut
the communications of Great Britain, therefore, the submarines do not have to patrol two or three thousand miles
of sea-coast, as would be necessary in the case of the
United States ; they merely need to hover around the
extremely restricted waters west and south of Ireland.

This was precisely the area which the Germans had
selected for their main field of activity. It was here that
their so-called U-boats were operating with the most deadly
effect ; these waters constituted their happy hunting
grounds, for here came the great cargo ships, with food and
supplies from America, which were bound for Liverpool and
the great Channel ports. The submarines that did destruction in this region were the type that have gained universal
fame as the U-boats. There were other types, which I
shall describe, but the U-boats were the main reliance of the
German navy ; they were fairly large vessels, of about 800
tons, and carried from eight to twelve torpedoes and enough
fuel and supplies to keep the sea for three or four weeks.
And here let me correct one universal misapprehension.
These U-boats did not have bases off the Irish and Spanish
coasts, as most people still believe. Such bases would have
been of no particular use to them. The cruising period of a
submarine did not depend, as is the prevailing impression,
upon its supply of fuel oil and food, for almost any under-
water boat was able to carry enough of these essential
materials for a practically indefinite period ; the average
U-boat, moreover, could easily make the voyage across the

Atlantic and back. The cruising period depended upon its supply of torpedoes. A submarine returned to its base only after it had exhausted its supply of these destructive missiles; if it should shoot them all in twenty-four hours, then a single day would end that particular cruise; if the torpedoes lasted a month, then the submarine stayed out for that length of time. For these reasons bases on the Irish coast would have been useful only in case they could replenish the torpedoes, and this was obviously an impossibility. No, there was not the slightest mystery concerning the bases of the U-boats. When the Germans captured the city of Bruges in Belgium they transformed it into a headquarters for submarines; here many of the U-boats were assembled, and here facilities were provided for docking, repairing, and supplying them. Bruges was thus one of the main headquarters for the destructive campaign which was waged against British commerce. Bruges itself is an inland town, but from it two canals extend, one to Ostend and the other to Zeebrugge, and in this way the interior submarine base formed the apex of a triangle. It was by way of these canals that the U-boats reached the open sea.

Once in the English Channel, the submarines had their choice of two routes to the hunting grounds off the west and south of Ireland. A large number made the apparently unnecessarily long detour across the North Sea and around Scotland, going through the Fair Island Passage, between the Orkney and the Shetland islands, along the Hebrides, where they sometimes made a landfall, and so around the west coast of Ireland. This looks like a long and difficult trip, yet the time was not entirely wasted, for the U-boats, as the map of sinkings shows, usually destroyed several vessels on the way to their favourite hunting grounds. But there was another and shorter route to this area available to the U-boats. And here I must correct another widely prevailing misapprehension. While the war was going on many accounts were published in the newspapers describing the barrage across the English Channel, from Dover to Calais, and the belief was general that this barrier kept the U-boats from passing through. Unfortunately this was not the case. The surface boats did succeed in transporting almost at will troops and supplies across this narrow passage-way; but the mines, nets, and other obstructions that were intended to prevent the passage of submarines were not particularly effective. The British navy knew little about mines in 1914 ; British naval men had always rather despised them as the "weapons of the weaker power," and it is therefore not surprising that the so-called mine barrage at the Channel crossing was not successful. A large part of it was carried away by the strong tide and storms, and the mines were so defective that oysters and other sea growths, which attached themselves to their prongs, made many of them harmless. In 1918, Admiral Sir Roger Keyes reconstructed this barrage with a new type of mine and transformed it into a really effective barrier ; but in the spring of 1917, the German U-boats had little difficulty in slipping through, particularly in the night time. And from this point the distance to the trade routes south and west of Ireland was relatively a short one.

Yet, terribly destructive as these U-boats were, the number which were operating simultaneously in this and in other fields was never very large. The extent to which the waters were infested with German submarines was another particularly ludicrous and particularly prevalent misapprehension. Merchant vessels constantly reported that they had been assailed by " submarines in shoals," and most civilians still believe that they sailed together in flotillas, like schools of fish. There is hardly an American doughboy who did not see at least a dozen submarines on his way across the Atlantic ; every streak of suds which was caused by a " tide rip," and every swimming porpoise, was immediately mistaken for the wake of a torpedo ; and every bit of driftwood, in the fervid imagination of trans-Atlantic voyagers, immediately assumed the shape of a periscope. Yet it is a fact that we knew almost every time a German submarine slunk from its base into the ocean. The Allied secret service was immeasurably superior to that of the Germans, and in saying this I pay particular tribute to the British Naval Intelligence Department. We always knew how many submarines the Germans had and we could usually tell pretty definitely their locations at a particular time ; we also had accurate information about building operations in Germany ; thus we could estimate how many they were building and where they were building them, and we could also describe their essential characteristics, and the stage of progress they which had reached at almost any day.

It was not the simplest thing to pilot a submarine out of
its base.   The Allies were constantly laying mines at these
outlets ; and before the U-boat could safely make its exit
elaborate sweeping operations were necessary.   It often
took a squadron of nine or ten surface ships, working for
several hours, to manœuvre a submarine out of its base and
to start it on its journey.   For these reasons we could keep
a careful watch upon its movements ; we always knew
when one of our enemies came out ; we knew which one it
was, and not infrequently we had learned the name of the
commander and other valuable details.   Moreover, we
knew where it went, and we kept charts on which we plotted
from day to day the voyage of each particular submarine.

" Why didn't you sink it then ? " is the question usually
asked when I make this statement—a question which, as I
shall show, merely reflects the ignorance which prevails
everywhere on the underlying facts of submarine warfare.

Now in this densely packed shipping area, which extended from the north of Ireland to Brest, there were
seldom more than eight or ten submarines engaged in their
peculiar form of warfare at one time.   The largest number
which I had any record of was fifteen ; and this was an
exceptional force ; the usual number was four, six, eight, or
perhaps ten.   Yet the men upon our merchant convoys and
troopships saw submarines scattered all over the sea.   We
estimated that the convoys and troopships reported that
they had sighted about 300 submarines for every submarine
which was actually in the field.   Yet we knew that for
every hundred submarines which the Germans possessed
they could keep only ten or a dozen at work in the open sea.
The rest were on their way to the hunting grounds, or
returning, or they were in port being refitted and taking on
supplies.   Could Germany have kept fifty submarines constantly at work on the great shipping routes in the winter
and spring of 1917—before we had learned how to handle
the situation—nothing could have prevented her from
winning the war.   Instead of sinking 850,000 tons in a
single month, she would have sunk 2,000,000 or 3,000,000
tons.   The fact is that Germany, with all her microscopic
preparations for war, neglected to provide herself with the
one instrumentality with which she might have won it.

This circumstance, that so few submarines could accomplish such destructive results, shows how formidable was

the problem which confronted us. Germany could do this, of course, because the restricted field in which she was able to operate was so constantly and so densely infested with valuable shipping.

In the above I have been describing the operations of the U-boats in the great area to the west and south of Ireland. But there were other hunting fields, particularly that which lay on the east coast of England, in the area extending from Harwich to Newcastle. This part of the North Sea was constantly filled with ships passing between the North Sea ports of England and Norway and Sweden, carrying essential products like lumber and many manufactured articles. Every four days a convoy of from forty to sixty ships left some port in this region for Scandinavia ; I use the word " convoy," but the operation was a convoy only in the sense that the ships sailed in groups, for the navy was not able to provide them with an adequate escort—seldom furnishing them more than one or two destroyers, or a few yachts or trawlers. Smaller types of submarines which were known as UB's and UC's and which issued from Wilhelmshaven and the Skager Rack constantly preyed upon this coastal shipping. These submarines differed from the U-boats in that they were smaller, displacing about 350 and 400 tons, and in that they also carried mines, which they were constantly laying. They were much handier than the larger types ; they could rush out much more quickly from their bases and get back, and they did an immense amount of damage to this coastal trade. The value of the shipping sunk in these waters was unimportant when compared with the losses which Great Britain was suffering on the great trans-Atlantic routes, but the problem was still a serious one, because the supplies which these ships brought from the Scandinavian countries were essential to the military operations in France.

Besides these two types, the U-boats and the UB's and UC's, the Germans had another type of submarine, the great ocean cruisers. These ships were as long as a small surface cruiser and were half again as long as a destroyer, and their displacement sometimes reached 3,000 tons. They carried crews of seventy men, could cross the Atlantic three or four times without putting into port, and some actually remained away from their bases for three or four months. But they were vessels very difficult to manage ;

it took them a relatively long time to submerge, and, for this reason, they could not operate around the Channel and other places where the anti-submarine craft were most numerous. In fact, these vessels, of which the Germans had in commission perhaps half a dozen when the armistice was signed, accomplished little in the war. The purpose for which they were built was chiefly a strategic one. One or two were usually stationed off the Azores, not in any expectation that they would destroy much shipping—the fact is that they sank very few merchantmen—but in the hope that they might divert anti-submarine craft from the main theatre of operations. In this purpose, however, they were not successful ; in fact, I cannot see that these great cruisers accomplished anything that justified the expense and the trouble which were involved in building them.

III

This, then, was the type of warfare which the German submarines were waging upon the shipping of the Allied nations. What were the Allied navies doing to check them in this terrible month of April, 1917 ? What anti-submarine methods had been developed up to that time ?

The most popular game on both sides of the Atlantic was devising means of checking the under-water ship. Every newspaper, every magazine, every public man, and every gentleman at his club had a favourite scheme for defeating the U-boat campaign. All that any one needed for this engaging pastime was a map of the North Sea, and the solution appeared to be as clear as daylight. As Sir Eric Geddes once remarked to me, nothing is quite so deceptive as geography. All of us are too likely to base our conception of naval problems on the maps which we studied at school. On these maps the North Sea is such a little place ! A young lady once declared in my hearing that she didn't see how the submarines could operate in the English Channel, it was so narrow ! She didn't see how there was room enough to turn around ! The fact that it is twenty miles wide at the shortest crossing and not far from two hundred at the widest is something which it is apparently difficult to grasp.

The plan which was most popular in those days was to pen the submarines in their bases and so prevent their egress into the North Sea. Obviously the best way to handle the situation was to sink the whole German submarine fleet ; that was apparently impossible, and the next best thing was to keep them in their home ports and prevent them from sailing the high seas. It was not only the man in the street who was advocating this programme. I had a long talk with several prominent Government officials, in which they asked me why this could not be done.

" I can give you fourteen reasons why it is impossible," I answered. " We shall first have to capture the bases, and it would be simply suicidal to attempt it, and it would be playing directly into Germany's hands. Those bases are protected by powerful 15-, 11-, and 8-inch guns. These are secreted behind hills or located in pits on the seashore, where no approaching vessel can see them. Moreover, those guns have a range of 40,000 yards, but the guns on no ships have a range of more than 30,000 yards ; they are stationary, whereas ours would be moving. For our ships to go up against such emplacements would be like putting a blind prize-fighter up against an antagonist who can see and who has arms twice as long as his enemy's. We can send as many ships as we wish on such an expedition, and they will all be destroyed. The German guns would probably get them on the first salvo, certainly on the second. There is nothing the Germans would so much like to have us try."

Another idea suggested by a glance at the map was the construction of a barrage across the North Sea from the Orkneys to the coast of Norway. The distance did not seem so very great—on the map ; in reality, it was two hundred and thirty miles and the water is from 360 to 960 feet in depth. If we cannot pen the rats up in their holes, said the newspaper strategist, certainly we can do the next best thing : we can pen them up in the North Sea. Then we can route all our shipping to points on the west coast of England, and the problem is solved.

I discussed this proposition with British navy men and their answer was quite to the point.

" If we haven't mines enough to build a successful barrage across the Straits of Dover, which is only twenty miles wide, how can we construct a barrage across the North Sea, which is 230 ? "

A year afterward, as will be shown later, this plan came

up in more practical form, but in 1917 the idea was not among the possibilities—there were not mines enough in the world to build such a barrage, nor had a mine then been invented that was suitable for the purpose.

The belief prevailed in the United States, and, to a certain extent, in England itself, that the most effective means of meeting the submarine was to place guns and gun crews on all the mercantile vessels. Even some of the old British merchant salts maintained this view. " Give us a gun, and we'll take care of the submarines all right," they kept saying to the Admiralty. But the idea was fundamentally fallacious. In the American Congress, just prior to the declaration of war, the arming of merchant ships became a great political issue ; scores of pages in the *Congressional Record* are filled with debates on this subject, yet, so far as affording any protection to shipping was concerned, all this was wasted oratory. Those who advocated arming the merchant ships as an effective method of counteracting submarine campaigns had simply failed to grasp the fundamental elements of submarine warfare. They apparently did not understand the all-important fact that the quality which makes the submarine so difficult to deal with is its invisibility. The great political issue which was involved in the submarine controversy, and the issue which brought the United States into the war, was that the Germans were sinking merchant ships without warning. And it was because of this very fact—this sinking without warning—that a dozen guns on a merchant ship afforded practically no protection. The look-out on a merchantman could not see the submarine, for the all-sufficient reason that the submarine was concealed beneath the water ; it was only by a happy chance that the most penetrating eye could detect the periscope, provided that one were exposed. The first intimation which was given the merchantman that a U-boat was in his neighbourhood was the explosion of the torpedo in his hull. In six weeks, in the spring and early summer of 1917, thirty armed merchantmen were torpedoed and sunk off Queenstown, and in no case was a periscope or a conning-tower seen. The English never trusted their battleships at sea without destroyer escort, and certainly if a battleship with its powerful armament could not protect itself from submarines, it was too much to expect that an ordinary armed merchantman would be able to do so. I think the fact that few American armed ships were attacked and sunk in 1917 created the impression that their guns afforded them some protection. But the apparent immunity extended to them was really policy on Germany's part. She expected, as I have said, that she would win the war long before the United States could play an effective rôle in the struggle. It was therefore good international politics to refrain from any unnecessary acts that would still further embitter the American people against her. There was also a considerable pacifist element in our country which Germany was coddling in the hope of preventing the United States from using against her such forces as we already had at hand. The reason American armed merchantmen were not sunk was simply because they were not seriously attacked; I have already shown how easily Germany could have sunk them if she had really tried. Any reliance upon armed guards as a protection against submarines would have been fundamentally a mistake, for the additional reason that it was a defensive measure; it must be apparent that the extremely grave situation which we were then facing demanded the most energetic offensive methods. Yet the arming of merchant ships was justified as a minor measure. It accomplished the one important end of forcing the submarine to submerge and to use torpedoes instead of gunfire. In itself this was a great gain; obviously the Germans would much prefer to sink ships with projectiles than with torpedoes, for their supply of these latter missiles was limited.[1]

In April, 1917, the British navy was fighting the submarine mainly in two ways: it was constantly sowing mines off the entrance to the submarine bases, such as Ostend and Zeebrugge, and in the Heligoland Bight—operations that accomplished little, for the Germans swept them up almost as fast as they were planted; and it was patrolling the submarine infested area with anti-submarine craft. The Admiralty was depending almost exclusively upon this patrol, yet this, the only means which then seemed to hold forth much promise of defeating the submarine, was making little progress.

[1] See Appendix IV for my statement to Washington on arming merchant ships.

For this patrol the navy was impressing into service all the destroyers, yachts, trawlers, sea-going tugs, and other light vessels which could possibly be assembled; almost any craft which could carry a wireless, a gun, and depth charges was boldly sent to sea. At this time the vessel chiefly used was the destroyer. The naval war had demonstrated that the submarine could not successfully battle with the destroyer; that any U-boat which came to the surface within fighting range of this alert and speedy little surface ship ran great risk of being sunk. This is the fundamental fact—that the destruction of the submarine was highly probable, in case the destroyer could get a fair chance at her—which regulated the whole anti-submarine campaign. It is evident, therefore, that a proper German strategy would consist in so disposing its submarines that they could conduct their operations with the minimum risk of meeting their most effective enemies, while a properly conceived Allied strategy would consist in so controlling the situation that the submarines would have constantly to meet them. Frankness compels me to say that, in the early part of 1917, the Germans were maintaining the upper hand in this strategic game; they were holding the dominating position in the campaign, since they were constantly attacking Allied shipping without having to meet the Allied destroyers, while the Allied destroyers were dispersing their energies over the wide waste of waters. But the facts in the situation, and not any superior skill on the part of the German navy, were giving the submarines this advantage. The British were most heroically struggling against the difficulties imposed by the mighty task which they had assumed. The British navy, like all other navies, was only partially prepared for this type of warfare; in 1917 it did not possess destroyers enough both to guard the main fighting fleet and to protect its commerce from submarines. Up to 1914, indeed, it was expected that the destroyers would have only one function to perform in warfare, that of protecting the great surface vessels from attack, but now the new kind of warfare which Germany was waging on merchant ships had laid upon the destroyer an entirely new responsibility; and the plain fact is that the destroyers, in the number which were required, did not exist. The problem which proved so embarrassing can be stated in the simple terms of arithmetic. Everything, as I have said, reduced itself to the question of destroyers. In April, 1917, the British navy had in commission about 200 ships of this indispensable type ; many of them were old and others had been pretty badly worn and weakened by three years of particularly racking service. It was the problem of the Admiralty to place these destroyers in those fields in which they could most successfully serve the Allied cause. The one requirement that necessarily took precedence over all others was that a flotilla of at least 100 destroyers must be continuously kept with the Grand Fleet, ready to go into action at a moment's notice. It is clear from this statement of the case that the naval policy of the Germans, which consisted in holding their high seas battle fleet in harbour and in refusing to fight the Allied navy, had an important bearing upon the submarine campaign. So long as there was the possibility of such an engagement, the British Grand Fleet had to keep itself constantly prepared for such a crisis ; and an indispensable part of this préparation was to maintain always in readiness its flotilla of protecting destroyers. Had the German fleet seriously engaged in a great sea battle, it would have unquestionably been defeated ; such a defeat would have meant an even greater disaster than the loss of the battleships, a loss which in itself would not greatly have changed the naval situation. But the really fatal effect of such a defeat would have been that it would no longer have been necessary for the British to sequestrate a hundred or more destroyers at Scapa Flow. The German battleships would have been sent to the bottom, and then these destroyers would have been used in the warfare against the submarines. By keeping its dreadnought fleet intact, always refusing to give battle and yet always threatening an engagement, the Germans thus were penning up 100 British destroyers in the Orkneys—destroyers which otherwise might have done most destructive work against the German submarines off the coast of Ireland. The mere fact that the German High Seas Fleet had once engaged the British Grand Fleet off Jutland was an element in the submarine situation, for this constantly suggested the likelihood that the attempt might be repeated, and was thus an influence which tended to keep these destroyers at Scapa Flow. Many times during that critical period the Admiralty discussed the question of releasing those destroyers, or a part of them, for the anti-submarine campaign; yet they always decided, and they decided wisely, against any such hazardous division. At that time the German dreadnought fleet was not immeasurably inferior in numbers to the British; it had a protecting screen of about 100 destroyers; and it would have been madness for the British to have gone into battle with its own destroyer screen placed several hundred miles away, off the coast of Ireland. I lay stress upon this circumstance because I find that in America the British Admiralty has been criticized for keeping a large destroyer force with the Grand Fleet, instead of detaching them for battle with the submarine. I think that I have made clear that this criticism is based upon a misconception of the whole naval campaign. Without this destroyer screen the British Grand Fleet might have been destroyed by the Germans; if the Grand Fleet had been destroyed, the war would have ended in the defeat of the Allies; not to have maintained these destroyers in northern waters would thus have amounted simply to betraying the cause of civilization and to making Germany a free gift of victory.

Germany likewise practically immobilized a considerable number of British destroyers by attacking hospital ships. When the news of such dastardly attacks became known, it was impossible for Americans and Englishmen to believe at first that they were intentional; they so callously violated all the rules of warfare and all the agreements for lessening the horrors of war to which Germany herself had become a party that there was a tendency in both enlightened countries to give the enemy the benefit of the doubt. As a matter of fact, not only were the submarine attacks on hospital ships deliberate, but Germany had officially informed us that they would be made! The reasons for this warning are clear enough; again, the all-important rôle which the destroyers were playing in anti-submarine warfare was the point at issue. Until we received such warning, hospital ships had put to sea unescorted by warships, depending for their safety upon the rules of the Hague Conference. Germany attacked these ships in order to make us escort them with destroyers, and thereby compel us to divert these destroyers from the anti-submarine campaign. And, of course, England was forced to acquiesce in this German programme. Had the Anglo-Saxon mind resembled the Germanie in all probability we should have accepted the logic of the situation; we should have refused to be diverted from the great strategic purpose which meant winning the war —that is, protecting merchant shipping; in other words, we should have left the hospital ships to their fate, and justified ourselves and stilled our consciences by the principle of the greater good. But the British and the American minds do not operate that way; it was impossible for us to leave sick and wounded men as prey to submarines. Therefore, after receiving the German warning, backed up, as it was, by the actual destruction of unprotected hospital ships, we began providing them with destroyer escorts. This greatly embarrassed us in the anti-submarine campaign, for at times, especially during the big drives, we had a large number of hospital ships to protect. As soon as we adopted this policy, Germany, having attained her end, which was to keep the destroyers out of the submarine area, stopped attacking sick and wounded soldiers. Yet we still were forced to provide these unfortunates with destroyer escorts, for, had we momentarily withdrawn these protectors, the German submarines would immediately have renewed their attacks on hospital ships.

Not only was the British navy at that time safeguarding the liberties of mankind at sea, but its army in France was doing its share in safeguarding them on land. And the fact that Britain had to support this mighty army had its part in making British shipping at times almost an easy prey for the German submarines. For next in importance to maintaining the British Grand Fleet intact it was necessary to keep secure the channel crossing. Over this little strip of water were transported the men and the supplies from England to France that kept the German army at bay; to have suspended these communications, even for a brief period, would have meant that the Germans would have captured Paris, overrun the whole of France, and ended the war, at least the war on land. In the course of four years Great Britain transported about 20,000,000 people across the Channel without the loss of a single soul. She accomplished this only by constantly using many destroyers and other light surface craft as escorts for the transports. But this was not the only responsibility of the kind that rested on the overburdened British shoulders. There was another part of the seas in which, for practical and political reasons, the British destroyer fleet had to do protective duty. In the Mediterranean lay not only the trade routes to the East, but also the lines of supply which extended to Italy, to Egypt, to Palestine, and to Mesopotamia. If Germany could have cut off Italy's food and materials Italy would have been forced to withdraw from the war. The German and Austrian submarines, escaping from Austria's Adriatic ports, were constantly assailing this commerce, attempting to do this very thing. Moreover, the success of the German submarine campaign in these waters would have compelled the Allies to abandon the Salonika expedition, which would have left the Central Powers absolute masters of the Balkans and the Middle East. For these reasons it was necessary to maintain a considerable force of destroyers in the Mediterranean.

For the British navy it was therefore a matter of choice what areas she would attempt to protect with her destroyer forces ; the one thing that was painfully apparent was that she could not satisfactorily safeguard all the danger zones. With the inadequate force at her disposal it was inevitable that certain areas should be left relatively open to the U-boats ; and the decision as to which ones these should be was simply a matter of balancing the several conflicting interests. In April, 1917, the Admiralty had decided to give the preference to the Grand Fleet, the hospital ships, the Channel crossing, and the Mediterranean, practically in the order mentioned. It is evident from these facts that nearly the entire destroyer fleet must have been disposed in these areas. This decision, all things considered, was the only one that was possible ; yet, after placing the destroyers in these selected areas, the great zone of trans-Atlantic shipping, west and south of Ireland, vitally important as it was, was necessarily left inadequately protected. So desperate was the situation that sometimes only four or five British destroyers were operating in this great stretch of waters ; and I do not think that the number ever exceeded fifteen. Inasmuch as that represented about the number of German submarines in this same area, the situation may strike the layman as not particularly desperate. But any such basis of comparison is absurd. The destroyers were operating on the surface in full view of the submarines ; the submarines could submerge at any time and make themselves invisible ; and herein we have the reason why the contest was so markedly unequal. But aside from all other considerations, the method of warfare adopted by the Allies against the U-boat was necessarily ineffective, but was the best that could be used until sufficient destroyers became available to convoy shipping. The so-called submarine patrol, under the circumstances which prevailed at that time, could accomplish very little. This little fleet of destroyers was based on Queenstown ; from this port they put forth and patrolled the English Channel and the waters about Ireland in the hope that a German submarine would stick its nose above the waves. The central idea of the destroyer patrol was this one of hunting ; the destroyer could have sunk any submarine or driven it away from shipping if the submarine would only have made its presence known. But of course this was precisely what the submarine declined to do. It must be evident to the merest novice that four or five destroyers, rushing around hunting for submarines which were lying a hundred feet or so under water, could accomplish very little. The under-water boat could always see its surface enemy long before it was itself seen and thus could save its life by the simple process of submerging. It must also be clear that the destroyer patrol could accomplish much only in case there were a very large number of destroyers. We figured that, to make the patrol system work with complete success, it would be necessary to have one destroyer for every square mile. The area of the destroyer patrol off Queenstown comprised about 25,000 square miles ; it is apparent that the complete protection of the trans-Atlantic trade routes would have taken about 25,000 destroyers. And the British, as I have said, had available anywhere from four to fifteen in this area.

The destroyer flotilla being so small, it is not surprising that the German submarines were making ducks and drakes of it. The map of the sinkings which took place in April brings out an interesting fact : numerous as these sinkings were, very few merchantmen were torpedoed, in this month, at the entrance to the Irish Sea or in the English Channel..

These were the narrow waters where shipping was massed and where the little destroyer patrol was intended to operate. The German submarines apparently avoided these waters, and made their attacks out in the open sea, sometimes two and three hundred miles west, and south of Ireland. Their purpose in doing this was to draw the destroyer patrol out into the open sea and in that way to cause its dispersal. And these tactics were succeeding. There were six separate steamship " lanes " by which the merchantmen could approach the English Channel and the Irish Sea. One day the submarines would attack along one of these lanes ; then the little destroyer fleet would rush to this scene of operations. Immediately the Germans would depart and attack another route many miles away ; then the destroyers would go pell-mell for that location. Just as they arrived, however, the U-boats would begin operating elsewhere ; and so it went on, a game of hide and seek in which the advantages lay all on the side of the warships which possessed that wonderful ability to make themselves unseen. At this period the submarine campaign and the anti-submarine campaign was really a case of blindman's buff ; the destroyer could never see the enemy while the enemy could always see the destroyer ; and this is the reason that the Allies were failing and that the Germans were succeeding.

IV

To show how serious the situation was, let me quote from the reports which I sent to Washington during this period. I find statements like these scattered everywhere in my despatches of the spring of 1917 :

" The military situation presented by the enemy submarine campaign is not only serious but critical."

" The outstanding fact which cannot be escaped is that we are not succeeding, or in other words, that the enemy's campaign is proving successful."

" The consequences of failure or partial failure of the Allied cause which we have joined are of such far-reaching character that I am deeply concerned in insuring that the part played by our country shall stand every test of analysis before the bar of history. The situation at present is exceedingly grave. If sufficient United States naval

4

forces can be thrown into the balance at the present critical time and place there is little doubt that early success will be assured."

" Briefly stated, I consider that at the present moment we are losing the war." [1]

And now came another important question : What should the American naval policy be in this crisis ? There were almost as many conflicting opinions as there were minds. Certain authorities believed that our whole North Atlantic Fleet should be moved immediately into European waters. Such a manœuvre was not only impossible but it would have been strategically very unwise ; indeed such a disposition would have been playing directly into Germany's hands. What naval experts call the " logistics " of the situation immediately ruled this idea out of consideration. The one fact which made it impossible to base the fleet in European waters at that time was that we could not have kept it supplied, particularly with oil. The German U-boats were making a particularly successful drive at tankers with the result that England had the utmost difficulty in supplying her fleet with this kind of fuel. It is indeed impossible to exaggerate the seriousness of this oil situation. " Orders have just been given to use three-fifths speed, except in case of emergency," I reported to Washington on June 29th, referring to scarcity of oil. " This simply means that the enemy is winning the war." It was lucky for us that the Germans knew nothing about this particular disability. Had they been aware of it, they would have resorted to all kinds of manœuvres in the attempt to keep the Grand Fleet constantly steaming at sea, and in this way they might so have exhausted our oil supply as possibly to threaten the actual command of the surface. Fortunately for the cause of civilization, there were certain important facts which the German Secret Service did not learn.

But this oil scarcity made it impossible to move the Atlantic Fleet into European waters, at least at that time. Since most oil supplies were brought from America, we simply could not have fuelled our super-dreadnoughts in Europe in the spring and summer of 1917. Moreover, if

[1] For specimens of my reports to the Navy Department in these early days see Appendices II and III.

we had sent all our big ships to England we should have been obliged to keep our destroyers constantly stationed with them ready for a great sea action ; and this would have completely fallen in with German plans, for then these destroyers could not have been used against her submarines. The British did indeed request that we send five coal-burning ships to reinforce her fleet and give her that preponderance which made its ascendancy absolutely secure, and these ships were subsequently sent ; but England could not have made provision for our greatest dreadnoughts, the oil burners. Indeed our big ships were of much greater service to the Allied cause stationed on this side than they would have been if they had been located at a European base. They were providing a reserve for the British fleet, precisely as our armies in France were providing a reserve for the Allied armies ; and meanwhile this disposition made it possible for us to send their destroyer escorts to the submarine zone, where they could participate in the anti-submarine campaign. In American waters these big ships could be kept in prime condition, for here they had an open, free sea for training, and here they could also be used to train the thousands of new men who were needed for the new ships constructed during the war.

I early took the stand that our forces should be considered chiefly in the light of reinforcements to the Allied navies, and that, ignoring all question of national pride and even what at first might superficially seem to be national interest, we should exert such offensive power as we possessed in the way that would best assist the Allies in defeating the submarine. England's naval resources were much greater than ours ; and therefore, in the nature of the case, we could not expect to maintain overseas anywhere near the number of ships which England had assembled ; consequently it should be our policy to use such available units as we possessed to strengthen the weak spots in the Allied line. There were those who believed that national dignity required that we should build up an independent navy in European waters, and that we should operate it as a distinct American unit. But that, I maintained, was not the way to win the war. If we had adopted this course, we should have been constructing naval bases and perfecting an organization when the armistice was signed ; indeed, the idea of operating independently of the Allied fleet was not for a moment to be considered.   There were others in America who thought that it was unwise to put any part of our fleet in European waters, in view of the dangers that might assail us on our own coast.   There was every expectation that Germany would send submarines to the western Atlantic, where they could prey upon our shipping and could possibly bombard our ports ; I have already shown that she had submarines which could make such a long voyage, and the strategy of the situation in April and May, 1917, demanded that a move of this kind be made.   The predominant element in the submarine defence, as I have pointed out, was the destroyer.   The only way in which the United States could immediately and effectively help the Allied navies was by sending our whole destroyer flotilla and all our light surface craft at once.   It was Germany's part, therefore, to resort to every manœuvre that would keep our destroyer force on this side of the Atlantic.   Such a performance might be expected to startle our peaceful American population and inspire a public demand for protection ; and in this way our Government might be compelled to keep all anti-submarine craft in our own waters.   I expected Germany to make such a demonstration immediately and I therefore cautioned our naval authorities at Washington not to be deceived.   I pointed out that Germany could accomplish practically nothing by sporadic attacks on American shipping in American waters ; that, indeed, if we could induce the German Admiralty to concentrate all its submarine efforts on the American coasts, and leave free the Irish Sea and the English Channel, the war practically would be won for the Allies.   Yet these facts were not apparent to the popular mind in 1917, and I shall always think that Germany made a great mistake in not sending submarines to the American coast immediately on our declaration of war, instead of waiting until 1918.   Such attacks, at that time, would have started a public demand for protection which the Washington authorities might have had great difficulty in resisting, and which might have actually kept our destroyer fleet in American waters, to the great detriment of the Allied cause.   Germany evidently refrained from doing so for reasons which I have already indicated—a desire to deal gently with the United States, and in that way to delay our military preparations and win the war without coming into bloody conflict with the American people.

There were others who thought it unwise to expose any part of our fleet to the dangers of the European contest; their fear was that, if the Allies should be defeated, we would then need all our naval forces to protect the American coast. This point of view, of course, was not only short-sighted and absurd, but it violated the fundamental principle of warfare, which is that a belligerent must assail his enemy as quickly as possible with the greatest striking power which he can assemble. Clearly our national policy demanded that we should exert all the force we could collect to make certain a German defeat. The best way to fight Germany was not to wait until she had vanquished the Allies, but to join hands with them in a combined effort to annihilate her military power on land and sea. The situation which confronted us in April, 1917, was one which demanded an immediate and powerful offensive; the best way to protect America was to destroy Germany's naval power in European waters and thus make certain that she could not attack us at home.

The fact is that few nations have ever been placed in so tragical a position as that in which Great Britain found herself in the spring and early summer of 1917. And I think that history records few spectacles more heroic than that of the great British navy, fighting this hideous and cowardly form of warfare in half a dozen places with pitifully inadequate forces, but with an undaunted spirit which remained firm even against the fearful odds which I have described. What an opportunity for America! And it was perfectly apparent what we should do. It was our duty immediately to place all our available antisubmarine craft in those waters west and south of Ireland in which lay the pathways of the shipping which meant life or death to the Allied cause—the area which England, because almost endless demands were being made upon her navy in other fields, was unable to protect.

The first four days in London were spent collecting all possible data; I had no desire to alarm Washington unwarrantably, yet I also believed that it would be a serious dereliction if all the facts were not presented precisely as they were. I consulted practically everyone who could give me essential details and wrote a cable despatch, filling four foolscap pages, which furnished Washington with its first detailed account of the serious state of the cause on which we had embarked.[1]

In this work I had the full co-operation of our Ambassador in London, Mr. Walter Hines Page. Mr. Page's whole heart and mind were bound up in the Allied cause ; he was zealous that his country should play worthily its part in this great crisis in history ; and he worked unsparingly with me to get the facts before our Government. A few days after sending a despatch it occurred to me that a message from our Ambassador might give emphasis to my own. I therefore wrote such a message and took it down to Brighton, where the American Ambassador was taking a little rest. I did not know just how strong a statement Mr. Page would care to become responsible for, and so I did not make this statement quite as emphatic as the circumstances justified.

Mr. Page took the paper and read it carefully. Then he looked up.

" It isn't strong enough," he said. " I think I can do better than this myself."

He sat down and wrote the following cablegram which was immediately sent to the President :

From : Ambassador Page.
To : Secretary of State.
Sent : 27 April 1917.
Very confidential for Secretary and President.

There is reason for the greatest alarm about the issue of the war caused by the increasing success of the German submarines. I have it from official sources that during the week ending 22nd April, 88 ships of 237,000 tons allied and neutral were lost. The number of vessels unsuccessfully attacked indicated a great increase in the number of submarines in action.

This means practically a million tons lost every month till the shorter days of autumn come. By that time the sea will be about clear of shipping. Most of the ships are sunk to the westward and southward of Ireland. The British have in that area every available anti-submarine

[1] See Appendix II.

craft, but their force is so insufficient that they hardly discourage the submarines.

The British transport of troops and supplies is already strained to the utmost, and the maintenance of the armies in the field is threatened. There is food enough here to last the civil population only not more than six weeks or two months.

Whatever help the United States may render at any time in the future, or in any theatre of the war, our help is now more seriously needed in this submarine area for the sake of all the Allies than it can ever be needed again, or anywhere else.

After talking over this critical situation with the Prime Minister and other members of the Government, I cannot refrain from most strongly recommending the immediate sending over of every destroyer and all other craft that can be of anti-submarine use. This seems to me the sharpest crisis of the war, and the most dangerous situation for the Allies that has arisen or could arise.

If enough submarines can be destroyed in the next two or three months the war will be won, and if we can contribute effective help immediately it will be won directly by our aid. I cannot exaggerate the pressing and increasing danger of this situation. Thirty or more destroyers and other similar craft sent by us immediately would very likely be decisive.

There is no time to be lost.   PAGE.

But Mr. Page and I thought that we had not completely done our duty even after sending these urgent messages. Whatever might happen, we were determined that it could never be charged that we had not presented the Allied situation in its absolutely true light. It seemed likely that an authoritative statement from the British Government would give added assurance that our statements were not the result of panic, and with this idea in mind, Mr. Page and I called upon Mr. Balfour, Foreign Secretary, who, in response to our request, sent a despatch to Washington describing the seriousness of the situation.

All these messages made the same point : that the United States should immediately assemble all its destroyers and other light craft, and send them to the port where they could render the greatest service in the anti-submarine campaign—Queenstown.

CHAPTER II

I

THE morning of May 4, 1917, witnessed an important event in the history of Queenstown. The news had been printed in no British or American paper, yet in some mysterious way it had reached nearly everybody in the city. A squadron of American destroyers, which had left Boston on the evening of April 24th, had already been reported to the westward of Ireland and was due to reach Queenstown that morning. At almost the appointed hour a little smudge of smoke appeared in the distance, visible to the crowds assembled on the hills ; then presently another black spot appeared, and then another ; and finally these flecks upon the horizon assumed the form of six rapidly approaching warships. The Stars and Stripes were broken out on public buildings, on private houses, and on nearly all the water craft in the harbour ; the populace, armed with American flags, began to gather on the shore ; and the local dignitaries donned their official robes to welcome the new friends from overseas. One of the greatest days in Anglo-American history had dawned, for the first contingent of the American navy was about to arrive in British waters and join hands with the Allies in the battle against the forces of darkness and savagery.

The morning was an unusually brilliant one. The storms which had tossed our little vessels on the seas for ten days, and which had followed them nearly to the Irish coast, had suddenly given way to smooth water and a burst of sunshine. The long and graceful American ships steamed into the channel amid the cheers of the people and the tooting of all harbour craft ; the sparkling waves, the greenery of the bordering hills, the fruit trees already in bloom, to say nothing of the smiling and cheery faces

40

of the welcoming Irish people, seemed to promise a fair beginning for our great adventure. " Welcome to the American colours," had been the signal of the *Mary Rose,* a British destroyer which had been sent to lead the Americans to their anchorage. " Thank you, I am glad of your company," answered the Yankee commander ; and these messages represented the spirit of the whole proceeding. Indeed there was something in these strange-looking American ships, quite unlike the British destroyers, that necessarily inspired enthusiasm and respect. They were long and slender ; the sunlight, falling upon their graceful sides and steel decks, made them brilliant objects upon the water ; and their business-like guns and torpedo tubes suggested efficiency and readiness. The fact that they had reached their appointed rendezvous exactly on time, and that they had sailed up the Queenstown harbour at almost precisely the moment that preparations had been made to receive them, emphasized this impression. The appearance of our officers on the decks in their un-familiar, closely fitting blouses, and of our men, in their neat white linen caps, also at once won the hearts of the populace.

" Sure an' it's our own byes comin' back to us," an Irish woman remarked, as she delightedly observed the unmis-takably Gaelic countenances of a considerable proportion of the crew. Indeed the natives of Queenstown seemed to regard these American bluejackets almost as their own. The welcome provided by these people was not of a formal kind ; they gathered spontaneously to cheer and to admire. In that part of Ireland there was probably not a family that did not have relatives or associations in the United States, and there was scarcely a home that did not possess some memento of America. The beautiful Queenstown Roman Catholic Cathedral, which stood out so conspicuously, had been built very largely with American dollars, and the prosperity of many a local family had the same trans-Atlantic origin. It was hardly surprising, therefore, that when our sailors landed for a few hours' liberty many hands were stretched out to welcome them. Their friends took them arm in arm, marched them to their homes, and enter-tained them with food and drink, all the time plying them with questions about friends and relatives in America. Most of these young Americans with Irish ancestry had never seen Ireland, but that did not prevent the warm-hearted people of Queenstown from hailing them as their own. This cordiality was appreciated, for the trip across the Atlantic had been very severe, with gales and rain-storms nearly every day.

The senior officer in charge was Commander Joseph K. Taussig, whose flagship was the *Wadsworth*. The other vessels of the division and their commanding officers were the *Conyngham*, Commander Alfred W. Johnson ; the *Porter*, Lieutenant-Commander Ward K. Wortman ; the *McDougal*, Lieutenant-Commander Arther P. Fairfield ; the *Davis*, Lieutenant-Commander Rufus F. Zogbaum ; and the *Wainwright*, Lieutenant-Commander Fred H. Poteet. On the outbreak of hostilities these vessels, com-prising our Eighth Destroyer Division, had been stationed at Base 2, in the York River, Virginia ; at 7 P.M. of April 6th, the day that Congress declared war on Germany, their commander had received the following signal from the *Pennsylvania*, the flagship of the Atlantic Fleet : " Mobilize for war in accordance with Department's confidential mobilization plan of March 21st." From that time events moved rapidly for the Eighth Division. On April 14th, the very day on which I sent my first report on submarine con-ditions to Washington, Commander Taussig received a message to take his flotilla to Boston and there fit out for " long and distant service." Ten days afterward he sailed, with instructions to go fifty miles due east of Cape Cod and there to open his sealed orders. At the indicated spot Commander Taussig broke the seal, and read the following document—a paper so important in history, marking as it does the first instructions any American naval or army officer had received for engaging directly in hostilities with Germany, that it is worth quoting in full :

NAVY DEPARTMENT
Office of Naval Operations
Washington, D. C.

Secret and Confidential

To : Commander, Eighth Division, Destroyer Force, Atlantic Fleet, U.S.S. *Wadsworth*, Flagship.

Subject : Protection of commerce near the coasts of Great Britain and Ireland.

1. The British Admiralty have requested **the co-operation of a** division of American destroyers in the protection of commerce near the coasts of Great Britain and France.

2. Your mission is to assist naval operations of Entente Powers in every way possible.

3. Proceed to Queenstown, Ireland. Report to senior British naval officer present, and thereafter co-operate fully with the British navy. Should it be decided that your force act in co-operation with French naval forces your mission and method of co-operation under French Admiralty authority remain unchanged.

Route to Queenstown.

> Boston to latitude 50 N—Long. 20 W to arrive at daybreak then to latitude 50 N—Long. 12 W thence to Queenstown.

When within radio communication of the British naval forces off Ireland, call G CK and inform the Vice-Admiral at Queenstown in British general code of your position, course, and speed. You will be met outside of Queenstown.

4. Base facilities will be provided by the British Admiralty.

5. Communicate your orders and operations to Rear-Admiral Sims at London and be guided by such instructions as he may give you. Make no reports of arrival to Navy Department direct.

JOSEPHUS DANIELS.

No happier selection for the command of this division could have been made than that of Commander Taussig. In addition to his qualities as a sailor, certain personal associations made him particularly acceptable to the British naval authorities. In 1900, Commander Taussig, then a midshipman, was a member of the naval forces which the United States sent to China to co-operate with other powers in putting down the Boxer Rebellion and rescuing the besieged legations in Pekin. Near Tientsin this international force saw its hardest fighting, and here Commander Taussig was wounded. While recovering from his injury, the young American found himself lying on a cot side by side with an English captain, then about forty years old, who was in command of the *Centurion* and chief-of-staff to Admiral Seymour, who had charge of the British forces. This British officer **was** severely wounded; a bullet had **pene**trated his lung, and **for** a considerable period he **was** tion. Naturally Taussig had watched Jellicoe's career with the utmost interest; since he was only twenty-one at the time, however, and the Englishman was twice his age, it had never occurred to him that the First Sea Lord would remember his youthful hospital companion. Yet the very first message he received, on arriving in Irish waters, was the following letter, brought to him by Captain Evans, the man designated by the British Admiralty as liaison officer with the American destroyers:

ADMIRALTY, WHITEHALL
1-5-17.

MY DEAR TAUSSIG:

I still retain very pleasant and vivid recollections of our association in China and I am indeed delighted that you should have been selected for the command of the first force which is coming to fight for freedom, humanity, and civilization. We shall all have our work cut out to subdue piracy. My experience in China makes me feel perfectly convinced that the two nations will work in the closest co-operation, and I won't flatter you by saying too much about the value of your help. I must say this, however. There is no navy in the world that can possibly give us more valuable assistance, and there is no personnel in any navy that will fight better than yours. My China experience tells me this.

If only my dear friend McCalla could have seen this day how glad I would have been!

I must offer you and all your officers and men the warmest welcome possible in the name of the British nation and the British Admiralty, and add to it every possible good wish from myself. May every good fortune attend you and speedy victory be with us.

Yours very sincerely,
J. R. JELLICOE.

At this same meeting Captain Evans handed **the Amer-**
tcan commander another letter which was just as characteristic as that of Admiral Jellicoe. The following lines
constitute our officers' first introduction to Vice-Admiral
Bayly, the officer who was to command their operations in
the next eighteen months, and, in its brevity, its entirely
business-like qualities, as well as in its genuine sincerity and
kindness, it gave a fair introduction to the man :

ADMIRALTY HOUSE,
QUEENSTOWN,
4-5-17.

DEAR LIEUTENANT-COMMANDER TAUSSIG :
I hope that you and the other five officers in command
of the U.S. destroyers in your flotilla will come and dine
here to-night, Friday, at 7.45, and that you and three others
will remain to sleep here so as to get a good rest after your
long journey. Allow me to welcome you and to thank you
for coming.

Yours sincerely,
LEWIS BAYLY.

Dine in undress ; no speeches.

The first duty of the officers on arrival was to make the
usual ceremonial calls. The Lord Mayor of Cork had
come down from his city, which is only twelve miles from
Queenstown, to receive the Americans, and now awaited
them in the American consulate ; and many other citizens
were assembled there to welcome them. One of the most
conspicuous features of the procession was the moving
picture operator, whose presence really had an international
significance. The British Government itself had detailed
him for this duty ; it regarded the arrival of our destroyers
as a great historical event and therefore desired to preserve
this animated record in the official archives. Crowds
gathered along the street to watch and cheer our officers as
they rode by ; and at the consulate the Lord Mayor, Mr.
Butterfield, made an eloquent address, laying particular
emphasis upon the close friendship that had always prevailed between the American and the Irish people. Other
dignitaries made speeches voicing similar sentiments.
This welcome concluded, Commander Taussig and his
brother officers started up the steep hill that leads to
Admiralty House, a fine and spacious old building.

Here, following out the instructions of the Navy Department, they were to report to Vice-Admiral Bayly for duty.
It is doing no injustice to Sir Lewis to say that our men
regarded this first meeting with some misgiving. The
Admiral's reputation in the British navy was well known to
them. They knew that he was one of the ablest officers in
the service; but they had also heard that he was an extremely exacting man, somewhat taciturn in his manner,
and not inclined to be over familiar with his subordinates—
a man who did not easily give his friendship or his respect,
and altogether, in the anxious minds of these ambitious
young Americans, he was a somewhat forbidding figure.
And the appearance of the Admiral, standing in his doorway
awaiting their arrival, rather accentuated these precon-
ceptions. He was a medium-sized man, with somewhat
swarthy, weatherbeaten face and black hair just turning
grey; he stood there gazing rather quizzically at the
Americans as they came trudging up the hill, his hands
behind his back, his bright eyes keenly taking in every detail
of the men, his face not showing the slightest trace of a smile.
This struck our young men at first as a somewhat grim
reception; the attitude of the Admiral suggested that he
was slightly in doubt as to the value of his new recruits, that
he was entirely willing to be convinced, but that only deeds
and not fine speeches of greeting would convince him. Yet
Admiral Bayly welcomed our men with the utmost courtesy
and dignity, and his face, as he began shaking hands, broke
into a quiet, non-committal smile; there was nothing about
his manner that was effusive, there were no unnecessary
words, yet there was a real cordiality that put our men at
ease and made them feel at home in this strange environ-
ment. They knew, of course, that they had come to Ireland,
not for social diversions, but for the serious business of
fighting the Hun, and that indeed was the only thought
which could then find place in Admiral Bayly's mind. Up
to this time the welcome to the Americans had taken the
form of lofty oratorical flights, with emphasis upon the
blood ties of Anglo-Saxondom, and the significance to
civilization of America and Great Britain fighting side by
side; but this was not the kind of a greeting our men
received from Admiral Bayly. The Admiral himself, with his
somewhat worn uniform and his lack of ceremony, formed
a marked contrast to the official reception by the Lord

Mayor and his suite in their insignia of office. Entirely characteristic also was the fact that, instead of making a long speech, he made no speech at all. His chief interest in the Americans at that time was the assistance which they were likely to bring to the Allied cause ; after courteously greeting the officers, the first question he asked about these forces was :

" When will you be ready to go to sea ? "

Even under the most favourable conditions that is an embarrassing question to ask of a destroyer commander. There is no type of ship that is so chronically in need of overhauling. Even in peace times the destroyer usually has under way a long list of repairs ; our first contingent had sailed without having had much opportunity to refit, and had had an extremely nasty voyage. The fact was that it had been rather severely battered up, although the flotilla was in excellent condition, considering its hard experience on the ocean and the six months of hard work which it had previously had on our coast. One ship had lost its fire-room ventilator, another had had condenser troubles on the way across, and there had been other difficulties. Commander Taussig, however, had sized up Admiral Bayly as a man to whom it would be a tactical error to make excuses, and promptly replied :

" We are ready now, sir, that is, as soon as we finish refuelling. Of course you know how destroyers are—always wanting something done to them. But this is war, and we are ready to make the best of things and go to sea immediately."

The Admiral was naturally pleased with the spirit indicated by this statement, and, with his customary consideration for his juniors, said :

" I will give you four days from the time of arrival. Will that be sufficient ? "

" Yes," answered Taussig, " that will be more than ample time."

As we discovered afterward, the Admiral had a system of always " testing out " new men, and it is not improbable that this preliminary interview was a part of this process.

During the period of preparation there were certain essential preliminaries : it was necessary to make and to receive many calls, a certain amount of tea drinking was inevitable, and there were many invitations to dinners and to clubs that could not be ignored. Our officers made a state visit to Cork, going up in Admiral Bayly's barge, and returned the felicitations of the Mayor and his retinue.

Naturally both the Americans and their ships became objects of great interest to their new allies. It was, I think, the first time that a destroyer flotilla had ever visited Great Britain, and the very appearance of the vessels themselves aroused the greatest curiosity. They bore only a general resemblance to the destroyers of the British navy. The shape of their hulls, the number and location of smoke pipes, the positions of guns, torpedo tubes, bridges, deckhouse, and other details gave them quite a contrasting profile. The fact that they were designed to operate under different conditions from the British ships accounted for many of these divergences. We build our destroyers with the widest possible cruising radius ; they are expected to go to the West Indies, to operate from the Atlantic to the Pacific, and in general to feel at home anywhere in the great stretch of waters that surround our country. British destroyers, on the other hand, are intended to operate chiefly in the restricted waters around the British Isles, where the fuelling and refitting facilities are so extensive that they do not have to devote much space to supplies of this kind. The result is that our destroyers can keep the sea longer than the British ; on the other hand, the British are faster than ours, and they can also turn more quickly. These differences were of course a subject of much discussion among the observers at Queenstown, and even of animated argument. Naturally, the interest of the destroyer officers of the two services in the respective merits of their vessels was very keen. They examined minutely all features that were new to them in the design and arrange- ment of guns, torpedoes, depth charges, and machines, freely exchanged information, and discussed proposed improvements in the friendliest possible spirit. Strangely enough, although the American destroyers carried greater fuel supplies than the British, they were rather more dainty and graceful in their lines, a fact which inspired a famous retort which rapidly passed through the ranks of both navies.

" You know," remarked a British officer to an American, " I like the British destroyers better than the American. They look so much sturdier. Yours seem to me rather feminine in appearance."

" Yes," replied the American, " that's so, but you must remember what Kipling says, ' The female of the species is more deadly than the male.' "

The work of the Americans really began on the Sunday which followed their arrival ; by this time they had established cordial relations with Admiral Bayly and were prepared to trust themselves unreservedly in his hands. He summoned the officers on this Sunday morning and talked with them a few moments before they started for the submarine zone ; the time of their departure had been definitely fixed for the next day. In the matter of cere-monial greetings the Admiral was not strong, but when it came to discussing the business in hand he was the master of a convincing eloquence. The subject of his discourse was the responsibility that lay before our men ; he spoke in sharp, staccato tones, making his points with the utmost precision, using no verbal flourishes or unnecessary words—looking at our men perhaps a little fiercely, and certainly impressing them with the fact that the work which lay before them was to be no summer holiday. As soon as the destroyers passed beyond the harbour defences, the Admiral began, death constantly lay before the men until they returned. There was only one safe rule to follow ; days and even weeks might go by without seeing a submarine, but the men must assume that one was constantly watching them, looking for a favourable opportunity to discharge its torpedo. " You must not relax attention for an instant, or you may lose an oppor-tunity to destroy a submarine or give her a chance to destroy you." It was the present intention to send the American destroyers out for periods of six days, giving them two days' rest between trips, and about once a month they were to have five days in port for boiler cleaning. And now the Admiral gave some details about the practical work at sea. Beware, he said, about ram-ming periscopes ; these were frequently mere decoys for bombs and should be shelled. In picking up survivors of torpedoed vessels the men must be careful not to stop until thoroughly convinced that there were no submarines

5

in the neighbourhood : " You must not risk the loss of your vessel in order to save the lives of a few people."

The Admiral proclaimed the grim philosophy of this war when he told our men that it would be their first duty, should they see a ship torpedoed, not to go to the rescue of the survivors, but to go after the submarine. The three imperative duties of the destroyers were, in the order named : first, to destroy submarines ; second, to convoy and protect merchant shipping ; and third, to save the lives of the passengers and crews of torpedoed ships. No commander should ever miss an opportunity to destroy a submarine merely because there were a few men and women in small boats or in the water who might be saved. Admiral Bayly explained that to do this would be false economy : sinking a submarine meant saving far more lives than might be involved in a particular instance, for this vessel, if spared, would simply go on constantly destroying human beings. The Admiral then gave a large number of instructions in short, pithy sentences : " Do not use searchlights ; do not show any lights whatever at night ; do not strike any matches ; never steam at a slower rate than thirteen knots ; always zigzag, thereby preventing the submarine from plotting your position ; always approach a torpedoed vessel with the sun astern ; make only short signals ; do not repeat the names of vessels ; carefully watch all fishing vessels—they may be submarines in disguise—they even put up masts, sails, and funnels in this attempt to conceal their true character." The Admiral closed his remarks with a warning based upon his estimate of the character and methods of the enemy. In substance he said that were it not for the violations of the dictates of humanity and the well-established chivalry of the sea, he would have the greatest respect for the German submarine commanders. He cautioned our officers not to underrate them, and particularly emphasized their cleverness at what he termed " the art of irregularity." He explained this by saying that up to that time he had been unable to deduce from their operations any definite plan or tactics, and advised our commanders also to guard against any regularity of movement ; they should never, for example, patrol from one corner to another of their assigned squares in the submarine zone, or adopt any other uniform practice which the enemy might soon perceive and of which he would probably take advantage.

At the very moment that Admiral Bayly was giving these impressive instructions the submarine campaign had reached its crisis ; the fortunes of the Allies had never struck so low a depth as at that time. An incident connected with our arrival, not particularly important in itself, brought home to our men the unsleeping vigilance of the enemy with whom they had to deal.

Perhaps the Germans did not actually have advance information of the arrival of this first detachment of our destroyers ; but they certainly did display great skill in divining what was to happen. At least it was a remarkable coincidence that for the first time in many months a submarine laid a mine-field directly off the entrance to Queenstown the day before our ships arrived. Soon afterward a parent ship of the destroyers reached this port and encountered the same welcome ; and soon after that a second parent ship found a similar mine-field awaiting her arrival. The news that our destroyers had reached Queenstown actually appeared in the German papers several days before we had released it in the British and American press. Thanks to the vigilance and efficiency of the British mine-sweepers, however, the enemy gained nothing from all these preparations, for the channel was cleared of German mines before our vessels reached port.

The night before the destroyers arrived, while some of the officers of my staff were dining with Admiral Bayly, the windows were shaken by heavy explosions made by the mines which the sweepers were dragging out. Admiral Bayly jokingly remarked that it was really a pity to interfere with such a warm welcome as had apparently been planned for our crusaders. Even the next night, while the destroyer officers were dining at Admiralty House, several odd mines exploded outside the channel that had been swept the previous day. This again impressed our men with the fact that the game which they had now entered was quite a different affair from their peace-time manœuvres.

The Germans at that time were jubilant over the progress of their submarine campaign and, indeed, they had good reason to be. The week that our first flotilla reached Irish waters their submarines had destroyed 240,000 tons of

Allied shipping; if the sinking should keep up at this rate, it meant losses of 1,000,000 tons a month and an early German victory.

In looking over my letters of that period, I find many references that picture the state of the official mind. All that time I was keeping closely in touch with Ambassador Page, who was energetically seconding all my efforts to bring more American ships across the Atlantic.

" It remains a fact," I wrote our Ambassador, " that at present the enemy is succeeding and that we are failing. Ships are being sunk faster than they can be replaced by the building facilities of the world. This simply means that the enemy is winning the war. There is no mystery about that. The submarines are rapidly cutting the Allies' lines of communication. When they are cut, or sufficiently interfered with, we must accept the enemy's terms."

Six days before our destroyers put in at Queenstown I sent this message to Mr. Page:

Allies do not now command the sea. Transport of troops and supplies strained to the utmost and the maintenance of the armies in the field is threatened.

Such, then, was the situation when our little destroyer flotilla first went to sea to do battle with the submarine.

II

Admiral Sir Lewis Bayly, who now became the commander of the American destroyers at Queenstown, so far as their military operations were concerned, had spent fifty years in the British navy, forty years of this time actually at sea. This ripe experience, combined with a great natural genius for salt water, had made him one of the most efficient men in the service. In what I have already said, I may have given a slightly false impression of the man; that he was taciturn, that he was generally regarded as a hard taskmaster, that he never made friends at the first meeting, that he was more interested in results than in persons—all this is true; yet these qualities merely concealed what was, at bottom, a generous, kindly, and even a warm-hearted character. Admiral Bayly was so retiring and so modest that he seemed almost to have assumed these exterior traits to disguise his real nature. When our men first met the Admiral they saw a man who would exact their last effort and accept no excuses for failure ; when admitted to more intimate association, however, they discovered that this weather-beaten sailor had a great love for flowers, for children, for animals, for pictures, and for books ; that he was deeply read in general literature, in history, and in science, and that he had a knowledge of their own country and its institutions which many of our own officers did not possess. Americans have great reason to be proud of the achievements of their naval men, and one of the most praiseworthy was the fact that they became such intimate friends of Admiral Bayly. For this man's nature was so sincere that he could never bring himself to indulge in friendships which he deemed unworthy. Early in his association with our men, he told them bluntly that any success he and they might have in getting on together would depend entirely upon the manner in which they performed their work. If they acquitted themselves creditably, well and good ; if not, he should not hesitate to find fault with them. It is thus a tribute to our officers that in a very short time they and Admiral Bayly had established relations which were not only friendly but affectionate. Not long after our destroyers arrived at Queenstown most of the British destroyers left to reinforce the hard-driven flotillas in the Channel and the North Sea, so that the destroyer forces at Queenstown under Admiral Bayly became almost exclusively American, though they worked with many British vessels—sloops, trawlers, sweepers, and mystery ships, in co-operation with British destroyers and other vessels in the north and other parts of Ireland. The Admiral watched over our ships and their men with the jealous eye of a father. He always referred to his command as " my destroyers " and " my Americans," and woe to anyone who attempted to interfere with them or do them the slightest injustice ! Admiral Bayly would fight for them, against the combined forces of the whole British navy, like a tigress for her cubs. He constantly had a weather eye on Plymouth, the main base of the British destroyers, to see that the vessels from that station did their fair share of the work. Once or twice a dispute arose between an American destroyer commander and a British; in such cases Admiral Bayly vigorously took the part of the American. "You did perfectly right," he would say to our men, and then he would turn all his guns against the interfering Britisher. Relations between the young Americans and the experienced Admiral became so close that they would sometimes go to him with their personal troubles; he became not only their commander, but their confidant and adviser.

There was something in these bright young chaps from overseas, indeed, so different from anything which he had ever met before, that greatly appealed to this seasoned Englishman. One thing that he particularly enjoyed was their sense of humour. The Admiral himself had a keen wit and a love of stories; and he also had the advantage, which was not particularly common in England, of understanding American slang and American anecdotes. There are certain stories which apparently only an upbringing on American soil qualifies one to appreciate; yet Admiral Bayly always instantly got the point. He even took a certain pride in his ability to comprehend the American joke. One of the regular features of life at Queenstown was a group of retired British officers—fine, white-haired old gentlemen who could take no active part in the war but who used to find much consolation in coming around to smoke their pipes and to talk things over at Admiralty House. Admiral Bayly invariably found delight in encouraging our officers to entertain these rare old souls with American stories; their utter bewilderment furnished him endless entertainment. The climax of his pleasure came when, after such an experience, the old men would get the Admiral in a corner, and whisper to him: "What in the world do they mean?"

The Admiral was wonderfully quick at repartee, as our men found when they began "joshing" him on British peculiarities, for as naval attaché he had travelled extensively in the United States, had observed most of our national eccentricities, and thus was able promptly "to come back." In such contests our men did not invariably come off with all the laurels. Yet, despite these modern tendencies, Admiral Bayly was a conservative of the conservatives, having that ingrained British respect for old things simply because they were old. An ancient British custom requires that at church on Sundays the leading dignitary in each community shall mount the reading desk and read the lessons of the day; Admiral Bayly would perform this office with a simplicity and a reverence which indicated the genuinely religious nature of the man. And in smaller details he was likewise the ancient, tradition-loving Briton. He would never think of writing a letter to an equal or superior officer except in longhand; to use a typewriter for such a purpose would have been profanation in his eyes. I once criticized a certain Admiral for consuming an hour or so in laboriously penning a letter which could have been dictated to a stenographer in a few minutes.

" How do you ever expect to win the war if you use up time this way ? " I asked.

" I'd rather lose the war," the Admiral replied, but with a twinkle in his eye, " than use a typewriter to my chiefs ! "

Our officers liked to chaff the Admiral quietly on this conservatism. He frequently had a number of them to breakfast, and upon one such occasion the question was asked as to why the Admiral ate an orange after breakfast, instead of before, as is the custom in America.

" I can tell you why," said Commander Zogbaum.

" Well, why is it ? " asked the Admiral.

" Because that's what William the Conqueror used to do."

" I can think of no better reason than that for doing it," the Admiral promptly answered. But this remark tickled him immensely, and became a byword with him. Ever afterward, whenever he proposed to do something which the Americans regarded as too conservative, he would say:

" You know that this is what William the Conqueror used to do ! "

Yet in one respect the Admiral was all American; he was a hard worker even to the point of hustle. He insisted on the strictest attention to the task in hand from his subordinates, but at least he never spared himself. After he had arrived at Queenstown, two years before our destroyers put in, he proceeded to reorganize Admiralty House on the most business-like basis. The first thing he pounced upon was the billiard-room in the basement. He decided that it would make an excellent plotting-room, and that the billiard-tables could be transformed into admirable drawing-boards for his staff; he immediately called the superintendent and told him to make the necessary transformations.

"All right," said the superintendent. "We'll start work on them to-morrow morning."

"No, you won't," Admiral Bayly replied. "We propose to be established in this room using these tables to-morrow morning. They must be all ready for use by eight o'clock."

And he was as good as his word; the workmen spent the whole night making the changes. At the expense of considerable personal comfort he also caused one half of the parlour of Admiralty House to be partitioned off as an office and the wall thus formed covered with war maps.

These incidents are significant, not only of Admiral Bayly's methods, but of his ideals. In his view, if a billiard room could be made to serve a war purpose, it had no proper place in an Admiralty house which was the headquarters for fighting German submarines. The chief duty of all men at that crisis was work, and their one responsibility was the defeat of the Hun. Admiralty House was always open to our officers; they spent many a delightful evening there around the Admiral's fire; they were constantly entertained at lunch and at dinner, and they were expected to drop in for tea whenever they were in port. But social festivities in the conventional sense were barred. No ladies, except the Admiral's relatives, ever visited the place. Some of the furnishings were rather badly worn, but the Admiral would make no requisitions for new rugs or chairs; every penny in the British exchequer, he insisted, should be used to carry on the war. He was scornfully critical of any naval officers who made a lavish display of silver on their tables; money should be spent for depth charges, torpedoes, and twelve-inch shells, not for ostentation. He was scrupulousness itself in observing all official regulations in the matter of food and other essentials.

For still another reason the Admiral made an ideal commander of American naval forces. He was a strict tectotaller. His abstention was not a war measure; he had always had a strong aversion to alcohol in any form and had never drank a cocktail or a brandy and soda in his

life. Dinners at Admiralty House, therefore, were absolutely " dry," and in perfect keeping with American naval
regulations.

Though Admiral Bayly was not athletic—his outdoor
games being limited to tip-and-run cricket in the Admiralty
grounds, which he played with a round bat and a tennis
ball—he was a man of wiry physique and a tireless walker.
Indeed the most active young men in our navy had great
difficulty in keeping pace with him. One of his favourite
diversions on a Saturday afternoon was to take a group on
a long tramp in the beautiful country surrounding Queenstown ; by the time the party reached home, the Admiral,
though sixty years old, was usually the freshest of the lot.
I still vividly remember a long walk which I took with him
in a pelting rain ; I recall how keenly he enjoyed it and
how young and nimble he seemed to be when we reached
home, drenched to the skin. A steep hill led from the
shore up to Admiralty House ; Sir Lewis used to say that
this was a valuable military asset—it did not matter how
angry a man might be with him when he started for
headquarters, by the time he arrived, this wearisome
climb always had the effect of quieting his antagonism.
The Admiral was fond of walking up this hill with our
young officers ; he himself usually reached the top as
fresh as a daisy, while his juniors were frequently puffing
for breath.

He enjoyed testing out our men in other ways ; nothing
delighted him more than giving them hard jobs to do—
especially when they accomplished the tasks successfully.
One day he ordered one of our officers, Lieutenant-Commander Roger Williams, captain of the *Duncan*, a recent
arrival at Queenstown, to cross the Irish Sea and bring
back a ship. The joke lay in the fact that this man's
destroyer had just come in with her steering gear completely out of commission—a circumstance which Admiral
Bayly well understood. Many officers would have
promptly asked to be excused on this ground, but not
this determined American. He knew that the Admiral
was trying to " put something over on him," and he rose
to the occasion. The fact that Queenstown Harbour is
long and narrow, not wide enough for a destroyer to turn
around in, made Commander Williams's problem still more
difficult, but by cleverly using his engines, he succeeded

in backing out—the distance required was five miles ; he took another mile and a half to turn his ship and then he went across the sea and brought back his convoy—all without any steering gear.   This officer never once mentioned to the Admiral the difficulties under which he had worked, but his achievement completely won Sir Lewis's heart, and from that time this young man became one of his particular favourites.   Indeed, it was the constant demonstration of this kind of fundamental character in our naval men which made the Admiral admire them so.

On occasions Admiral Bayly would go to sea himself— something quite unprecedented and possibly even reprehensible, for it was about the same thing as a commanding general going into the front-line trenches.   But the Admiral believed that doing this now and then helped to inspire his men ; and, besides that, he enjoyed it—he was not made for a land sailor.   He had as flagship a cruiser of about 5,000 tons ; he had a way of jumping on board without the slightest ceremony and taking a cruise up the west coast of Ireland.   On occasion the Admiral would personally lead an expedition which was going to the relief of a torpedoed vessel, looking for survivors adrift in small boats.   One day Admiral Bayly, Captain Pringle of the U.S.S. *Melville*, Captain Campbell, the Englishman whose exploits with mystery ships had given him worldwide fame, and myself went out on the *Active* to watch certain experiments with depth charges.   It was a highly imprudent thing to do, because a vessel of such draft was an excellent target for torpedoes, but that only added to the zest of the occasion from Admiral Bayly's point of view.

" What a bag this would be for the Hun ! " he chuckled. " The American Commander-in-Chief, the British Admiral commanding in Irish waters, a British and an American captain ! "

In our mind's eye we could see our picture in the Berlin papers—four distinguished prisoners standing in a row.

A single fact shows with what consideration Admiral Bayly treated his subordinates.   The usual naval regulation demands that an officer, coming in from a trip, shall immediately seek out his commander and make a verbal report.   Frequently the men came in late in the evening, extremely fatigued ; to make the visit then was a hardship and might deprive them of much-needed sleep.   Admiral

Bayly therefore had a fixed rule that such visits should be
made at ten o'clock of the morning following the day of
arrival. On such occasions he would often be found seated
somewhat grimly behind his desk wholly absorbed in the
work in hand. If he were writing or reading his mail he
would keep steadily at it, never glancing up until he had
finished. He would listen to the report stoically, possibly
say a word of praise, and then turn again to the business
in hand. Occasionally he would notice that his abruptness
had perhaps pained the young American ; then he would
break into an apologetic smile, and ask him to come up
to dinner that evening, and even—this was the greatest
honour of all—to spend the night at Admiralty House.

These dinners were great occasions for our men, particularly as they were presided over by Miss Voysey, the Admiral's niece. Miss Voysey, the little spaniel, Patrick, and
the Admiral constituted the " family," and the three were
entirely devoted to one another. Pat in particular was an
indispensable part of this menage; I have never seen any
object quite so crestfallen and woe-begone as this little dog
when either Miss Voysey or the Admiral spent a day or two
away from the house. Miss Voysey was a young woman of
great personal charm and cultivation ; probably she was the
influence that most contributed to the happiness and comfort of our officers at Queenstown. From the day of their
arrival she entered into the closest comradeship with the
Americans. She kept open house for them : she was
always on hand to serve tea in the afternoon, and she never
overlooked an opportunity to add to their well-being. As a
result of her delightful hospitality Admiralty House really
became a home for our officers. Miss Voysey had a genuine
enthusiasm for America and Americans ; possibly the fact
that she was herself an Australian made her feel like one of
us ; at any rate, there were certain qualities in our men that
she found extremely congenial, and she herself certainly
won all their hearts. Anyone who wishes to start a burst of
enthusiasm from our officers who were stationed at Queenstown need only to mention the name of Miss Voysey. The
dignity with which she presided over the Admiral's house,
and the success with which she looked out for his comfort,
also inspired their respect. Miss Voysey was the leader in
all the war charities at Queenstown, and she and the Admiral
made it their personal duty to look out for the victims of

torpedoed ships. At whatever hour these survivors arrived they were sure of the most warm-hearted attentions from headquarters. In a large hall in the Custom House at the landing the Admiral kept a stock of cigarettes and tobacco, and the necessary gear and supplies for making and serving hot coffee at short notice, and nothing ever prevented him and his people from stationing themselves there to greet and serve the survivors as soon as they arrived—often wet and cold, and sometimes wounded. Even though the Admiral might be at dinner he and Miss Voysey would leave their meal half eaten and hurry to the landing to welcome the survivors. The Admiral and his officers always insisted on serving them, and they would even wash the dishes and put them away for the next time. The Admiral, of course, might have ordered others to do this work, but he preferred to give this personal expression of a real seaman's sympathy for other seamen in distress. It is unnecessary to say that any American officers who could get there in time always lent a hand. I am sure that long after most of the minor incidents of this war have faded from my memory, I shall still keep a vivid recollection of this kindly gentleman, Admiral Sir Lewis Bayly, K.C.B., K.C.M.G., C.V.O., Royal Navy, serving coffee to wretched British, American, French, Italian, Japanese, or negro sailors, with a cheering word for each, and afterward, with sleeves tucked up, calmly washing dishes in a big pan of hot water.

I have my fears that the Admiral will not be particularly pleased by the fact that I have taken all these pains to introduce him to the American public. Excessive modesty is one of his most conspicuous traits. When American correspondents came to Queenstown, Admiral Bayly would receive them courteously. " You can have all you want about the navy," he would say, " but remember—not a word about Lewis Bayly." He was so reticent that he was averse to having his picture taken ; even the moving picture operator detailed to get an historic record of the arrival of our destroyers did not obtain a good view of the Admiral, for whenever Sir Lewis saw him coming he would turn his back to the camera ! My excuse for describing this very lovable man, however, is because he became almost an object of veneration to our American officers, and because, since for eighteen months he was the commander of the American forces based on Queenstown, he is an object of legitimate

interest to the American people.   The fact that the Admiral
was generally known to our officers as " Uncle Lewis," and
that some of those who grew to know him best even called
him that to his face, illustrates the delightful relations
which were established.   Any account of the operations of
our navy in the European War would thus be sadly incomplete which ignored the splendid sailor who was largely
responsible for their success.

Another officer who contributed greatly to the efficiency
of the American forces was Captain E. R. G. R. Evans, R.N.,
who was detailed by Admiral Jellicoe at my request to act
as liaison officer with our destroyers.   No more fortunate
selection could have been made.   Captain Evans had
earned fame as second in command of the Scott Antarctic
expedition ; he had spent much time in the United States
and knew our people well ; indeed when war broke out he
was lecturing in our country on his polar experiences.   A
few days before our division arrived Captain Evans had
distinguished himself in one of the most brilliant naval
actions of the war.   He was commander of the destroyer-
leader *Broke*—a " destroyer-leader " being a destroyer of
unusually large size—and in this battle three British vessels
of this type had fought six German destroyers.   Captain
Evans's ship sank one German destroyer and rammed
another, passing clear over its stern and cutting it nearly in
two.   The whole of England was ringing with this exploit,
and it was a decided tribute to our men that Admiral Jellicoe
consented to detail the commander of the *Broke*.   He was
a man of great intelligence, great energy, and, what was
almost equally to the point, he was extremely companion-
able ; whether he was relating his experiences at the South
Pole, or telling us of active life on a destroyer, or swapping
yarns with our officers, or giving us the value of his practical
experiences in the war, Captain Evans was always at home
with our men—indeed, he seemed to be almost one of us.

The fact that these American destroyers were placed
under the command of a British admiral was somewhat
displeasing to certain Americans.   I remember that one
rather bumptious American correspondent, on a visit to
Queenstown, was loud in expressing his disapproval of this
state of affairs, and even threatened to " expose " us all in
the American press.   The fact that I was specifically commissioned as destroyer commander also confused **the**

situation. Yet the procedure was entirely proper, and, in fact, absolutely necessary. My official title was "Commander of the U.S. Naval Forces Operating in European Waters"; besides this, I was the representative of our Navy Department at the British Admiralty and American member of the Allied Naval Council. These duties required my presence in London, which became the centre of all our operations. I was commander not only of our destroyers at Queenstown, but of a destroyer force at Brest, another at Gibraltar, of subchaser forces at Corfu and Plymouth, of a mixed force at the Azores, of the American battle squadrons at Scapa Flow and Berehaven, Ireland, certain naval forces at Murmansk and Archangel in north Russia, and of many other contingents. Clearly it was impossible for me to devote all my time exclusively to any one of these commands; so far as actual operations were concerned it was necessary that particular commanders should control them. All these destroyer squadrons, including that at Queenstown, were under the command of the American Admiral stationed in London; whenever they sailed from Queenstown on specific duty, however, they sailed under orders from Admiral Bayly. Any time, however, I could withdraw these destroyers from Queenstown and send them where the particular necessities required. My position, that is, was precisely the same as that of General Pershing in France. He sent certain American divisions to the British army; as long as they acted with the British they were subject to the orders of Sir Douglas Haig; but General Pershing could withdraw these men at any time for use elsewhere. The actual supreme command of all our forces, army and navy, rested in the hands of Americans; but, for particular operations, they naturally had to take their orders from the particular officer under whom they were stationed.

III

On May 17th a second American destroyer flotilla of six ships arrived at Queenstown. From that date until July 5th a new division put in nearly every week. The six destroyers which escorted our first troopships from America to France were promptly assigned to duty with our forces in Irish waters. Meanwhile other ships were added. On May 22nd the *Melville*, the "Mother Ship" of the destroyers, arrived and became the flagship of all the American vessels which were stationed at Queenstown. This repair and supply ship practically took the place of a dockyard, so far as our destroyer forces were concerned. Queenstown had been almost abandoned as a navy yard many years before the European War and its facilities for the repair of warships were consequently very inadequate. The *Melville* relieved the British authorities of many responsibilities of this kind. She was able to do three-quarters of all this work, except major repairs and those which required docking. Her resources for repairing destroyers, and for providing for the wants and comforts of our men, aroused much admiration in British naval circles. The rapidity with which our forces settled down to work, and the seamanly skill which they manifested from the very beginning, likewise made the most favourable impression. By July 5th we had thirty-four destroyers at Queenstown—a force that remained practically at that strength until November. In 1918 much of the work of patrolling the seas and of convoying ships to the west and south of Ireland—the area which, in many ways, was the most important field of submarine warfare—fell upon these American ships. The officers and crews began this work with such zest that by June 1st I was justified in making the following statement to the Navy Department : " It is gratifying to be able to report that the operations of our forces in these waters have proved not only very satisfactory, but also of marked value to the Allies in overcoming the submarine menace. The equipment and construction of our ships have proved adequate and sufficient, and the personnel has shown an unusually high degree of enthusiasm and ability to cope with the situation presented."

It is impossible to exaggerate the enthusiasm which the arrival of these vessels produced upon the British public. America itself experienced something of a thrill when the news was first published that our destroyers had reached European waters, but this was mild compared with the joy which spread all over the British Isles. The feeling of Americans was mainly one of pride ; our people had not yet suffered much from the European cataclysm, and despite the fact that we were now active participants, the war still seemed very far off and unreal. The fact that a German victory would greatly endanger our national freedom had hardly entered our national consciousness ; the idea seemed

dim, abstract, perhaps even absurd ; but in Great Britain,
with the guns constantly booming almost within earshot of
the people, the horrors of the situation were acutely realized.
For this reason those American destroyers at Queenstown
immediately became a symbol in the minds of the British
people.   They represented not only the material assistance
which our limitless resources and our almost inexhaustible
supply of men would bring to a cause which was really in
desperate straits ; but they stood also for a great spiritual
fact ; for the kinship of the two great Anglo-Saxon peoples,
which, although separated politically, had now joined hands
to fight for the ideals upon which the civilization of both
nations rested.   In the preceding two years Great Britain
had had her moments of doubt—doubt as to whether the
American people had remained true to the principles that
formed the basis of their national life ; the arrival of these
ships immediately dispelled all such misgivings.

Almost instinctively the minds of the British people
turned to the day, nearly three hundred years before, when
the *Mayflower* sailed for the wilderness beyond the seas. The
moving picture film, which depicted the arrival of our first
destroyer division, and which was exhibited all over Great
Britain to enthusiastic crowds, cleverly accentuated this
idea.   This film related how, in 1620, a few Englishmen had
landed in North America ; how these adventurers had laid
the foundations of a new state based on English conceptions
of justice and liberty ; how they had grown great and
prosperous; how the stupidity of certain British statesmen
had forced them to declare their independence ; how they
had fought for this independence with the utmost heroism ;
how out of these disjointed British colonies they had founded
one of the mightiest nations of history; and how now, when
the liberties of mankind were endangered, the descendants
of the old *Mayflower* pioneers had in their turn crossed the
ocean—this time going eastward—to fight for the traditions of their race.   Had Americans been making this film,
they would have illustrated another famous episode in our
history that antedated, by thirteen years, the voyage of
the *Mayflower*—that is, the landing of British colonists
in Virginia, in 1607 ; but in the minds of the English
people the name *Mayflower* had become merely a symbol
of American progress and all that it represented.   This
whole story appealed to the British masses as one of the

great miracles of history—a single, miserable little settlement in Massachusetts Bay expanding into a continent overflowing with resources and wealth ; a shipload of men, women, and children developing, in less than three centuries, into a nation of more than 100,000,000 people. And the arrival of our destroyers, pictured on the film, informed the British people that all this youth and energy had been thrown upon their side of the battle.

One circumstance gave a particular appropriateness to the fact that I commanded these forces. In 1910 I had visited England as captain of the battleship *Minnesota*, a unit in a fleet which was then cruising in British and French waters. It was apparent even at that time that preparations were under way for a European war ; on every hand there were plenty of evidences that Germany was determined to play her great stroke for the domination of the world. In a report to the Admiral commanding our division I gave it as my opinion that the great European War would begin within four years. In a speech at the Guildhall, where 800 of our sailors were entertained at lunch by the Lord Mayor, Sir Vezey Strong, I used the words which involved me in a good deal of trouble at the time and which have been much quoted since. The statement then made was purely the inspiration of the moment ; it came from the heart, not from the head ; probably the evidences that Germany was stealthily preparing her great blow had something to do with my outburst. I certainly spoke without any authorization from my Government, and realized at once that I had committed a great indiscretion. " If the time should ever come," I said, " when the British Empire is menaced by a European coalition, Great Britain can rely upon the last ship, the last dollar, the last man, and the last drop of blood of her kindred beyond the sea." It is not surprising that the appearance of American ships, commanded by the American who had spoken these words seven years before, strongly appealed to the British sense of the dramatic. Indeed, it struck the British people as a particularly happy fulfilment of prophecy. These sentences were used as an introduction to the moving picture film showing the arrival of our first destroyer division, and for weeks after reaching England I could hardly pick up a newspaper without these words of my Guildhall speech staring me in the face.

6

Of course, any American admiral then commanding American naval forces in European waters would have been acclaimed as the living symbol of Anglo-American co-operation ; and it was simply as the representative of the American people and the American navy that the British people received me so appreciatively. At first the appearance of our uniforms aroused much curiosity ; our tightly fitting blouses were quite different from the British sack coats, and few people in London, in fact, knew who we were. After our photographs had appeared in the press, however, the people always recognized us in the streets. And then something quite unusual happened. That naval and military men should salute my staff and me was to have been expected, but that civilians should show this respect for the American uniform was really unprecedented. Yet we were frequently greeted in this way. It indicated, almost more than anything else, how deeply affected the British people were by America's entrance into the war. All classes and all ages showed this same respect and gratitude to our country. Necessarily I had to attend many public dinners and even to make many speeches ; the people gathered on such occasions always rose *en masse* as a tribute to the uniform which I wore. Sometimes such meetings were composed of boy scouts, of schoolboys or schoolgirls, of munition workers, of journalists, or of statesmen ; and all, irrespective of age or social station or occupation, seemed delighted to pay respect to the American navy. There were many evidences of interest in the " American Admiral " that were really affecting. Thus one day a message came from Lady Roberts, widow of the great soldier, Field-Marshal Earl Roberts, saying that she was desirous of meeting the " American Admiral." I was very glad to go out in the country and spend a Sunday afternoon with her. This charming, white-haired old lady was very feeble, and had to spend most of her time in a wheel-chair. But her mind was bright as ever, and she had been following the war with the closest attention. She listened with keen interest as I told her all about the submarines, and she asked innumerable questions concerning them. She was particularly affected when she spoke about the part the United States was playing in the war, and remarked how much our participation would have delighted the Field-Marshal.

I have already given my first impressions of Their Majesties the King and Queen, and time only confirmed them. Neither ever missed an opportunity to show their appreciation of the part that we were playing. The zeal with which the King entered into the celebration of our Fourth of July made him very popular with all our men. He even cultivated a taste for our national game. Certain of our early contingents of soldiers encamped near Windsor; here they immediately laid out a baseball diamond and daily engaged in their favourite sport. The Royal Family used to watch our men at their play, became interested in the game, and soon learned to follow it. The Duke of Connaught and the Princess Patricia, his daughter, had learned baseball through their several years' residence in Canada, and could watch a match with all the understanding and enthusiasm of an American "fan." As our sailors and soldiers arrived in greater numbers, the interest and friendliness of the Royal Family increased. One of the King's most delightful traits is his sense of humour. The Queen also showed a great fondness for stories, and I particularly remember her amusement at the famous remark of the Australians—perhaps the most ferocious combatants on the Western Front—about the American soldier, " a good fighter, but a little rough." Of all the anecdotes connected with our men, none delighted King George so much as those concerning our coloured troops. A whole literature of negro yarns spread rapidly over Europe; most of them, I find, have long since reached the United States. The most lasting impression which I retain of the head of the British Empire is that he is very much of a human being. He loved just about the same things as the normal American or Englishman loves—his family, his friends, his country, a good story, a pleasant evening with congenial associates. And he had precisely the same earnestness about the war which one found in every properly constituted Briton or American; the victories of the Allies exhilarated King George just as they exhilarated the man in the street, and their defeats saddened him just as they saddened the humblest citizen. I found in His Majesty that same solemn sense of comradeship with America which I found in the English civilians who saluted the American uniform in the street.

As an evidence of the exceedingly cordial relations existing between the two navies the Admiralty proposed, in the latter part of May, that I should assume Admiral Bayly's command for several days while he took a little vacation on the west coast of Ireland. Admiral Bayly was the Commander-in-Chief of all the British forces operating on the Irish coast. This command thus included far more than that at Queenstown ; it comprised several naval stations and the considerable naval forces in Irish waters. Never before, so I was informed, had a foreign naval officer commanded British naval forces in time of war. So far as exercising any control over sea operations was concerned, this invitation was not particularly important. Matters were running smoothly at the Queenstown station ; Admiral Bayly's second in command could easily have kept the machine in working order ; it was hardly likely, in the few days that I was to command, that any changes in policy would be initiated. The British Admiralty merely took this way of showing a great courtesy to the American navy, and of emphasizing to the world the excellent relations that existed between the two services. The act was intended to symbolize the fact that the British and the American navies were really one in the thoroughness of their co-operation in subduing the Prussian menace. Incidentally the British probably hoped that the publication of this news in the German press would not be without effect in Germany. On June 18th, therefore, I went to Queenstown, and hoisted my flag on the staff in front of Admiralty House. I had some hesitation in doing this, for American navy regulations stipulate that an Admiral's flag shall be raised only on a ship afloat, but Admiral Bayly was insistent that his flag should come down and that mine should go up, and I decided that this technicality might be waived. The incident aroused great interest in England, but it started many queer rumours in Queenstown. One was that Admiral Bayly and I had quarrelled, the British Admiral, strangely enough, having departed in high dudgeon and left me serenely in control. Another was that I had come to Queenstown, seized the reins out of Admiral Bayly's hands, thrown him out of the country, and taken over the government of Ireland on behalf of the United States, which had now determined to free the island from British oppression ! However, in a few days Admiral Bayly returned and all went on as before.

During the nearly two years which the American naval forces spent in Europe only one element in the population showed them any hostility or even unfriendliness. At the moment when these lines are being written a delegation claiming to represent the " Irish Republic " is touring the United States, asking Americans to extend their sympathy and contribute money toward the realization of their project. I have great admiration for the mass of the Irish people, and from the best elements of these people the American sailors received only kindness. I have therefore hesitated about telling just how some members of the Sinn Fein Party treated our men. But it seems that now when this same brotherhood is attempting to stir up hatred in this country against our Allies in the war, there is a certain pertinence in informing Americans just what kind of treatment their brave sailors met with at the hands of the Sinn Fein in Ireland.

The people of Queenstown and Cork, as already described, received our men with genuine Irish cordiality. Yet in a few weeks evidence of hostility in certain quarters became apparent. The fact is that the part of Ireland in which the Americans were stationed was a headquarters of the Sinn Fein. The members of this organization were not only openly disloyal ; they were openly pro-German. They were not even neutral ; they were working day and night for a German victory, for in their misguided minds a German victory signified an Irish Republic. It was no secret that the Sinn Feiners were sending information to Germany and constantly laying plots to interfere with the British and American navies. At first it might be supposed that the large number of sailors—and some officers —of Irish extraction on the American destroyers would tend to make things easier for our men. Quite the contrary proved to be the case. The Sinn Feiners apparently believed that these so-called Irish-Americans would sympathize with their cause ; in their wildest moments they even hoped that our naval forces might champion it. But these splendid sailors were Americans before they were anything else ; their chief ambition was the defeat of the Hun and they could not understand how any man anywhere could have any other aim in life. They were disgusted at the large numbers of able-bodied men whom they saw in the streets, and did not hesitate to ask some of them why they were not fighting on the Western Front. The behaviour of the American sailors was good ; but the mere fact that they did not openly manifest a hatred of Great Britain and a love of Germany infuriated the Sinn Feiners. And the eternal woman question also played its part. Our men had much more money than the native Irish boys, and could entertain the girls more lavishly at the movies and ice-cream stands. The men of our fleet and the Irish girls became excellent friends ; the association, from our point of view, was a very whole-some one, for the moral character of the Irish girls of Queenstown and Cork—as, indeed, of Irish girls everywhere —is very high, and their companionship added greatly to the well-being and contentment of our sailors, not a few of whom found wives among these young women. But when the Sinn Fein element saw their sweethearts desert-ing them for the American boys their hitherto suppressed anger took the form of overt acts.

Occasionally an American sailor would be brought from Cork to Queenstown in a condition that demanded pressing medical attention. When he regained consciousness he would relate how he had suddenly been set upon by half a dozen roughs and beaten into a state of insensibility. Several of our men were severely injured in this way. At other times small groups were stoned by Sinn Fein sym-pathizers, and there were many hostile demonstrations in moving-picture houses and theatres. Even more fre-quently attacks were made, not upon the American sailors, but upon the Irish girls who accompanied them. These chivalrous pro-German agitators would rush up and attempt to tear the girls away from our young men ; they would pull down their hair, slap them, and even kick them. Naturally American sailors were hardly the type to tolerate behaviour of this kind, and some bloody battles took place. This hostility was increased by one very regrettable occurrence in Queenstown. An American sailor was promenading the main thoroughfare with an Irish girl, when an infuriated Sinn Feiner rushed up, began to abuse his former sweetheart in vile language, and attempted to lay hands on her. The American struck this hooligan a terrific blow ; he fell backward and struck his head on the curb. The fall fractured the assailant's skull and in a few hours he was dead. We handed our man over to the civil authorities for trial, and a jury, composed entirely of Irishmen, acquitted him. The action of this jury in itself indicated that there was no sympathy among the decent Irish element, which constituted the great majority, with this sort of tactics, but naturally it did not improve relations between our men and the Sinn Fein. The importance of another incident which took place at the cathedral has been much exaggerated. It is true that a priest in his Sunday sermon denounced the American sailors as vandals and betrayers of Irish womanhood, but it is also true that the Roman Catholics of that section were themselves the most enraged at this absurd proceeding. A number of Roman Catholic officers who were present left the church in a body; the Catholic Bishop of the Diocese called upon Admiral Bayly and apologized for the insult, and he also punished the offending priest by assigning him to new duties at a considerable distance from the American ships.

But even more serious trouble was brewing, for our officers discovered that the American sailors were making elaborate plans to protect themselves. Had this discovery not been made in time, something like an international incident might have resulted. Much to our regret, therefore, it was found necessary to issue an order that no naval men, British or American, under the rank of Commander, should be permitted to go to Cork. Ultimately we had nearly 8,000 American men at this station; Queenstown itself is a small place of 6,000 or 7,000, so it is apparent that it did not possess the facilities for giving such a large number of men those relaxations which were necessary to their efficiency. We established a club in Queenstown, provided moving pictures and other entertainments, and did the best we could to keep our sailors contented. The citizens of Cork also keenly regretted our action. The great majority had formed a real fondness for our boys; and they regarded it as a great humiliation that the rowdy element had made it necessary to keep our men out of their city. Many letters were printed in the Cork newspapers apologizing to the Americans and calling upon the people to take action that would justify us in rescinding our order. The loss to Cork tradesmen was great; our men received not far from $200,000 to $300,000 a month in pay; they were free spenders, and their presence in the neighbourhood for nearly two years would have meant a fortune to many of the local merchants. Yet we were obliged to refuse to accede to the numerous requests that the American sailors be permitted to visit this city.

A committee of distinguished citizens of Cork, led by the Lord Mayor, came to Admiralty House to plead for the rescinding of this order. Admiral Bayly cross-examined them very sharply. It appeared that the men who had committed these offences against American sailors had never been punished.

Unless written guarantees were furnished that there would be no hostile demonstrations against British or Americans, Admiral Bayly refused to withdraw the ban, and I fully concurred in this decision. Unfortunately the committee could give no such guarantee. We knew very well that the first appearance of Americans in Cork would be the signal for a renewal of hostilities, and the temper of our sailors was such that the most deplorable consequences might have resulted. We even discovered that the blacksmiths on the U.S.S. *Melville* were surreptitiously manufacturing weapons which our men could conceal on their persons and with which they proposed to sally forth and do battle with the Sinn Fein ! So for the whole period of our stay in Queenstown our sailors were compelled to keep away from the dangerous city. But the situation was not without its humorous aspects. Thus the pretty girls of Cork, finding that the Americans could not come to them, decided to come to the Americans ; every afternoon a trainload would arrive at the Queenstown station, where our sailors would greet them, give them a splendid time, and then, in the evening, escort them to the station and send a happy crowd on their way home.

But the Sinn Feiners interfered with us in much more serious ways than this. They were doing everything in their power to help Germany. With their assistance German agents and German spies were landed in Ireland. At one time the situation became so dangerous that I had to take experienced officers whose services could ill be spared from our destroyers and assign them to our outlying air stations in Ireland. This, of course, proportionately weakened our fleet and did its part in prolonging the war.

CHAPTER III

I

ALL this time that we were seeking a solution for the submarine problem we really had that solution in our hands. The seas presented two impressive spectacles in those terrible months of April, May, and June, 1917. One was the comparative ease with which the German submarines were sinking merchant vessels; the other was their failure materially to weaken the Allied fleets. If we wish a counter-picture to that presented by the Irish Sea and the English Channel, where merchant shipping was constantly going down, we should look to the North Sea, where the British Grand Fleet, absolutely intact, was defiantly riding the waves. The uninformed public explained this apparent security in a way of its own; it believed that the British dreadnoughts were anchored behind booms, nets, and mine-fields, through which the submarines could not penetrate. Yet the fact of the matter was that the Grand Fleet was frequently cruising in the open sea, in the waters which were known to be the most infested with submarines. The German submarines had been attempting to destroy this fleet for two and a half years. It had been their plan to weaken this great battle force by " attrition "; to sink the great battleships one by one, and in this way to reduce the fighting power of the fleet to such a point that the German dreadnoughts could have some chances of success. Such had been the German programme, widely heralded at the beginning of the war; nearly three years had now passed, but how had this pretentious scheme succeeded? The fact was that the submarines had not destroyed a single dreadnought. It was certainly a profitable study in contrasts— that of merchant ships constantly being torpedoed and that of battleships constantly repelling such attacks.

been solved. The explanation was found in tr
circumstance that, whenever the dreadnoughts
sea, they were preceded by a screen of cruisers
stroyers. It almost seemed as though these surf
were serving as a kind of impenetrable wall agair
the German U-boats were beating themselves in va
to the casual observer there seemed to be no rea
the submarines should stand in any particular ter:
destroyers. Externally they looked like the leas
sive war vessels afloat. When they sailed ahea
battle squadrons, the destroyers were ungracefu
upon the surface of the water; the impression wl
conveyed was that of fragility rather than of strer
the idea that they could ever be the guardiar
mighty battleships which sailed behind them
seemed almost grotesque. Yet these little vesse
possessed the power of overcoming the submari
war had not progressed far when it became appa
the U-boat could not operate anywhere near th
little surface vessel without running serious ri:
struction.

Until the reports of submarine fighting bega:
their way into the papers, however, the destr
probably the one type of warship in which the p
the smallest interest. It had become, indeed, a
ugly duckling of the Navy. Our Congress had
neglected it; year after year our naval experts ha
mended that four destroyers be built for ever
ship, and annually Congress had appropriated
one or two. The war had also found Great Brit
out a sufficient number of destroyers for the p
anti-submarine warfare. The Admiralty had
enough for screening the Grand Fleet in cruisi:
battle, but it had been called upon to divert so
the protection of troop transportation, supply :
commerce generally that the efficiency of the
been greatly undermined. Thus Britain foui

without enough destroyers to meet the submarine campaign; this situation was not due to any lack of foresight, but to a failure to foresee that any civilized nation could ever employ the torpedo in unrestricted warfare against merchant ships and their crews.

The one time that this type of vessel had come prominently into notice was in 1904, when several of them attacked the Russian fleet at Port Arthur, damaging several powerful vessels and practically ending Russian sea power in the Far East. The history of the destroyer, however, goes back much further than 1904. It was created to fulfil a duty not unlike that which it has played so gloriously in the World War. In the late seventies and early eighties a new type of war vessel, the torpedo boat, caused almost as much perturbation as the submarine has caused in recent years. This speedy little fighter was invented to serve as a medium for the discharge of a newly perfected engine of naval warfare, the automobile torpedo. It was its function to creep up to a battleship, preferably under cover of darkness or in thick weather, and let loose this weapon against her unsuspecting hulk. The appearance of the torpedo boat led to the same prediction as that which has been more recently inspired by the submarine; in the eyes of many it simply meant the end of the great surface battleship. But naval architects, looking about for the " answer " to this dangerous craft, designed another type of warship and appropriately called it the " torpedo boat destroyer." This vessel was not only larger and speedier than its appointed antagonist, but it possessed a radius of action and a seaworthiness which enabled it to accompany the battle fleet. Its draft was so light that a torpedo could pass harmlessly under the keel, and it carried an armament which had sufficient power to end the career of any torpedo boat that came its way. Few types have ever justified their name so successfully as the torpedo boat destroyer. So completely did it eliminate that little vessel as a danger to the fighting ships that practically all navies long since ceased to build torpedo boats. Yet the destroyer promptly succeeded to the chief function of the discarded vessel, that of attacking capital ships with torpedoes; and, in addition to this, it assumed the duty of protecting battleships from similar attack by enemy vessels of the same type.

It surprises many people to learn that the destroyer is not a little boat but a warship of considerable size. This vessel to-day impresses most people as small only because all ships, those which are used for commerce and those which are used for war, have increased so greatly in displacement. The latest specimens of the destroyer carry four- or five-inch guns and twelve torpedo tubes, each of which launches a torpedo that weighs more than a ton, and runs as straight as an arrow for more than six miles. The *Santa Maria*, the largest vessel of the squadron with which Columbus made his first voyage to America, had a displacement of about five hundred tons, and thus was about half as large as a destroyer ; and even at the beginning of the clipper ship era few vessels were much larger.

Previous to 1914 it was generally believed that torpedo attacks would play a large part in any great naval engagement, and this was the reason why all naval advisers insisted that a large number of these vessels should be constructed as essential units of the fleet. Yet the war had not made much progress when it became apparent that this versatile craft had another great part to play, and that it would once more justify its name in really heroic fashion. Just as it had proved its worth in driving the surface torpedo boat from the seas, so now it developed into a very dangerous foe to the torpedo boat that sailed beneath the waves. Events soon demonstrated that, in all open engagements between submarine and destroyer, the submarine stood very little chance. The reason for this was simply that the submarine had no weapon with which it could successfully resist the attack of the destroyer, whereas the destroyer had several with which it could attack the submarine. The submarine had three or four torpedo tubes, and only one or two guns, and with neither could it afford to risk attacking the more powerfully armed destroyer. The U-boat was of such a fragile nature that it could never afford to engage in a combat in which it stood much chance of getting hit. A destroyer could stand a comparatively severe pounding and still remain fairly intact, but a single shell, striking a submarine, was a very serious matter ; even though the vessel did not sink as a result, it was almost inevitable that certain parts of its machinery would be so injured that it would have difficulty in getting into port. It therefore became necessary for the submarine always to play safe, to fight only under conditions in which it had the enemy at such a disadvantage that it ran little risk itself; and this was the reason why it preferred to attack merchant and passenger ships rather than vessels, such as the destroyer, that could energetically defend themselves.

The comparatively light draft of the destroyer, which is about nine or ten feet, pretty effectually protects it from the submarine's torpedo, for this torpedo, to function with its greatest efficiency, must take a course about fifteen feet under water; if it runs nearer the surface than this, it comes under the influence of the waves, and does not make a straight course. More important still, the speed of the destroyer, the ease with which it turns, circles, and zigzags, makes it all but impossible for a torpedo to be aimed with much chance of hitting her. Moreover, the discharge of this missile is a far more complicated undertaking than is generally supposed. The submarine commander cannot take position anywhere and discharge his weapon more or less wildly, running his chances of hitting; he must get his boat in place, calculate range, course, and speed, and take careful aim. Clearly it is difficult for him to do this successfully if his intended victim is scurrying along at the rate of thirty or forty miles an hour. Moreover, the destroyer is constantly changing its course, making great circles and indulging in other disconcerting movements. So well did the Germans understand the difficulty of torpedoing a destroyer that they practically never attempted so unprofitable and so hazardous an enterprise.

Torpedoes are complicated and expensive mechanisms; each one costs about $8,000 and the average U-boat carried only from eight to twelve; it was therefore necessary to husband these precious weapons, to use them only when the chances most favoured success; the U-boat commander who wasted them in attempts to sink destroyers would probably have been court-martialled.

But while the submarine had practically no means of successfully fighting the destroyer, the destroyer had several ways of putting an end to the submarine. The advantage which really made the destroyer so dangerous, as already intimated, was its excessive speed. On the surface the U-boat made little more than fifteen miles an hour, and under the surface it made little more than seven or eight. If the destroyer once discovered its presence, therefore, it could reach its prey in an incredibly short time. It could attack with its guns, and, if conditions were favourable, it could ram ; and this was no trifling accident, for a destroyer going at thirty or forty miles could cut a submarine nearly in two with its strong, razor-like bow. In the early days of the war these were the main methods upon which it relied to attack, but by the time that I had reached London, another and much more frightful weapon had been devised. This was the depth charge, a large can containing about three hundred pounds of TNT, which, if it exploded anywhere within one hundred feet of the submarine, would either destroy it entirely or so injure it that the victim usually had to come to the surface and surrender.

I once asked Admiral Jellicoe who was the real inventor of this annihilating missile.

"No man in particular," he said. "It came into existence almost spontaneously, in response to a pressing need. Gunfire can destroy submarines when they are on the surface, but you know it can accomplish nothing against them when they are submerged. This fact made it extremely difficult to sink them in the early days of the war. One day, when the Grand Fleet was cruising in the North Sea, a submarine fired a torpedo at one of the cruisers. The cruiser saw the periscope and the wake of the torpedo, and had little difficulty in so manœuvring as to avoid being struck. She then went full speed to the spot from which the submarine had fired its torpedo, in the hope of ramming it. But by the time she arrived the submarine had submerged so deeply that the cruiser passed over her without doing her any harm. Yet the officers and crew could see the submerged hull ; there the enemy lay in full view of her pursuers, yet perfectly safe ! The officers reported this incident to me in the presence of Admiral Madden, second in command.

" ' Wouldn't it have been fine,' said Madden, ' if they had had on board a mine so designed that, when dropped overboard, it would have exploded when it reached the depth at which the submarine was lying ? '

"That remark," continued Admiral Jellicoe, "gave us the germinal idea of the depth charge. I asked the

Admiralty to get to work and produce a 'mine' that would act in the way that Admiral Madden had suggested. It proved to be very simple to construct—an ordinary steel cylinder filled with TNT; this was fitted with a simple firing appliance which was set off by the pressure of the water, and could be so adjusted that it would explode the charge at any depth desired. This apparatus was so simple and so necessary that we at once began to manufacture it."

The depth charge looked like the innocent domestic ash can, and that was the name by which it soon came to be popularly known. Each destroyer eventually carried twenty or thirty of these destructive weapons at the stern; a mere pull on a lever would make one drop into the water. Many destroyers also carried strange-looking howitzers, which were made in the shape of a Y, and from which one ash can could be hurled fifty yards or more from each side of the vessel. The explosion, when it took place within the one hundred feet which I have mentioned as usually fatal to the submarine, would drive the plates inward and sometimes make a leak so large that the vessel would sink almost instantaneously. At a somewhat greater distance it frequently produced a leak of such serious proportions that the submarine would be forced to blow her ballast tanks, come to the surface, and surrender. Even when the depth charge exploded considerably more than a hundred feet away, the result might be equally disastrous, for the concussion might distort the hull and damage the horizontal rudders, making it impossible to steer, or it might so injure the essential machinery that the submarine would be rendered helpless. Sometimes the lights went out, leaving the crew groping in blackness; necessary parts were shaken from their fastenings; and in such a case the commander had his choice of two alternatives, one to be crushed by the pressure of the water, and the other to come up and be captured or sunk by his surface foe. It is no reflection upon the courage of the submarine commanders to say that in this embarrassing situation they usually preferred to throw themselves upon the mercy of the enemy rather than to be smashed or to die a lingering and agonizing death under the water. Even when the explosion took place at a distance so great that the submarine was not

seriously damaged, the experience was a highly disconcerting one for the crew. If a dozen depth charges were
dropped, one after the other, the effect upon the men in
the hunted vessel was particularly demoralizing. In
the course of the war several of our own submarines were
depth-charged by our own destroyers, and from our crews
we obtained graphic descriptions of the sensations which
resulted. It was found that men who had passed through
such an ordeal were practically useless for several days,
and that sometimes they were rendered permanently unfit
for service. The state of nerves which followed such an
experience was not unlike that new war psychosis known
as shell-shock. One of our officers who had had such an
adventure told me that the explosion of a single depth
charge under the water might be compared to the concussion produced by the simultaneous firing of all the
fourteen-inch guns of a battleship. One can only imagine
what the concussion must have been when produced by
ten or twenty depth charges in succession. Whether or
not the submarine was destroyed or seriously injured, a
depth-charged crew became extremely cautious in the
future about getting anywhere in the neighbourhood of
a destroyer ; and among the several influences which
ultimately disorganized the *moral* of the German U-boat
service these contacts with depth charges were doubtless
the most important. The hardiest under-water sailor did
not care to go through such frightful moments a second
time.

This statement makes it appear as though the depth
charge had settled the fate of the submarine. Yet that
was far from being the case, for against the ash can,
with its 300 pounds of TNT, the submarine possessed
one quality which gave it great defensive power. That
was ability to make itself unseen. Strangely enough,
the average layman is inclined to overlook this fairly
apparent fact, and that is the reason why, even at the
risk of repeating myself, I frequently refer to it. Indeed,
the only respect in which the subsurface boat differs
essentially from all other war vessels is in this power of
becoming invisible. Whenever it descries danger from
afar, the submarine can disappear under the water in
anywhere from twenty seconds to a minute. And its
great advantage is that it can detect its enemy long before

that enemy can detect the submarine. A U-boat, sailing awash, or sailing with only its conning-tower exposed, can see a destroyer at a distance of about fifteen miles if the weather is clear ; but, under similar conditions, the destroyer can see the submarine at a distance of about four miles. Possessing this great advantage, the submarine can usually decide whether it will meet the enemy or not ; if it decides that it is wise to avoid an encounter, all it has to do is to duck, remain submerged until the destroyer has passed on, entirely unconscious of its presence, and then to resume its real work, which is not that of fighting warships, but of sinking merchantmen. The chief anxiety of the U-boat commander is thus to avoid contact with its surface foe and its terrible depth charge, whereas the business of the destroyer commander is to get within fighting distance of his quarry.

Ordinarily, conditions favour the U-boat in this game, simply because the ocean is so large a place. But there is one situation in which the destroyer has more than a fighting chance, for the power of the submarine to keep its presence secret lasts only so long as it remains out of action. If it makes no attempt to fight, its presence can hardly ever be detected ; but just as soon as it becomes belligerent, it immediately reveals its whereabouts. If it comes to the surface and fires its guns, naturally it advertises to its enemy precisely where it is; but it betrays its location almost as clearly when it discharges a torpedo. Just as soon as the torpedo leaves the submarine, a wake, clearly marking its progress, appears upon the surface of the water. Though most newspaper readers have heard of this tell-tale track, I have found few who really understand what a conspicuous disturbance it is. The torpedo is really a little submarine itself ; it is propelled by compressed air, the exhaust of which stirs up the water and produces a foamy, soapy wake, which is practically the same as that produced by the propeller of an ocean liner. This trail is four or five feet wide ; it is as white and is as distinct as a chalk line drawn upon a blackboard, provided the weather is clear and the sun is in the right direction. Indeed, it is sometimes so distinct that an easily manœuvred ship, and even sometimes a merchantman, can avoid the torpedo which it sees advancing merely by putting over the helm and turning out of its

7

course. But the chief value of this wake to the submarine hunters is that it shows the direction in which the submarine was located when the torpedo started on its course. It stands out on the surface of the water like a long, ghostly finger pointing to the spot where the foe let loose its shaft.

As soon as the destroyer sees this betraying disturbance, the commander rings for full speed ; and one of the greatest advantages of this type of vessel is that it can attain full speed in an incredibly short time. The destroyer then dashes down the wake until it reaches the end, which indicates the point where the submarine lay when it discharged its missile. At this point the surface vessel drops a depth charge and then begins cutting a circle, say, to the right. Pains are taken to make this circle so wide that it will include the submarine, provided it has gone in that direction. The destroyer then makes another circle to the left. Every ten or fifteen seconds, while describing these circles, it drops a depth charge ; indeed, not infrequently it drops twenty or thirty in a few minutes. If there is another destroyer in the neighbourhood it also follows up the wake and when it reaches the indicated point, it circles in the opposite direction from the first. Sometimes more than two may start for the suspected location and, under certain conditions, the water within a radius of half a mile or more may be seething with exploding depth charges.

It is plain from this description that the proceeding develops into an exceedingly dangerous game for the attacking submarine. It is a simple matter to calculate the chances of escaping which the enemy has under these conditions. That opportunity is clearly measured by the time which elapses from the moment when it discharges its torpedo to the moment when the destroyer has reached the point at which it was discharged. This interval gives the subsurface boat a certain chance to get away ; but its under-water speed is moderate, and so by the time the destroyer reaches the critical spot, the submarine has advanced but a short distance away from it. How far has she gone ? In what direction did she go ? These are the two questions which the destroyer commander must answer, and the success with which he answers them accurately measures his success in sinking or damaging his enemy, or in giving him a good scare. If he always decided these two points accurately, he would almost always " get " his submarine ; the chances of error are very great, however, and that is the reason why the submarine in most cases gets away. All that the surface commander knows is that there is a U-boat somewhere in his neighbourhood, but he does not know its precise location and so he is fighting more or less in the dark. In the great majority of cases the submarine does get away, but now and then the depth charge reaches its goal and ends its career.

If only one destroyer is hunting, the chances of escape strongly favour the under-water craft ; if several pounce upon her at once, however, the chances of escaping are much more precarious. If the water is shallow the U-boat can sometimes outwit the pursuer by sinking to the bottom and lying there in silent security until its surface enemy tires of the chase. But in the open sea there is no possibility of concealing itself and so saving itself in this fashion, for if the submarine sinks beyond a certain depth the pressure of the water will crush it.

While the record shows that the U-boat usually suc-ceeded in evading the depth charges, there were enough sunk or seriously damaged or given a bad shake-up to serve as a constant reminder to the crews that they ran great danger in approaching waters which were protected by destroyers. The U-boat captains, as will appear, avoided such waters regularly ; they much preferred to attack their merchant prey in areas where these soul-racking depth charges did not interfere with their opera-tions.

It is now becoming apparent why the great battle fleet, which always sailed behind a protecting screen of such destroyers, was practically immune from torpedo attack. In order to assail these battleships the submarine was always compelled to do the one thing which, above all others, it was determined to avoid—to get within depth-charge radius of the surface craft. In discharging the torpedo, distance, as already intimated, is the all-impor-tant consideration. The U-boat carries a torpedo which has a much shorter range than that of the destroyer ; it was seldom effective if fired at more than 2,000 yards, and beyond that distance its chances of hitting became very slight. Indeed, a much shorter distance than that was desirable if the torpedo was to accomplish its most destructive purpose. So valuable were these missiles and so necessary was it that every one should be used to good advantage, that the U-boat's captain had instructions to shoot at no greater distance than 300 yards, unless the conditions were particularly favourable. In the early days, the torpedoes which were fired at a greater distance would often hit the ships on the bow or the stern, and do comparatively little damage ; such vessels could be brought in, repaired in a short time, and again put to sea. The German Admiralty discovered that in firing from a comparatively long distance it was wasting its torpedoes ; it therefore ordered its men to get so near the prey that it could strike the vessel in a vital spot, preferably in the engine-room ; and to do this it was necessary to creep up within 300 yards. But to get as close as that to the destroyers which screened the battleships meant almost certain destruction. Thus the one method of attack which was left to the U-boat was to dive under the destroyer screen and come up in the midst of the battle fleet itself. A few minutes after its presence should become known, however, a large number of destroyers would be dropping depth charges in its neighbourhood, and its chances of escaping destruction would be almost nil, to say nothing of its chances of destroying ships.

The Germans learned the futility of this kind of an operation early in the war, and the man who taught them this lesson was Commander Weddingen, the same officer who had first demonstrated the value of the submarine in practical warfare. It was Otto Weddingen who, in September, 1914, sank the old British cruisers, the *Hogue*, the *Cressy*, and the *Aboukir*, an exploit which made him one of the great popular heroes of Germany. A few months afterward Commander Weddingen decided to try an experiment which was considerably more hazardous than that of sinking three unescorted cruisers ; he aspired to nothing less ambitious than an attack upon the Grand Fleet itself. On March 18th a part of this fleet was cruising off Cromarty, Scotland ; here Weddingen came with the *U*-29, dived under the destroyer screen and fired one torpedo, which passed astern of the *Neptune*. The alarm was immediately sounded, and presently the battle-ship *Dreadnought*, which had seen the periscope, started at full speed for the submarine, rammed the vessel and sent it promptly to the bottom. As it was sinking the bow rose out of the water, plainly disclosing the number *U*-29. There was not one survivor. Weddingen's attempt was an heroic one, but so disastrous to himself and to his vessel that very few German commanders ever tried to emulate his example. It clearly proved to the German Admiralty that it was useless to attempt to destroy the Grand Fleet with submarines, or even to weaken it piecemeal, and probably this experience had much to do with this new kind of warfare—that of sub-marines against unprotected merchant ships—which the Germans now proceeded to introduce.

The simple fact is that the battle fleet was never so safe as when it was cruising in the open sea, screened by de-stroyers. It was far safer when it was sailing thus defiantly, constantly inviting attack, than when it was anchored at its unprotected base at Scapa Flow. Indeed, until Scapa Flow was impregnably protected by booms and mines, the British commanders recognized that cruising in the open sea was its best means of avoiding the German U-boats. No claim is made that the sub-marine cannot dive under the destroyer screen and attack a battle fleet, and possibly torpedo one or more of its vessels. The illustration which has been given shows that Weddingen nearly " got " the *Neptune* ; and had this torpedo gone a few feet nearer, his experiment might have shown that, although he subsequently lost his own life, crew, and ship, he had sunk one British battleship, a pro-ceeding which, in war, might have been recognized as a fair exchange. But the point which I wish to emphasize is that the chances of success were so small that the Germans decided that it was not worth while to make the attempt. Afterward, when merchant vessels were formed into convoys, a submarine would occasionally dive under the screen and destroy a ship ; but most such attacks were unsuccessful, and experience taught the Germans that a persistent effort of this kind would cause the destruction of so many submarines that their campaign would fail. So the U-boat commanders left the Grand Fleet alone, either because they lacked nerve or because their instructions from Berlin were explicit to that effect.

II

Having constantly before my eyes this picture of the Grand Fleet immune from torpedo attack, naturally the first question I asked, when discussing the situation with Admiral Jellicoe and others, was this : " Why not apply this same principle to merchant ships ? "

If destroyers could keep the submarines away from battleships, they could certainly keep them away from merchantmen. It is clear, from the description already given, precisely how the battleships had been made safe from submarines ; they had proceeded, as usual, in a close formation, or " convoy," and their destroyer screen had proved effective. Thus logic apparently indicated that the convoy system was the " answer " to the sub-marine.

Yet the convoy, as used in previous wars, differed materially from any application of the idea which could possibly be made to the present contest. This scheme of sailing vessels in groups, and escorting them by warships, is almost as old as naval warfare itself. As early as the thirteenth century, the merchants of the Hanseatic League were compelled to sail their ships in convoy as a protection against the pirates who were then constantly lurking in the Baltic Sea. The Government of Venice used this same device to protect its enormous commerce. In the fifteenth century the large trade in wool and wine which existed between England and the Moorish ports of Spain was safeguarded by convoys, and in the sixteenth century Spain herself regularly depended upon massing her ships to defend her commerce with the West Indies against the piratical attacks of English and French adventurers. The escorts provided for these " flotas " really laid the foundation of the mighty Spanish fleet which threatened England's existence for more than a hundred years. By the time of Queen Elizabeth the convoy had thus become the all-prevailing, method of safeguarding merchant shipping, but it was in the Napoleonic wars that it had reached its greatest usefulness. The convoys of that period were managed with some military precision ; there were carefully stipulated methods of collecting the ships, of meeting the cruiser escorts at the appointed rendezvous, and of dispersing them when the danger zone was passed ; and naval officers were systematically put in charge. The convoys of this period were very large ; from 200 to 300 ships were not an unusual gathering, and sometimes 500 or more would get together at certain important places, such as the entrance to the Baltic. But these ships, of course, were very small compared with those of the present time. It was only necessary to supply such aggregations of vessels with enough protecting cruisers to overwhelm any raiders which the enemy might send against them. The merchantmen were not required to sail in any particular formation, nor were they required to manœuvre against unseen mysterious foes. Neither was it absolutely essential that they should keep constantly together ; and they could even spread themselves somewhat loosely over the ocean. If an enemy raider appeared on the horizon, the escorting cruiser or cruisers left the convoy and began chase ; a battle ensued, the convoy meanwhile passing on its voyage unharmed. When its protecting vessels had disposed of the attackers, they rejoined the merchantmen. No unusual seamanship was demanded of the merchant captains, for the whole responsibility for their safety rested with the escorting cruisers.

But the operation of beating off an occasional surface raider, which necessarily fights in the open, is quite a different procedure from that of protecting an aggregation of vessels from enemies that discharge torpedoes under the water. As part protection against such insidious attacks both the merchant ships and the escorting men-of-war of to-day had in this war to keep up a perpetual zigzagging. This zigzag, indeed, was in itself an efficacious method of protection. As already said, the submarine was forced to attain an advantageous position before it could discharge its torpedo ; it was its favourite practice to approach to within a few hundred yards in order to hit its victim in a vital spot. This mere fact shows that zigzagging in itself was one of the best methods of avoiding destruction. Before this became the general rule, the task of torpedoing a vessel was comparatively easy. All it was necessary for the submarine to do was to bring the vessel's masts in line ; that is, to get directly ahead of her, submerge with the small periscope showing only occasionally, and to fire the torpedo at short range as the ship passed by. Except in the case of very slow vessels, she could of course do this only when she was not far from the course of her advancing prey when she first sighted her. If, however, the vessel was zigzagging, this pretty game was usually defeated ; the submarine never knew in what direction to go in order to get within torpedoing distance, and she could not go far because her speed under water is so slow. The same conditions apply to a zigzagging convoy. This explained why, as soon as the merchant vessel or convoy entered the submarine zone, or as soon as a submarine was sighted, it began zigzagging, first on one side and then on the other, and always irregularly, its course comprising a disjointed line, which made it a mere chance whether the submarine could get into a position from which to fire with any certainty of obtaining results. A vessel sailing alone could manœuvre in this way without much difficulty, but it is apparent that twenty or thirty vessels, sailing in close formation, would not find the operation a simple one. It was necessary for them to sail in close and regular formation in order to make it possible to manœuvre them and screen them with destroyers, so it is evident that the closer the formation the fewer the destroyers that would be needed to protect it. These circumstances make the modern convoy quite a different affair from the happy-go-lucky proceeding of the Napoleonic era.

It is perhaps not surprising that the greatest hostility to the convoys has always come from the merchant captains themselves. In old days they chafed at the time which was consumed in assembling the ships, at the necessity for reducing speed to enable the slower vessels to keep up with the procession, and at the delay in getting their cargoes into port. In all wars in which convoys have been used it has been very difficult to keep the merchant captains in line. In Nelson's day these fine old salts were constantly breaking away from their convoys and taking their chances of running into port unescorted. If the merchant master of a century ago rebelled at the comparatively simply managed convoy of those days it is not strange that their successors of the present time should not have looked with favour upon the relatively complicated and difficult arrangement required of them in this war. In the early discussions with these men at the Admiralty they showed themselves almost unanimously opposed to the convoy.

"The merchantmen themselves are the chief obstacle to the convoy," said Admiral Jellicoe. "We have discussed it with them many times and they declare that it is impossible. It is all right for war vessels to manœuvre in close formation, they say, for we spend our time practising in these formations, and so they think that it is second nature to us. But they say that they cannot do it. They particularly reject the idea that when in formation they can manœuvre their ships in the fog or at night without lights. They believe that they would lose more ships through collisions than the submarines would sink."

I was told that the whole subject had been completely threshed out at a meeting which had been held at the Admiralty on February 23, 1917, about six weeks before America had entered the war. At that time ten masters of merchant ships had met Admiral Jellicoe and other members of the Admiralty and had discussed the convoy proposition at length. In laying the matter before these experienced seamen Admiral Jellicoe emphasized the necessity of good station-keeping, and he described the close formation which the vessels would have to maintain. It would be necessary for the ships to keep together, he explained, otherwise the submarines could pick off the stragglers. He asked the masters whether eight merchant ships, which had a speed varying perhaps two knots, could keep station in line ahead (that is, in single file or column) 500 yards apart, and sail in two columns down the Channel.

"It would be absolutely impossible," the ten masters replied, almost in a chorus.

A discouraging fact, they said, was that many of the ablest merchant captains had gone into the navy, and that many of those who had replaced them could not be depended on to handle their ships in such a formation.

"We have so few competent deck officers that the captain would have to be on the bridge the whole twenty-four hours," they said. And the difficulty was not only with the bridge, but with the engine-room. In order to keep the ships constantly the same distance apart it would be necessary accurately to regulate their speed ; the battleships could do this because they had certain elaborate devices, which the merchant vessels lacked, for timing the revolutions of the engines. The poor quality of the coal which they were obtaining would also make it difficult to maintain a regular speed.

Admiral Jellicoe then asked the masters whether they could sail in twos or threes and keep station.

" Two might do it, but three would be too many," was the discouraging verdict. But the masters were positive that even two merchantmen could not safely keep station abreast in the night-time without lights ; two such vessels would have to sail in single file, the leading ship showing a stern light. The masters emphasized their conviction that they preferred to sail alone, each ship for herself, and to let each one take her chances of getting into port.

And there the matter rested. I had the opportunity of discussing the convoy system with several merchant captains, and in these discussions they simply echoed the views which had been expressed at this formal conference. I do not believe that British naval officers came in contact with a single merchant master who favoured the convoy at that time. They were not doubtful about the idea ; they were openly hostile. The British merchant captains are a magnificent body of seamen ; their first thought was to serve their country and the Allied cause ; their attitude in this matter was not obstinacy ; it simply resulted from their sincere conviction that the convoy system would entail greater shipping losses than were then being inflicted by the German submarines.

Many naval officers at that time shared the same view. They opposed the convoy not only on these grounds ; its introduction would mean immediately cutting down the tonnage 15 or 20 per cent., because of the time which would be consumed in assembling the ships and awaiting escorts and in the slower average speed which they could make. Many ship owners and directors of steamship companies expressed the same opinions. They also objected to the convoy on the ground that it would cause considerable delay and hence would result in loss of earnings. Yet the attitude of the merchant marine had not entirely eliminated the convoy from consideration. At the time when I arrived the proposal was still being discussed ; the rate at which the Germans were sinking merchantmen made this inevitable. And there seemed to be two schools among Allied naval men, one of which was opposed to the convoy, while the other insisted that it should be given a trial.   The convoy had one irresistible attraction for the officer which seemed to counterbalance all the objections which were being urged against it.   Its adoption would mean taking the offensive against the German submarines.   The essential defect of the patrol system, as it was then conducted, was that it was primarily a defensive measure.   Each destroyer cruised around in an assigned area, ready to assist vessels in distress, escort ships through her own " square " and, incidentally, to attack a submarine when the opportunity was presented. But the mere fact that a destroyer was patrolling a particular area meant only, as already explained, that the submarine had occasionally to sink out of sight until she had passed by. Consequently the submarine proceeded to operate whenever a destroyer was not in sight, and this was necessarily most of the time, for the submarine zone was such a big place and the Allied destroyer fleet was so pitifully small that it was impossible to cover it effectively.   Under these conditions there were very few encounters between destroyers and submarines, at least in the waters south and west of Ireland, for the submarines took all precautions against getting close enough to be sighted by the destroyers.

But the British and French navies were not the only ones which, at this time, were depending upon the patrol as a protection against the subsurface boat.   The American navy was committing precisely the same error off our Atlantic coast.   As soon as Congress declared war against Germany we expected that at least a few of the U-boats would cross the Atlantic and attack American shipping ; indeed, many believed that some had already crossed in anticipation of war ; the papers were filled with silly stories about " submarine bases " in Mexican waters, on the New England coast, and elsewhere ; submarines were even reported entering Long Island Sound ; nets were stretched across the Narrows to keep them out of New York Harbour ; and our coasting vessels saw periscopes and the wakes of torpedoes everywhere from Maine to Florida.   So prevalent was this apprehension that, in the early days of the war, American destroyers regularly patrolled our coast looking for these far-flung submarines.   Yet the idea of seeking them this way was absurd.   Even had we known where the submarine was located there would have been little likelihood that we could ever have sighted it, to say nothing of getting near it. We might have learned that a German U-boat was operating off Cape Cod ; we might have had the exact latitude and longitude of the location which it was expected that it would reach at a particular moment. At the time the message was sent the submarine might have been lying on the surface ready to attack a passing merchantman, but even under these conditions the destroyer could never have reached her quarry, for as soon as the U-boat saw the enemy approaching it would simply have ducked under the water and remained there in perfect safety. When all danger had passed it would again have bobbed up to the surface as serenely as you please, and gone ahead with its appointed task of sinking merchant ships. One of the astonishing things about this war was that many of the naval officers of all countries did not seem to understand until a very late date that it was utterly futile to send anti-submarine surface craft out into the wide ocean to attack or chase away submarines. The thing to do, of course, was to make the submarines come to the anti-submarine craft and fight in order to get merchantmen.

I have made this point before, and I now repeat the explanation to emphasize that the patrol system was necessarily unsuccessful, because it made almost impossible any combats with submarines and afforded very little protection to shipping. The advantage of the convoy system, as its advocates now urged, was precisely that it made such combats inevitable. In other words, it meant offensive warfare. It was proposed to surround each convoy with a protecting screen of destroyers in precisely the same way that the battle fleet was protected. Thus we should compel any submarine which was planning to torpedo a convoyed ship to do so only in waters that were infested with destroyers. In order to get into position to discharge its missile the submarine would have to creep up close to the rim that marked the circle of these destroyers. Just as soon as the torpedo started on its course and the tell-tale wake appeared on the surface the protecting ships would immediately begin sowing the waters with their depth charges. Thus in the future the Germans would be compelled to fight for every ship which they should attempt to sink, instead of sinking them conveniently in waters that were free of destroyers, as had hitherto been their privilege. Already the British had demonstrated that such a screen of destroyers could protect merchant ships as well as war vessels. They were making this fact clear every day in the successful transportation of troops and supplies across the Channel. In this region they had established an immune zone, which was constantly patrolled by destroyers and other anti-submarine craft, and through these the merchant fleets were constantly passing with complete safety. The proposal to convoy all merchant ships was a proposal to apply this same system on a much broader scale. If we should arrange our ships in compact convoys and protect them with destroyers we would really create another immune zone of this kind, and this would be different from the one established across the Channel only in that it would be a movable one. In this way we should establish about a square mile of the surface of the ocean in which submarines could not operate without great danger, and then we could move that square mile along until port was reached.

The advantages of the convoy were thus so apparent that, despite the pessimistic attitude of the merchant captains, there were a number of officers in the British navy who kept insisting that it should be tried. In this discussion I took my~stand emphatically with these officers. From the beginning I had believed in this method of combating the U-boat warfare. Certain early experiences had led me to believe that the merchant captains were wrong in under-estimating the quality of their own seamanship. It was my conviction that these intelligent and hardy men did not really know how capable they were at handling ships. In my discussions with them they disclosed an exaggerated idea of the seamanly ability of naval officers in manœuvring their large fleets. They attributed this to the superior training of the men and to the special manœuvring qualities of the ship. "Warships are built so that they can keep station, and turn at any angle at a moment's notice," they would say, "but we haven't any men on our ships who can do these things." As a matter of fact, these men were entirely in error and I knew it. Their practical experience in handling ships of all sizes, shapes, and speeds under a great variety of conditions is in reality much more extensive than naval officers can possibly enjoy. I learned this more than thirty years ago, when stationed on the Pennsylvania schoolship, teaching the boys navigation. This was one of the most valuable experiences of my life, for it brought me in every-day contact with merchant seamen, and it was then that I made the discovery which proved so valuable to me now.

It is true that merchant captains had much to learn about steaming and manœuvring in formation, but I was sure they could pick it up quickly and carry it out successfully under the direction of naval officers—the convoy commander being always a naval officer.

The naval officer not only has a group of vessels that are practically uniform in speed and ability to turn around quickly, but he is provided also with various instruments which enable him to keep the revolutions of his engines constant, to measure distances and the like. Moreover, as a junior officer, he is schooled in manœuvring these very ships for some years before he is trusted with the command of one of them, and he, therefore, not only knows their peculiarities, but also those of their captains—the latter very useful information, by the way.

Though it was necessary for the merchantmen, on the other hand, to bring their much clumsier ships into formation with perhaps thirty entirely strange vessels of different sizes, shapes, speeds, nationalities, and manœuvring qualities, yet I was confident that they were competent to handle them successfully under these difficult conditions. Indeed, afterward, one of my most experienced destroyer commanders reported that while he was escorting a convoy of twenty-eight ships they kept their stations quite as well as battleships, while they were executing two manœuvres to avoid a submarine.

Such influence as I possessed at this time, therefore, I threw in with the group of British officers which was advocating the convoy.

There was, however, still one really serious impediment to adopting this convoy system, and that was that the number of destroyers available was insufficient. The British, for reasons which have been explained, did not have the necessary destroyers for this work, and this was what made so very important the participation of the United States in the naval war—for our navy possessed the additional vessels that would make possible the immediate adoption of the convoy system. I do not wish to say that the convoy would not have been established had we not sent destroyers for that purpose, yet I do not see how otherwise it could have been established in any complete and systematic way at such an early date. And we furnished other ships than destroyers, for besides providing what I have called the modern convoy—that which protects the compact mass of vessels from submarines—it was necessary also to furnish escorts after the old Napoleonic plan. It was the business of the destroyers to conduct the merchantmen only through the submarine zone. They did not take them the whole distance across the ocean, for there was little danger of submarine attack until the ships had arrived in the infested waters. This would have been impossible in any case with the limited number of destroyers. But from the time the convoys left the home port there was a possibility that the same kind of attack would be launched as that to which convoys were subjected in Nelsonian days ; there was the danger, that is, that surface war vessels, raiders or cruisers, might escape from their German bases and swoop down upon them. We always had before our minds the activities of the *Moewe*, and we therefore deemed it necessary to escort the convoys across the ocean with battleships and cruisers, just as was the practice a century ago. The British did not have ships enough available for this purpose, and here again the American navy was able to supply the lack ; for we had a number of pre-dreadnoughts and cruisers that were ideally adapted to this kind of work.

III

On April 30th I received a message from Admiral Jellicoe requesting me to visit him at the Admiralty. When I arrived he said that the projected study of the convoy system had been made, and he handed me a copy of it. It had been decided to send one experimental convoy from Gibraltar. The Admiralty, he added, had not yet definitely decided that the convoy system should be adopted, but there was every intention of giving it a thorough and fair trial. That same evening at dinner I met Mr. Lloyd George, Sir Edward Carson, and Lord Milner, and once more discussed with them the whole convoy idea. I found the Prime Minister especially favourable to the plan and, in fact, civilians in general were more kindly disposed toward the convoy than seamen, because they were less familiar with the nautical and shipping difficulties which it involved.

Naval officers were immediately sent to Gibraltar to instruct the merchant masters in the details of assembling and conducting vessels. Eight-knot ships were selected for the experiment, and a number of destroyers were assigned for their protection. The merchant captains, as was to be expected, regarded the whole enterprise suspiciously, but entered into it with the proper spirit.

On May 20th that first convoy arrived at its English destination in perfect condition. The success with which it made the voyage disproved all the pessimistic opinions which the merchant sailors had entertained about themselves. They suddenly discovered, as I had contended, that they could do practically everything which, in their conferences with the Admiralty, they had declared that they were unable to do. In those meetings they had asserted that not more than two ships could keep station ; but now they discovered that the whole convoy could sail with stipulated distances between the vessels and keep this formation with little difficulty. They were drilled on the way in zigzagging and manœuvring—a practice carried out subsequently with all convoys—and by the time they reached the danger zone they found that, in obedience to a prearranged signal, all the ships could turn as a single one, and perform all the zigzag evolutions which the situation demanded. They had asserted that they could not sail at night without lights and that an attempt to do so would result in many collisions, but the experimental convoy proved that this was merely another case of self-delusion. Naturally the arrival of this convoy caused the greatest satisfaction in the Admiralty, but the most delighted men were the merchant captains themselves, for the whole thing was to them a complete revelation of their seamanly ability, and naturally it flattered their pride. The news of this arrival naturally travelled fast in shipping circles ; it completely changed the attitude of the merchant sailors, and the chief opponents of the convoy now became its most enthusiastic advocates.

Outside shipping circles, however, nothing about this convoy was known at that time. Yet May 20th, the date when it reached England safely, marked one of the great turning-points of the war. That critical voyage meant nothing less than that the Allies had found the way of defeating the German submarine. The world might still clamour for a specific " invention " that would destroy all the submarines overnight, or it might demand that the Allies should block them in their bases, or suggest that they might do any number of impossible things, but the naval chiefs of the Allies discovered, on May 20, 1917, that they could defeat the German campaign even without these rather uncertain aids. The submarine danger was by no means ended when this first convoy arrived ; many anxious months still lay ahead of us ; other means would have to be devised that would supplement the convoy ; yet the all-important fact was that the Allied chiefs now realized, for the first time, that the problem was not an insoluble one ; and that, with hard work and infinite patience, they could keep open the communications that were essential to victory. The arrival of these weather-beaten ships thus brought the assurance that the armies and the civilian populations could be supplied with food and materials, and that the seas could be kept open for the transportation of American troops to France. In fine, it meant that the Allies could win the war.

On May 21st the British Admiralty, which this experimental convoy had entirely converted, voted to adopt the convoy system for all merchant shipping. Not long afterward the second convoy arrived safely from Hampton Roads, and then other convoys began to put in from Scandinavian ports. On July 21st I was able definitely to report to Washington that " the success of the convoys so far brought in shows that the system will defeat the submarine campaign if applied generally and in time."

But while we recognize the fact that the convoy preserved our communications and so made possible the continuation of the war, we must not overlook a vitally important element in its success. In describing the work of the destroyer, which was the protecting arm of the convoy, I have said nothing about the forces that really laid the whole foundation of the anti-submarine campaign. All the time that these destroyers were fighting off the submarines the power that made possible their operations was cruising quietly in the North Sea, doing its work so inconspicuously that the world was hardly aware of its existence. For back of all these operations lay the mighty force of the Grand Fleet. Admiral Beatty's dreadnoughts and battle cruisers, which were afterward supplemented

8

by a fine squadron of American ships, kept the German surface vessels penned in their harbours and in this way left the ocean free for the operations of the Allied surface craft. I have already said that, in April, 1917, the Allied navies, while they controlled the surface of the water, did not control the subsurface, which at that time was practically at the disposition of the Germans. Yet the determining fact, as we were now to learn, was that this control of the surface was to give us the control of the subsurface also. Only the fact that the battleships kept the German fleet at bay made it possible for the destroyers and other surface craft to do their beneficent work. In an open sea battle their surface navies would have disposed of the German fleet; but let us suppose for a moment that an earthquake, or some other great natural disturbance, had engulfed the British fleet at Scapa Flow. The world would then have been at Germany's mercy and all the destroyers the Allies could have put upon the sea would have availed them nothing, for the German battleships and battle cruisers could have sunk them or driven them into their ports. Then Allied commerce would have been the prey, not only of the submarines, which could have operated with the utmost freedom, but of the German surface craft as well. In a few weeks the British food supplies would have been exhausted. There would have been an early end to the soldiers and munitions which Britain was constantly sending to France. The United States could have sent no forces to the Western Front and the result would have been the surrender which the Allies themselves, in the spring of 1917, regarded as not a remote possibility. America would then have been compelled to face the German power alone, and to face it long before we had had an opportunity of assembling our resources and of equipping our armies. The world was preserved from all these calamities because the destroyer and the convoy solved the problem of the submarine and because back of these agencies of victory lay Admiral Beatty's squadrons, holding at arm's length the German surface ships while these comparatively fragile craft were saving the liberties of the world.

CHAPTER IV

I

OUR first division of destroyers reached Queenstown on a Friday morning, May 4, 1917; the following Monday they put to sea on the business of hunting the submarine and protecting commerce. For the first month or six weeks they spent practically all their time on patrol duty in company with British destroyers, sloops, and other patrol vessels. Though the convoy system was formally adopted in the latter part of May, it was not operating completely and smoothly until August or September. Many troop and merchant convoys were formed in the intervening period and many were conducted through the submarine zone by American destroyers; but our ships spent much time sailing singly, hunting for such enemies as might betray their presence, or escorting individual cargoes. The early experiments had demonstrated the usefulness of the convoy system, yet a certain number of pessimists still refused to accept it as the best solution of the shipping problem; and to reorganize practically all the shipping of the world, scattered everywhere on the seven seas, necessarily took time.

But this intervening period furnished indispensable training for our men. They gained an every-day familiarity with the waters which were to form the scene of their operations and learned many of the tricks of the German submarines. It was a strange world in which these young Americans now found themselves. The life was a hard one, of course, in those tempestuous Irish waters, with the little destroyers jumping from wave to wave, sometimes showing daylight beneath their keels, their bows frequently pointing skyward, or plunged deep into heavy seas, and their sides occasionally ploughing along under the foamy waves. For days the men lived in a world of fog and mist ; rain in those regions seemed to be almost the normal state of nature. Much has been written about the hardships of life aboard the destroyer, and to these narratives our men could add many details of their own. These hardships, however, did not weigh heavily upon them, for existence in those waters, though generally monotonous, possessed at times plenty of interest and excitement. The very appearance of the sea showed that our men were engaging in a kind of warfare very different from that for which they had been trained. The enormous amount of shipping seemed to give the lie to the German reports that British commerce had been practically arrested. A perpetual stream of all kinds of vessels, liners, tramps, schooners, and fishing boats, was passing toward the Irish and the English coasts. Yet here and there other floating objects on the surface told the story. Now it was a stray boat filled with the survivors of a torpedoed vessel ; now a raft on which lay the bodies of dead men ; now the derelict hulk of a ship which the Germans had abandoned as sunk, but which persisted in floating aimlessly around, a constant danger to navigation. Loose mines, bobbing in the water, hinted at the perils that were constantly threatening our forces. In the tense imagination of the lookouts floating spars or other débris easily took the form of periscopes. Queer-looking sailing vessels, at a distance, aroused suspicions that they might be submarines in disguise. A phosphorescent trail in the water was sometimes mistaken for the wake of a torpedo. The cover of a hatchway floating on the surface, if seen at a distance of a few hundred yards, looked much like the conning-tower of a submarine, while the back of an occasional whale gave a life-like representation of a U-boat awash—in fact, so life-like was it that on one occasion several of our submarine chasers on the English coast dropped depth charges on a whale and killed it.

But it was the invisible rather than the visible evidences of warfare that especially impressed our men. The air all around them was electric with life and information. One had only to put the receiver of the wireless to his ear to find himself in a new and animated world. The atmosphere was constantly spluttering messages of all kinds coming from all kinds of places. Sometimes these were sent by Admiral Bayly from Queenstown; they would direct our men to go to an indicated spot and escort an especially valuable cargo ship; they would tell a particular commander that a submarine was lying at a designated latitude and longitude and instruct him to go and " get " it. Running conversations were frequently necessary between destroyers and the ships which they had been detailed to escort. " Give me your position," the destroyer would ask. " What is the name of your assistant surgeon, and who is his friend on board our ship ? " the suspicious vessel would reply—such precaution being necessary to give assurance that the query had not come from a German submarine. " Being pursued by a submarine Lat. 50 N., Long. 15 W."—cries of distress like this were common. Another message would tell of a vessel that was being shelled; another would tell of a ship that was sinking; while other messages would give the location of lifeboats which were filled with survivors and ask for speedy help. Our wireless operators not only received the news of friends, but also the messages of enemies. Conversations between German submarines frequently filled the air. They sometimes attempted to deceive us by false " S.O.S." signals, hoping that in this way they could get an opportunity to torpedo any vessel that responded to the call. But these attempts were unsuccessful, for our wireless operators had no difficulty in recognizing the " spark " of the German instruments. At times the surface of the ocean might be calm; there would not be a ship in sight or a sign of human existence anywhere; yet the air itself would be uninterruptedly filled with these reminders of war.

The duties of our destroyers, in these earliest days, were to hunt for submarines, to escort single ships, to pick up survivors in boats, and to go to the rescue of ships that were being attacked. For the purpose of patrol the sea was divided into areas thirty miles square; and to each of these one destroyer, sloop, or other vessel was assigned. The ship was required to keep within its allotted area, unless the pursuit of a submarine should lead it into a neighbouring one. This patrol, as I have described, was not a satisfactory way of fighting submarines. A vessel would occasionally get a distant glimpse of the enemy, but that was all; as soon as the U-boat saw the ship, it simply dived to security beneath the waves. Our destroyers had many chances to fire at the enemy but usually at very long ranges; some of them had lively scraps, which perhaps involved the destruction of U-boats, though this was always a difficult thing to prove. Yet the mere fact that submarines were seldom sunk by destroyers on patrol, either by ourselves or by the Allies, did not mean that the latter accomplished nothing. The work chiefly expected of destroyers on patrol was that they should keep the U-boats under the surface as much as possible and protect commerce. Normally the submarine sails on top of the water, looking for its prey. As long as it is beyond the merchantmen's range of vision, it uses its high surface speed of about 14 knots to attain a position ahead of the advancing vessel; before the surface vessel reaches a point where its lookout can see the submarine, the U-boat dives and awaits the favourable moment for firing its torpedo. It cannot take these preliminary steps if there is a destroyer anywhere in the neighbourhood; the mere presence of such a warship therefore constitutes a considerable protection to any merchant ship that is within sight. The submarine normally prefers to use its guns on merchant ships, for the torpedoes are expensive and comparatively few in number. Destroyers constantly interfered with these gunning operations. A long distance shot usually was sufficient to make the under-water vessel submerge and thus lose its power for doing harm. The early experiences of our destroyers with submarines were of this kind; but the work of chasing U-boats under the water, escorting a small proportion of the many cargo ships, and picking up survivors, important as it was, did not really constitute effective anti-submarine warfare. It gave our men splendid training, it saved many a merchant ship, it rescued many victims from the extreme dangers of German ruthlessness, it sank a small number of submarines, but it could never have won the war.

This patrol by destroyers and light surface vessels has been criticized as affording an altogether ineffective method of protecting shipping, especially when compared with the convoy system. This criticism is, of course, justified; still we must understand that it was the only possible method until we had enough anti-submarine craft to make the convoy practicable. Nor must we forget that this Queenstown patrol was organized systematically and operated with admirable skill and tireless energy. Most of this duty fell at this time upon the British destroyers, sloops, and other patrol vessels, which were under the command of Admiral Bayly, and these operations were greatly aided by the gallant actions of the British Q-ships, or " mystery ships." Though some of the admirable exploits of these vessels will be recorded in due time, it may be said here that the record which these ships made was not only in all respects worthy of the traditions of their great service, but also that they exhibited an endurance, a gallantry, and seamanlike skill that has few parallels in the history of naval warfare.

II

The headquarters of the convoy system was a room in the British Admiralty ; herein was the mainspring of the elaborate mechanism by which ten thousand ships were conducted over the seven oceans. Here every morning those who had been charged with the security of the Allies' lines of communication reviewed the entire submarine situation. Vice-Admiral Sir Alexander L. Duff, R.N., bore this heavy responsibility, ably assisted by a number of British officers. Captain Byron A. Long, U.S.N., a member of my staff, was associated with Admiral Duff in this important work. It was Captain Long's duty to co-ordinate the movements of our convoys with the much more numerous convoys of the Allies ; he performed this task so efficiently that, once the convoy organization was in successful operation, I eliminated the whole subject from my anxieties and requested Captain Long not to inform me when troop convoys sailed from the United States or when they were due to arrive in France or England. There seemed to be no reason why both of us should lose sleep over the same cause.

The most conspicuous feature of the convoy room was a huge chart, entirely covering the wall on one side of the office ; access to this chart was obtained by ladders not unlike those which are used in shoe stores. It gave a comprehensive view of the North and South American coast, the Atlantic Ocean, the British Isles, and a considerable part of Europe and Africa. The ports which it especially emphasized were Sydney (Cape Breton), Halifax, New York, Hampton Roads, Gibraltar, and Sierra Leone and Dakar, ports on the west coast of Africa. Thin threads were stretched from each one of these seven points to certain positions in the ocean just outside the British Isles, and on these threads were little paper boats, each one of which represented a convoy. When a particular convoy started from New York, one of these paper boats was placed at that point ; as it made its way across the ocean, the boat was moved from day to day in accordance with the convoy's progress. At any moment, therefore, a mere glance at this chart, with its multitude of paper boats, gave the spectator the precise location of all the commerce which was then *en route* to the scene of war.

But there were other exhibits on the chart which were even more conspicuous than these minute representations of convoys. Little circles were marked off in the waters surrounding the British Isles, each one of which was intended to show the location of a German submarine. From day to day each one of these circles was moved in accordance with the ascertained positions of the submarine which it represented, a straight line indicating its course on the chart. Perhaps the most remarkable fact about the Allied convoy service was the minute information which it possessed about the movements of German submarines. A kind of separate intelligence bureau devoted its entire attention to this subject. Readers of detective stories are familiar with the phenomenon known as " shadowing." It is a common practice in the detective's fascinating profession to assign a man, known as a " shadow," to the duty of keeping a particular person under constant observation. With admirable patience and skill an experienced " shadow " keeps in view this object of his attention for twenty-four hours ; he dogs him through crowded streets, tracks him up and down high office buildings, accompanies him to restaurants, trolley cars, theatres, and hotels, and unobtrusively chases him through dense thoroughfares in cabs and automobiles. " We get him up in the morning and we put him to bed at night " is the way the " shadow " describes the assiduous care which he bestows upon his unsuspecting victim. In much the same fashion did the Allied secret service

" shadow " German submarines ; it got each submarine " up in the morning and put it to bed at night." That is to say, the intelligence department took charge of Fritz and his crew as they emerged from their base, and kept an unwearied eye upon them until they sailed back home. The great chart in the convoy room of the Admiralty showed, within the reasonable limits of human fallibility, where each submarine was operating at a particular moment, and it also kept minute track of its performances.

Yet it was not so difficult to gather this information as may at first be supposed. I have already said that there were comparatively few submarines, perhaps not more than an average of eight or nine, which were operating at the same time in the waters south and west of Ireland, the region with which we Americans were most concerned. These boats betrayed their locations in a multitude of ways. Their commanders were particularly careless in the use of wireless. The Germanic passion for conversation could not be suppressed even on the U-boats, even though this national habit might lead to the most serious consequences. Possibly also the solitary submarine felt lonely ; at any rate, as soon as it reached the Channel or the North Sea, it started an almost uninterrupted flow of talk. The U-boats communicated principally with each other, and also with the Admiralty at home ; and, in doing this, they gave away their positions to the assiduously listening Allies. The radio-direction finder, an apparatus by which we can instantaneously locate the position from which a wireless message is sent, was the mechanism which furnished us much of this information. Of course, the Germans knew that their messages revealed their locations, for they had direction finders as well as we, but the fear of discovery did not act as a curb upon a naturally loquacious nature. And we had other ways of following their movements. The submarine spends much the larger part of its time on the surface. Sailing thus conspicuously, it was constantly being sighted by merchant or military ships, which had explicit instructions to report immediately the elusive vessel, and to give its exact location. Again it is obvious that a submarine could not fire at a merchantman or torpedo one, or even attempt to torpedo one, without revealing its presence. The wireless operators of all merchant vessels were supplied at all times with the longitude and latitude of their ships ; their instructions required them immediately to send out this information whenever they sighted a submarine or were attacked by one. In these several ways we had little difficulty in " shadowing " the U-boats. For example, we would hear that the *U-53* was talking just outside of Heligoland ; this submarine would be immediately plotted on the chart. As the submarine made only about ten knots on the surface, in order to save fuel oil, and much less under the surface, we could draw a circle around this point, and rest assured that the boat must be somewhere within this circle at a given time. But in a few hours or a day we would hear from this same boat again ; perhaps it was using its wireless or attacking a merchantman ; or perhaps one of our vessels had spotted it on the surface. The news of this new location would justify the convoy officers in moving this submarine on our chart to this new position. Within a short time the convoy officers acquired an astonishingly intimate knowledge of these boats and the habits of their commanders. Indeed, the personalities of some of these German officers ultimately took shape with surprising clearness ; for they betrayed their presence in the ocean by characteristics that often furnished a means of identifying them. Each submarine behaved in a different way from the others, the difference, of course, representing the human element in control. One would deliver his attacks in rapid succession, boldly and almost recklessly ; another would approach his task with the utmost caution ; certain ones would display the meanest traits in human nature ; while others—let us be just—were capable of a certain display of generosity, and possibly even of chivalry. By studying the individual traits of each commander we could often tell just which one was operating at a given time ; and this information was extremely valuable in the game in which we were engaged.

" Old Hans is out again," the officers in the convoy room would remark.

They were speaking of Hans Rose, the commander of the *U-53* ; this was that same submarine officer who, in the fall of 1916, brought that boat to Newport, Rhode Island, and torpedoed five or six ships off Nantucket. **Our** men never saw Hans Rose face to face ; they had

not the faintest idea whether he was fat or lean, whether
he was fair or dark ; yet they knew his military characteristics intimately. He became such a familiar personality
in the convoy room and his methods of operation were so
individual, that we came to have almost a certain liking
for the old chap. Other U-boat commanders would appear
off the hunting grounds and attack ships in more or less
easy-going fashion. Then another boat would suddenly
appear, and—bang ! bang ! bang ! Torpedo after torpedo would fly, four or five ships would sink, and then this
disturbing person would vanish as unexpectedly as he
had arrived. Such an experience informed the convoy
officers that Hans Rose was once more at large. We
acquired a certain respect for Hans because he was a
brave man who would take chances which most of his
compatriots would avoid ; and, above all, because he
played his desperate game with a certain decency. Sometimes, when he torpedoed a ship, Rose would wait around
until all the lifeboats were filled ; he would then throw
out a tow line, give the victims food, and keep all the
survivors together until the rescuing destroyer appeared
on the horizon, when he would let go and submerge. This
humanity involved considerable risk to Captain Rose,
for a destroyer anywhere in his neighbourhood, as he well
knew, was a serious matter. It was he who torpedoed
our destroyer, the *Jacob Jones*. He took a shot at her
from a distance of two miles—a distance from which a
hit is a pure chance ; and the torpedo struck and sank the
vessel within a few minutes. On this occasion Rose acted
with his usual decency. The survivors of the *Jacob Jones*
naturally had no means of communication, since the
wireless had gone down with their ship ; and now Rose,
at considerable risk to himself, sent out an " S.O.S." call,
giving the latitude and longitude, and informing Queenstown that the men were floating around in open boats.
It is perhaps not surprising that Rose is one of the few
German U-boat commanders with whom Allied naval
officers would be willing to-day to shake hands. I have
heard naval officers say that they would like to meet him
after the war.

We were able to individualize other commanders ; the
business of acquiring this knowledge, learning the location
of their submarines and the characteristics of their boats,

and using this vital information in protecting convoys, was all part of the game which was being played in London. It was the greatest game of " chess " which history has known—a game that exacted not only the most faithful and studious care, but one in which it was necessary that all the activities should be centralized in one office. This small group of officers in the Admiralty convoy room, composed of representatives of all the nations concerned, exercised a control which extended throughout the entire convoy system. It regulated the dates when convoys sailed from America or other ports and when they arrived ; if it had not taken charge of this whole system, congestion and confusion would inevitably have resulted. We had only a limited number of destroyers to escort all troops and other important convoys arriving in Europe ; it was therefore necessary that they should arrive at regular and predetermined intervals. It was necessary also that one group of officers should control the routing of all convoys, otherwise there would have been serious danger of collisions between outward and inward bound ships, and no possibility of routing them clear of the known positions of submarines. The great centre of all this traffic was not New York or Hampton Roads, but London. It was inevitable, if the convoy system was to succeed, that it should have a great central headquarters, and it was just as inevitable that this headquarters should be London.

On the huge chart already described the convoys, each indicated by a little boat, were shown steadily making their progress toward the appointed rendezvous. Eight or nine submarines, likewise indicated on the chart, were always waiting to intercept them. On that great board the prospective tragedies of the seas were thus unfolding before our eyes. Here, for example, was a New York convoy of twenty ships, steaming toward Liverpool, but steering straight toward the position of a submarine. The thing to do was perfectly plain. It was a simple matter to send the convoy a wireless message to take a course fifty miles to the south where, according to the chart, there were no hidden enemies. In a few hours the little paper boat, which represented this group of ships and which was apparently headed for destruction, would suddenly turn southward, pass around the entirely unconscious submarine, and then take an unobstructed course for its destination. The Admiralty convoy board knew so accurately the position of all the submarines that it could almost always route the convoys around them. It was an extremely interesting experience to watch the paper ships on this chart deftly turn out of the course of U-boats, sometimes when they seemed almost on the point of colliding with them. That we were able constantly to save the ships by sailing the convoys around the submarines brings out the interesting fact that, even had there been no destroyer escort, the convoy in itself would have formed a great protection to merchant shipping. There were times when we had no escorting vessels to send with certain convoys ; and in such instances we simply routed the ships in masses, directed them on courses which we knew were free of submarines, and in this way brought them safely into port.

III

The Admiralty in London was thus the central nervous system of a complicated but perfectly working organism which reached the remotest corners of the world. Wherever there was a port, whether in South America, Australia, or in the most inaccessible parts of India or China, from which merchantmen sailed to any of the other countries which were involved in the war, representatives of the British navy and the British Government were stationed, all working harmoniously with shipping men in the effort to get their cargoes safely through the danger zones. These danger zones occupied a comparatively small area surrounding the belligerent countries, but the safeguarding of the ships was an elaborate process which began far back in the countries from which the commerce started. Until about July, 1917, the world's shipping for the most part had been unregulated ; now for the first time it was arranged in hard and fast routes and despatched in accordance with schedules as fixed as those of a great railroad. The whole management of convoys, indeed, bore many resemblances to the method of handling freight cars on the American system of trans-continental lines. In the United States there are several great headquarters of freight, sometimes known as " gateways," places, that is, at which freight cars are assembled from a thousand places, and from which the great accumulations are routed to their destinations. Such places are Pittsburg, Buffalo, St. Louis, Chicago, Minneapolis, Denver, San Francisco—to mention only a few. Shipping destined for the belligerent nations was similarly assembled, in the years 1917 and 1918, at six or eight great ocean "gateways," and there formed into convoys for "through routing" to the British Isles, France, and the Mediterranean. Only a few of the ships that were exceptionally fast—speed in itself being a particularly efficacious protection against submarines—were permitted to ignore this routing system, and dash unprotected through the infested area. This was a somewhat dangerous procedure even for such ships, however, and they were escorted whenever destroyers were available. All other vessels, from whatever parts of the world they might come, were required to sail first for one of these great assembling points, or "gateways"; and at these places they were added to one of the constantly forming convoys. Thus all shipping which normally sailed to Europe around the Cape of Good Hope proceeded up the west coast of Africa until it reached the port of Dakar or Sierra Leone, where it joined the convoy. Shipping from the east coast of South America —ports like Rio de Janeiro, Bahia, Buenos Aires, and Montevideo—instead of sailing directly to Europe, joined the convoy at this same African town. Vessels which came to Britain and France by way of Suez and Mediterranean ports found their great stopping place at Gibraltar —a headquarters of traffic which, in the huge amount of freight which it " created," became almost the Pittsburg of this mammoth transportation system. The four "gateways" for North America and the west coast of South America were Sydney (Cape Breton), Halifax, New York, and Hampton Roads. The grain-laden merchantmen from the St. Lawrence valley rendezvoused at Sydney and Halifax. Vessels from Portland, Boston, New York, Philadelphia, and other Atlantic points found their assembling headquarters at New York, while ships from Baltimore, Norfolk, the Gulf of Mexico, and the west coast of South America proceeded to the great convoy centre which had been established at Hampton Roads.

In the convoy room of the Admiralty these aggregations of ships were always referred to as the " Dakar convoy," the " Halifax convoy," the " Hampton Roads convoy," and the like. When the system was completely established the convoys sailed from their appointed headquarters on regular schedules, like railroad trains. From New York one convoy departed every sixteen days for the west coast of England and one left every sixteen days for the east coast. From Hampton Roads one sailed every eight days to the west coast and one every eight days to the east coast, and convoys from all the other convoy points maintained a similarly rigid schedule. The dates upon which these sailings took place were fixed, like the arrivals and departures of trains upon a railroad time-table, except when it became necessary to delay the sailing of a convoy to avoid congestion of arrivals. According to this programme, the first convoy to the west coast left New York on August 14, 1917, and its successors thereafter sailed at intervals of about sixteen days. The instructions sent to shipmasters all over the world, by way of the British consulates, gave explicit details concerning the method of assembling their convoys.

Here, for example, was a ship at New York, all loaded and ready to sail for the war zone. The master visited the port officer at the British consulate, who directed him to proceed to Gravesend Bay, anchor his vessel, and report to the convoy officers for further instructions. The merchant captain, reaching this indicated spot, usually found several other vessels on hand, all of them, like his ship, waiting for the sailing date. The commander of the gathering convoy, under whose instructions all the merchantmen were to operate, was a naval officer, usually of the rank of commodore or captain, who maintained constant cable communication with the convoy room of the Admiralty and usually used one of the commercial vessels as his flagship. When the sailing day arrived usually from twenty to thirty merchantmen had assembled ; the commander summoned all their masters, gave each a blue book containing instructions for the management of convoyed ships, and frequently delivered something in the nature of a lecture. Before the aggregation sailed it was joined by a cruiser or pre-dreadnought battleship of the American navy, or by a British or French cruiser. This ship was to accompany the convoy across the Atlantic as far as the danger zone ; its mission **was** not, as most people mistakenly believed, to protect the convoy from submarines, but to protect it from any surface German raider that might have escaped into the high seas. The Allied navies constantly had before their minds the exploits of the *Emden*; the opportunity to break up a convoy in mid-ocean by dare-devil enterprises of this kind was so tempting that it seemed altogether likely that Germany might take advantage of it. To send twenty or thirty merchant ships across the Atlantic with no protection against such assaults would have been to invite a possible disaster. As a matter of fact, the last German raider that even attempted to gain the high seas was sunk in the North Sea by the British Patrol Squadron in February, 1917.

On the appointed day the whole convoy weighed anchor and silently slipped out to sea. To such spectators as observed its movements it seemed to be a rather limping, halting procession. The speed of a convoy was the speed of its slowest ship, and vessels that could easily make twelve or fourteen knots were obliged to throttle down their engines, much to the disgust of their masters, in order to keep formation with a ship that made only eight or ten; though whenever possible vessels of nearly equal speed sailed together. Little in the newly assembled group suggested the majesty of the sea. The ships formed a miscellaneous and ill-assorted company, rusty tramps shamefacedly sailing alongside of spick-and-span liners; miserable little two- or three-thousand ton ships attempting to hold up their heads in the same company with other ships of ten or twelve. The whole mass was sprawled over the sea in most ungainly fashion; twenty or thirty ships, with spaces of nine hundred or a thousand yards stretching between them, took up not far from ten square miles of the ocean surface. Neither at this stage of the voyage did the aggregation give the idea of efficiency. It presented about as desirable a target as the submarine could have desired. But the period taken in crossing the ocean was entirely devoted to education. Under the tutorship of the convoy commander, the men composing the twenty or thirty crews went every day to school. For fifteen or twenty days upon the broad Atlantic they were trained in all the evolutions which were necessary for coping with the submarine. Every possible situation that could arise in the danger zone was anticipated and the officers and the crews were trained to meet it. They perfected themselves in the signal code ; they learned the art of making the sudden manœuvres which were instantaneously necessary when a submarine was sighted ; they acquired a mastery in the art of zigzagging ; and they became accustomed to sailing at night without lights. The crews were put through all the drills which prepared them to meet such crises as the landing of a torpedo in their engine-room or the sinking of the ship ; and they were thoroughly schooled in getting all hands safely into the boats. Possibly an occasional scare on the way over may have introduced the element of reality into these exercises ; though no convoys actually met submarines in the open ocean, the likelihood that they might do so was never absent, especially after the Germans began sending out their huge under-water cruisers.

The convoy commander left his port with sealed orders, which he was instructed not to open until he was a hundred miles at sea. These orders, when the seal was broken, gave him the rendezvous assigned by Captain Long of the convoy board in London. The great chart in the convoy room at the Admiralty indicated the point to which the convoy was to proceed and at which it would be met by the destroyer escorts and taken through the danger zone. This particular New York convoy commander was now perhaps instructed to cross the thirtieth meridian at the fifty-second parallel of latitude, where he would be met by his escort. He laid his course for that point and regulated his speed so as to reach it at the appointed time. But he well knew that these instructions were only temporary. The precise point to which he would finally be directed to sail depended upon the movement and location of the German submarines at the time of his arrival. If the enemy became particularly active in the region of this tentative rendezvous, then, as the convoy approached it, a wireless from London would instruct the commander to steer abruptly to another point, perhaps a hundred miles to north or south.

" Getting your convoy " was a searching test of destroyer seamanship, particularly in heavy or thick weather. It was not the simplest thing to navigate a group of destroyers through the tempestuous waters of the North Atlantic, with

9

no other objective than the junction point of a certain meridian and parallel, and reach the designated spot at a certain hour.   Such a feat demanded navigation ability of a high order ; and the skill which our American naval officers displayed in this direction aroused great admiration, especially on the part of the merchant skippers ; in partieular it aroused the astonishment of the average doughboy. Many destroyer escorts that went out to meet an incoming convoy also took out one which was westward bound.   A few mishaps in the course of the war, such as the sinking of the *Justicia*, which was sailing from Europe to America, created the false notion that outward-bound convoys were not escorted.   It was just as desirable, of course, to escort the ships going out as it was to escort those which were coming in.   The mere fact that the inbound ships carried troops and supplies gave stronger reasons, from the humane standpoint, for heavier escorts, but not from the standpoint of the general war situation.   The Germans were not sinking our ships because they were carrying men and supplies ; they were sinking them simply because they were ships. They were not seeking to destroy American troops and munitions exclusively ; they were seeking to destroy tonnage.   They were aiming to reduce the world's supply of ships to such a point that the Allies would be compelled to abandon the conflict for lack of communications.   It was therefore necessary that they should sink the empty ships, which were going out, as well as the crowded and loaded ships which were coming in.   For the same reason it was necessary that we should protect them, and we did this as far as practicable without causing undue delays in forming outward-bound convoys.   The *Justicia*, though most people still think that she was torpedoed because she was unescorted, was, in fact, protected by a destroyer escort of considerable size.   This duty of escorting outward-bound ships increased considerably the strain on our destroyer force.   The difficulty was that the inbound convoy arrived in a body, but that the ships could not be unloaded and sent back in a body without detaining a number of them an undue length of time—and time was such an important factor in this war that it was necessary to make the " turn-around " of each important transport as quickly as possible.   The consequence was that returning ships were often despatched in small convoys as fast as they were unloaded. The escorts which we were able to supply for such groups were thus much weaker than absolute safety required, and sometimes we were even forced to send vessels across the submarine zone with few, if any, escorting warships. This explains why certain homeward-bound transports were torpedoed, and this was particularly true of troop and munition convoys to the western ports of France. Only when we could assemble a large outgoing convoy and despatch it at such a time that it could meet an incoming one at the western edge of the submarine zone could we give these vessels the same destroyer escort as that which we always gave for the loaded convoys bound for European ports.

As soon as the destroyers made contact with an inward-bound convoy, the ocean escort, the cruiser or pre-dreadnought, if an American, abandoned it and started it back home, sometimes with a westbound convoy if one had been assembled in time. British escorts went ahead at full speed into a British port, usually escorted by one or more destroyers. This abandonment sometimes aroused the wrath of the passengers on the inbound convoy. Their protector had dropped them just as they had entered the submarine zone, the very moment its services were really needed ! These passengers did not understand, any more than did the people at home, that the purpose of the ocean escort was not to protect them from submarines, but from possible raiders. Inside the danger zone this ocean escort would become part of the convoy itself and require protection from submarines, so that its rather summary departure really made the merchantmen more secure. As the convoy approached the danger zone, after being drilled all the way across the ocean, its very appearance was more taut and business-like. The ships were closed up into a much more compact formation, keeping only such distances apart as were essential for quick manœuvring. Generally the convoy was formed in a long parallelogram, the distance across the front of which was much longer than the depth or distance along the sides. Usually the formation was a number of groups of four vessels each, in column or " Indian file," at a distance of about five hundred yards from ship to ship, and all groups abreast of each other and about half a mile apart. Thus a convoy of twenty-four vessels, or six groups of four, would have a width of about three miles and a depth of one. Most of the destroyers were stationed on the narrow sides, for it was only on the side, or the beam, that the submarines could attack with much likelihood of succeeding. It was usually necessary for a destroyer to be stationed in the rear of a convoy, for, though the speed of nearly all convoys was faster than that of a submarine when submerged, the latter while running on the surface could follow a convoy at night with a fair chance of torpedoing a vessel at early daylight and escaping to the rear if unhampered by the presence of a rear-guard destroyer. It was generally impracticable and dangerous for the submarine to wait ahead, submerge, and launch its torpedoes as the convoy passed over it. The extent to which purely mechanical details protected merchant ships is not understood, and this inability to attack successfully from the front illustrates this point. The submarine launches its torpedoes from tubes in the bow or stern ; it has no tubes on the beam. If it did possess such side tubes, it could lie in wait ahead and shoot its broadsides at the convoy as it passed over the spot where it was concealed. Its length in that case would be parallel to that of the merchant ships, and thus it would have a comparatively small part of its area exposed to the danger of ramming. The mere fact that its torpedo tubes are placed in the bow and stern makes it necessary for the submarine, if it wishes to attack in the fashion described, to turn almost at right angles to the course of the convoy, and to manœuvre into a favourable position from which to discharge its missile—a procedure so altogether hazardous that it almost never attempts it. With certain reservations, which it is hardly necessary to explain in detail at this point, it may be taken at least as a general rule that the sides of the convoy not only furnish the U-boats much the best chance to torpedo ships, but also subject them to the least danger ; and this is the reason why, in the recent war, the destroyers were usually concentrated at these points.

I have already compared the convoy system to a great aggregation of railroads. This comparison holds good of its operation after it had entered the infested zone. Indeed the very terminology of our railroad men was used. Every convoy nearly followed one of two main routes, known at convoy headquarters as the two " trunk lines." The trunk line which reached the west coast of England usually passed north of Ireland through the North Channel and down the Irish Sea to Liverpool. Under certain conditions these convoys passed south of Ireland and thence up the Irish Sea. The convoys to the east coast took a trunk line that passed up the English Channel. Practically all shipping from the United States to Great Britain and France took one of these trunk lines. But, like our railroad systems, each of these main routes had branch lines. Thus shipping destined for French ports took the southern route until off the entrance to the English Channel ; here it abandoned the main line and took a branch route to Brest, Bordeaux, Nantes, and other French ports. In the Channel likewise several " single-track " branches went to various English ports, such as Plymouth, Portsmouth, Southampton, and the like. The whole gigantic enterprise flowed with a precision and a regularity which I think it is hardly likely that any other transportation system has ever achieved.

IV

A description of a few actual convoys, and the experiences of our destroyers with them, will perhaps best make clear the nature of the mechanism which protected the world's shipping. For this purpose I have selected typical instances which illustrate the every-day routine experiences of escorting destroyers, and other experiences in which their work was more spectacular.

One day in late October, 1917, a division of American destroyers at Queenstown received detailed instructions from Admiral Bayly to leave at a certain hour and escort the outward convoy " O Q 17 " and bring into port the inbound convoy " H S 14." These detailed instructions were based upon general instructions issued from the Admiralty, where my staff was in constant attendance and co-operation. The symbols by which these two groups of ships were designated can be easily interpreted. The O Q simply meant that convoy " No. 17 "—the seventeenth which had left that port—was Outward bound from Queenstown, and the H S signified that convoy " No. 14 " was Homeward bound from Sydney, Cape Breton. Queenstown during the first few months was one of those places at which ships, having discharged their cargoes, assembled in groups for despatching back to the United States. Later

Milford Haven, Liverpool, and other ports were more often used for this purpose. Vessels had been arriving here for several days from ports of the Irish Sea and the east coast of England. These had now been formed into convoy " O Q 17 " ; they were ready for a destroyer escort to take them through the submarine zone and start them on the westward voyage to American ports.

This escort consisted of eight American destroyers and one British " special service ship " ; the latter was one of that famous company of decoy vessels, or " mystery ships," which, though to all outward appearances unprotected merchantmen, really carried concealed armament of sufficient power to destroy any submarine that came within range. This special service ship, the *Aubrietia*, was hardly a member of the protective escort. Her mission was to sail about thirty miles ahead of the convoy ; when observed from the periscope or the conning-tower of a submarine, the *Aubrietia* seemed to be merely a helpless merchantman sailing alone, and as such she presented a particularly tempting target to the U-boat. But her real purpose in life was to be torpedoed. After landing its missile in a vessel's side, the submarine usually remained submerged for a period, while the crew of its victim was getting off in boats ; it then came to the surface, and the men prepared to board the disabled ship and search her for valuables and delicacies, particularly for information which would assist them in their campaign, such as secret codes, sailing instructions, and the like. The mystery ship had been preparing for this moment, and as soon as the submarine broke water, the gun ports of the disguised merchantman dropped, and her hitherto concealed guns began blazing away at the German. By October, 1917, these special service ships had already accounted for several submarines ; and it had now become a frequent practice to attach one or more to a convoy, either ahead, where she might dispose of the submarine lying in wait for the approaching aggregation, or in the rear, where a U-boat might easily mistake her for one of those stragglers which were an almost inevitable part of every convoy.

Trawlers and mine-sweepers, as was the invariable custom, spent several hours sweeping the Queenstown Channel before the sailing of convoy " O Q 17 " and its escort. Promptly at the appointed time the eight American ships sailed out in " Indian file," passing through the net which was always kept in place at the entrance to the harbour. Their first duty was to patrol the waters outside for a radius of twelve miles ; it was not improbable that the Germans, having learned that this convoy was to sail, had stationed a submarine not far from the harbour entrance. Having finally satisfied himself that there were no lurking enemies in the neighbourhood, the commander of the destroyer flagship signalled to the merchant ships, which promptly left the harbour and entered the open sea. The weather was stormy ; the wind was blowing something of a gale and head seas were breaking over the destroyers' decks. But the convoy quickly manoeuvred into three columns, the destroyers rapidly closed around them, and the whole group started for " Rendezvous A "—this being the designation of that spot on the ocean's surface where the fourteenth meridian of longitude crosses the forty-ninth parallel of latitude—a point in the Atlantic about three hundred miles south-west of Queenstown, regarded at that time as safely beyond the operating zone of the submarine. Meanwhile, the " mystery ship," sailing far ahead, disappeared beneath the horizon.

Convoying ships in the stormy autumn and winter waters, amid the fog and rain of the eastern Atlantic, was a monotonous and dreary occupation. Only one or two incidents enlivened this particular voyage. As the *Parker*, Commander Halsey Powell, was scouting ahead at about two o'clock in the afternoon, her lookout suddenly sighted a submarine, bearing down upon the convoy. Immediately the news was wirelessed to every vessel. As soon as the message was received, the whole convoy, at a signal from the flagship, turned four points to port. For nearly two hours the destroyers searched this area for the submerged submarine, but that crafty boat kept itself safely under the water, and the convoy now again took up its original course. About two days' sailing brought the ships to the point at which the protecting destroyers could safely leave them, as far as submarines were concerned, to continue unescorted to America ; darkness had now set in, and, under its cover, the merchantmen slipped away from the warships and started westward. Meantime, the destroyer escort had received a message from the *Cumberland*, the British cruiser which was acting as the time of arrival up to noon. The destroyers, slowing down so that they would not arrive ahead of time, started for the designated spot.

Sometimes thick weather made it impossible to fix the position by astronomical observations, and the convoy might not be at its appointed rendezvous. For this reason the destroyers now deployed on a north and south line about twenty miles long for several hours. Somewhat before the appointed time one of the destroyers sighted a faint cloud of smoke on the western horizon, and soon afterward thirty-two merchantmen, sailing in columns of fours, began to assume a definite outline. At a signal from this destroyer the other destroyers of the escort came in at full speed and ranged themselves on either side of the convoy—a manœuvre that always excited the admiration of the merchant skippers. This mighty collection of vessels, occupying about ten or twelve square miles on the ocean, skilfully maintaining its formation, was really a beautiful and inspiring sight. When the destroyers had gained their designated positions on either side, the splendid cavalcade sailed boldly into the area which formed the favourite hunting grounds for the submarine.

As soon as this danger zone was reached the whole aggregation, destroyers and merchant ships, began to zigzag. The commodore on the flagship hoisted the signal, " Zigzag A," and instantaneously the whole thirty-two ships began to turn twenty-five degrees to starboard. The great ships, usually so cumbersome, made this simultaneous turn with all the deftness, and even with all the grace of a school of fish into which one has suddenly cast a stone. All the way across the Atlantic they had been practising such an evolution ; most of them had already sailed through the danger zone more than once, so that the manœuvre was by this time an old story. For ten or fifteen minutes they proceeded along this course, when immediately, like one vessel, the convoy turned twenty degrees to port, and started in a new direction. And so on for hours, now a few minutes to the right, now a few minutes to the left, and now again straight ahead, while all the time the destroyers were cutting through the water, every eye of the skilled lookouts in each crew fixed upon the surface for the first glimpse of a periscope. This zigzagging was carried out according to comprehensive plans which enabled the convoy to zigzag for hours at a time without signals, the courses and the time on each course being designated in the particular plan ordered, all ships' clocks being set exactly alike by time signal. Probably I have made it clear why these zigzagging evolutions constituted such a protective measure. All the time the convoy was sailing in the danger zone it was assumed that a submarine was present, looking for a chance to torpedo. Even though the officers might know that there was no submarine within three hundred miles, this was never taken for granted ; the discipline of the whole convoy system rested upon the theory that the submarine was there, waiting only the favourable moment to start the work of destruction. But a submarine, as already said, could not strike without the most thorough preparation. It must get within three or four hundred yards or the torpedo would stand little chance of hitting the mark in a vital spot. The commander almost never shot blindly into the convoy, on the chance of hitting some ship ; he carefully selected his victim ; his calculation had to include its speed, the speed of his own boat and that of his torpedo ; above all, he had to be sure of the direction in which his intended quarry was steaming ; and in this calculation the direction of the merchantman formed perhaps the most important element. But if the ships were constantly changing their direction, it is apparent that the submarine could make no calculations which would have much practical value.

In the afternoon the *Aubrietia*, the British mystery ship which was sailing thirty miles ahead of the convoy, reported that she had sighted a submarine. Two or three destroyers dashed for the indicated area, searched it thoroughly, found no traces of the hidden boat, and returned to the convoy. The next morning six British destroyers and one cruiser arrived from Devonport. Up to this time the convoy had been following the great " trunk line " which led into the Channel, but it had now reached the point where the convoys split up, part going to English ports and part to French. These British destroyers had come to take over the twenty ships which were bound for their own country, while the American destroyers were assigned to escort the rest to Brest. The following conversation —typical of those that were constantly filling the air in that area—now took place between the American flagship and the British :

Conyngham to *Achates :* This is the *Conyngham*, Commander Johnson. I would like to keep the convoy together until this evening. I will work under your orders until I leave with convoy for Brest.

Achates to *Conyngham :* Please make your own arrangements for taking French convoy with you to-night.

Achates to *Conyngham :* What time do you propose leaving with French convoy to-night ?

Conyngham to *Achates :* About 5 P.M. in order to arrive in Brest to-night.

Devonport Commander-in-chief to *Conyngham :* Proceed in execution Admiralty orders *Achates* having relieved you. Submarine activity in Lat. 48.41, Long. 4.51.

The *Aubrietia* had already given warning of the danger referred to in the last words of this final message. It had been flashing the news in this way :

1.15 P.M. *Aubrietia* to *Conyngham :* Submarine sighted 49.30 N 6.8 W. Sighted submarine on surface. Speed is not enough. Course south-west by south magnetic.

1.30 P.M. *Conyngham* to *Achates :* *Aubrietia* to all men-of-war and Land's End. Chasing submarine on the surface 49.30 N 6.8 W, course south-west by south. Waiting to get into range. He is going faster than I can.

2.00 P.M. *Aubrietia* to all men-of-war. Submarine submerged 49.20 N 6.12 W. Still searching.

The fact that nothing more was seen of that submarine may possibly detract from the thrill of the experience, but in describing the operations of this convoy I am not attempting to tell a story of wild adventure, but merely to set forth what happened ninety-nine out of a hundred times. What made destroyer work so exasperating was that, in the vast majority of cases, the option of fighting or not fighting lay with the submarine. Had the submarine decided to approach and attack the convoy, the chances would have been more than even that it would have been destroyed. In accordance with its usual practice, however, it chose to submerge, and that decision ended the affair for the moment. This was the way in which merchant ships were protected. At the time this submarine was sighted it was headed directly for this splendid aggregation of cargo vessels; had not the *Aubrietia* discovered it and had not one of the American destroyers started in pursuit, the U-boat would have made an attack and possibly would have sent one or more ships to the bottom. The chief business of the escorting ships, all through the war, was this unspectacular one of chasing the submarines away; and for every under-water vessel actually destroyed there were hundreds of experiences such as the one which I have just described.

The rest of this trip was uneventful. Two American destroyers escorted **H.M.S.** *Cumberland*—the ocean escort which had accompanied the convoy from Sydney—to Devonport; the rest of the American escort took its quota of merchantmen into Brest, and from that point sailed back to Queenstown, whence, after three or four days in port, it went out with another convoy. This was the routine which was repeated until the end of the war.

The " O Q 17 " and the " H S 14 " form an illustration of convoys which made their trips successfully. Yet these same destroyers had another experience which pictures other phases of the convoy system.

On the morning of October 19th, Commander Johnson's division was escorting a great convoy of British ships on its way to the east coast of England. Suddenly out of the air came one of those calls which were daily occurrences in the submarine zone. The *J. L. Luckenback* signalled her position, ninety miles ahead of the convoy, and that she was being shelled by a submarine. In a few minutes the *Nicholson*, one of the destroyers of the escort, started to the rescue. For the next few hours our ships began to pick out of the air the messages which detailed the progress of this adventure—messages which tell the story so graphically, and which are so typical of the events

9.25 *Conyngham* to *Nicholson :* Proceed to assistance of S.O.S. ship.

9.30 *Luckenback* to U.S.A. : Am manœuvring around.

9.35 *Luckenback* to U.S.A. : How far are you away ?

9.40 *Luckenback* to U.S.A. : Code books thrown overboard. How soon will you arrive ?

Nicholson to *Luckenback :* In two hours.

9.41 *Luckenback* to U.S.A. : Look for boats. They are shelling us.

Nicholson to *Luckenback :* Do not surrender !

Luckenback to *Nicholson :* Never !

11.01 *Nicholson* to *Luckenback :* Course south magnetic.

12.36 P.M. *Nicholson* to *Conyngham :* Submarine submerged 47.47 N 10.00 W at 11.20.

1.23 *Conyngham* to *Nicholson* : What became of steamer ?

3.41 *Nicholson* to Admiral (at Queenstown) and *Conyngham :* *Luckenback* now joining convoy. Should be able to make port unassisted.

I have already said that a great part of the destroyer's duty was to rescue merchantmen that were being attacked by submarines : this *Luckenback* incident vividly illustrates this point. Had the submarine used its torpedo upon this vessel, it probably would have disposed of it summarily ; but it was the part of wisdom for the submarine to economize in these weapons because they were so expensive and so comparatively scarce, and to use its guns whenever the opportunity offered. The *Luckenback* was armed, but the fact that the submarine's guns easily outranged hers made her armament useless. Thus all the German had to do in this case was to keep away at a safe distance and bombard the merchantman. The U-boat had been doing this for more than three hours when the destroyer reached the scene of operations ; evidently the marksmanship was poor, for out of a great many shots fired by the submarine only about a dozen had hit the vessel. The *Luckenback* was on fire, a shell having set aflame her cargo of cotton ; certain parts of the machinery had been damaged, but, in the main, the vessel was intact. The submarine was always heroic enough when it came to shelling defenceless merchantmen, but the appearance of a destroyer anywhere in her neighbourhood made her resort to the one secure road to safety—diving for protection. The *Nicholson* immediately trained her guns on the U-boat, which, on the second shot, disappeared under the water. The destroyer despatched men to the disabled vessel, the fire was extinguished, necessary repairs to the machinery were made, and in a few hours the *Luckenback* had become a member of the convoy.

Hardly had she joined the merchant ships and hardly had the *Nicholson* taken up her station on the flank when an event still more exciting took place. It was now late in the afternoon; the sea had quieted down; the whole atmosphere was one of peace; and there was not the slightest sign or suggestion of a hostile ship. The *Orama*, the British warship which had accompanied the convoy from its home port as ocean escort, had taken up her position as leading ship in the second column. Without the slightest warning a terrific explosion now took place on her starboard bow. There was no mystery as to what had happened; indeed, immediately after the explosion the wake of the torpedo appeared on the surface; there was no periscope in sight, yet it was clear, from the position of the wake, that the submarine had crept up to the side of the convoy and delivered its missile at close range. There was no confusion in the convoy or its escorting destroyers but there were scenes of great activity. Immediately after the explosion, a periscope appeared a few inches out of the water, stayed there only a second or two, and then disappeared. Brief as was this exposure, the keen eyes of the lookout and several sailors of the *Conyngham*, the nearest destroyer, had detected it; it disclosed the fact that the enemy was in the midst of the convoy itself, looking for other ships to torpedo. The *Conyngham* rang for full speed, and dashed for the location of the submarine. Her officers and men now saw more than the periscope; they saw the vessel itself. The water was very clear; as the *Conyngham* circled around the *Orama* her officers and men sighted a green, shining, cigar-shaped thing under the water not far from the starboard side. As she sped by, the destroyer dropped a depth charge almost directly on top of the object. After the waters had quieted down pieces of débris were seen floating upon the surface—boards, spars, and other miscellaneous wreckage, evidently scraps of the damaged deck of a submarine. All attempts to save the *Orama* proved fruitless : the destroyers stood by for five hours, taking off survivors, and making all possible efforts to salvage the ship, but at about ten o'clock that evening she disappeared under the water. In rescuing the survivors the seamanship displayed by the *Conyngham* was particularly praiseworthy. The little vessel was skilfully placed alongside the *Orama* and some three hundred men were taken off without accident or casualty while the ship was sinking.

One of the things that made the work of the destroyer such a thankless task was that only in the rarest cases was it possible to prove that she had destroyed the submarine. Only the actual capture of the enemy ship or some of its crew furnished irrefutable proof that the action had been successful. The appearance of oil on the surface after a depth charge attack was not necessarily convincing, for the submarine early learned the trick of pumping overboard a little oil after such an experience ; in this way it hoped to persuade its pursuer that it had been sunk and thus induce it to abandon the chase. Even the appearance of wreckage, such as arose on the surface after this *Conyngham* attack, did not absolutely prove that the submarine had been destroyed. Yet, as this submarine was never heard of again, there is little doubt that Commander Johnson's depth charge performed its allotted task. The judgment of the British Government, which awarded him the C.M.G. for his achievement, may be accepted as final. The Admiralty citation for this decoration reads as follows :

" At 5.50 P.M. H.M.S. *Orama* was torpedoed in convoy. *Conyngham* went full speed, circled bow of *Orama*, saw submarine between lines of convoy, passed right over it so that it was plainly visible and dropped depth charge. Prompt and correct action of Commander Johnson saved more ships from being torpedoed and probably destroyed the submarine."

One of the greatest difficulties of convoy commanders, especially during the first months the system was in operation, was with " slacker " merchantmen ; these were vessels which, for various reasons, fell behind the convoy, a tempting bait for the submarine. At this time certain of the merchant captains manifested an incurable obstinacy; they affected to regard the U-boats with contempt, and insisted rather on taking chances instead of playing the game. In such cases a destroyer would often have to leave the main division, go back several miles, and attempt to prod the straggler into joining the convoy, much as a shepherd dog attempts to force the laggard sheep to keep within the flock. In some cases, when the merchantman proved particularly obdurate, the destroyer would slyly drop a depth charge, near enough to give the backward vessel a considerable shaking up without doing her any injury; usually such a shock caused the merchantman to start full speed ahead to rejoin her convoy, firmly believing that a submarine was giving chase. In certain instances the merchantman fell behind the convoy because the machinery had broken down or because she had suffered other accidents. The submarines would follow for days in the track of convoys, looking for a straggler of this kind, just as a shark will follow a vessel in the hope that something will be thrown overboard; and for this reason one destroyer at least was often detached from the escorting division as a rear guard. In this connection we must keep in mind that at no time until the armistice was signed was any escort force strong enough to insure entire safety. If we had had destroyers enough to put a close screen, or even a double screen, around every convoy, there would have been almost no danger from submarines. The fact that all escort forces were very inadequate placed a very heavy responsibility upon the escort commanders, and made them think twice before detaching a destroyer in order to protect stragglers.

One late summer afternoon the American converted yacht *Christabel* was performing this duty for the British merchantman *Danae*, a vessel which had fallen eight miles behind her convoy, bound from La Pallice, France, to Brest. It was a beautiful evening; the weather was clear, the sea smooth, and there was not a breath of wind. Under such conditions a submarine could conceal its presence only with great difficulty; and at about 5.30 the lookout on the *Christabel* detected a wake, some six hundred yards on the port quarter. The *Christabel* started

at full speed ; the wake suddenly ceased, but a few
splotches of oil were seen, and she was steered in the
direction of this disturbance. A depth charge was dropped
at the spot where the submarine ought to have been, but
it evidently did not produce the slightest result. The
Christabel rejoined the *Danae,* and the two went along
peacefully for nearly four hours, when suddenly a periscope appeared about two hundred yards away, on the
starboard side. Evidently this persistent German had
been following the ships all that time, looking for a favourable opportunity to discharge his torpedo. That moment
had now arrived ; the submarine was at a distance where
a carefully aimed shot meant certain destruction ; the
appearance of the periscope meant that the submarine
was making observations in anticipation of delivering this
shot. The *Christabel* started full speed for the wake of
the periscope ; this periscope itself disappeared under the
water like a guilty thing, and a disturbance on the surface
showed that the submarine was making frantic efforts to
submerge. The destroyer dropped its depth charge, set
to explode at seventy feet, its radio meantime sending
signals broadcast for assistance. Immediately after the
mushroom of water arose from this charge a secondary
explosion was heard ; this was a horrible and muffled
sound coming from the deep, more powerful and more
terrible than any that could have been caused by the
destroyer's " ash can." An enormous volcano of water
and all kinds of débris arose from the sea, half-way between
the *Christabel* and the spot where it had dropped its
charge. This secondary explosion shook the *Christabel*
so violently that the officers thought at first that the ship
had been seriously damaged, and a couple of men were
knocked sprawling on the deck. As soon as the water
subsided great masses of heavy black oil began rising to
the surface, and completely splintered wood and other
wreckage appeared. In a few minutes the sea, for a space
many hundred yards in diameter, was covered with dead
fish—about ten times as many, the officers reported, as
could have been killed by the usual depth charge. The
Christabel and the ship she was guarding started to rejoin
the main convoy, entirely satisfied with the afternoon's
work. Indeed, they had good reason to be ; a day or
two afterward a battered submarine, the *U C*-56, crept

painfully into the harbour of Santander, Spain ; it was the boat which had had such an exciting contest with the *Christabel.* She was injured beyond the possibility of repair ; besides, the Spanish Government interned her for " the duration of the war " ; so that for all practical purposes the vessel was as good as sunk.

V

Discouraging as was this business of hunting an invisible foe, events occasionally happened with all the unexpectedness of real drama. For the greater part of the time the destroyers were engaged in battle with oil slicks, wakes, tide rips, streaks of suds, and suspicious disturbances on the water ; yet now and then there were engagements with actual boats and flesh and blood human beings. To spend weeks at sea with no foe more substantial than an occasional foamy excrescence on the surface was the fate of most sailormen in this war ; yet a few exciting moments, when they finally came, more than compensated for long periods of monotony.

One afternoon in November, 1917, an American destroyer division, commanded by Commander Frank Berrien, with the *Nicholson* as its flagship, put out of Queenstown on the usual mission of taking a westbound convoy to its rendezvous and bringing in one that was bound for British ports. This outward convoy was the " O Q 20 " and consisted of eight fine ships. After the usual preliminary scoutings the vessels passed through the net in single file, sailed about ten miles to sea, and began to take up the stipulated formation, four columns of two ships each. The destroyers were moving around ; they were even mingling in the convoy, carrying messages and giving instructions ; by a quarter past four all the ships had attained their assigned positions, except one, the *René,* which was closing up to its place as the rear ship of the first column. Meanwhile, the destroyer *Fanning* was steaming rapidly to its post on the rear flank. Suddenly there came a cry from the bridge of the *Fanning,* where Coxswain David D. Loomis was on lookout :

" Periscope ! "

Off the starboard side of the *Fanning,* glistening in the smooth water, a periscope of the " finger " variety, one

10

so small that it could usually elude all but the sharpest eyes, had darted for a few seconds above the surface and had then just as suddenly disappeared. Almost directly ahead lay the *Welshman,* a splendid British merchant ship ; the periscope was so close that a torpedo would almost inevitably have hit this vessel in the engine-room. The haste with which the German had withdrawn his periscope, after taking a hurried glance around, was easily explained ; for his lens had revealed not only this tempting bait, but the destroyer *Fanning* close aboard and bearing down on him. Under these circumstances it was not surprising that no torpedo was fired ; it was clearly military wisdom to beat a quick retreat rather than attempt to attack the merchantman. Lieut. Walter S. Henry, who was the officer of the deck, acted with the most commendable despatch. It is not the simplest thing, even when the submarine is so obviously located as this one apparently was, to reach the spot accurately.

The destroyer has to make a wide and rapid turn, and there is every danger, in making this manœuvre, that the location will be missed. Subsequent events disclosed that the *Fanning* was turned with the utmost accuracy. As the ship darted by the spot at which the periscope had been sighted, a depth charge went over the stern, and exploded so violently that the main generator of the *Fanning* herself was temporarily disabled. Meanwhile the *Nicholson* had dashed through the convoy, made a rapid detour to the left, and dropped another depth charge a short distance ahead of the *Fanning.*

The disturbances made on the water by these " ash cans " gradually subsided ; to all outward appearances the submarine had escaped unharmed. The *Fanning* and the *Nicholson* completed their circles and came back to the danger spot, the officers and crew eagerly scanning the surface for the usual oil patch and air bubbles, even hoping for a few pieces of wreckage—those splintered remnants of the submarine's wooden deck that almost invariably indicated a considerable amount of damage. But none of these evidences of success, or half-success, rose to the surface ; for ten or fifteen minutes everything was as quiet as the grave. Then something happened which occurred only a few times in this strange war. The stern of a submarine appeared out of the water, tilted at about thirty degrees, clearly revealing its ugly torpedo tubes. Then came the conning-tower and finally the entire boat, the whole hull taking its usual position on the surface as neatly and unconcernedly as though no enemies were near. So far as could be seen the U-boat was in perfect condition. Its hull looked intact, showing not the slightest indication of injury; the astonished officers and men on the destroyers could easily understand now why no oil or wreckage had risen to the top, for the *U-58*—they could now see this inscription plainly painted on the conning-tower—was not leaking, and the deck showed no signs of having come into contact even remotely with a depth charge. The *Fanning* and the *Nicholson* began firing shells at the unexpected visitant, and the *Nicholson* extended an additional welcome in the form of a hastily dropped " ash can."

Suddenly the conning-tower of the submarine opened and out popped the rotund face and well-fed form of Kapitän-Leutnant Gustav Amberger, of the Imperial German Navy. The two arms of the Herr Kapitän immediately shot heavenward and the Americans on the destroyers could hear certain guttural ejaculations :

" Kamerad ! Kamerad ! "

A hatchway now opened, and a procession of German sailors emerged, one after the other, into the sunshine, like ants crawling out of their hole. As each sailor reached the deck he straightened up, lifted his arms, and shouted :

" Kamerad ! Kamerad ! Kamerad ! "

In all four officers and thirty-five men went through this ceremony. Were they really surrendering themselves and their boat, or did these gymnastic exercises conceal some new form of German craftiness ? The American ships ceased firing ; the *Fanning* gingerly approached the submarine, while the *Nicholson* stood by, all her four-inch guns trained upon the German boat, and the machine-guns pointed at the kamerading Germans, ready to shoot them into ribbons at the first sign that the surrender was not a genuine one.

While these preliminaries were taking place, a couple of German sailors disappeared into the interior of the submarine, stayed there a moment or two, and then returned to the deck. They had apparently performed a duty that was characteristically German ; for a few minutes after they appeared again, the *U-58* began to settle in the water, and soon afterward sank. These men, obeying orders, had opened the cocks and scuttled the ship—this after the officers had surrendered her ! As the submarine disappeared, the men and officers dived and started swimming toward the *Fanning*; four of them became entangled in the radio antennæ and were dragged under the waves ; however, in a few minutes these men succeeded in disentangling themselves and joined the swimmers. As the thirty-nine men neared the *Fanning* it was evident that most of them were extremely wearied and that some were almost exhausted. The sailors from the *Fanning* threw over lines ; some still had the strength to climb up these to the deck, while to others it was necessary to throw other lines which they could adjust under their arms. These latter, limp and wet figures, the American sailors pulled up, much as the fisherman pulls up the inert body of a monster fish. And now an incident took place which reveals that the American navy has rather different ideals of humanity from the German. One of the sailors was so exhausted that he could not adjust the life-lines around his shoulders ; he was very apparently drowning. Like a flash Elxer Harwell, chief pharmacist mate, and Francis G. Conner, coxswain, jumped overboard, swam to this floundering German, and adjusted the line around him as solicitously as though he had been a shipmate. The poor wretch—his name was Franz Glinder—was pulled aboard, but he was so far gone that all attempts to resuscitate him failed, and he died on the deck of the *Fanning*.

Kapitän Amberger, wet and dripping, immediately walked up to Lieut. A. S. Carpender, the commander of the *Fanning*, clicked his heels together, saluted in the most ceremonious German fashion, and surrendered himself, his officers, and his crew. He also gave his parole for his men. The officers were put in separate staterooms under guard and each of the crew was placed under the protection of a well-armed American jackie—who, it may be assumed, immensely enjoyed this new duty. All the " survivors " were dressed in dry, warm clothes, and good food and drink were given them. They were even supplied with cigarettes and something which they valued more than all the delicacies in the world—soap for a washing, the first soap which they had had for months, as this was an article which was more scarce in Germany than even copper or rubber. Our physicians gave the men first aid, and others attended to all their minor wants. Evidently the fact that they had been captured did not greatly depress their spirits, for, after eating and drinking to their heart's content, the assembled Germans burst into song.

But what was the explanation of this strange proceeding ? The German officers, at first rather stiff and sullen, ultimately unbent enough to tell their story. Their submarine had been hanging off the entrance to Queenstown for nearly two days, waiting for this particular convoy to emerge. , The officers admitted that they were getting ready to torpedo the *Welshman* when the discovery that the *Fanning* was only a short distance away compelled a sudden change in their plans. Few " ash cans " dropped in the course of the war reached their objective with the unerring accuracy of the one which now came from this American destroyer. It did not crush the submarine but the concussion wrecked the motors, making it impossible . for it to navigate, jammed its diving rudders, making the boat uncontrollable under the water, and broke the oil leads, practically shutting off the supply of this indispensable fuel. Indeed, it would be impossible to conceive of a submarine in a more helpless and unmanageable state. The officers had the option of two alternatives : to sink until the pressure of the water crushed the boat like so much paper, or to blow the ballast tanks, rise to the surface, and surrender. Even while the commander was mentally debating this problem, the submarine was rapidly descending to the bottom ; when it reached a depth of two hundred feet, which was about all that it could stand, the commander decided to take his chances with the Americans. Rising to the top involved great dangers ; but the guns of the destroyers seemed less formidable to these cornered Germans than the certainty of the horrible death that awaited them under the waves.

Admiral Bayly came to meet the *Fanning* as she sailed into Queenstown with her unexpected cargo. He went on board the destroyer to congratulate personally the officers and men upon their achievement. He published to the assembled company a cablegram just received from the Admiralty in London :

Express to commanding officers and men of the United States ship *Fanning* their Lordships' high appreciation of their successful action against enemy submarine.

I added a telegram of my own, ending up with the words, which seemed to amuse the officers and men : " Go out and do it again."

For this action the commanding officer of the *Fanning*, Lieutenant-Commander Carpender, was recommended by the Admiralty for the D.S.O., which was subsequently conferred upon him by the King at Buckingham Palace.

Only one duty remained : the commanding officer read the burial service over the body of poor Franz Glinder, the German sailor who had been drowned in his attempt to swim to the *Fanning*. The *Fanning* then steamed out to sea with the body and buried it with all the honours of war. A letter subsequently written by Kapitän Amberger to a friend in Germany summed up his opinion of the situation in these words :

" The Americans were much nicer and more obliging than expected."

VI

So far as convoying merchant ships was concerned, Queenstown was the largest American base ; by the time the movement of troops laid heavy burdens on the American destroyers Brest became a headquarters almost equally important.

In July, 1917, the British Government requested the co-operation of the American navy in the great work which it had undertaken at Gibraltar ; and on August 6th the U.S.S. *Sacramento* reached that port, followed about a week afterward by the *Birmingham* flying the flag of Rear-Admiral Henry B. Wilson. Admiral Wilson remained as commander of this force until November, when he left to assume the direction of affairs at Brest. On November 25th Rear-Admiral Albert P. Niblack succeeded to this command, which he retained throughout the war.

Gibraltar was the " gateway " for more traffic than any other port in the world. It was estimated that more than one quarter of all the convoys which reached the Entente nations either rendezvoused at this point or passed through these Straits. This was the great route to the East by way of the Suez Canal. From Gibraltar extended the Allied lines of communication to southern France, Italy, Salonika, Egypt, Palestine, and Mesopotamia. There were other routes to Bizerta (Tunis), Algiers, the island of Milo, and a monthly service to the Azores.

The Allied forces that were detailed to protect this shipping were chiefly British and American, though they were materially assisted by French, Japanese, and Italian vessels. They consisted of almost anything which the hard-pressed navies could assemble from all parts of the world—antiquated destroyers, yachts, sloops, trawlers, drifters, and the like. The Gibraltar area was a long distance from the main enemy submarine bases. The enemy could maintain at sea at any one time only a relatively small number of submarines; inasmuch as the zone off the English Channel and Ireland was the most critical one, the Allies stationed their main destroyer force there. Because of these facts, we had great difficulty in finding vessels to protect the important Gibraltar area, and the force which we ultimately got together was therefore a miscellaneous lot. The United States gathered at this point forty-one ships, and a personnel which averaged 314 officers and 4,660 men. This American aggregation contained a variegated assortment of scout cruisers, gunboats, coastguard cutters, yachts, and five destroyers of antique type. The straits to which we were reduced for available vessels for the Gibraltar station—and the British navy was similarly hard pressed—were illustrated by the fact that we placed these destroyers at Gibraltar. They were the *Decatur* and four similar vessels, each of 420 tons—the modern destroyer is a vessel of from 1,000 to 1,200 tons—and were stationed, when the war broke out, at Manila, where they were considered fit only for local service; yet the record which these doughty little ships made is characteristic of the spirit of our young officers. This little squadron steamed 12,000 miles from Manila to Gibraltar, and that they arrived in condition immediately to take up their duties was due to the excellent judgment and seamanship displayed by their commanding officer, Lieutenant-Commander (now Commander) **Har**old R. Stark. Subsequently they made **48,000** miles on escort duty. This makes 60,000 miles for vessels which in peace time had been consigned to minor duties ! Unfortunately one of these gallant little vessels was subsequently cut down and sunk by a merchant ship while escorting a convoy.

For more than a year the Gibraltar force under Admiral Niblack performed service which reflected high credit upon that commander, his officers, and his men. During this period of time it escorted, in co-operation with the British forces, 562 convoys, comprising a total of 10,478 ships. Besides protecting commerce, chasing submarines, and keeping them under the surface, many of the vessels making up this squadron had engagements with submarines that were classified as " successful." On May 15, 1918, the *Wheeling*, a gunboat, and the *Surveyor* and *Venetia*, yachts, while escorting a Mediterranean convoy, depth-charged a submarine which had just torpedoed one of the convoyed vessels ; we credited these little ships with sinking their enemy. The *Venetia*, under the command of Commander L. B. Porterfield, U.S.N., had an experience not unlike that of the *Christabel*, already described. On this occasion she was part of the escort of a Gibraltar-Bizerta convoy. A British member of this convoy, the *Surveyor*, was torpedoed at six in the evening ; at that time the submarine gave no further evidence of its existence. The *Venetia*, however, was detailed to remain in the neighbourhood, attempt to locate the mysterious vessel, and at least to keep it under the water. The *Venetia* soon found the wake of the submerged enemy and dropped the usual depth charges. Three days afterward a badly injured U-boat put in at Carthagena, Spain, and was interned for the rest of the war. Thus another submarine was as good as sunk. The *Lydonia*, a yacht of 500 tons, in conjunction with the British ship *Basilisk*, sank another U-boat in the western Mediterranean. This experience illustrates the doubt that enshrouded all such operations, for it was not until three months after the *Lydonia* engagement took place that the Admiralty discovered that the submarine had been destroyed and recommended Commander Richard P. McCullough, U.S.N., for a decoration.

Thus from the first day that this method of convoying ships was adopted it was an unqualified success in defeating the submarine campaign. By August 1, 1917, more than 10,000 ships had been convoyed, with losses of only one-half of 1 per cent. Up to that same date not a single ship which had left North American ports in convoy had been lost. By August 11th, 261 ships had been sent in convoy from North American ports, and of these only one had fallen a prey to the submarines. The convoy gave few opportunities for encounters with their enemies. I have already said that the great value of this system as a protection to shipping was that it compelled the underwater boats to fight their deadliest enemies, the destroyers, every time they tried to sink merchant ships in convoy, and they did not attempt this often on account of the danger. There were destroyer commanders who spent months upon the open sea, convoying huge aggregations of cargo vessels, without even once seeing a submarine. To a great extent the convoy system did its work in the same way that the Grand Fleet performed its indispensable service—silently, unobtrusively, making no dramatic bids for popular favour, and industriously plodding on, day after day and month after month. All this time the world had its eyes fixed upon the stirring events of the Western Front, almost unconscious of the existence of the forces that made those land operations possible. Yet a few statistics eloquently disclose the part played by the convoy system in winning the war. In the latter months of the struggle from 91 to 92 per cent. of Allied shipping sailed in convoys. The losses in these convoys were less than 1 per cent. And this figure includes the ships lost after the dispersal of the convoys; in convoys actually under destroyer escort the losses were less than one-half of 1 per cent. Military experts would term the convoy system a defensive-offensive measure. By this they mean that it was a method of taking a defensive position in order to force the enemy to meet you and give you an opportunity for the offensive. It is an old saying that the best defensive measure is a vigorous offensive one. Unfortunately, owing to the fact that the Allies had not prepared for the kind of warfare which the Germans saw fit to employ against them, we could not conduct purely offensive operations; that is, we could not employ our anti-submarine forces exclusively in the effort to destroy the submarines. Up to the time of the armistice, despite all the assistance rendered to the navies by the best scientific brains of the world, no sure means had been found of keeping track of the submarine once he submerged. The convoy system was, therefore, our only method of bringing him into action. I lay stress on this point and reiterate it because many critics kept insisting during the war—and their voices are still heard—that the convoy system was purely a defensive or passive method of opposing the submarine, and was, therefore, not sound tactics. It is quite true that we had to defend our shipping in order to win the war, but it is wrong to assume that the method adopted to accomplish this protection was a purely defensive and passive one.

As my main purpose is to describe the work of the American navy I have said little in the above about the activities of the British navy in convoying merchant ships. But we should not leave this subject with a false perspective. When the war ended we had seventy-nine destroyers in European waters, while Great Britain had about 400. These included those assigned to the Grand Fleet, to the Harwich force, to the Dover patrol, to Gibraltar and the Mediterranean, and other places, many of which were but incidentally making war on the submarines. As to minor ships—trawlers, sloops, Q-boats, yachts, drifters, tugs, and the other miscellaneous types used in this work—the discrepancy was even greater. In absolute figures our effort thus seems a small one when compared with that of our great ally. In tonnage of merchant ships convoyed, the work of the British navy was far greater than ours. Yet the help which we contributed was indispensable to the success that was attained. For, judging from the situation before we entered the war, and knowing the inadequacy of the total Allied anti-submarine forces even after we had entered, it seems hardly possible that, without the assistance of the United States navy, the vital lines of communication of the armies in the field could have been kept open, the civil populations of Great Britain supplied with food, and men and war materials sent from America to the Western Front. In other words, I think I am justified in saying that without the co-operation of the American navy, the Allies could not have won the war. Our forces stationed at Queenstown actually escorted through the danger zone about 40 per cent. of all the cargoes which left North American ports. When I describe the movement of American troops, it will appear that our destroyers located at Queenstown and Brest did even a larger share of this work. The latest reports show that about 205 German submarines were destroyed. Of these it seems probable that thirteen can be credited to American efforts, the rest to Great Britain, France, and Italy—the greatest number, of course, to Great Britain. When we take into consideration the few ships that we had on the other side, compared with those of the Allies, and the comparatively brief period in which we were engaged in the war, this must be regarded as a highly creditable showing.

I regret that I have not been able to describe the work of all of our officers and men ; to do this, however, would demand more than a single volume. One of the disappointing aspects of destroyer work was that many of the finest performances were those that were the least spectacular. The fact that an attack upon a submarine did not result in a sinking hardly robbed it of its importance ; many of the finest exploits of our forces did not destroy the enemy, but they will always hold a place in our naval annals for the daring and skill with which they were conducted. In this class belong the achievements of the *Sterrett*, under Lieutenant-Commander Farquhar ; of the *Benham*, under Lieutenant-Commander D. Lyons ; of the *O'Brien*, under Lieutenant-Commander C. A. Blakeley ; of the *Parker*, under Lieutenant-Commander H. Powell ; of the *Jacob Jones*, under Lieutenant-Commander D. W. Bagley ; of the *Wadsworth*, under Lieutenant-Commander Taussig, and afterward I. F. Dortch ; of the *Drayton*, under Lieutenant-Commander D. L. Howard ; of the *McDougal*, under Commander A. L. Fairfield ; and of the *Nicholson*, under Commander F. D. Berrien. The senior destroyer commander at Queenstown was Commander David C. Hanrahan of the *Cushing*, a fine character and one of the most experienced officers of his rank in the Navy. He was a tower of strength at all times, and I shall have occasion to mention him later in connection with certain important duties. The Chief-of-Staff at Queenstown, Captain J. R. P. Pringle, was especially commended by Admiral Bayly for his " tact, energy, and ability." The **American** naval forces at Queenstown were under my immediate command. Necessarily, however, I had to spend the greater part of my time at the London head-quarters, or at the Naval Council in Paris, and it was therefore necessary that I should be represented at Queenstown by a man of marked ability. Captain Pringle proved equal to every emergency. He was responsible for the administration, supplies, and maintenance of the Queenstown forces, and the state of readiness and efficiency in which they were constantly maintained was the strongest possible evidence of his ability. To him was chiefly due also the fact that our men co-operated so harmoniously and successfully with the British.

As an example of the impression which our work made I can do no better than to quote the message sent by Admiral Sir Lewis Bayly to the Queenstown forces on May 4, 1918 :

" On the anniversary of the arrival of the first United States men-of-war at Queenstown, I wish to express my deep gratitude to the United States officers and ratings for the skill, energy, and unfailing good-nature which they have all consistently shown and which qualities have so materially assisted in the war by enabling ships of the Allied Powers to cross the ocean in comparative freedom.

" To command you is an honour, to work with you is a pleasure, to know you is to know the best traits of the Anglo-Saxon race."

CHAPTER V

DECOYING SUBMARINES TO DESTRUCTION

I

My chief purpose in writing this book is to describe the activities during the World War of the United States naval forces operating in Europe. Yet it is my intention also to make clear the several ways in which the war against the submarine was won ; and in order to do this it will be necessary occasionally to depart from the main subject and to describe certain naval operations of our allies. The most important agency in frustrating the submarine was the convoy system. An examination of the tonnage losses in 1917 and in 1918, however, discloses that this did not entirely prevent the loss of merchant ships. From April, 1917, to November, 1918, the monthly losses dropped from 875,000 to 101,168 tons. This decrease in sinkings enabled the Allies to preserve their communications and so win the war ; however, it is evident that these losses, while not necessarily fatal to the Allied cause, still offered a serious impediment to success. It was therefore necessary to supplement the convoy system in all possible ways. Every submarine that could be destroyed, whatever the method of destruction, represented just that much gain to the Allied cause. Every submarine that was sent to the bottom amounted in 1917 to a saving of many thousands of tons per year of the merchant shipping that would have been sunk by the U-boat if left unhindered to pursue its course. Besides escorting merchant ships, therefore, the Allied navies developed several methods of hunting individual submarines ; and these methods not only sank a considerable number of U-boats, but played an important part in breaking down the German submarine *moral*. For the greater part of the war the utmost secrecy was observed regarding these expedients ; it was not until the early part of 1918, indeed, that the public heard anything of the special service vessels that came to be known as the " mystery " or " Q-ships "—although these had been operating for nearly three years. It is true that the public knew that there was something in the wind, for there were announcements that certain naval officers had received the Victoria Cross, but as there was no citation explaining why these coveted rewards were given, they were known as " mystery V.C.'s."

On one of my visits to Queenstown Admiral Bayly showed me a wireless message which he had recently received from the commanding officer of a certain mystery ship operating from Queenstown, one of the most successful of these vessels. It was brief but sufficiently eloquent.

" Am slowly sinking," it read. " Good-bye, I did my best."

Though the man who had sent that message was apparently facing death at the time when it was written, Admiral Bayly told me that he had survived the ordeal, and that, in fact, he would dine at Admiralty House that very night. Another fact about this man lifted him above the commonplace : he was the first Q-boat commander to receive the Victoria Cross, and one of the very few who wore both the Victoria Cross and the Distinguished Service Order ; and he subsequently won bars for each, not to mention the Croix de Guerre and the Legion of Honour. When Captain Gordon Campbell arrived, I found that he was a Britisher of quite the accepted type. His appearance suggested nothing extraordinary. He was a short, rather thick-set, phlegmatic Englishman, somewhat non-committal in his bearing ; until he knew a man well, his conversation consisted of a few monosyllables, and even on closer acquaintance his stolidity and reticence, especially in the matter of his own exploits, did not entirely disappear. Yet there was something about the Captain which suggested the traits that had already made it possible for him to sink three submarines, and which afterward added other trophies to his record. It needed no elaborate story of his performances to inform me that Captain Campbell was about as cool and determined a man as was to be found in the British navy. His associates declared that his physical system absolutely lacked nerves ; that, when it came to pursuing a German submarine, his patience and his persistence knew no bounds ; and that the extent to which his mind concentrated upon the task in hand amounted to little less than genius. When the war began, Captain Campbell, then about thirty years old, was merely one of several thousand junior officers in the British navy. He had not distinguished himself in any way above his associates ; and probably none of his superiors had ever regarded him as in any sense an unusual man. Had the naval war taken the course of most naval wars, Campbell would probably have served well, but perhaps not brilliantly. This conflict, however, demanded a new type of warfare and at the same time it demanded a new type of naval fighter. To go hunting for the submarine required not only courage of a high order, but analytical intelligence, patience, and a talent for preparation and detail. Captain Campbell seemed to have been created for this particular task. That evening at Queenstown he finally gave way to much urging, and entertained us for hours with his adventures ; he told the stories of his battles with submarines so quietly, so simply and, indeed, so impersonally, that at first they impressed his hearers as not particularly unusual. Yet, after the recital was finished, we realized that the mystery ship performances represented some of the most admirable achievements in the whole history of naval warfare. We have laid great emphasis upon the brutalizing aspects of the European War ; it is well, therefore, that we do not forget that it had its more exalted phases. Human nature may at times have manifested itself in its most cowardly traits, but it also reached a level of courage which, I am confident, it has seldom attained in any other conflict. It was reserved for this devastating struggle to teach us how brave modern men could really be. And when the record is complete it seems unlikely that it will furnish any finer illustration of the heroic than that presented by Captain Campbell and his compatriots of the mystery ships.

This type of vessel was a regular ship of His Majesty's navy, yet there was little about it that suggested warfare. To the outward eye it was merely one of those several thousand freighters or tramps which, in normal times, sailed sluggishly from port to port, carrying the larger part of the world's commerce. It looked like a particularly dirty and uninviting specimen of the breed. Just who invented this grimy enemy of the submarine is unknown, as are the inventors of many other devices developed by the war. It was, however, the natural outcome of a close study of German naval methods. The man who first had the idea well understood the peculiar mentality of the U-boat commanders. The Germans had a fairly easy time in the early days of submarine warfare on merchant shipping. They sank as many ships as possible with gunfire and bombs. The prevailing method then was to break surface, and begin shelling the defenceless enemy. In case the merchant ship was faster than the submarine she would take to her heels; if, as was usually the case, she was slower, the passengers and crews lowered the boats and left the vessel to her fate. In such instances the procedure of the submarine was invariably the same. It ceased shelling, approached the lifeboats filled with survivors, and ordered them to take a party of Germans to the ship. This party then searched the vessel for all kinds of valuables, and, after depositing time bombs in the hold, rowed back to the submarine. This procedure was popular with the Germans, because it was the least expensive form of destroying merchant ships. It was not necessary to use torpedoes or even a large number of shells; an inexpensive bomb, properly placed, did the whole job. Even when the arming of merchant ships interfered with this simple programme, and compelled the Germans to use long-range gunfire or torpedoes, the submarine commanders still persisted in rising to the surface near the sinking ship. Torpedoes were so expensive that the German Admiralty insisted on having every one accounted for. The word of the commander that he had destroyed a merchant ship was not accepted at its face value; in order to have the exploit officially placed to his credit, and so qualify the commander and crew for the rewards that came to the successful, it was necessary to prove that the ship had actually gone to the bottom. A prisoner or two furnished unimpeachable evidence, and, in default of such trophies, the ship's papers would be accepted. In order to obtain such proofs of success the submarine had to rise to the surface and approach its victim. The search for food, especially for alcoholic liquor, was another motive that led to such a manœuvre; and sometimes mere curiosity, the desire to come to close quarters and inspect the consequences of his handiwork, also impelled the Hun commander to take what was, as events soon demonstrated, a particularly hazardous risk.

This simple fact that the submarine, even when the danger had been realized, insisted on rising to the surface and approaching the vessel which it had torpedoed, offered the Allies an opportunity which they were not slow in seizing. There is hardly anything in warfare which is more vulnerable than a submarine on the surface within a few hundred yards of a four-inch gun. A single, well-aimed shot will frequently send it to the bottom. Indeed, a U-boat caught in such a predicament has only one chance of escaping : that is represented by the number of seconds which it takes to get under the water. But before that time has expired rapidly firing guns can put a dozen shots into its hull ; with modern, well-trained gun crews, therefore, a submarine which exposes itself in this way stands practically no chance of getting away. Clearly, the obvious thing for the Allies to do was to send merchant ships, armed with hidden guns, along the great highways of commerce. The crews of these ships should be naval officers and men disguised as merchant masters and sailors. They should duplicate in all details the manners and the " technique " of a freighter's crew, and, when shelled or torpedoed by a submarine, they should behave precisely like the passengers and crews of merchantmen in such a crisis ; a part—the only part visible to the submarine—should leave the vessel in boats, while the remainder should lie concealed until the submarine rose to the surface and approached the vessel. When the enemy had come within two or three hundred yards, the bulwarks should fall down, disclosing the armament, the white battle ensign go up, and the guns open fire on the practically helpless enemy.

II

Such was the mystery ship idea in its simplest form. In the early days it worked according to this programme. The trustful submarine commander who approached a mystery ship in the manner which I have described promptly found his resting-place on the bottom of the sea. I have frequently wondered what must have been the emotions of this first submarine crew, when, standing on the deck of their boat, steaming confidently toward their victim, they saw its bulwarks suddenly drop, and beheld the ship, which

11

to all outward appearances was a helpless, foundering hulk, become a mass of belching fire and smoke and shot. The picture of that first submarine, standing upright in the water, reeling like a drunken man, while the apparently innocent merchant ship kept pouring volley after volley into its sides, is one that will not quickly fade from the memory of British naval men. Yet it is evident that the Allies could not play a game like this indefinitely. They could do so just as long as the Germans insisted on delivering themselves into their hands. The complete success of the idea depended at first upon the fact that the very existence of mystery ships was unknown to the German navy. All that the Germans knew, in these early days, was that certain U-boats had sailed from Germany and had not returned. But it was inevitable that the time should come when a mystery ship attack would fail ; the German submarine would return and report that this new terror of the seas was at large. And that is precisely what happened. A certain submarine received a battering which it seemed hardly likely that any U-boat could survive ; yet, almost by a miracle, it crept back to its German base and reported the manner of its undoing. Clearly the mystery ships in future were not to have as plain sailing as in the past ; the game, if it were to continue, would become more a battle of wits ; henceforth every liner and merchantman, in German eyes, was a possible enemy in disguise, and it was to be expected that the U-boat commanders would resort to every means of protecting their craft against them. That the Germans knew all about these vessels became apparent when one of their naval publications fell into our hands, giving complete descriptions and containing directions to U-boat commanders how to meet this new menace. The German newspapers and illustrated magazines also began to devote much space to this kind of anti-submarine fighting, denouncing it in true Germanic fashion as " barbarous " and contrary to the rules of civilized warfare. The great significance of this knowledge is at once apparent. The mere fact that a number of Q-ships were at sea, even if they did not succeed in sinking many submarines, forced the Germans to make a radical change in their submarine tactics. As they could no longer bring to, board, and loot merchant ships, and sink them inexpensively and without danger by the use of bombs, they were obliged not only to use their precious torpedoes, but also to torpedo without warning. This was the only alternative except to abandon the submarine campaign altogether.

Berlin accordingly instructed the submarine commanders not to approach on the surface any merchant or passenger vessel closely enough to get within range of its guns, but to keep at a distance and shell it. Had the commanders always observed these instructions the success of the mystery ship in sinking submarines would have ended then and there, though the influence of their presence upon tactics would have remained in force. The Allied navies now made elaborate preparations, all for the purpose of persuading Fritz to approach in the face of a tremendous risk concerning which he had been accurately informed. Every submarine commander, after torpedoing his victim, now clearly understood that it might be a decoy despatched for the particular purpose of entrapping him ; and he knew that an attempt to approach within a short distance of the foundering vessel might spell his own immediate destruction. The expert in German mentality must explain why, under these circumstances, he should have persisted in walking into the jaws of death. The skill with which the mystery ships and their crews were disguised perhaps explains this in part. Anyone who might have happened in the open sea upon Captain Campbell and his slow-moving freighter could not have believed that they were part and parcel of the Royal Navy. Our own destroyers were sometimes deceived by them. The *Cushing* one day hailed Captain Campbell in the *Pargust*, having mistaken him for a defenceless tramp. The conversation between the two ships was brief but to the point :

Cushing : What ship ?
Pargust : Gordon Campbell ! Please keep out of sight.

The next morning another enemy submarine met her fate at the hands of Captain Campbell, and although the *Cushing* had kept far enough away not to interfere with the action, she had the honour of escorting the injured mystery ship into port and of receiving as a reward three rousing cheers from the crew of the *Pargust* led by Campbell. A more villainous-looking gang of seamen than the crews of these ships never sailed the waves. All men on board were naval officers or enlisted men; they were all volunteers and comprised men of all ranks—admirals, captains, commanders, and midshipmen. All had temporarily abandoned His Majesty's uniform for garments picked up in second-hand clothing stores. They had made the somewhat disconcerting discovery that carefully trained gentlemen of the naval forces, when dressed in cast-off clothing and when neglectful of their beards, differ little in appearance from the somewhat rough-and-tumble characters of the tramp service. To assume this external disguise successfully meant that the volunteers had also to change almost their personal characteristics as well as their clothes. Whereas the conspicuous traits of a naval man are neatness and order, these counterfeit merchant sailors had to train themselves in the casual ways of tramp seamen. They had also to accustom themselves to the conviction that a periscope was every moment searching their vessel from stem to stern in an attempt to discover whether there was anything suspicious about it; they therefore had not only to dress the part of merchantmen, but to act it, even in its minor details. The genius of Captain Campbell consisted in the fact that he had made a minute study of merchantmen, their officers and their crews, and was able to reproduce them so literally on this vessel that even the expert eye was deceived. Necessarily such a ship carried a larger crew than the merchant freighter; nearly all, however, were kept constantly concealed, the number appearing on deck always representing just about the same number as would normally have sailed upon a tramp steamer. These men had to train themselves in slouchiness of behaviour; they would hang over the rails, and even use merchant terms in conversation with one another; the officers were " masters," " mates," " pursers," and the like, and their principal gathering-place was not a wardroom, but a saloon. That scrupulous deference with which a subordinate officer in the navy treats his superior was laid aside in this service. It was no longer the custom to salute before addressing the commander; more frequently the sailor would slouch up to his superior, his hands in his pockets and his pipe in his mouth. This attempt to deceive the Hun observer at the periscope sometimes assumed an even more ludicrous form.

When the sailor of a warship dumps ashes overboard he does it with particular care, so as not to soil the sides of his immaculate vessel ; but a merchant seaman is much less considerate ; he usually hurls overboard anything he does not want and lets the ship's side take its chances. To have followed the manner of the navy would at once have given the game away ; so the sailors, in carrying out this domestic duty, performed the act with all the nonchalance of merchant seamen. To have messed in naval style would also have been betraying themselves. The ship's cook, therefore, in a white coat, would come on deck, and have a look around, precisely as he would do on a freighter. Even when in port officers and men maintained their disguise. They never visited hotels or clubs or private houses ; they spent practically all their time on board ; if they occasionally went ashore, their merchant outfit so disguised them that even their best friends would not have recognized them in the street.

The warlike character of their ships was even more cleverly hidden. In the early days the guns were placed behind the bulwarks, which, when a lever was pulled, would fall down, thus giving them an unobstructed range at the submarine. In order to make the sides of the ships collapsible, certain seams were unavoidably left in the plates, where the detachable part joined the main struc-ture. The U-boat commanders soon learned to look for these betraying seams before coming to the surface. They would sail submerged around the ship, the periscope minutely examining the sides, much as a scientist examines his specimens with a microscope. This practice made it necessary to conceal the guns more carefully. The places which were most serviceable for this purpose were the hatchways—those huge wells, extending from the deck to the bottom, which are used for loading and unloading cargo. Platforms were erected in these openings, and on these guns were emplaced ; a covering of tarpaulin com-pletely hid them ; yet a lever, pulled by the gun crews, would cause the sides of the hatchway covers to fall instantaneously. Other guns were placed under lifeboats, which, by a similar mechanism, would fall apart, or rise in the air, exposing the gun. Perhaps the most deceptive device of all was a gun placed upon the stern, and, with its crew, constantly exposed to public gaze. Since most merchantmen carried such a gun, its absence on a mystery ship would in itself have caused suspicion ; this armament not only helped the disguise, but served a useful purpose in luring the submarine. At the first glimpse of a U-boat on the surface, usually several miles away, the gun crew would begin shooting ; but they always took care that the shots fell short, thus convincing the submarine that it had the advantage of range and so inducing it to close.

Captain Campbell and his associates paid as much attention to details in their ships as in their personal appearance. The ship's wash did not expose the flannels that are affected by naval men but the dungarees that are popular with merchant sailors. Sometimes a side of beef would be hung out in plain view ; this not only kept up the fiction that the ship was an innocent tramp, but it served as a tempting bait to the not too well-fed crew of the submarine. Particularly tempting cargoes were occasionally put on deck. One of the ships carried several papier-mâché freight cars of the small European type covered with legends which indicated that they were loaded with ammunition and bound for Mesopotamia. It is easy to imagine how eagerly the Hun would wish to sink that cargo !

These ships were so effectively disguised that even the most experienced eyes could not discover their real character. For weeks they could lie in dock, the dockmen never suspecting that they were armed to the teeth. Even the pilots who went aboard to take them into harbour never discovered that they were not the merchant ships which they pretended to be. Captain Hanrahan, who commanded the U.S. mystery ship *Santee*, based on Queenstown, once entertained on board an Irishman from Cork. The conversation which took place between this American naval officer—who, in his disguise, was indistinguishable from a tramp skipper of many years' experience—disclosed the complete ignorance of the guest concerning the true character of the boat.

" How do you like these Americans ? " Captain Hanrahan innocently asked.

" They are eating us out of house and home ! " the indignant Irishman remarked. The information was a little inaccurate, since all our food supplies were brought from the United States ; but the remark was reassuring as proving that the ship's disguise had not been penetrated. Such precautions were the more necessary in a port like Queenstown where our forces were surrounded by spies who were in constant communication with the enemy.

I can personally testify to the difficulty of identifying a mystery ship. One day Admiral Bayly suggested that we should go out in the harbour and visit one of these vessels lying there preparatory to sailing on a cruise. Several merchantmen were at anchor in port. We steamed close around one in the Admiral's barge and examined her very carefully through out glasses from a short distance. Concluding that this was not the vessel we were seeking, we went to another merchantman. This did not show any signs of being a mystery ship ; we therefore hailed the skipper, who told us the one which we had first visited was the mystery ship. We went back, boarded her, and began examining her appliances. The crew was dressed in the ordinary sloppy clothes of a merchantman's deck-hands ; the officers wore the usual merchant ship uniform, and everything was as unmilitary as a merchant ship usually is. The vessel had quite a long deckhouse built of light steel. The captain told us that two guns were concealed in this structure ; he suggested that we should walk all around it and see if we could point out from a close inspection the location of the guns. We searched carefully, but were utterly unable to discover where the guns were. The captain then sent the crew to quarters and told us to stand clear. At the word of command one of the plates of the perpendicular side of the deckhouse slid out of the way as quickly as a flash. The rail at the ship's side in front of the gun fell down and a boat davit swung out of the way. At the same time the gun crew swung the gun out and fired a primer to indicate how quickly they could have fired a real shot. The captain also showed us a boat upside down on the deckhouse—merchantmen frequently carry one boat in this position. At a word a lever was pulled down below and the boat reared up in the air and revealed underneath a gun and its crew. On the poop was a large crate about $6 \times 6 \times 8$ or 10 feet. At a touch of the lever the sides of this crate fell down and revealed another gun.

III

For the greater part of 1917 from twenty to thirty of these ships sailed back and forth in the Atlantic, always choosing those parts of the seas where they were most likely to meet submarines. They were " merchantmen " of all kinds—tramp steamers, coasting vessels, trawlers, and schooners. Perhaps the most distressing part of existence on one of these ships was its monotony : day would follow day ; week would follow week ; and sometimes months would pass without encountering a single submarine. Captain Campbell himself spent nine months on his first mystery ship before even sighting an enemy, and many of his successors had a similar experience. The mystery boat was a patient fisherman, constantly expecting a bite and frequently going for long periods without the slightest nibble. This kind of an existence was not only disappointing but also exceedingly nerve racking ; all during this waiting period the officers and men had to keep themselves constantly at attention ; the vaudeville show which they were maintaining for the benefit of a possible periscope had to go on continuously ; a moment's forgetfulness or relaxation might betray their secret, and make their experiment a failure. The fearful tediousness of this kind of life had a more nerve-racking effect upon the officers and men than the most exciting battles, and practically all the mystery ship men who broke down fell victims not to the dangers of their enterprise, but to this dreadful tension of sailing for weeks and months without coming to close quarters with their enemy.

About the most welcome sight to a mystery ship, after a period of inactivity, was the wake of a torpedo speeding in its direction. Nothing could possibly disappoint it more than to see this torpedo pass astern or forward without hitting the vessel. In such a contingency the genuine merchant ship would make every possible effort to turn out of the torpedo's way : the helmsman of the mystery ship, however, would take all possible precautions to see that his vessel was hit. This, however, he had to do with the utmost cleverness, else the fact that he was attempting to collide with several hundred pounds of gun-cotton would in itself betray him to the submarine.

Not improbably several members of the crew might be killed when the torpedo struck, but that was all part of the game which they were playing. More important than the lives of the men was the fate of the ship ; if this could remain afloat long enough to give the gunners a good chance at the submarine, everybody on board would be satisfied. There was, however, little danger that the mystery ship would go down immediately ; for all available cargo space had been filled with wood, which gave the vessel sufficient buoyancy sometimes to survive many torpedoes.

Of course this, as well as all the other details of the vessel, was unknown to the skipper of the submerged submarine. Having struck his victim in a vital spot, he had every reason to believe that it would disappear beneath the waves within a reasonable period. The business of the disguised merchantman was to encourage this delusion in every possible way. From the time that the torpedo struck, the mystery ship behaved precisely as the everyday cargo carrier, caught in a similar predicament, would have done. A carefully drilled contingent of the crew, known as the " panic party," enacted the rôle of the men on a torpedoed vessel. They ran to and fro on the deck, apparently in a state of high consternation, now rushing below and emerging with some personal treasure, perhaps an old suit of clothes tucked under the arm, perhaps the ship's cat or parrot, or a small handbag hastily stuffed with odds and ends. Under the control of the navigating officer these men would make for a lifeboat, which they would lower in realistic fashion—sometimes going so far, in their stage play, as to upset it, leaving the men puffing and scrambling in the water. One member of the crew, usually the navigator, dressed up as the " captain," did his best to supervise these operations. Finally, after everybody had left, and the vessel was settling at bow or stern, the " captain " would come to the side, cast one final glance at his sinking ship, drop a roll of papers into a lifeboat—ostensibly the precious documents which were so coveted by the submarine as an evidence of success —lower himself with one or two companions, and row in the direction of the other lifeboats. Properly placing these lifeboats, after " abandoning ship," was itself one of the finest points in the plot. If the submarine rose

to the surface it would invariably steer first for those
little boats, looking for prisoners or the ship's papers;
the boats' crews, therefore, had instructions to take up
a station on a bearing from which the ship's guns could
most successfully rake the submarine. That this manœuvre
involved great danger to the men in the lifeboats was a
matter of no consideration in the desperate enterprise in
which they were engaged.

Thus to all outward appearance this performance was
merely the torpedoing of a helpless merchant vessel. Yet
the average German commander became altogether too
wary to accept the situation in that light. He had no
intention of approaching either lifeboats or the ship until
entirely satisfied that he was not dealing with one of the
decoy vessels which he so greatly feared. There was
only one way of satisfying himself: that was to shell the
ship so mercilessly that, in his opinion, if any human
beings had remained aboard, they would have been killed
or forced to surrender. The submarine therefore arose
at a distance of two or three miles. Possibly the mystery
ship, with one well-aimed shot, might hit the submarine
at this distance, but the chances were altogether against
her. To fire such a shot, of course, would immediately
betray the fact that a gun crew still remained on board,
and that the vessel was a mystery ship; and on this discovery the submarine would submerge, approach the
vessel under water, and give her one or two more torpedoes.
No, whatever the temptation, the crew must " play
'possum," and not by so much as a wink let the submarine
know that there was any living thing on board. But this
experience demanded heroism that almost approaches the
sublime. The gun crews lay prone beside their guns,
waiting the word of command to fire; the captain lay on
the screened bridge, watching the whole proceeding
through a peephole, with voice tubes near at hand with
which he could constantly talk to his men. They maintained these positions sometimes for hours, never lifting
a finger in defence, while the submarine, at a safe distance,
showered hundreds of shells upon the ship. These horrible
missiles would shriek above their heads; they would land
on the decks, constantly wounding the men, sometimes
killing whole gun crews—yet, although the ship might
become a mass of blood and broken fragments of human

bodies, the survivors would lie low, waiting, with infinite patience, until the critical moment arrived. This was the way they took to persuade the submarine that their ship was what it pretended to be, a tramp, that there was nothing alive on board, and that it could safely come near. The still cautious German, after an hour or so of this kind of execution, would submerge and approach within a few hundred yards. All that the watchful eye at the peephole could see, however, was the periscope ; this would sail all around the vessel, sometimes at a distance of fifty or a hundred feet. Clearly the German was taking no chances ; he was examining his victim inch by inch, looking for the slightest sign that the vessel was a decoy. All this time the captain and crew were lying taut, holding their breath, not moving a muscle, hardly winking an eyelid, the captain with his mouth at the voice pipe ready to give the order to let the false works drop the moment the submarine emerged, the gun crews ready to fire at a second's warning. But the cautious periscope, having completed the inspection of the ship, would start in the direction of the drifting lifeboats. This ugly eye would stick itself up almost in the faces of the anxious crew, evidently making a microscopical examination of the clothes, faces, and general personnel, to see if it could detect under their tramp steamer clothes any traces of naval officers and men.

Still the anxious question was, would the submarine emerge ? Until it should do so the ship's crew was absolutely helpless. There was no use in shooting at the submerged boat, as shots do not penetrate the water but bounce off the surface as they do off solid ice. Everybody knew that the German under the water was debating that same question. To come up to the surface so near a mystery ship he knew meant instant death and the loss of his submarine ; yet to go away under water meant that the sinking ship, if a merchantman, might float long enough to be salvaged, and it meant also that he would never be able to prove that he had accomplished anything with his valuable torpedo. Had he not shelled the derelict so completely that nothing could possibly survive ? Had he not examined the thing minutely and discovered nothing amiss ? It must be remembered that in 1917 a submarine went through this same procedure with every ship that did not sink very soon after being torpedoed, and that, in nearly every case, it discovered, after emerging, that it had been dealing with a real merchantman. Already this same submarine had wasted hours and immense stores of ammunition on véssels that were not mystery ships, but harmless tramps, and all these false alarms had made it impatient and careless. In most cases, therefore, the crew had only to bide its time. The captain knew that his hidden enemy would finally rise.

" Stand by ! "

This command would come softly through the speaking tubes to the men at the guns. The captain on the bridge had noticed the preliminary disturbance on the water that preceded the emergence of the submarine. In a few seconds the whole boat would be floating on top, and the officers and crews would climb out on the deck, eager for booty. And this within a hundred yards of four or five guns !

" Let go ! "

This command came at the top of the voice, for concealment was now no longer necessary. In a twinkling up went the battle flag, bulwarks fell down, lifeboats on decks collapsed, revealing guns, sides dropped from deckhouses, hen-coops, and other innocent-looking structures. The apparently sinking merchantman became a volcano of smoke and fire ; scores of shells dropped upon the submarine, punching holes in her frail hull, hurling German sailors high into the air, sometimes decapitating them or blowing off their arms or legs. The whole horrible scene lasted only a few seconds before the helpless vessel would take its final plunge to the depths, leaving perhaps two or three survivors, a mass of oil and wood, and still more ghastly wreckage, to mark the spot where another German submarine had paid the penalty of its crimes.

IV

It was entirely characteristic of this strange war that the greatest exploit of any of the mystery ships was in one sense a failure—that is, it did not succeed in destroying the submarine which attacked it.

On an August day in 1917 the British "merchant steamer" *Dunraven* was zigzagging across the Bay of Biscay. Even to the expert eye she was a heavily laden cargo vessel bound for Gibraltar and the Mediterranean, probably carrying supplies to the severely pressed Allies in Italy and the East. On her stern a $2\frac{1}{2}$-pounder gun, clearly visible to all observers, helped to emphasize this impression. Yet the apparently innocent *Dunraven* was a far more serious enemy to the submarine than appeared on the surface. The mere fact that the commander was not an experienced merchant salt, but Captain Gordon Campbell, of the Royal Navy, in itself would have made the *Dunraven* an object of terror to any lurking submarine, for Captain Campbell's name was a familiar one to the Germans by this time. Yet it would have taken a careful investigation to detect in the rough and unkempt figure of Captain Campbell any resemblance to an officer of the British navy, or to identify the untidy seamen as regularly enrolled British sailors. The armament of the *Dunraven*, could one have detected it, would have provided the greatest surprises. This vessel represented the final perfection of the mystery ship. Though seemingly a harmless tramp she carried a number of guns, also two torpedo tubes, and several depth charges; but even from her deck nothing was visible except the usual merchant gun aft. The stern of the *Dunraven* was a veritable arsenal. Besides the guns and depth charges, the magazine and shell-rooms were concealed there; on each side of the ship a masked torpedo tube held its missile ready for a chance shot at a submarine; and the forward deck contained other armament. Such was the *Dunraven*, ploughing her way along, quietly and indifferently, even when, as on this August morning, a submarine was lying on the horizon, planning to make her its prey.

As soon as the disguised merchantman spotted this enemy she began to behave in character. When an armed merchant ship got within range of a submarine on the surface she frequently let fly a shot on the chance of a hit. That was therefore the proper thing for the *Dunraven* to do; it was really all a part of the game of false pretence in which she was engaged. However, she took pains that the shell should not reach the submarine; this was her means of persuading the U-boat that it outranged the *Dunraven's* gun and could safely give chase. The decoy merchantman apparently put on extra steam when the submarine started in her direction at top speed; here, again, however, the proper manœuvre was not to run too fast, for her real mission was to get caught. On the other hand, had she slowed down perceptibly, that in itself would have aroused suspicion; her game, therefore, was to decrease speed gradually so that the U-boat would think that it was overtaking its enemy by its own exertions. All during this queer kind of a chase the submarine and the cargo ship were peppering each other with shells, one seriously, the other merely in pretence. The fact that a naval crew, with such a fine target as an exposed submarine, could shoot with a conscious effort not to hit, but merely to lure the enemy to a better position, in itself is an eloquent evidence of the perfect discipline which prevailed in the mystery ship service. Not to aim a fair shot upon the detested vessel, when there was a possibility of hitting it, was almost too much to ask of human nature. But it was essential to success with these vessels never to fire with the intention of hitting unless there was a practical certainty of sinking the submarine; all energies were focussed upon the supreme task of inducing the enemy to expose itself completely within three or four hundred yards of the disguised freighter.

In an hour or two the submarine landed a shot that seemed to have done serious damage. At least huge clouds of steam arose from the engine-room, furnishing external evidence that the engines or boilers had been disabled. The submarine commander did not know that this was a trick; that the vessel was fitted with a specially arranged pipe around the engine-room hatch which could emit these bursts of steam at a moment's notice, all for the purpose of making him believe that the vitals of the ship had been irreparably damaged. The stopping of the ship, the blowing off of the safety valve, and the appearance of the " panic party " immediately after this ostensible hit made the illusion complete. This " panic party " was particularly panicky; one of the lifeboats was let go with a run, one fall at a time, thus dumping its occupants into the sea. Ultimately, however, the struggling swimmers were picked up and the boat rowed away, taking up a position where a number of the *Dunraven's* guns could get a good shot at the submar ne should the Germans follow their usual plan of inspecting the lifeboats before visiting the sinking merchant-man.

So far everything was taking place according to pro-gramme ; but presently the submarine reopened fire and scored a shot which gave the enemy all the advantages of the situation. I have described in some detail the stern of the ship—a variegated assortment of depth charges, shell, guns, and human beings. The danger of such an una-voidable concentration of armament and men was that a lucky shot might land in the midst of it. And this is precisely what now happened. Not only one, but three shells from the submarine one after the other struck this hidden mass of men and ammunition. The first one exploded a depth charge—300 pounds of high explosive—which blew one of the officers out of the after-control station where he lay concealed and landed him on the deck several yards distant. Here he remained a few moments unconscious ; then his associates saw him, wounded as he was, creeping inch by inch back into his control position, fortunately out of sight of the Germans. The seaman who was stationed at the depth charges was also wounded by this shot, but, despite all efforts to remove him to a more comfortable place, he insisted on keeping at his post.

" 'Ere I was put in charge of these things," he said, " and 'ere I stays."

Two more shells, one immediately after the other, now landed on the stern. Clouds of black smoke began to rise, and below tongues of flame presently appeared, licking their way in the direction of a large quantity of ammunition, cordite, and other high explosives. It was not decoy smoke and decoy flame this time. Captain Campbell, watching the whole proceeding from the bridge, perhaps felt some-thing in the nature of a chill creeping up his spine when he realized that the after-part of the ship, where men, explo-sives, and guns lay concealed in close proximity, was on fire. Just at this moment he observed that the submarine was rapidly approaching ; and in a few minutes it lay within 400 yards of his guns. Captain Campbell was just about to give the orders to open fire when the wind took up the dense smoke of the fire and wafted it between his ship and the submarine. This precipitated one of the crises which tested to the utmost the discipline of the mystery ship. The captain had two alternatives : he could fire at the submarine through the smoke, taking his chances of hitting an unseen and moving target, or he could wait until the enemy passed around the ship and came up on the other side, where there would be no smoke to interfere with his view. It was the part of wisdom to choose the latter course ; but under existing conditions such a decision involved not only great nerve, but absolute confidence in his men. For all this time the fire at the stern was increasing in fierceness ; in a brief period, Captain Campbell knew, a mass of ammunition and depth charges would explode, probably killing or frightfully wounding every one of the men who were stationed there. If he should wait until the U-boat made the tour of the ship and reached the side that was free of smoke the chances were that this explosion would take place before a gun could be fired. On the other hand, if he should fire through the smoke, there was little likelihood of hitting the submarine.

Those who are acquainted with the practical philosophy which directed operations in this war will readily foresee the choice which was now made. The business of mystery ships, as of all anti-submarine craft, was to sink the enemy. All other considerations amounted to nothing when this supreme object was involved. The lives of officers and men, precious as they were under ordinary circumstances, were to be immediately sacrificed if such a sacrifice would give an opportunity of destroying the submarine. It was therefore Captain Campbell's duty to wait for the underwater boat to sail slowly around his ship and appear in clear view on the starboard side, leaving his brave men at the stern exposed to the fire, every minute raging more fiercely, and to the likelihood of a terrific explosion. That he was able to make this decision, relying confidently upon the spirit of his crew and their loyal devotion to their leader, again illustrates the iron discipline which was maintained on the mystery ships. The first explosion had destroyed the voice tube by means of which Captain Campbell communicated with this gun crew. He therefore had to make his decision without keeping his men informed of the progress of events—information very helpful to men under such a strain ; but he well knew that these men would understand his action and cheerfully accept their rôle in the game. Yet the agony of their position tested their self-control to the utmost. The deck on which they lay every moment became hotter; the leather of their shoes began to smoke, but they refused to budge—for to flee to a safer place meant revealing themselves to the submarine and thereby betraying their secret. They took the boxes of cordite shells in their arms and held them up as high as possible above the smouldering deck in the hope of preventing an explosion which seemed inevitable. Never did Christian martyrs, stretched upon a gridiron, suffer with greater heroism.

V

It was probably something of a relief when the expected explosion took place. The submarine had to go only 200 yards more to be under the fire of three guns at a range of 400 yards, but just as it was rounding the stern the German officers and men, standing on the deck, were greeted with a terrific roar. Suddenly a conglomeration of men, guns, and unexploded shells was hurled into the air. The German crew, of course, had believed that the vessel was a deserted hulk, and this sudden manifestation of life on board not only tremendously startled them, but threw them into a panic. The four-inch gun and its crew were blown high into the air, the gun landing forward on the well deck, and the crew in various places. One man fell into the water; he was picked up, not materially the worse for his experience, by the *Dunraven's* lifeboat, which, all this time, had been drifting in the neighbourhood. It is one of the miracles of this war that not one of the members of that crew was killed. The gashed and bleeding bodies of several were thrown back upon the deck; but there were none so seriously wounded that they did not recover. In the minds of these men, however, their own sufferings were not the most distressing consequences of the explosion; the really unfortunate fact was that the sudden appearance of men and guns in the air informed the Germans that they had to deal with one of the ships which they so greatly dreaded. The game, so far as the *Dunraven* was concerned, was apparently up. The submarine vanished under the water; and the Englishmen well knew that the next move would be

12

the firing of the torpedo which could confidently be expected
to end the Q-boat's career. Some of the crew who were
not incapacitated got a hose and attempted to put out the
fire, while others removed their wounded comrades to as
comfortable quarters as could be found. Presently the
wake of the torpedo could be seen approaching the ship;
the explosion that followed was a terrible one. The concussion of the previous explosion had set off the " open-
fire " buzzers at the gun positions—these buzzers being the
usual signals for dropping the false work that concealed the
guns and beginning the fight. The result was that, before
the torpedo had apparently given the *Dunraven* its quietus,
all the remaining guns were exposed with their crews.
Captain Campbell now decided to fight to the death. He
sent out a message notifying all destroyers and other anti-
submarine craft, as well as all merchant ships, not to
approach within thirty miles. A destroyer, should she
appear, would force the German to keep under water, and
thus prevent the *Dunraven* from getting a shot. Another
merchant ship on the horizon might prove such a tempting
bait to the submarine that it would abandon the *Dunraven*,
now nearly done for—all on fire at one end as she was and
also sinking from her torpedo wound—and so prevent any
further combat. For the resourceful Captain Campbell had
already formulated another final plan by which he might
entice the submarine to rise within range of his guns. To
carry out this plan, he wanted plenty of sea room and no
interference; so he drew a circle in the water, with a radius
of thirty miles, inclosing the space which was to serve as the
" prize ring " for the impending contest.

His idea was to fall in with the German belief that the
Dunraven had reached the end of her tether. A hastily
organized second " panic party " jumped into a remaining
lifeboat and a raft and rowed away from the sinking,
burning ship. Here was visible evidence to the Germans
that their enemies had finally abandoned the fight after
nearly four hours of as frightful gruelling as any ship had
ever received. But there were still two guns that were concealed and workable; there were, as already said, two
torpedo tubes, one on each beam; and a handful of men
were kept on board to man these. Meanwhile, Captain
Campbell lay prone on the bridge, looking through a peephole for the appearance of the submarine, constantly talking

to his men through the tubes, even joking them on their painful vigil.

" If you know a better 'ole," he would say, quoting Bairnsfather, " go to it ! "

" Remember, lads," he would call at another time, " that the King has given this ship the V.C."

Every situation has its humorous aspects. Thus one gun crew could hardly restrain its laughter when a blue-jacket called up to Captain Campbell and asked if he could not take his boots off. He came of a respectable family, he explained, and did not think it becoming to die with his boots on. But the roar of the fire, which had now engulfed the larger part of the ship, and the constantly booming shells, which were exploding, one after another, like mammoth fire-crackers, interfered with much conversation. For twenty minutes everybody lay there, hoping and praying that the U-boat would emerge.

The German ultimately came up, but he arose cautiously at the stern of the ship, at a point from which the guns of the *Dunraven* could not bear. On the slim chance that a few men might be left aboard, the submarine shelled it for several minutes, fore and aft, then, to the agony of the watching Englishmen, it again sank beneath the waves. Presently the periscope shot up, and began moving slowly around the blazing derelict, its eye apparently taking in every detail ; he was so cautious, that submarine commander, he did not propose to be outwitted again ! Captain Campbell now saw that he had only one chance ; the conflagration was rapidly destroying his vessel, and he could spend no more time waiting for the submarine to rise. But he had two torpedoes and he determined to use these against the submerged submarine. As the periscope appeared abeam, one of the *Dunraven's* torpedoes started in its direction ; the watching gunners almost wept when it missed by a few inches. But the submarine did not see it, and the periscope calmly appeared on the other side of the ship. The second torpedo was fired ; this also passed just about a foot astern, and the submarine saw it. The game was up. What was left of the *Dunraven* was rapidly sinking, and Captain Campbell sent out a wireless for help. In a few minutes the U.S. armed yacht *Noma* and the British destroyers *Alcock* and *Christopher*, which had been waiting outside the " prize ring," arrived and took off the crew.

The tension of the situation was somewhat relieved when a " jackie " in one of the " panic " boats caught sight of his beloved captain, entirely uninjured, jumping on one of the destroyers.

" Gawd ! " he shouted, in a delighted tone, " if there ain't the skipper still alive ! "

" We deeply regret the loss of His Majesty's ship," said Captain Campbell, in his report, " and still more the escape of the enemy.   We did our best, not only to destroy the enemy and save the ship, but also to show ourselves worthy of the Victoria Cross which the King recently bestowed on the ship."

They did indeed.   My own opinion of this performance I expressed in a letter which I could not refrain from writing to Captain Campbell :

My dear Captain :

I have just read your report of the action between the *Dunraven* and a submarine on August 8th last.

I have had the benefit of reading the reports of some of your former exploits, and Admiral Bayly has told me about them all ; but in my opinion this of the *Dunraven* is the finest of all as a military action and the most deserving of complete success.

It was purely incidental that the sub escaped.   That was due, moreover, to an unfortunate piece of bad luck. The engagement, judged as a skilful fight, and not measured by its material results, seems to me to have been perfectly successful, because I do not think that even you, with all your experience in such affairs, could conceive of any feature of the action that you would alter if you had to do it over again.   According to my idea about such matters, the standard set by you and your crew is worth infinitely more than the destruction of a submarine. Long after we both are dust and ashes, the story of this last fight will be a valuable inspiration to British (and American) naval officers and men—a demonstration of the extraordinary degree to which the patriotism, loyalty, personal devotion, and bravery of a crew may be inspired. I know nothing finer in naval history than the conduct of the after-gun's crew—in fact, the entire crew of the *Dunraven*.   It goes without saying that the credit of this behaviour is chiefly yours. . . .

With my best wishes for your future success, believe me, my dear Captain,

Faithfully yours,

WM. S. SIMS.

The records show that the mystery ships sank twelve submarines, of which Captain Campbell accounted for four; yet this was perhaps not their most important achievement. From the German standpoint they were a terribly disturbing element in the general submarine situation. Externally a mystery ship, as already described, was indistinguishable from the most harmless merchantman. The cleverness with which the Allied officers took advantage of the vicious practices of the submarine commanders bewildered them still further. Nothing afloat was sacred to the Hun; and he seemed to take particular pride in destroying small vessels, even little sailing vessels. The Navy decided to turn this amiable trait to good account, and fitted out the *Prize*, a topsail schooner of 200 tons, and placed her under the command of Lieut. William Sanders, R.N.R. This little schooner, as was expected, proved an irresistible bait. A certain submarine, commanded by one of the most experienced U-boat captains, attacked her by gun fire from a safe distance and, after her panic party had left, shelled her until she was in a sinking condition; many of her crew had been killed and wounded, when, confident that she could not be a Q-ship, the enemy came within less than 100 yards. It was promptly fired on and disappeared beneath the surface. The panic party picked up the German captain and two men, apparently the only survivors, who expressed their high admiration for the bravery of the crew and assisted them to get their battered craft into port. The captain said to Lieutenant Sanders: "I take off my hat to you and your men. I would not have believed that any men could stand such gun fire." For this exploit Lieutenant Sanders was awarded the Victoria Cross. Within about four days from the time of this action the Admiralty received an inquiry via Sweden through the Red Cross asking the whereabouts of the captain of this submarine. This showed that the vessel had reached her home port, and illustrated once more the necessity for caution in claiming the destruction of U-boats and the wisdom of declining to publish the figures of sinkings. Unfortunately, the plucky little *Prize* was subsequently lost with her gallant captain and crew.

So great was the desire of our people to take some part in the mystery ship campaign that I took steps to satisfy their legitimate ambition. As the Navy had fitted out no mystery ships of our own, I requested the Admiralty to assign one for our use. This was immediately agreed to by Admiral Jellicoe and, with the approval of the Navy Department, the vessel was delivered and named the *Santee*, after our old sailing man-of-war of that name. We called for volunteers, and practically all the officers and men of the forces based on Queenstown clamoured for this highly interesting though hazardous service. Commander David C. Hanrahan was assigned as her commander, and two specially selected men were taken from each of our vessels, thus forming an exceedingly capable crew. The ship was disguised with great skill and, with the invaluable advice of Captain Campbell, the crew was thoroughly trained in all the fine points of the game.

One December evening the *Santee* sailed from Queenstown for Bantry Bay to carry out intensive training. A short time after she left port she was struck by a torpedo which caused great damage, but so solidly was her hull packed with wood that she remained afloat. The panic party got off in most approved style, and for several hours the *Santee* awaited developments, hoping for a glimpse of the submarine. But the under-water boat never disclosed its presence ; not even the tip of a periscope showed itself ; and the *Santee* was towed back to Queenstown.

The *Santee's* experience was that of many mystery ships of 1918. The Germans had learned their lesson.

For this reason it is desirable to repeat and emphasize that the most important accomplishment of the mystery ships was not the actual sinking of submarines, but their profound influence upon the tactics of the U-boats. It was manifest in the beginning that the first information reaching Germany concerning the mystery ships would greatly diminish the chances of sinking submarines by this means, for it would cause all submarines to be wary of all mercantile craft. They were therefore obliged largely to abandon the easy, safe, and cheap methods of sinking ships by bombs or gun fire, and were consequently forced to incur the danger of attacking with the scarce and expensive torpedo. Moreover, barring the very few vessels that could be sunk by long-range gun fire, they were practically restricted to this method of attack on pain of abandoning the submarine campaign altogether.

CHAPTER VI

I

WHO would ever have thought that a little wooden vessel, displacing only sixty tons, measuring only 110 feet from bow to stern, and manned by officers and crew very few of whom had ever made an ocean voyage, could have crossed more than three thousand miles of wintry sea, even with the help of the efficient naval officers and men who, after training there, convoyed and guided them across, and could have done excellent work in hunting the submarines? We built nearly 400 of these little vessels in eighteen months; and we sent 170 to such widely scattered places as Plymouth, Queenstown, Brest, Gibraltar, and Corfu. Several enemy submarines now lie at the bottom of the sea as trophies of their offensive power; and on the day that hostilities ceased, the Allies generally recognized that this tiny vessel, with the " listening devices " which made it so efficient, represented one of the most satisfactory direct " answers " to the submarine which had been developed by the war. Had it not been that the war ended before enough destroyers could be spared from convoy duty to assist, with their greater speed and offensive power, hunting groups of these tiny craft, it is certain that they would soon have become a still more important factor in destroying submarines and interfering with their operations.

The convoy system, as I have already explained, was essentially an offensive measure; it compelled the submarine to encounter its most formidable antagonist, the destroyer, and to risk destruction every time that it attacked merchant vessels. This system, however, was an indirect offensive, or, to use the technical phrase, it was a defensive-offensive. Its great success in protecting merchant shipping, and the indispensable service which it performed to the cause of civilization, I have already described. But the fact remained that there could be no final solution of the submarine problem, barring breaking down the enemy *moral*, until a definite, direct method of attacking these boats had been found. A depth charge, fired from the deck of a destroyer, was a serious matter for the submarine ; still the submarine could avoid this deadly weapon at any time by simply concealing its whereabouts when in danger of attack. The destroyer could usually sink the submarine whenever it could get near enough ; it was for the under-water boat, however, to decide whether an engagement should take place. That great advantage in warfare, the option of fighting or of running away, always lay with the submarine. Until it was possible for our naval forces to set out to sea, find the enemy that was constantly assailing our commerce, and destroy him, it was useless to maintain that we had discovered the anti-submarine tactics which would drive this pest from the ocean for all time. Though the convoy, the mine-fields, the mystery ships, the airplane, and several other methods of fighting the under-water boat had been developed, the submarine could still utilize that one great quality of invisibility which made any final method of attacking it such a difficult problem.

Thus, despite the wonderful work which had been accomplished by the convoy, the Allied effort to destroy the submarine was still largely a game of blind man's buff. In our struggle against the German campaign we were deprived of one of the senses which for ages had been absolutely necessary to military operations—that of sight. We were constantly attempting to destroy an enemy whom we could not see. So far as this offensive on the water was concerned, the Allies found themselves in the position of a man who has suddenly gone blind. I make this comparison advisedly, for it at once suggests that our situation was not entirely hopeless. The man who loses the use of his eyes suffers a terrible affliction ; yet this calamity does not completely destroy his usefulness. Such a person, if normally intelligent, gradually learns how to find his way around in darkness ; first he slowly discovers how to move about his room ; then about his house, then about his immediate neighbourhood ; and ultimately he becomes so expert that he can be trusted to walk alone in crowded streets, to pilot himself up and down strange buildings, and even to go on long journeys. In time he learns to read, to play cards and chess, and not infrequently even to resume his old profession or occupation; indeed his existence, despite the deprivation of what many regard as the most indispensable of the senses, becomes again practically a normal process. His whole experience, of course, is one of the most beautiful demonstrations we have of the exquisite economy of Nature. What has happened in the case of this stricken man is that his other senses have come to fill the place of the one which he has lost. Deprived of sight, he is forced to form his contacts with the external world by using his other senses, especially those of touch and hearing. So long as he could see clearly these senses had lain half developed; he had never used them to any extent that remotely approached their full powers; but now that they are called into constant action they gradually increase in strength to a degree that seems abnormal, precisely as a disused muscle, when regularly exercised, acquires a hitherto unsuspected vigour.

This illustration applies to the predicament in which the Allied navies now found themselves. When they attempted to fight the submarine they discovered that they had gone hopelessly blind. Like the sightless man, however, they still had other senses left; and it remained for them to develop these to take the place of the one of which they had been deprived. The faculty which it seemed most likely that they could increase by stimulation was that of hearing. Our men could not detect the presence of the submarine with their eyes; could they not do so with their ears? Their enemy could make himself unseen at will, but he could not make himself unheard, except by stopping his motors. In fact, when the submarine was under water the vibrations, due to the peculiar shape of its propellers and hull, and to its electric motors, produced sound waves that resembled nothing else in art or nature. It now clearly became the business of naval science to take advantage of this phenomenon to track the submarine after it had submerged. Once this feat had been accomplished, the only advantage which the under-water boat possessed over other warcraft, that of invisibility, would be overcome ; and, inasmuch as the submarine, except for this quality of invisibility, was a far weaker vessel than any other afloat, the complete elimination of this advantage would dispose of it as a formidable enemy in war.

A fact that held forth hopes of success was that water is an excellent conductor of sound—far better than the atmosphere itself. In the air there are many cross-currents and areas of varying temperature which make sound waves frequently behave in most puzzling fashion, sometimes travelling in circles, sometimes moving capriciously up or down or even turning sharp corners. The mariner has learned how deceptive is a foghorn ; when it is blowing he knows that a ship is somewhere in the general region, but usually he has no definite idea where. The water, however, is uniform in density and practically uniform in temperature, and therefore sound in this medium always travels in straight lines. It also travels more rapidly in water than in the air, it travels farther, and the sound waves are more distinct. American inventors have been the pioneers in making practical use of this well-known principle. Before the war its most valuable applications were the submarine bell and the vibrator. On many Atlantic and Pacific points these instruments had been placed under the water, provided with mechanisms which caused them to sound at regular intervals ; an ingenious invention, installed aboard ships, made it possible for trained listeners to pick up these noises, and so fix positions, long before lighthouses or lightships came into view in any but entirely clear weather. For several years the great trans-Atlantic liners have frequently made Nantucket Lightship by listening for its submarine bell. From the United States this system was rapidly extending all over the world.

American inventors were therefore well qualified to deal with this problem of communicating by sound under the water. A listening device placed on board ship, which would reveal to practised ears the noise of a submarine at a reasonable distance, and which would at the same time give its direction, would come near to solving the most serious problem presented by the German tactics. Even before the United States entered the war, American specialists had started work on their own initiative. In particular the General Electric Company, the Western Electric Company, and the Submarine Signal Company had taken up the matter at their own expense ; each had a research department and an experimental station where a large amount of preliminary work had been done. Soon a special board was created at Washington to study detection devices, to which each of these companies was invited to send a representative ; the board eventually took up its headquarters at New London, and was assisted in this work by some of the leading physicists of our universities. All through the summer and autumn of 1917 these men kept industriously at their task ; to such good purpose did they labour that by October of that year several devices had been invented which seemed to promise satisfactory results. In beginning their labours they had one great advantage : European scientists had already made considerable progress in this work, and the results of their studies were at once placed at our disposal by the Allied Admiralties. Moreover, these Admiralties sent over several of their experts to co-operate with us. About that time Captain Richard H. Leigh, U.S.N., who had been assigned to command the subchaser detachments abroad, was sent to Europe to confer with the Allied Admiralties, and to test, in actual operations against submarines, the detection devices which had been developed at the New London station. Captain Leigh, who after the armistice became my chief-of-staff at London, was not only one of our ablest officers, but he had long been interested in detection devices, and was a great believer in their possibilities.

The British, of course, received Captain Leigh cordially and gave him the necessary facilities for experimenting with his devices, but it was quite apparent that they did not anticipate any very satisfactory results. The trouble was that so many inventors had presented new ideas which had proved useless that we were all more or less doubtful. They had been attempting to solve this problem ever since the beginning of the war ; British inventors had developed several promising hydrophones, but these instruments had not proved efficient in locating a submarine with sufficient accuracy to enable us to destroy it with depth charges. These disappointments quite naturally created an atmosphere of scepticism which, however, did not diminish the energy which was devoted to the solution of this important problem. Accordingly, three British trawlers and a " P " [1] boat were assigned to Captain Leigh, and with these vessels he spent ten days in the Channel, testing impartially both the British and American devices. No detailed tactics for groups of vessels had yet been elaborated for hunting by sound. Though the ships used were not particularly suitable for the work in hand, these few days at sea demonstrated that the American contrivances were superior to anything in the possession of the Allies. They were by no means perfect ; but the ease with which they picked up all kinds of noises, particularly those made by submarines, astonished everybody who was let into the secret ; the conviction that such a method of tracking the hidden enemy might ultimately be used with the desired success now became more or less general. In particular the American " K-tubes " and the " C-tubes " proved superior to the " Nash-fish " and the " Shark-fin," the two devices which up to that time had been the favourites in the British navy. The " K-tubes " easily detected the sound of large vessels at a distance of twenty miles, while the " C-tubes " were more useful at a shorter distance. But the greatest advantage which these new listening machines had over those of other navies was that they could more efficiently determine not only the sound but also the direction from which it came. Captain Leigh, after this demonstration, visited several British naval stations, consulting with the British officers, explaining our sound-detection devices, and testing the new appliances in all kinds of conditions. The net result of his trip was a general reversal of opinion on the value of this method of hunting submarines. The British Admiralty ordered from the United States large quantities of the American mechanisms, and also began manufacturing them in England.

About the time that it was shown that these listening devices would probably have great practical value, the first " subchasers " were delivered at New London, Conn. The design of the subchaser type was based upon what proved to be a misconception as to the cruising possi-

[1] A " P " boat is a special type of anti-submarine craft smaller and slower than a destroyer and having a profile especially designed to resemble that of a submarine.

bilities of the submarine. Just before the beginning of the Great War most naval officers believed that the limitations of the submarine were such that it could not operate far from coastal waters. Hardly any one, except a few experienced submarine officers, had regarded it as possible that these small boats could successfully attack vessels upon the high seas or remain for any extended period away from their base. High authorities condemned them. This is hard to realize, now that we know so well the offensive possibilities of submarines, but we have ample evidence as to what former opinions were. For example, a distinguished naval writer says that at that time " The view of the majority of admirals and captains probably was that submersible craft were ' just marvellous toys, good for circus performances in carefully selected places in fine weather.' " He adds that certain very prominent naval men of great experience declared that the submarine " could operate only by day in fair weather ; that it was practically useless in misty weather " ; that it had to come to the surface to fire its torpedo ; that its " crowning defect lay in its want of habitability " ; that " a week's peace manœuvres got to the bottom of the health of officers and men " ; and that " on the high seas the chances [of successful attack] will be few, and submarines will require for their existence parent ships." The first triumph of Otto Weddingen, that of sinking the *Cressy,* the *Hogue,* and the *Aboukir,* did not change this conviction, for these three warships had been sunk in comparatively restricted waters under conditions which were very favourable to the submarine. It was not until the *Audacious* went to the bottom off the north-west coast of Ireland, many hundreds of miles from any German submarine base, that the possibilities of this new weapon were partially understood ; for it was clear that the *Audacious* had been sunk by a mine, and that that mine must have been laid by a submarine. Even then many doubted the ability of the U-boats to operate successfully in the open sea westward of the British Isles. Therefore the subchaser was designed to fight the submarine in restricted waters ; Great Britain and France ordered more than 500 smaller (80-foot) vessels of this type, or of approximately this type, built in the United States ; and just before our declaration of war the United States had

designed and contracted for several hundred of a somewhat larger size (the 110-foot chasers) with the original
idea of using them as patrol boats near the harbours and
coastal waters of our own country. Long before these
vessels were finished, however, it became apparent that
Germany could not engage in any serious, extensive
campaign on this side ; it was also evident that any vessel
as small as the subchaser had little value in convoy work,
notwithstanding the excellence of its sea-keeping qualities ;
and we were all rather doubtful as to just what use we
could make of these new additions to our navy.

The work of pushing the design and construction of
these boats reflects great credit upon those who were
chiefly responsible. The designs were drawn and the first
contracts were placed before the United States had declared
war. The credit for this admirable work belongs chiefly
to Commander Julius A. Furer (Construction Corps) U.S.
Navy, and to Mr. A. Loring Swasey, a yacht architect of
Boston, who was enrolled as a lieutenant-commander in
the reserves, and who served throughout the war as an
adviser and assistant to Commander Furer in his specialty
as a small vessel designer, particularly in wood. It speaks
well for the ability of these officers that the small subchasers exhibited such remarkable sea-keeping qualities ;
this fact was a pleasant surprise to all seagoing men, particularly to naval officers who had had little experience
with that type of craft. The listening devices had not
been perfected when they were designed, and this innovation opened up possibilities for their employment which
had not been anticipated ; for these reasons it inevitably
took a large amount of time, after the subchasers had
been delivered, to provide the hydrophones and all the
several appliances which were necessary for hunting submarines. Apparently those who were responsible for constructing these boats had a rocky road to travel ; with
the great demand for material and labour for building
destroyers, merchant ships, and for a multitude of war
supplies, it was natural that the demands for the subchasers in the early days were viewed as a nuisance ; the
responsible officers, therefore, deserve credit for delivering
these boats in such an efficient condition and in such a
remarkably short time. That winter, as everyone will
recall, was the coldest in the memory of the present

generation. Day after day the poor subchasers, coated with ice almost a foot thick, many with their engines wrecked, their planking torn and their propellers crumpled, were towed into the harbour and left at the first convenient mooring, where the ice immediately began to freeze them in. As was inevitable under such conditions, the crews, for the most part, suffered acutely in this terrible weather ; they had had absolutely no training in ordinary seamanship, to say nothing of the detailed tactics demanded by the difficult work in which they were to engage.

I do not think that the whole lot contained 1 per cent. of graduates of Annapolis or 5 per cent. of experienced sailors ; for the greater number that terrible trip in the icy ocean, with the thermometer several degrees below zero, and with very little artificial heat on board, was their first experience at sea. Yet there was not the slightest sign of whimpering or discouragement. Ignorant of salt water as these men at that time were, they really represented about the finest raw material in the nation for this service. Practically all, officers and men, were civilians ; a small minority were amateur yachtsmen, but the great mass were American college undergraduates. Boys of Yale, Harvard, Princeton—indeed, of practically every college and university in the land—had dropped their books, left the comforts of their fraternity houses, and abandoned their athletic fields, eager for the great adventure against the Hun. If there is any man who still doubts what the American system of higher education is doing for our country, he should have spent a few days at sea with these young men. That they knew nothing at first about navigation and naval technique was not important ; the really important fact was that their minds were alert, their hearts filled with a tremendous enthusiasm for the cause, their souls clean, and their bodies ready for the most exhausting tasks. Whenever I get to talking of the American college boys and other civilians in our navy, I find myself indulging in what may seem extravagant praise. I have even been inclined to suggest that it would be well, in the training of naval officers in future, to combine a college education with a shorter intensive technical course at the Naval Academy. For these college men have what technical academies do not usually succeed in giving—a general education and a general training, which develops the power of initiative, independent thought, an ability quickly to grasp intricate situations, and to master, in a short time, almost any practical problem. At least this proved to be the case with our subchaser forces. So little experience did these boys have of seafaring that, as soon as they had completed their first voyage, we had to place a considerable portion in hospital to recover from seasickness. Yet, a few months afterward, we could leave these same men on the bridge at night in command of the ship. When they reached New London they knew no more of seamanship and navigation than so many babies, but so well were these boys instructed and trained within a few weeks by the regular officers in charge that they learned their business sufficiently well to cross the Atlantic safely in convoy. The early 80-foot subchasers which we built for Great Britain and France crossed the ocean on the decks of ocean liners; for it would have been a waste of time, even if international law had permitted it, to send them under their own power; but all of the 110-footers which these young men commanded crossed the ocean under their own power and many in the face of the fierce January and February gales, almost constantly tossed upon the waves like pieces of cork. As soon as they were sufficiently trained and prepared to make the trip, groups were despatched under escort of a naval vessel fitted to supply them with gasolene at sea. Such matters as gunnery these young men also learned with lightning speed. The most valuable were those who had specialized in mathematics, chemistry, and general science; but they were all a splendid lot, and to their spirit and energy are chiefly due their remarkable success in learning their various duties.

"Those boys can't bring a ship across the ocean!" someone remarked to Captain Cotten, who commanded the first squadron of subchasers to arrive at Plymouth, after he had related the story of one of these voyages.

"Perhaps they can't," replied Captain Cotten—himself an Annapolis man who admires these reservists as much as I do. "But they have."

And he pointed to thirty-six little vessels lying at anchor in Plymouth Harbour, just about a hundred yards from the monument which marks the spot from which the

Mayflower sailed for the new world—all of which were navigated across by youngsters of whom almost none, officers or men, had had any nautical training until the day the United States declared war on Germany.

Capable as they were, however, I am sure that these reservists would be the first to acknowledge their obligations to the loyal and devoted regular officers of the Navy, who laboured so diligently to train them for their work. One of the minor tragedies of the war is that many of our Annapolis men, whose highest ambition it was to cross the ocean and engage in the " game," had to stay on this side, in order to instruct these young men from civil life.

I wish that I had the space adequately to acknowledge the work in organization done by Captain John T. Tompkins ; in listening devices by Rear-Admiral S. S. Robison, Captains Frank H. Schofield, Joseph H. Defrees, Commanders Clyde S. McDowell, and Miles A. Libbey, and the many scientists who gave us the benefit of their knowledge and experience. It is impossible to overpraise the work of such men as Captains Arthur J. Hepburn, Lyman A. Cotten, and William P. Cronan, in " licking " the splendid raw material into shape. Great credit is also due to Rear-Admiral T. P. Magruder, Captains David F. Boyd, S. V. Graham, Arthur Crenshaw, E. P. Jessop, C. M. Tozer, H. G. Sparrow, and C. P. Nelson, and many others who had the actual responsibility of convoying these vessels across the ocean.

I assume that they will receive full credit when the story of the work of the Navy at home is written ; meanwhile, they may be assured of the appreciation of those of us on the other side who depended so much for success upon their thorough work of preparation.

II

The sea qualities which the subchaser displayed, and the development of listening devices which made it possible to detect all kinds of sounds under water at a considerable distance, immediately laid before us the possibility of direct offensive operations against the submarine. It became apparent that these listening devices could be used to the greatest advantage on these little craft. The tactics which were soon developed for their use made it necessary that we should have a large number of vessels ; nearly all the destroyers were then engaged in convoy duty, and we could not entertain the idea of detailing many of them for this more or less experimental work. Happily the subchasers started coming off the ways just in time to fill the need ; and the several Allied navies began competing for these new craft in lively fashion. France demanded them in large numbers to work in co-operation with the air stations and also to patrol her coastal waters, and there were many requests from stations in England, Ireland, Gibraltar, Portugal, and Italy. The question of where we should place them was therefore referred to the Allied Naval War Council, which, at my suggestion, considered the matter, not from the standpoint of the individual nation, but from the standpoint of the Allied cause as a whole.

A general survey clearly showed that there were three places where the subchasers might render the most efficient service. The convoy system had by this time not only greatly reduced the losses, but it was changing the policy of the submarines. Until this system was adopted, sinkings on a great scale were taking place far out at sea, sometimes three or four hundred miles west of Ireland. The submarines had adopted the policy of meeting the unescorted ships in the Atlantic and of torpedoing them long before they could reach the zones where the destroyer patrol might possibly have protected them. But sailing great groups of merchantmen in convoys, surrounded by destroyers, made this an unprofitable adventure, and the submarines therefore had to change their programme. The important point is that the convoys, so long as they could keep formation, and so long as protecting screens could be maintained on their flanks, were virtually safe. Under these conditions sinkings, as already said, were less than one-half of 1 per cent. These convoys, it will be recalled, came home by way of two " trunk lines," a southern one extending through the English Channel and a northern one through the so-called " North Channel "— the latter being the passage between Ireland and Scotland. As soon as the inward-bound southern " trunk-line " convoys reached the English Channel they broke up, certain ships going to Plymouth, Portsmouth, Southampton, and other Channel ports, and others sailing to Brest, Cherbourg, Havre, and other harbours in France. In the same fashion, convoys which came in by way of the North Channel split up as soon as they reached the Irish Sea. In other words, the convoys, as convoys, necessarily ceased to exist the moment that they entered these inland waters, and the ships, as individual ships, or small groups of ships, had to find their way to their destinations unescorted by destroyers, or escorted most inadequately. This was the one weak spot in the convoy system, and the Germans were not slow to turn it to their advantage. They now proceeded to withdraw most of their submarines from the high seas and to concentrate them in these restricted waters. In April, 1917, the month which marked the high tide of German success, not far from a hundred merchant ships were sunk in an area that extended about 300 miles west of Ireland and about 300 miles south. A year afterward —in the month of April, 1918—not a single ship was sent to the bottom in this same section of the sea. That change measures the extent to which the convoy saved Allied shipping. But if we examine the situation in inclosed waters—the North Channel, the Irish Sea, St. George's Channel, and the English Channel—we shall find a less favourable state of affairs. Practically all the sinkings of April, 1918, occurred in these latter areas. In April, 1917, the waters which lay between Ireland and England were practically free from depredations ; in the spring of 1918, however, these waters had become a favourite hunting ground for submarines ; while in the English Channel the sinkings were almost as numerous in April, 1918, as they had been in the same month the year before.

Thus we had to deal with an entirely new phase of the submarine campaign ; the new conditions made it practicable to employ light vessels which existed in large numbers, and which could aggressively hunt out the submarines even though they were sailing submerged. The subchaser, when fitted with its listening devices, met these new requirements, though of course not to the desirable degree of precision we hoped soon to attain with still further improved hydrophones and larger vessels of the Eagle class then being built.

The matter was presented to the Allied Naval Council and, in accordance with the unanimous opinion of all of the members, they recommended that of the subchasers then available, a squadron should be based on Plymouth, where it could be advantageously used against the German submarines which were still doing great damage in the English Channel, and that another squadron, based on Queenstown, should similarly be used against the submarines in the Irish Sea.

I was therefore requested to concentrate the boats at these two points, and at once acquiesced in this recommendation.

But another point, widely separated from British waters, also made a powerful plea for consideration. In the Mediterranean the submarine campaign was still a menace. The spring and early summer of 1918 witnessed large losses of shipping destined to southern France, to Italy, and to the armies at Salonika and in Palestine. Austrian and German submarines, operating from their bases at Pola and Cattaro in the Adriatic, were responsible for this destruction. If we could pen these pests in the Adriatic, the whole Mediterranean Sea would become an unobstructed highway for the Allies. A glance at the map indicated the way in which such a desirable result might be accomplished. At its southern extremity the Adriatic narrows to a passage only forty miles wide—the Strait of Otranto—and through this restricted area all the submarines were obliged to pass before they could reach the water where they could prey upon Allied commerce. For some time before the Allied Naval Council began to consider the use of the American subchasers, the British navy was doing its best to keep submarines from passing this point. A defensive scheme known, not very accurately, as the " Otranto barrage " was in operation. The word " barrage " suggests an effective barrier, but this one at the base of the Adriatic consisted merely of a few British destroyers of ancient type and a large number of drifters, which kept up a continuous patrolling of the gateway through which the submarines made their way into the Mediterranean. It is no reflection upon the British to say that this barrage was unsatisfactory and inadequate, and that, for the first few months, it formed a not particularly formidable obstruction. So many demands were made upon the British navy in northern waters that it could not spare many vessels for this work ; the Italian navy was holding the majority of its destroyers intact, momentarily prepared for a sortie by the Austrian battle fleet ; the Otranto barrage, therefore, important as it was to the Allied cause, was necessarily insufficient. The Italian representatives at the Allied Council made a strong plea for a contingent of American subchasers to reinforce the British ships, and the British and French delegates seconded this request.

In the spring of 1918 I therefore sent Captain Leigh to southern Italy to locate and construct a subchaser base in this neighbourhood. After inspecting the territory in detail Captain Leigh decided that the Bay of Govino, in the island of Corfu, would best meet our requirements. The immediate connection which was thus established between New London and this ancient city of classical Greece fairly illustrates how widely the Great War had extended the horizon of the American people. There was a certain appropriateness in the fact that the American college boys who commanded these little ships—not much larger than the vessel in which Ulysses had sailed these same waters three thousand years before—should have made their base on the same island which had served as a naval station for Athens in the Peloponnesian War, and which, several centuries afterward, had been used for the same purpose by Augustus in the struggle with Antony. And probably the sight of the Achelleion, the Kaiser's palace, which was not far from this new American base, was not without its influence in constantly reminding our young men of the meaning of this unexpected association of Yankee-land with the ancient world.

III

By June 30, 1918, two squadrons of American chasers, comprising thirty-six boats, had assembled at Plymouth, England, under the command of Captain Lyman A. Cotten, U.S.N. The U.S. destroyer *Parker*, commanded by Commander Wilson Brown, had been assigned to this detachment as a supporting ship. The area which now formed the new field of operations was one which was causing great anxiety at that time. It comprehended that section of the Channel which reached from Start Point to Lizard Head, and included such important shipping ports as Plymouth, Devonport, and Falmouth. This was the region in which the convoys, after having been escorted through the submarine zone, were broken up, and from which the individual ships were obliged to find their way to their destinations with greatly diminished protection. It was one of the most important sections in which the Germans, forced to abandon their submarine campaign on the high seas, were now actively concentrating their efforts. Until the arrival of the subchasers sinkings had been taking place in these waters on a considerable scale. In company with a number of British hunting units, Captain Cotten's detachment kept steadily at work from June 30th until the middle of August, when it became necessary to send it elsewhere. The historical fact is that not a single merchant ship was sunk between Lizard Head and Start Point as long as these subchasers were assisting in the operations. The one sinking which at first seemed to have broken this splendid record was that of the *Stockforce*; this merchantman was destroyed off Dartmouth; but it was presently announced that the *Stockforce* was in reality a " mystery " ship, sent out for the express purpose of being torpedoed, and that she " got " the submarine which had ended her own career. This happening therefore hardly detracted from our general satisfaction over the work done by our little vessels. Since many ships had been sunk in this area in the month before they arrived, and since the sinkings started in again after they had left, the immunity which this region enjoyed during July and August may properly be attributed largely to the American navy. Not only were no bona-fide merchant ships destroyed, but no mines were laid from Start Point to Lizard Head during the time that the American forces maintained their vigil there. That this again was probably not a mere coincidence was shown by the fact that, the very night after these chasers were withdrawn from Plymouth, five mines were laid in front of that harbour, in preparation for a large convoy scheduled to sail the next day.

By the time that Captain Cotten's squadron began work the hunting tactics which had been developed during their training at New London had been considerably improved. Their procedure represented something entirely new in naval warfare. Since the chasers had to depend for the detection of the foe upon an agency so uncertain as the human ear, it was thought to be necessary, as a safeguard against error, and also to increase the chances of successful attack, that they should hunt in groups of at least three. The fight against the submarine, under this new system, was divided into three parts—the search, the pursuit, and the attack. The first chapter included those weary hours which the little group spent drifting on the ocean, the lookout in the crow's nest scanning the surface for the possible glimpse of a periscope, while the trained listeners on deck, with strange little instruments which somewhat resembled telephone receivers glued to their ears, were kept constantly at tension for any noise which might manifest itself under water. It was impossible to use these listening devices while the boats were under way, for the sound of their own propellers and machinery would drown out any other disturbances. The three little vessels therefore drifted abreast—at a distance of a mile or two apart—their propellers hardly moving, and the decks as silent as the grave; they formed a new kind of fishing expedition, the officers and crews constantly held taut by the expectation of a " bite." And frequently their experience was that of the proverbial " fisherman's luck." Hours passed sometimes without even the encouragement of a " nibble "; then, suddenly, one of the listeners would hear something which his experienced ear had learned to identify as the propellers and motors of a submarine. The great advantage possessed by the American tubes, as already said, was that they gave not only the sound, but its direction. The listener would inform his commanding officer that he had picked up a submarine. " Very faint," he would perhaps report, " direction 97 "—the latter being the angle which it made with the north and south line. Another appliance which now rendered great service was the wireless telephone. The commanding officer at once began talking with the other two boats, asking if they had picked up the noise. Unless all three vessels had heard the disturbance, nothing was done; but if all identified it nearly simultaneously, this unanimity was taken as evidence that something was really moving in the water.

When all three vessels obtained the direction as well as the sound it was a comparatively simple matter to define pretty accurately its location. The middle chaser of the three was the flagship and her most interesting feature was the so-called plotting-room. Here one officer received constant telephone reports from all three boats, giving the nature of the sounds, and, more important still, their directions. He transferred these records to a chart as soon as they came in, rapidly made calculations, and in a few seconds he was able to give the location of the submarine. This process was known as obtaining a " fix." The reports of our chaser commanders are filled constantly with reference to these " fixes "—the " fix " being that point on the surface of the ocean where three lines, each giving the direction of the detected sound, cross one another. The method can be most satisfactorily illustrated by the following diagram :

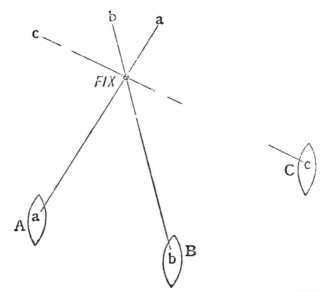

HOW THE LISTENING DEVICES LOCATED A SUBMARINE.

In this demonstration the letters A, B, and C, each represent a subchaser, the central one, B, being the flagship of the division. The listener on A has picked up a noise, the direction of which is indicated by the line *a a*. He telephones by wireless this information to the plotting-room aboard the flagship B. The listeners on this vessel have picked up the same sound, which comes from the direction indicated by the line *b b*. The point at which these two lines cross is the " fix " ; it shows the spot in the ocean where the submarine was stationed when the sound was first detected. The reason for having a report from the third subchaser C is merely for the purpose of corroborating the work of the other two ; if three observations, made independently, agree in locating the enemy at this point, the commanding officer may safely assume that he is not chasing a will o' the wisp.

But this " fix " is merely the location of the submarine at the time when it was first heard. In the great majority of cases, however, the submerged vessel is moving ; so, rapidly as the men in the plotting-room may work, the German has advanced beyond this point by the time they have finished their calculations. The subchasers, which have been drifting while these observations were being made, now start their engines at full speed, and rush up to the neighbourhood of their first " fix." Arrived there, they stop again, put over their tubes, and begin listening once more. The chances are now that the noise of the submarine is louder ; the chasers are getting " warmer." It is not unlikely, however, that the direction has changed, for the submarine, which has listening devices of its own —though the German hydrophones were decidedly inferior to the American—may have heard the subchasers and may be making frantic efforts to elude them. But changing the course will help it little, for the listeners easily get the new direction, and send the details to the plotting-room, where the new " fix " is obtained in a few moments. Thus the subchasers keep inching up to their prey ; at each new " fix " the noise becomes louder, until the hunters are so near that they feel justified in attacking. Putting on full speed, all three rush up to the latest " fix," drop depth charges with a lavish hand, fire the " Y " howitzers, each one of which carries two depth charges, meanwhile manning their guns on the chance that the submarine may decide to rise to the surface and give battle. In many of these hunts a destroyer accompanies the sub-chasers, always keeping at a considerable distance, so that the noise of its propellers will not interfere with the game ; once the chasers determine the accurate " fix," they wire the position to this larger ship, which puts on full steam and dashes with the speed of an express train to the indicated spot, and adds ten or a dozen depth charges to those deposited by the chasers.

Such were the subchaser tactics in their perfection; yet it was only after much experience that the procedure began to work with clock-like regularity. At first the new world under the water proved confusing to the listeners at the tubes. This watery domain was something entirely new in human experience. When Dr. Alexander Bell invented his first telephone an attempt was made to establish a complete circuit by using the earth itself; the result was that a conglomerate of noises—moanings, shriekings, howlings, and humming sounds—came over the wire, which seemed to have become the playground of a million devils. These were the noises, hitherto unknown, which are constantly being given out by Mother Earth herself. And now it was discovered that the under-ocean, which we usually think of as a silent place, is in reality extremely vocal. The listeners at the C- and K-tubes heard many sounds in addition to the ones which they were seeking. On the K-tubes a submarine running at full speed was audible from fifteen to twenty miles, but louder noises could be heard much farther away. The day might be bright, the water quiet, and there might not be a ship anywhere within the circle of the horizon, but suddenly the listener at the tube would hear a terrific explosion, and he would know that a torpedo, perhaps forty or fifty miles distant, had blown up a merchantman, or that some merchantman had struck a mine. Again he would catch the unmistakable " chug! chug! chug! " which he learned to identify as indicating the industrious and slow progress of a convoy of twenty or thirty ships. Then a rapid humming noise would come along the wire; that was the whirling propeller of a destroyer. A faint moan caused some bewilderment at first; but it was ultimately learned that this came from a wreck, lying at the bottom, and tossed from side to side by the current; it sounded like the sigh of a ghost, and the frequency with which it was heard told how densely the floor of the ocean was covered with victims of the submarines. The larger animal life of the sea also registered itself upon the tubes. Our listeners, after a little training, could identify a whale as soon as the peculiar noise it made in swimming reached the receivers. At first a school of porpoises increased their perplexities. The " swish ! swish ! " which marked their progress so closely resembled the noise of a submarine that it used to lead our men astray. But practice in this game was everything ; after a few trips the listener easily distinguished between the porpoise and the submarine, though the distinction was so fine that he had difficulty in telling just how he made it. In fact, our men became so expert that, out of the miscellaneous noises which overwhelmed their ears whenever the tubes were dropped into the water, they were able almost invariably to select that of the U-boat.

In many ingenious ways the chasers supplemented the work of other anti-submarine craft. Destroyers and other patrol boats kept track of the foe pretty well so long as he remained on the surface ; the business of the chaser, we must remember, was to find him after he had submerged. The Commander-in-Chief on shore sometimes sent a radio that a German had appeared at an indicated spot, and disappeared beneath the waves ; the chasers would then start for this location and begin hunting with their listeners. Aircraft which sighted submarines would send similar messages ; convoys that had been attacked, individual ships that had been torpedoed, destroyers which had spotted their prey, only to lose track of it as soon as it submerged, would call upon the chasers to take up the battle where they had abandoned it.

As long as the chasers operated in the waters which I have indicated, those between Start Point and Lizard Head, they " got " no submarine ; the explanation was simple, for as soon as the chasers and British hunting vessels became active here, the Germans abandoned this field of operations. This was the reason that the operative area of the Plymouth detachment was extended. Some of the chasers were now sent around Land's End and up the north Cornish coast, where colliers bound from Wales to France were proving tempting bait for the U-boats ; others operated farther out to sea, off the Scilly Islands and west of Brest. In these regions their contacts with the submarine were quite frequent.

There was no U-boat in the German navy which the Allied forces were so ambitious to " get " as the *U-53*. I have already referred to this celebrated vessel and its still more celebrated commander, Captain Hans Rose. It was this submarine, it will be recalled, which had suddenly paid a ceremonious visit to Newport, R.I., in the autumn of 1916, and which, on its way back to Germany, had paused long enough off Nantucket to sink half a dozen British cargo ships. It was the same submarine which sank our own destroyer, the *Jacob Jones*, by a chance shot with a torpedo. Thus Americans had a peculiar reason for wishing to see it driven from the seas. About the middle of August, 1918, we discovered that the *U-53* was operating in the Atlantic about 250 miles west of Brest. At the same time we learned that two German submarines were coming down the west coast of Ireland. We picked up radio messages which these three boats were exchanging ; this made it quite likely that they proposed to form a junction west of Brest, and attack American transports, which were then sailing to France in great numbers. Here was an opportunity for the sub-chasers. The distance—250 miles to sea—would be a severe strain upon their endurance, but we assigned four hunting units, twelve boats in all, to the task, and also added to this contingent the destroyers *Wilkes* and *Parker*. On the morning of September 2nd one of these subchaser units picked up a suspicious sound. A little later the look-out on the *Parker* detected on the surface an object that looked like a conning-tower, with an upright just forward which seemed to be a mast and sail ; as it was the favourite trick of the *U-53* to disguise itself in this way, it seemed certain that the chasers were now on the track of this esteemed vessel. When this mast and sail and conning-tower suddenly disappeared under the water, these suspicions became still stronger. The *Parker* put on full speed, found an oilslick where the submarine had evidently been pumping its bilges, and dropped a barrage of sixteen depth charges. But had these injured the submarine ? Under ordinary conditions there would have been no satisfactory answer to this question ; but now three little wooden boats came up, advanced about 2,000 yards ahead of the *Parker*, stopped their engines, put over their tubes, and began to listen. In a few minutes they conveyed the disappointing news to the *Parker* that the depth charges had gone rather wild, that the submarine was still steaming ahead, and that they had obtained a " fix " of its position. But the *U-53*, as always, was exceedingly crafty. It knew that the chasers were on the trail ; its propellers were revolving so slowly that almost no noise was made ; the U-boat was stealthily trying to throw its pursuers off the scent. For two and a half hours the chasers kept up the hunt, now losing the faint noise of the *U-53*, now again picking it up, now turning in one direction, then abruptly in another. Late in the afternoon, however, they obtained a " fix," which disclosed the welcome fact that the submarine was only about 300 yards north of them. In a few minutes four depth charges landed on this spot.

When the waters had quieted the little craft began listening. But nothing was heard. For several days afterward the radio operators could hear German submarines calling across the void to the *U-53*, but there was no answer to their call. Naturally, we believed that this long-sought enemy had been destroyed ; about a week later, however, our radios caught a message off the extreme northern coast of Scotland, from the *U-53*, telling its friends in Germany that it was on its way home. That this vessel had been seriously damaged was evident, for it had made no attacks after its experience with the subchasers ; but it apparently had as many lives as a cat, for it was able, in its battered condition, to creep back to Germany around the coast of Scotland, a voyage of more than a thousand miles. The subchasers, however, at least had the satisfaction of having ended the active career of this boat. It was damaged two months before the armistice was signed, but it never recovered sufficiently from its injuries to make another voyage. Yet I must do justice to Captain Rose—he did not command the *U-53* on this last voyage. It was its only trip during the whole course of the war when he had not commanded it !

The story of the *U-53* ends with a touch which is characteristically German. It was one of the submarines which were surrendered to the Allies at the signing of the armistice. Its first visitors, on this occasion, were the Americans ; they were eager to read its log-book, and to find out just what had happened on this final voyage. The book was on board, and it contained a record of the *U-53's* voyages from the day when it was commissioned up to the day when it was surrendered. Two or three pages only were missing ; the Germans had ripped out that part which described the encounter with the American subchasers ! They were evidently determined that we should never have the satisfaction of knowing to just what extent we had damaged the boat ; this was the only revenge they could take on us.

IV

On the morning of September 6th three subchaser units, under the command of Ensign Ashley D. Adams, U.S.N.R.F., were listening at a point about 150 miles west of Land's End. At about eleven-thirty two of these units detected what was unquestionably the sound of a submarine. Moreover, the usual " fixes " disclosed that the enemy was close at hand ; so close that two of the units ran up and dropped their charges. This first attack produced no result on the submarine ; the depth charge from one of the howitzers, however, unfortunately landed near one of the chasers, and, though it injured no one, it put that particular unit out of commission. However, for two hours Ensign Adams's division kept closely on the heels of the quarry, now stopping to obtain a " fix," now running full speed to catch up with the fleeing prey. At one o'clock the plotting-room reported that the submerged boat was just about a hundred yards ahead. The three chasers laid barrages according to pattern, and the three " Y " guns shot their depth charges ; the region of the " fix " was so generously sowed with these bombs that it seemed an impossibility that the German could have escaped.

As soon as the tumult quieted down, the chasers put out their tubes and listened. For twenty minutes not a sound issued from the scene of all this activity. Then a propeller was heard faintly turning or attempting to turn. The noise this time was not the kind which indicated an effort to steal away furtively ; it conveyed rather the impression of difficulty and strain. There was a slight grating and squeaking such as might have been made by damaged machinery. This noise lasted for a few seconds and then ceased. Presently it started up again and then once more it stopped. The submarine was making a little progress, but fitfully ; she would go a few yards and then pause. A slight wake now appeared upon the surface, such as a submerged U-boat usually left when the water was calm ; the listeners at the tube were pleased to note that the location of this disturbance coincided precisely with their " fix," and thus, in a way, confirmed their calculations. One of the subchasers promptly ran ahead and began to drop depth charges on this wake. There was not the slightest doubt that the surface boat was now directly on top of the submarine. After one of the depth charges was dropped, a black cylindrical object, about thirty inches long, suddenly rose from the depths and jumped sixty feet into the air ; just what this unexpected visitant was no one seems to know, but that it came from the hunted submarine was clear.

Under such distressing conditions the U-boat had only a single chance of saving itself ; when the water was sufficiently shallow—not deeper than three hundred feet—it could safely sink to the bottom and " play dead," hoping that the chasers, with their accursed listening devices, would tire of the vigil and return to port. A submarine, if in very good condition, could remain silently on the bottom for two or three days. The listeners on the chaser tubes presently heard sounds which suggested that their enemy was perhaps resorting to this manœuvre. But there were other noises which indicated that possibly this sinking to the bottom was not voluntary. The listeners clearly heard a scraping and a straining as though the boat was making terrific attempts to rise. There was a lumbering noise, such as might be made by a heavy object trying to drag its hulk along the muddy bottom ; this was followed by silence, showing that the wounded vessel could advance only a few yards. A terrible tragedy was clearly beginning down there in the slime of the ocean floor ; a boat, with twenty-five or thirty human beings on board, was hopelessly caught, with nothing in sight except the most lingering death. The listeners on the chasers could follow events almost as clearly as though the inside of the U-boat could be seen ; for every motion the vessel made, every effort that the crew put forth to rescue itself from this living hell, was registered on the delicate wires which reached the ears of the men on the surface.

Suddenly sharp metallic sounds came up on the wires. They were clearly made by hammers beating on the steel body of the U-boat.

"They are trying to make repairs," the listeners reported.

If our subchasers had had any more depth charges,

they would have promptly put these wretches out of their misery, but they had expended all their ammunition. Darkness was now closing in ; our men saw that their vigil was to be a long one ; they sent two chasers to Penzance, to get a new supply of bombs, and also sent a radio call for a destroyer. The spot where the submarine had bottomed was marked by a buoy; lanterns were hung out on this buoy; and two units of chasers, six boats in all, prepared to stand guard. At any moment, of course, the struggling U-boat might come to the surface, and it was necessary to have forces near by to fight or to accept surrender. All night long the chasers stood by ; now and then the listeners reported scraping and straining noises from below, but these grew· fainter and fainter, seeming almost to register the despair which must be seizing the hearts of the imprisoned Germans.

At three o'clock in the morning a British destroyer arrived and presently the two chasers returned from Penzance with more ammunition. Meanwhile, the weather had thickened, a fog had fallen, the lights on the buoy had gone out, and the buoy itself had been pulled under by the tide. The watching subchasers were tossed about by the weather, and lost the precise bearing of the sunken submarine. When daylight returned and the weather calmed down the chasers again put over their tubes and attempted to " fix " the U-boat. They listened for hours without hearing a sound ; but about five o'clock in the afternoon a sharp piercing noise came ringing over the wires. It was a sound that made the listeners' blood run cold.

Only one thing in the world could make a sound like that. It was the crack of a revolver. The first report had hardly stilled when another shot was heard ; and then there were more in rapid succession. The listeners on two different chasers heard these pistol cracks and counted them ; the reports which these two men independently made agreed in every detail. In all, twenty-five shots came from the bottom of the sea. As there were from twenty-five to thirty men in a submarine crew the meaning was all too evident. The larger part of officers and men, finding themselves shut tightly in their coffin of steel, had resorted to that escape which was not uncommonly availed of by German submarine crews in

14

this hideous war. Nearly all of them had committed suicide.

V

Meanwhile, our subchaser detachment at Corfu was performing excellent service. In these southern waters Captain C. P. Nelson commanded two squadrons, comprising thirty-six vessels. Indeed, the American navy possessed few officers more energetic, more efficient, more lovable, or more personally engaging than Captain Nelson. The mere fact that he was known among his brother officers as " Juggy Nelson " gives some notion of the affection which his personality inspired. This nickname did not indicate, as might at first be suspected, that Captain Nelson possessed qualities which flew in the face of the prohibitory regulations of our navy : it was intended, I think, as a description of the physical man. For Captain Nelson's rotund figure, jocund countenance, and always buoyant spirits were priceless assets to our naval forces at Corfu. Living conditions there were not of the best ; disease was rampant among the Serbians, Greeks, and Albanians who made up the civil population ; there were few opportunities for entertainment or relaxation ; it was, therefore, a happy chance that the commander was a man whose very presence radiated an atmosphere of geniality and enthusiasm. His conversational powers for many years had made him a man of mark ; his story-telling abilities had long delighted naval officers and statesmen at Washington ; no other selection for commander could have been made that would have met with more whole-hearted approval from the college boys and other high-type civilians who so largely made up our forces in these flotillas. At Corfu, indeed, Captain Nelson quickly became a popular favourite ; his mind was always actively forming plans for the discomfiture of the German and Austrian submarines ; and all our Allies were as much impressed with his energy as were our own men. For Captain Nelson was more than a humorist and entertainer : he was pre-eminently a sailor of the saltest type, and he had a real barbaric joy in a fight. Even in his official communications to his officers and men he invariably referred to the enemy as the " Hun " ; the slogan on which he insisted as the guiding principle of his flotilla was " get the Hun before he has a chance to get us." He had the supreme gift of firing his subordinates with the same spirit that possessed himself ; and the vigilance, the constant activity, and the courage of the subchasers' crews admirably supplemented the sailor-like qualities of the man who commanded them.

I have already referred to the sea-going abilities of the subchasers ; but the feat accomplished by those that made the trip to Corfu was the most admirable of all. These thirty-six boats, little more than motor launches in size, sailed from New London to Greece—a distance of 6,000 miles ; and, a day or two after their arrival, they began work on the Otranto barrage. Of course they could not have made this trip without the assistance of vessels to supply them with gasolene, make the necessary routine repairs, care for the sick and those suffering from the inevitable minor accidents ; and it is greatly to the credit of the naval officers who commanded the escorting vessels that they shepherded these flotillas across the ocean with practically no losses. On their way through the Straits of Gibraltar they made an attack on a submarine which so impressed Admiral Niblack that he immediately wired London headquarters for a squadron to be permanently based on that port.

As already said, the Otranto Strait was an ideal location for this type of anti-submarine craft. It was so narrow— about forty miles—that a force of moderate size could keep practically all of the critical zone under fairly close observation. Above all, the water was so deep—nearly 600 fathoms (3,600 feet)—that a submarine, once picked up by the listening devices, could not escape by the method which was so popular in places where the water was shallow—that of sinking to the bottom and resting there until the excitement was over. On the other hand, this great depth made it very difficult to obstruct the passage by a fixed barrier—a difficulty that was being rapidly over- come by a certain Franco-Italian type of torpedo net. This barrage, after the arrival of our chasers, was so reorganized as to make the best use of their tactical and listening qualities. The several lines of patrolling vessels extended about thirty-five miles ; there were vessels of several types, the whole making a formidable gauntlet, which the submarines had to run before they could get from the Adriatic to the Mediterranean. First came a line of British destroyers ; it was their main duty to act as protectors and to keep the barrage from being raided, by German and Austrian surface ships—a function which they fulfilled splendidly. Next came a line of trawlers, then drifters, motor launches, and chasers, the whole being completed by a line of kite balloon sloops. Practically all these vessels, British as well as American, were provided with the American devices ; and so well did these ingenious mechanisms function that it was practically impossible for any submarine to pass through the Otranto barrage in calm weather without being heard. In fact, it became the regular custom for the enemy to wait for stormy weather before attempting to slip through this dangerous area, and even under these conditions he had great difficulty in avoiding detection.

From July, 1918, until the day of the armistice, our flotilla at this point kept constantly at work ; and the reports of our commanders show that their sound contacts with the enemy were very frequent. There were battles that unquestionably ended in the destruction of the submarines ; just how much we had accomplished, however, we did not know until the Austrians surrendered and our officers, at Cattaro and other places, came into touch with officers of the Austrian navy. These men, who showed the most friendly disposition toward their American enemies, though they displayed the most bitter hostility toward the r German allies, expressed their admiration for the work of our subchasers. These little boats, the Austrians now informed us, were responsible for a mutiny in the Austrian submarine force. Two weeks after their arrival it was impossible to compel an Austrian crew to take a vessel through the straits, and from that time until the ending of the war not a single Austrian submarine ventured upon such a voyage. All the submarines that essayed the experiment after this Austrian mutiny were German. And the German crews, the Austrian officers said, did not enjoy the experience any more than their own. There was practically no case in which a submarine crossed the barrage without being bombed in consequence ; the *moral* of the German crews steadily went to pieces,

until, in the last month of the war, their officers were
obliged to force them into the submarines at the point of
a pistol. The records showed, the Austrian high officers
said, that the Germans had lost six submarines on the
Otranto barrage in the last three months of the war.
These figures about correspond with the estimates which
we had made ; just how many of these the British sank
and just how many are to be attributed to our own forces
will probably never be known, but the fact that American
devices were attached to all the Allied ships on this duty
should be considered in properly distributing the credit.

We have evidence—conclusive even though somewhat
ludicrous—that the American device on a British destroyer
" got " one of these submarines. One dark night this
vessel, equipped with the C-tube, had pursued a submarine
and bombed it with what seemed to have been satisfactory
results. However, I have several times called attention
to one of the most discouraging aspects of anti-submarine
warfare : that only in exceptional circumstances did we
know whether the submarine had been destroyed. This
destroyer was now diligently searching the area of the battle,
the listeners straining every nerve for traces of her foe.
For a time everything was utterly silent ; then, suddenly,
the listener picked up a disturbance of an unusual kind.
The noise rapidly became louder, but it was still something
very different from any noise ever heard before. The
C-tube consisted of a lead pipe—practically the same as a
water pipe—which was dropped over the side of the ship
fifteen or twenty feet into the sea ; this pipe contained
the wires which, at one end, were attached to the devices
under the water, and which, at the other end, reached the
listener's ears. In a few seconds this tube showed signs
of lively agitation. It trembled violently and made a
constantly increasing hullabaloo in the ears of the listener.
Finally a huge German, dripping with water like a sea lion,
appeared over the side of the destroyer and astounded our
British Allies by throwing up his arms with " Kamerad ! "
This visitant from the depths was the only survivor of
the submarine which it now appeared had indubitably
been sunk. He had been blown through the conning
tower, or had miraculously escaped in some other way—
he did not himself know just what had taken place—and
while floundering around in the water in the inky dark-

This survivor, after shaking off the water, sat down and became very sociable. He did not seem particularly to dislike the British and Americans, but he was extremely bitter against the Italians and Austrians—the first for " deserting " the Germans, the latter for proving bad allies.

" How do you get on with the Italians ? " he asked the British officer.

" Very well indeed," the latter replied, giving a very flattering account of the Italian allies.

" I guess the Italians are about as useful to you as the Austrians are to us," the German sea lion replied.

In writing to our officers about this episode, the British commander said :

" We have found a new use for your listening devices—salvaging drowning Huns."

VI

On September 28, 1918, Captain Nelson received the following communication from the commander of the Allied naval forces at Brindisi, Commodore W. A. H. Kelly, R.N. :

" Can you hold twelve chasers ready to leave Corfu to-morrow (Sunday) for special service ? They should have stores for four days. If unavoidable, barrage force may be reduced during their absence. Request reply. Further definite orders will be sent Sunday afternoon."

To this Captain Nelson sent an answer which was entirely characteristic :

" Yes."

The Captain well knew what the enterprise was to which this message referred. The proposed undertaking was one which was very close to his heart and one which he had constantly urged. The Austrian port of Durazzo, on the Adriatic, at that time was playing an important part in the general conflict.   It was a base by which Germany and Austria had sent supplies to their ally Bulgaria ; and in September the Entente had started the campaign against Bulgaria which finally ended in the complete humiliation of that country.   The destruction of Durazzo as a base would greatly assist this operation.   Several ships lay in the harbour ; there were many buildings used for army stores ; the destruction of all these, as well as the docks and military works, would render the port useless.   The bombardment of Durazzo was, therefore, the undertaking for which the assistance of our subchasers had been requested.   It was estimated that about one hour's heavy shelling would render this port valueless as an Austrian base ; and to accomplish this destruction the Italians had detailed three light cruisers, the *San Giorgio*, the *Pisa*, and the *San Marco*, and the British three light scout cruisers, the *Lowestoft*, the *Dartmouth*, and the *Weymouth*.   According to the plan agreed upon the Italian ships would arrive at Durazzo at about ten o'clock on Wednesday morning, October 2nd, bombard the works for an hour, and then return to Brindisi ; when they had finished, it was proposed that the British cruisers should take their places, bombard for an hour, and likewise retire.   The duty which had been assigned to the subchasers in this operation was an important one.   The Austrians had a considerable force of submarines at Durazzo ; and it was to be expected that they would send them to attack the bombarding warships.   The chasers, therefore, were to accompany the cruisers, in order to fight any submarine which attempted to interfere with the game.   " Remember the life of these cruisers depends upon your vigilance and activity," said Captain Nelson in the instructions issued to the officers who commanded the little vessels.

At nine o'clock that Sunday evening twelve chasers slipped through the net at Corfu and started across the Adriatic ; they sailed " in column," or single file, Captain Nelson heading the procession in subchaser *No*. 95, his second in command, Lt.-Comdr. Paul H. Bastedo, coming next in chaser *No*. 215.   The tiny fleet hardly suggested to the observer anything in the nature of military operations ; they looked more like a group of motor launches out for a summer cruise.   The next morning they arrived at Brindisi, the gathering place of all the Allied vessels which were to participate in the operation—that same Brindisi (or Brundisium) which was one of the most famous ports of antiquity, the town from which Augustus and Antony, in 42 B.C., started on the expedition which, at the battle of Philippi, was to win them the mastery of the ancient world. Upon arriving Captain Nelson went ashore for a council with Commodore Kelly, who commanded the British cruisers, and other Allied officers. When he returned Captain Nelson's face was glowing with happiness and expectation.

" It's going to be a real party, boys," he informed his subordinate officers.

Two days were spent at Brindisi, completing preparations ; on Tuesday evening Captain Nelson called all his officers for a meeting on board the British destroyer *Badger*, to give them all the details of the forthcoming " party." If there had been any flagging spirits in that company when the speech began—which I do not believe —all depression had vanished when " Juggy " had finished his remarks ; every officer left with his soul filled by the same joy of approaching battle as that which possessed his chief.

At 2.30 Wednesday morning the chasers left Brindisi, steering a straight course to Durazzo. The night was very dark ; the harbour was black also with the smoke from the cruisers and other craft which were making preparations to get away. After steaming a few hours the officers obtained with their glasses their first glimpse of Durazzo ; at this time there were no fighting ships in sight except the chasers, as the larger ships had not yet arrived. Captain Nelson knew that there were two or three Austrian destroyers at Durazzo, and his first efforts were devoted to attempts to persuade them to come out and give battle. With this idea in mind, the chasers engaged in what they called a " war dance " before the port ; they began turning rapidly in a great circle, but all to no purpose, for the Austrian ships declined to accept the challenge. After a time the smoke of the Italian cruisers appeared above the horizon ; this was the signal for the chasers to take their stations. Durazzo is located in an indentation of the coast ; at the southern extremity of the little gulf the land juts out to a point, known as

Cape Laghi ; at the northern extremity the corresponding
point is Cape Pali ; the distance between these two points
is about fifteen miles. Two subchaser units, six boats,
were assigned as a screen to the Italian cruisers while the
bombardment was under way. One unit, three boats,
was stationed at Cape Pali, to the north, to prevent any
submarines leaving Durazzo from attacking the British
cruisers, which were to approach the scene of activities
from that quarter, and another unit, three boats, was
stationed off Cape Laghi. Thus the two critical capes
were covered against submarine surprises, and the attacking vessels themselves were effectively screened.

The Italian cruisers sailed back and forth for about an
hour, blazing away at Durazzo, destroying shipping in
the harbour, knocking down military buildings, and
devastating the place on a liberal scale, all the time
screened in this operation by our chasers. Meantime,
unit B, commanded by Lieutenant-Commander Bastedo,
had started for its station at Cape Pali. The Austrian
shore batteries at once opened upon the tiny craft, the
water in their neighbourhood being generously churned
up by the falling shells. Meanwhile, the British cruisers,
after steaming for a while east, turned south in order to
take up the bombarding station which, according to the
arranged programme, the Italian warships were about to
abandon. The three screening chasers were steaming in
column, *No.* 129, commanded by Ensign Maclair Jacoby,
U.S.N.R.F., bringing up the rear. Suddenly this little
boat turned to the right and started scampering in the
direction of some apparently very definite object. It
moved so abruptly and hastily that it did not take the time
even to signal to its associates the cause of its unexpected
manœuvre.

On board *No.* 215 there was some question as to what
should be done.

" Let's go," said Commander Bastedo. " Perhaps he's
after a submarine."

No. 215 was immediately turned in the direction of the
busy *No.* 129, when the interest of its officers was aroused
by a little foamy fountain of spray moving in the water
slightly forward of its port beam. There was no mystery
as to the cause of that feathery disturbance. It was
made by a periscope ; it was moving with considerable

speed also, entirely ignoring the subchasers, and shaping its course directly toward the advancing British cruisers. Commander Bastedo forgot all about subchaser *No.* 129, which apparently was after game of its own, and headed his own boat in the direction of this little column of spray. In a few seconds the periscope itself became visible ; Commander Bastedo opened fire at it with his port gun ; at the second shot a column of water and air arose about six feet—a splendid geyser which informed the pursuer that the periscope had been shattered. By this time the third chaser, *No.* 128, was rushing at full speed. The submarine now saw that all chance of attacking the British ships had gone, and turned to the south in an effort to get away with a whole skin. But the two subchasers, 215 and 128, quickly turned again and started for their prey ; soon both were dropping depth charges and shooting their " Y " guns ; and a huge circle of the sea was a mass of explosions, whirling water, mighty eruptions of foam, mist, and débris—and in the mass, steel plates and other wreckage flew from the depths into the air.

"That got him ! " cried the executive officer from the deck of *No.* 215, while the crew lifted up its voices in a shout that was reminiscent of a college yell.

It was not until this moment that Commander Bastedo and his associates remembered the 129, which, when last observed, was speeding through the water on an independent course of her own. In the midst of the excitement there came a message from this boat :

" Submarine sighted ! "

Then a second afterward came another message.

" My engines are disabled."

In a short time Bastedo had reached the boat.

" Where is the submarine ? "

" We just sank it," was the answer. *No.* 129 had dropped eight depth charges, one directly over the Austrian boat ; in the water thrown up the officers had counted seven pieces of metal plates, and the masses of oil and bubbles that presently arose completed the story of the destruction. Meanwhile, the British cruisers had taken up their station at Durazzo and were finishing the work that made this place useless as a military headquarters.

Not a man in the whole American force was injured ; in a brief time the excitement was all over, and the great

ships, screened again by the wasps of chasers, started
back to Brindisi. The impression made upon our Allies
was well expressed in the congratulatory message sent to
me in London by Commodore Kelly, who commanded the
British cruisers in this action.

" Their conduct," he said, " was beyond praise. They
all returned safely without casualties. They thoroughly
enjoyed themselves."

And from the Italians came this message :

" Italian Naval General Staff expresses highest appreciation of useful and efficient work performed by United
States chasers in protecting major vessels during action
against Durazzo ; also vivid admiration of their brilliant
and clever operations which resulted in sinking two enemy
submarines."

The war was now drawing to a close ; a day before the
Allied squadrons started for Durazzo Bulgaria surrendered ;
about two weeks after the attack Austria had given up
the ghost. The subchasers were about this time just
getting into their stride ; the cessation of hostilities,
however, ended their careers at the very moment when
they had become most useful. A squadron of thirty-six
under the command of Captain A. J. Hepburn reached
Queenstown in September, but though it had several
interesting contacts with the enemy, and is credited with
sending one German home badly damaged, the armistice
was signed before it had really settled down to work.
The final spectacular appearance was at Gibraltar, in the
last four days of the war. The surrender of Austria had
left the German submarines stranded in the Adriatic
without a base ; and they started home by way of the
Mediterranean and Gibraltar. A squadron of eighteen
chasers had just arrived at the Azores, on the way to
reinforce the flotilla at Plymouth ; seven of these were at
once despatched to Gibraltar on the chance that they
might bar the passage of these U-boats. They reached
this port at the storm season ; yet they went out in the
hardest gales and had several exciting contacts with the
fleeing Germans. The records show that five submarines
attempted to get through the straits ; there is good evidence that two of these were sunk, one by the British
patrol and one by our chasers.

CHAPTER VII

I

WHILE our naval forces were thus playing their parts in several areas, the work of creating the central staff of a great naval organization was going forward in London. The headquarters for controlling extensive naval operations in many widely dispersed areas, like the headquarters of an army extending over a wide front, must necessarily be located far behind the scene of battle. Thus, a number of remodelled dwelling-houses in Grosvenor Gardens contained the mainspring for an elaborate mechanism which reached from London to Washington and from Queenstown to Corfu. On the day of the armistice the American naval forces in European waters comprised about 370 vessels of all classes, more than 5,000 officers, regulars and reserves, and more than 75,000 men ; we had established about forty-five bases and were represented in practically every field of naval operations. The widespread activities of our London headquarters on that eventful day presented a striking contrast to the humble beginnings of eighteen months before.

From April to August, 1917, the American navy had a very small staff organization in Europe. During these extremely critical four months the only American naval representatives in London, besides the regular Naval Attaché and his aides, were my personal aide, Commander J. V. Babcock, and myself; and our only office in those early days was a small room in the American Embassy. For a considerable part of this time we had no stenographers and no clerical assistance of our own, though of course the Naval Attaché, Captain W. D. MacDougall, and his personnel gave us all the assistance in their power. Commander Babcock had a small typewriter, which he was able to work with two fingers, and on this he laboriously pounded out the reports which first informed the Navy Department of the seriousness of the submarine situation. The fact that Commander Babcock was my associate during this critical period was a fortunate thing for me, and a still more fortunate thing for the United States. Commander Babcock and I had been closely associated for several years ; in that early period, when we, in our two persons, represented the American naval forces at the seat of Allied naval activity, we not only worked together in that little room but we lived together. Our office was alternately this room in the American Embassy and our quarters in an hotel. I had already noted Commander Babcock's abilities when he was on my staff in the Atlantic Torpedo Flotilla and when he was a student at the Naval War College ; but our constant companionship throughout the war, especially during these first few strenuous months in London, gave me a still greater respect for his qualities. Many men have made vital contributions to our success in the war of whom the public scarcely ever hears even the name. A large part of the initiative and thinking which find expression in successful military action originates with officers of this type. They labour day after day and night after night, usually in subordinate positions, unselfishly doing work which is necessarily credited to other names than their own, daily lightening the burden of their chiefs, and constantly making suggestions which may control military operations or affect national policy. Commander Babcock is a striking representative of this type. My personal obligations to him are incalculable ; and I am indebted to him not only for his definite services, but for the sympathy, the encouragement, and the kindly and calculated pessimism which served so well to counterbalance my temperamental optimism.

Our relations were so close, working and living together as we did, that I find it difficult to speak of " Babby's " services with restraint. But there are particular accomplishments to his credit which should go down upon this popular record. I have described the first consultations with the British naval chiefs. These were the meetings which formed the basis of the reports recommending the conditions upon which the American navy should co-operate with the Allies. Commander Babcock was constantly at my elbow during all these consultations, and was all the time independently conducting investigations in the several departments of the Admiralty. The original drafts of all my written and cabled communications to the department—reports which form a connected story of our participation in the naval war during this period—were prepared by him.

Able as Commander Babcock was, human endurance still had its limitations. A public-spirited American business man in London, Mr. R. E. Gillmor, who had formerly been an officer in the navy, begged to be accepted as. a volunteer ; he brought two of his best stenographers, English girls, and personally paid their salaries for several weeks while they were devoting all their time to the American navy. Subsequently he was enlisted in the naval reserves and performed very valuable services on the staff throughout nearly the entire period of the war—until ordered to America, where his technical knowledge was required in connection with certain important appliances with which he was familiar. His experience as a business man in London was of great value to our forces, and his time and energy were devoted to our service with a zeal and loyalty that endeared him to us all.

Soon afterward a number of Rhodes scholars and other young Americans then in Europe, G. B. Stockton, E. H. McCormick, T. B. Kittredge, P. F. Good, R. M. D. Richardson, H. Millard, L. S. Stevens, and J. C. Baillargeon, joined our forces as unpaid volunteers and gave us the benefit of their trained minds and European experience. Two of these, Kittredge and Stockton, both valuable workers, had been serving under Hoover in Belgium. They were all later enrolled as reserves and continued their work throughout the war. Lieutenant Stockton performed the arduous and important duties of chief business manager, or executive officer, of headquarters in a most efficient manner, and throughout the war Kittredge's previous historical training, European experience, and fine intellectual gifts made his services very valuable in the Intelligence Department.

Mr. Page, the American Ambassador, aided and encouraged us in all possible ways. Immediately after my arrival in London he invited me to call upon him and his

staff for any assistance they could render. In his enthusiastic and warm-hearted way, he said : " Everything we
have is yours. I will turn the Embassy into the street
if necessary " ; and throughout the war he was a tower
of strength to the cause. He gave us his time and the
benefit of his great experience and personal prestige in
establishing cordial relations with the various branches of
the British Government—and all this with such an absence
of diplomatic formality, such courteous and forceful
efficiency, and such cordial sympathy and genuine kindness that he immediately excited not only our sincere
admiration but also our personal affection.

During all this period events of the utmost importance
were taking place ; it was within these four months that
the convoy system was adopted, that armed guards were
placed on merchant ships, that the first American troops
were escorted to France, and that our destroyers and
other warships began arriving in European waters. In
July it became apparent that the strain of doing the work
of a dozen men, which had been continuous during the
past four months, could no longer be supported by my
aide, Commander Babcock. When the destroyers and
other ships arrived, we went through their lists ; here
and there we hit upon a man whom we regarded as qualified
for responsible staff duty, and transferred him to the London headquarters. This proceeding was necessary if our
essential administrative work was to be done. Among
the reserves who were subsequently assigned to our
forces many excellent staff officers also were developed
for handling the work of communications, cipher codes,
and the like. When the Colonel House Commission came
over in October, 1917, I explained our necessities to the
" skippers " of the two cruisers that brought the party,
who promptly gave us all the desks and office equipment
they could spare and sent them to Grosvenor Gardens.

In August, however, additional ships and forces began
to arrive from America, and it became necessary to have
larger quarters than those available in the Embassy for
handling the increasing administrative work. At one time
the British Government contemplated building us a temporary structure near the Admiralty, but this was abandoned because there was a shortage of material. We
therefore moved into an unoccupied dwelling near the

American Embassy that seemed adapted to our needs. We rented this house furnished, just as it stood; a first glimpse of it, however, suggested refined domesticity rather than naval operations. We quickly cleared the building of rugs, tapestries, lace curtains, pictures, and expensive furniture, reduced the twenty-five rooms to their original bareness, and filled every corner with office equipment. In a few days the staff was installed in this five-story residence and the place was humming with the noise of typewriters. At first we regarded the leasing of this building as something of an extravagance ; it seemed hardly likely that we should ever use it all ! But in a few weeks we had taken the house adjoining, cut holes through the walls and put in doors ; and this, too, was filled up in an incredibly short time, so rapidly did the administrative work grow. Ultimately we had to take over six of these private residences and make alterations which transformed them into one. From August our staff increased at a rapid rate until, on the day the armistice was signed, we had not far from 1,200 officers, enlisted men, and clerical force, working in our London establishment, the commissioned staff consisting of about 200 officers, of which sixty were regulars and the remainder reserves.

I find that many people are surprised that I had my headquarters in London. The historic conception of the commander-in-chief of a naval force located on the quarter-deck of his flagship still holds the popular imagination. But controlling the operations of extensive and widely dispersed forces in a campaign of this kind is quite a different proceeding from that of directing the naval campaigns of Nelson's time, just as making war on land has changed somewhat from the method in vogue with Napoleon. The opinion generally prevails that my principal task was to command in person certain naval forces afloat. The fact is that this was really no part of my job during the war. The game in which several great nations were engaged for four years was a game involving organized direction and co-operation. It is improbable that any one nation could have won the naval war ; that was a task which demanded not only that we should all exert our fullest energies, but that, so far as it was humanly possible, we should exert them as a unit. It was the duty of the United States above all nations to manifest this spirit.

We had entered the war late ; we had entered it in a condition of unpreparedness; our naval forces, when compared to those which had been assembled by the Allies, were small ; we had not been engaged for three years combating an enemy using new weapons and methods of naval warfare. It was not unlikely that we could make some original contributions to the Allied effort ; indeed, we early did so ; yet it was natural to suppose that the navies which had been combating the submarines so long understood that game better than did we, and it was our duty to assist them in this work, rather than to operate independently. Moreover, this question as to whether any particular one of our methods might be better or might be worse than Great Britain's was not the most important one. The point was that the British navy had developed its own methods of working and that it was a great "going concern." The crisis was so pressing that we simply did not have the time to create a separate force of our own ; the most cursory examination of conditions convinced me that we could hope to accomplish something worth while only by playing the game as it was then being played, and that any attempt to lay down new rules would inevitably decrease the effectiveness of our co-operation, and perhaps result in losing the war. We can even admit, for the sake of the argument, that the Americans might have created a better organization than the British ; but the question of improving on their methods, or of not improving on them, was a point that was not worth considering ; long before we could have developed an efficient independent machine the war would have come to an end. It was thus our duty to take things as they were, to plunge immediately into the conflict, and to make every ship and every man tell in the most effective way and in the shortest possible time. Therefore I decided that our forces should become, for the purpose of this war, virtually a part of the Allied navies ; to place at the disposal of the Allies our ships to reinforce the weak part of their lines ; to ignore such secondary considerations as national pride, naval prestige, and personal ambitions ; and to subordinate every other consideration to that of defeating the Hun. I have already described how in distributing our subchasers I practically placed them at the disposal of the Allied

15

Council ; and this represents the policy that was followed
in all similar matters.

The naval high commands were located at Washington,
London, Paris, and Rome. Necessarily London was the
headquarters of the naval war. Events which had long
preceded the European conflict had made this choice inevitable. The maritime development of four centuries
had prepared London for the rôle which she was now
called upon to play. From all over the world naval and
maritime information flowed to this great capital as
though in obedience to the law of gravity. Even in peace
times London knew where every ship in the world was
at any particular time. All other machinery for handling
this great mass of detail was necessarily accumulated in
this great city, and Lloyd's, the world headquarters for
merchant shipping, had now become practically a part
of the British Admiralty. In this war the matter of
information and communications was supremely important. Every decision that was made and every order
that was issued, even those that were the least conse-
quential, rested upon complete information which was
obtainable, in time to be useful, only in London. I could
not have made my headquarters in Washington, or Paris,
or Rome because these cities could not have furnished the
military intelligence which was needed as a preliminary to
every act. For the same reason I could not have efficiently
controlled the operations of all our forces from Queenstown,
or Brest, or Gibraltar ; the staff controlling the whole had
necessarily to be located in London, and the tactical commands at these other bases must be exercised by subordinates. The British placed all their sources of information and their communications at our disposal. They
literally opened their doors and made us part of their
organization. I sat daily in consultation with British
naval chiefs, and our officers had access to all essential
British information just as freely as did the British naval
officers themselves. On the day of my arrival Admiral
Jellicoe issued orders that the Americans should be shown
anything which they wished to see. With all this information, the most complete and detailed in the world,
constantly placed at our disposal, and a spirit of confidence and friendship always prevailing which has no
parallel in history, it would have defeated the whole

purpose of our participation in the war had the American high command taken up its headquarters anywhere except in London.

Incidentally, there was an atmosphere in the London Admiralty which made a strong appeal to anyone who is interested in naval history. Everything about the place is reminiscent of great naval achievements. The room in which our councils met was the same old Admiralty Board room that had been used for centuries. In accordance with the spirit of British conservatism, this room is almost exactly the same now, even in its furnishings, as it was in Nelson's time. The same old wood carvings hang over the same old fireplace ; the table at which we sat is the identical one at which Nelson must have sat many times, and the very silver inkstand which Nelson used was used by his successors in this war. The portrait of this great naval chieftain looked down upon us during our deliberations. Above the fireplace is painted a huge compass, and about the centre of this swings an arrow. This was a part of the Admiralty equipment of a hundred years ago, though it has no usefulness now except a sentimental one. In old days this arrow was geared to a weather vane on the roof of the Admiralty, and it constantly showed to the chiefs assembled in the council room the direction of the wind—a matter of great importance in the days of sailing ships.

All general orders and plans concerning the naval operations of British and American forces came from the Admiralty, and here officers of my staff were constantly at work. The commanders-in-chief at the various bases commanded the combined British and American ships based on those ports only in the sense that they carried out the general instructions and policies which were formulated in London. These orders, so far as they affected American forces, could be issued to the commanders-in-chief only after American headquarters in London had viséd them. Thus the American staff held the ultimate command over all the American forces which were based in British waters. The same was true of those at Brest, Gibraltar, and other stations. The commanders-in-chief executed them, and were responsible for the manner in which the forces were used in combating the enemy. The operations of which I was the commander extended over an immense area. The Plymouth and Queenstown forces represented only a part of the ultimate American naval strength in European waters and not the most important part; before the war ended, Brest, as I shall show, developed into a greater naval base than any of those which we maintained in the British Isles. Convoys were not only coming across the Atlantic but they were constantly arriving from the Mediterranean and from the South Sea, and it was the duty of headquarters in London, and not the duty of local commanders, to route these precious argosies, except in special cases, just before they reached their port of destination. Not infrequently, as previously described, it was necessary to change destinations, or to slow down convoys, or to make any number of decisions based on new information; naturally only the centre of information, the Admiralty convoy room, could serve as a clearing house for such operations. The point is that it was necessary for me to exercise the chief command of American forces through subordinates. My position in this respect was precisely the same as that of Generals Haig and Pershing; I had to maintain a great headquarters in the rear, and to depend upon subordinates for the actual execution of orders.

The American headquarters in London comprised many separate departments, each one of which was directly responsible to me as the Force Commander, through the Chief of Staff; they included such indispensable branches as the office of the Chief of Staff, Captain N. C. Twining, Chief of Staff; Assistant Chief of Staff, Captain W. R. Sexton; Intelligence Department, Commander J. V. Babcock, who also acted as Aide; Convoy Operations Section, Captain Byron A. Long; Anti-submarine Section, Captain R. H. Leigh; Aviation Section, Captain H. I. Cone, and afterward, Lieutenant-Commander W. A. Edwards; Personnel Section, Commander H. R. Stark; Communication Section, Lieutenant-Commander E. G. Blakeslee; Material Section, Captain E. C. Tobey (S.C.); Repair Section, Captain S. F. Smith (C.C.), and afterward, L. B. McBride (C.C.); Ordnance Section, Commander G. L. Schuyler, and afterward, Commander T. A. Thomson; Medical Section, Captain F. L. Pleadwell (M.C.), and afterward, Commander Edgar Thompson (M.C.); Legal Section, Commander W. H. McGrann;

and the Scientific Section, Professor **H. A. Bumstead, Ph.D.**

I was fortunate in all of my departmental chiefs. The Chief of Staff, Captain N. C. Twining, would certainly have been a marked man in any navy ; he had a genius for detail, a tireless energy, and a mastery of all the problems that constantly arose. I used to wonder when Captain Twining ever found an opportunity to sleep ; he seemed to be working every hour of the day and night ; yet, so far as was observable, he never wearied of his task, and never slackened in his devotion to the Allied cause. As soon as a matter came up that called for definite decision, Captain Twining would assemble from the several departments all data and information which were available concerning the question at issue, spend a few hours studying this information, and then give his judgment—an opinion which was invariably sound and which was adopted in the vast majority of cases ; in fact, in all cases except those in which questions of policy or extraneous considerations dictated a different or modified decision. Captain Twining is a man of really fine intellect combined with a remarkable capacity for getting things done ; without his constant presence at my elbow, my work would have been much heavier and much less successful than it was. He is an officer of such exceptional ability, such matured experience, and such forceful character as to assure him a brilliant career in whatever duty he may be called upon to perform. I can never be sufficiently grateful to him for his loyalty and devotion and for his indispensable contribution to the efficiency of the forces I had the honour to command.

In accordance with my habitual practice, I applied the system of placing responsibility upon my carefully selected heads of departments, giving them commensurate authority, and holding them to account for results. Because the task was such a great one, this was the only possible way in which the operations of the force could have been successfully conducted. I say, successfully conducted, because in a " business " of this kind, " good enough " and " to-morrow " may mean disaster ; that is, it is a case of keeping both information and operations up to the minute. If the personnel and equipment of the staff are not completely capable of this, it is more than a partial failure, and the result is an ever-present danger.   There were men in this great war who " went to pieces " simply because they tried to do everything themselves.   This administrative vice of attempting to control every detail, even insignificant ones, to which military men seem particularly addicted, it had always been my policy to avoid.   Business at Grosvenor Gardens developed to such an extent that about a thousand messages were every day received in our office or sent from it ; and of these 60 per cent. were in code.   Obviously it was impossible for the Force Commander to keep constantly at his finger ends all these details.   All department heads, therefore, were selected because they were officers who could be depended upon to handle these matters and make decisions independently ; they were all strong men, and it is to their combined efforts that the success of our operations was due.   You would have to search a long time among the navies of the world before you could find an abler convoy officer than Captain Byron A. Long ; an abler naval constructor than Captain L. B. McBride ; an abler man to have charge of the finances of our naval forces, the purchase of supplies and all kinds of material than Captain (S.C.) Eugene C. Tobey ; abler aviation officers than Captain H. I. Cone and Lieutenant-Commander W. A. Edwards ; an abler chief of operations than Captain R. H. Leigh, or an abler intelligence officer than Commander J. V. Babcock. These men, and others of the fourteen department heads, acted as a kind of cabinet.   Many of them handled matters which, though wholly essential to the success of the forces, were quite outside of my personal knowledge or experience, and consequently they had to be men in whose ability to guide me in such matters I could place complete confidence. As an example of this I may cite one of the duties of Captain Tobey.   Nearly all of the very considerable financial transactions he was entrusted with were " Greek " to me, but he had only to show me the right place on the numerous documents, and I signed my name in absolute confidence that the interests of the Government were secure.

All cables, reports, and other communications were referred each day to the department which they concerned. The head of each department studied them, attended to the great majority on his own responsibility, and selected the few that needed more careful attention.   A meeting of the Chief of Staff and all department heads was held each day, at which these few selected matters were discussed in council and decisions made. The final results of these deliberations were the only matters that were referred to me. This system of subdividing responsibility and authority not only promoted efficiency but it left the Force Commander time to attend to vitally important questions of general policy, to keep in personal touch with the high command of the Allied navies, to attend the Allied naval councils, and, in general, to keep his finger constantly on the pulse of the whole war situation. Officers of our own and other navies who were always coming in from the outlying stations, and who could immediately be placed in touch with the one man who could answer all their questions and give immediate decisions, testified to the efficient condition in which the American headquarters was maintained.

One of our departments was so novel, and performed such valuable service, that I must describe it in some detail. We took over into our London organization an idea that is advantageously used in many American industrial establishments, and had a Planning Section, the first, I think, which had ever been adopted by any navy. I detached from all other duties five officers : Captain F. H. Schofield, Captain D. W. Knox, Captain H. E. Yarnell (who exchanged places afterward with Captain L. McNamee of the Plans Section of the Navy Department), and Colonel R. H. Dunlap (of the Marines), who was succeeded by Colonel L. McC. Little, when ordered to command a regiment of Marines in France. These men made it their business to advise the Commander-in-Chief on any questions that might arise. All were graduates of the Naval War College at Newport, and they applied to the consideration of war problems the lessons which they had learned at that institution. The business of the Planning Section was to make studies of particular problems, to prepare plans for future operations, and also to criticize fully the organization and methods which were already in existence. The fact that these men had no administrative duties and that they could therefore devote all their time to surveying our operations, discovering mistakes, and suggesting better ways of doing things, as well as the fact that they were themselves scholarly students of naval warfare, made their labours exceedingly valuable. I gave them the utmost freedom in finding fault with the existing regime ; there was no department and no office, from that of the Commander-in-Chief down, upon whose activities they were not at liberty to submit the fullest and the frankest reports.   If anything could be done in a better way, we certainly wanted to know it.   Whenever any specific problem of importance came up, it was always submitted to these men for a report.   The value of such a report depended upon the completeness and accuracy of the information available, and it was the business of the Intelligence Department of the staff to supply this.   If the desired information was not in their files, or the files of the Allied admiralties, or was not up to date, it was their duty to obtain it at once.   The point is that the Planning Section had no other duties beyond rendering a decision, based upon a careful analysis of the facts bearing upon the case, which they submitted in writing.   There was no phase of the naval warfare upon which the officers of the Planning Section did not give us reports.   One of their favourite methods was to place themselves in the position of the Germans and to decide how, if they were directing German naval operations, they would frustrate the tactics of the Allies.   Their records contain detailed descriptions of how merchant ships could be sunk by submarines, and these methods, our officers believed, represented a great improvement over those used by the Germans.   Indeed, I think that many of these reports, had they fallen into the hands of the Germans, would have been found by them exceedingly useful.   There was a general impression, in our own navy as well as in the British, that most of the German submarine commanders handled their boats unskilfully and obtained inadequate results.   All these documents were given to the responsible men in our forces, as well as to the British, and had a considerable influence upon operations.   The British also established a Planning Section, which worked harmoniously with our own.

A subject upon which our Planning Section liked to speculate was the possible sortie of the German fleet.   The possibility of a great naval engagement filled the minds of most naval officers ; and, after we had sent five of our battleships to reinforce Admiral Beatty's fleet, this topic became even more interesting to American naval men. Would the Germans ever come out ?   What had they to gain or to lose by such an undertaking ?   What were their chances of victory ?   Where would the engagement be fought, and what part would the several elements of modern naval warfare play in it : mines, submarines, battle-cruisers, airplanes, dirigibles, and destroyers ? These were among the questions with which the Planning Section busied itself, and this problem, like many others, they approached from the German standpoint. They placed themselves in the position of the German High Command, and peered into the Grand Fleet looking for a weakness, which, had they been Germans, they might turn to account in a general engagement. The only weak spot our Planning Section could find was one which reflected the greatest credit upon the British forces. The British commander, Admiral Sir David Beatty, was a particularly dashing and heroic fighter ; could not these splendid qualities really be turned to the advantage of the Germans ? That Admiral Beatty would fight at the first opportunity, and that he would run all justifiable risks, if a chance presented of defeating the German fleet, was as well known to the Germans as to ourselves. The British Admiral, it was also known, did not entertain much respect for mines and torpedoes. All navies possessed what was known as a " torpedo flag." This was an emblem which was to be displayed in case torpedoes were sighted, for the purpose of warning the ships to change course or, if necessary, to desist from an attack. It was generally reported that Admiral Beatty had ordered all these torpedo flags to be destroyed ; in case he once started in pursuit of the German fleet, he proposed to take his chances, dive straight through a school of approaching torpedoes, or even to rush full speed over a mine-field, making no efforts to avoid these hidden dangers. That he would probably lose some ships the Admiral well knew, but he figured—and probably correctly—that he would certainly have enough vessels left to annihilate the enemy. Still, in the judgment of our Planning Section, Admiral Beatty's assumed attitude toward " torpedo flags " gave the Germans their only possible chance of seriously injuring the Grand Fleet. They drew up a plan of attack on the Scapa Flow forces based upon this assumption. Imagining themselves directors of the German navy, they constructed large numbers of torpedo boats, submarines, and mine-fields and stationed them in a particularly advantageous position ; they then proposed to send the German fleet in the direction of Scapa Flow, draw the Grand

Fleet to the attack, and then lead it in the direction of the torpedoes and mines.   Probably such a scheme would never have succeeded ; but it represented, in the opinion of our Planning group, Germany's only chance of crippling the Grand Fleet and winning the war.   In other words, had my staff found itself in Germany's position, that is the strategy which it would probably have used.   I gave this report unofficially to the British Admiralty simply because I thought it might afford British officers reading that would possibly be entertaining.   It is an evidence of the co-operation that existed between the two forces, and of the British disposition to accept suggestions, that this document was immediately sent to Admiral Beatty.

II

The fact that I was able ultimately to create such an organization and leave the administration of its individual departments so largely to their respective heads was especially fortunate because it gave me time for what was perhaps the most important of my duties.   This was my attendance at the meetings of the Allied Naval Council, not to mention daily conferences with various officials of the Allies.   This naval council was the great headquarters for combined Allied operations against the enemy on the sea. It was not officially constituted by the Allied governments until November 29, 1917, but it had actually been in con-tinuous operation since the beginning of the war, the heads of the Allied admiralties having met frequently in con-ference.   At these meetings every phase of the situation was discussed, and the methods finally adopted represented the mature judgment of the Allied naval chiefs who partici-pated in them.   Without this council, and without the co-operation for which it stood, our efforts would have been so dispersed and would have so overlapped that their efficiency would have been greatly decreased.   This inter-national naval conference not only had to decide questions of naval strategy, but it also had to concern itself with a multitude of practical matters which have little interest for the public, but which are exceedingly important in war. In this struggle coal, oil, and other materials played a part almost as important as ships and men ; these materials, like ships and men, were limited in quantity; and it was necessary to apportion them as deliberately and as economically as the seemingly more important munitions of warfare. The Germans were constantly changing their tactics; sometimes they would make their concentrations in a certain area; while at other times their strength would appear in another field far distant from the first. These changes made it necessary that we should in each case readjust our forces to counteract the enemy's tactics. It was a vital necessity that these readjustments should be made immediately when the enemy's changes of tactics became known. It is evident that the element necessary to success was that the earliest and most complete possible information should be followed by prompt decision and action; and it is manifest that these requirements could have been satisfied only by a council which was fully informed and which was on the spot momentarily ready to act. The Allied Naval Council responded to all these requirements. One of my first duties, after my arrival, was to attend one of these councils in Paris; and immediately afterward the meetings became much more frequent.

Not only were the proceedings interesting because of the vast importance of the issues which were discussed, but because they brought me into intimate contact with some of the ablest minds in the European navies. Over the first London councils Admiral Jellicoe presided. I have already given my first impressions of this admirable sailor; subsequent events only increased my respect for his character and abilities. An English woman once described Admiral Jellicoe as " a great gentleman "; it is a description upon which I can hardly improve. The First Lord, Sir Eric Geddes, though he was by profession an engineer and had been transferred from the business of building roads and assuring the communications behind the armies in France to become the civilian head of the British navy, acquired, in an astonishingly short time, a mastery of the details of naval administration. Sir Eric is a type of man that we like to think of as American; perhaps the fact that he had received his business training in this country, and had served an apprenticeship on the Baltimore and Ohio Railroad, strengthened this impression. The habitués of the National Sporting Club in London—of whom I was one—used to look reproachfully at the giant figure of the First Lord ; in their opinion he had sadly missed his calling. His mighty frame, his hard and supple muscles, his power of vigorous and rapid movement, his keen eye and his quick wit—these qualities, in the opinion of those best qualified to judge, would have made this stupendous Briton one of the greatest heavyweight prize-fighters in the annals of pugilism. With a little training I am sure that Sir Eric would even now make a creditable showing in the professional ring. However, the paths of this business man and statesman lay in other fields. After returning from America he had had a brilliant business career in England ; he repre-sented the type which we call " self-made men " ; that is, he fought his way to the top without the aid of influ-ential friends. His elevation to the Admiralty, in succession to Sir Edward Carson, was something new in British public life, for Sir Eric had never dabbled in politics, and, until the war started, he was practically unknown in political circles. But this crisis in British affairs made it necessary for the Ministry to " draft " the most capable executives in the nation, irrespective of political considerations ; and Sir Eric, therefore, quite naturally found himself at the head of the navy. In a short time he had acquired a knowledge of the naval situation which enabled him to preside over an inter-national naval council with a very complete grasp of all the problems which were presented. I have heard the great naval specialists who attended say that, had they not known the real fact, they would hardly have suspected that Sir Eric was not a naval man. We admired not only his ability to direct the course of discussion, and even to take an important part in it, but also his skill at summing up the results of the whole proceeding in a few terse and masterly phrases. In fine, the First Lord was a man after Roosevelt's heart—big, athletic, energetic, with a genius for reaching the kernel of a question and of getting things done.

When it came to facility of exposition, however, we Anglo-Saxons made a poor showing in comparison with most French naval officers and in particular with Admirals Lacaze and de Bon. Both these gentlemen represented the Gallic type in its finest aspects. After spending a few moments with Rear-Admiral Lacaze, it was easy to understand the real affection which all French naval officers felt for him. He is a small, slight man, with a grey, pointed beard, and he possesses that earnestness of spirit, that courtesy of manner, and that sympathy and charm which we regard as the finest attributes of the cultured Frenchman. Admiral Lacaze has also a genuine French facility of speech and that precision of statement which is so characteristic of the French intellect. A slight acquaintance would make one believe that Admiral Lacaze would be a model husband and father, perhaps grandfather ; it was with surprise, however, that I learned that he was a bachelor, but I am sure that he is that kind of bachelor who is an uncle to all of the children of his acquaintance. As Minister of Marine he was the presiding officer of the council when it met in Paris.

In Vice-Admiral de Bon, chief of the French naval staff, Admiral Lacaze had a worthy colleague ; he was really a man of heroic mould, and he certainly looked the part. His white hair and his white beard, cut square, gave at first glance an impression of age ; yet his clear, pink skin, not ruffled by a trace of wrinkle, his erect figure, his bright blue eyes, the vigour of his conversation and the energy of his movements, betokened rather perpetual youth. Compared with the naval forces of Great Britain, the French navy was of inconsiderable size, but in Admiral de Bon it made a contribution to Allied naval strength which was worth many dreadnoughts. The reputation of this man has scarcely reached this side of the Atlantic ; yet it was the general opinion of practically all naval men that his was the keenest mind at the Allied Naval Council. It was certainly the most persuasive in argument, and the one that had most influence in determining our conclusions. Not that there was anything about this great French sailor that was arrogant or offensively self-assertive. On the contrary, his manner was all compact of charm and courtesy. He was about the most persuasive person I have ever met. Whenever an important matter arose, there was some influence that made us turn instinctively to Admiral de Bon for enlightenment ; and, when he rose to talk, the council hung upon his every word. For the man was a consummate orator. Those who understood French even slightly had little difficulty in following the Admiral, for he spoke his delightful language

with a precision, a neatness of phrase, and a clearness of
enunciation which made every syllable intelligible. So
perfect did these speeches seem that one would have
suspected that Admiral de Bon had composed them at
his leisure, but this was not the case ; the man apparently
had only to open his mouth, and his speech spontaneously
flowed forth ; he never hesitated for a word. And his
words were not only eloquent, but, as I have said, they
were full of substance. The charm which he manifested
on these public occasions he carried likewise into his
domestic life. Whenever the council met in Paris the
Admiral's delightful wife and daughters entertained us at
luncheon—an experience which caused many of us to
regret that it did not always meet in that city.

The other two members of this interesting group were
Rear-Admiral Funakoshi, representing the Japanese navy,
and Vice-Admiral di Revel, representing the Italian.
The Japanese was also naval attaché at London, and the
popularity which he had acquired in this post he also
won in the larger field. In some respects, he was not like
the conventional notion of a Japanese ; physically he did
not fulfil the accepted rôle, for he was tall and heavily
built ; nor was there anything about him that was " in-
scrutable " ; the fact was that he was exceedingly frank
and open, and apparently loved nothing so much as a good
joke. The remark of a London newspaper that Admiral
di Revel, the Italian, " unlike Admiral Sims, looks every
inch the sailor," caused Admiral Funakoshi much amusement ; he could not resist the temptation to chaff me
about it. We all became so well acquainted that, in our
lighter moments, we did not mind having a little fun at
one another's expense ; and in these passages the Japanese
representative did not always make the poorest showing.
The Italian, di Revel, was a source of continual delight.
Someone remarked that he was in reality an Irishman
who had escaped into Italy ; and this facetious charac-
terization was really not inapt. His shock of red hair, his
reddish beard, and his short, stocky figure almost per-
suaded one that County Cork was his native soil. He
delivered his opinions with an insistence which indicated
that he entertained little doubt about their soundness ;
he was not particularly patient if they were called in
question ; yet he was so courteous, so energetic, and so

entertaining that he was a general favourite. That his Government appreciated his services is shown by the fact that it made di Revel a full admiral, a rank which is rarely bestowed in Italy.

Such, then, were the men who directed the mighty forces that defeated the German submarines. The work at the councils was arduous, yet the opportunity of associating with such men in such a task is one that comes to few naval officers. They all worked with the most indomitable spirit; not one of them ever for a moment showed the slightest discouragement over a situation which was at times disquieting, to say the least; not one faltered in the determination to force the issue to the only logical end. History has given few examples of alliances that worked harmoniously. The Allied Naval Council did its full share in making harmonious the Allied effort against the submarine.

CHAPTER VIII

SUBMARINE AGAINST SUBMARINE

I

It is not improbable that I have given a false impression concerning the relative merits of the several methods which were developed for fighting the submarine. Destroyers, patrol boats, subchasers, and mystery ships all accomplished great things in solving the most baffling problem presented by the war. The belief is general that the most successful hunter of the submarine was the destroyer, and, so far as absolute figures are concerned, this is true. Destroyers, with their depth charges and their gunfire, sank more U-boats than any other agency. One type of craft, however, proved a more destructive enemy of the submarine than even the destroyer. That was a warship of whose achievements in this direction little has so far been heard. The activities of the German submarine have completely occupied public attention; and this is perhaps the reason why few newspaper readers have suspected that there were other than German and Austrian submarines constantly operating at sea. Everyone has heard of the U-boats, yet how many have heard anything of the H-boats, the E-boats, the K-boats, and the L-boats ? The H-, E-, and K-boats were British submarines, and the L-boats were American submarines. In the destruction of the German under-water craft these Allied submarines proved more successful than any kind of surface ship. The Allied destroyers, about 500 in number, sank 34 German submarines with gunfire and depth charges ; auxiliary patrol craft, such as trawlers, yachts, and the like, about 3,000 in number, sank 31 ; while the Allied submarines, which were only about 100 in number, sank 20. Since, therefore, the Allies had about five times as many destroyers as submarines at work, it is evident that the record of the latter vessels surpasses that of the most formidable surface anti-submarine craft.

Thus the war developed the fact that the most deadly enemy of the submarine is the submarine itself. Underwater warfare is evidently a disease in which like cures like. In a way this is the most astonishing lesson of the naval operations. It is particularly interesting, because it so completely demolishes all the ideas on this subject with which we entered the war. From that day in history when the submarine made its first appearance, the one quality which seemed to distinguish it from all other kinds of warship was that it could not be used to fight itself. Writers were fond of pointing out that battleship could fight battleship, that cruiser could fight cruiser, that destroyer could fight destroyer, but that submarine could not fight submarine. This supposed quality, which was constantly emphasized, was what seemed to make the introduction of this strange vessel such a dangerous thing for the British Empire. For more than a hundred years the under-water boat was a weapon which was regarded as valuable almost exclusively to the weaker sea powers. In the course of the nineteenth century this engine of sea fighting made many spectacular appearances ; and significantly it was always heralded as the one effective way of destroying British domination at sea.

The inventor of the modern submarine was an undergraduate of Yale named David Bushnell ; his famous *Turtle*, according to the great British authority, Sir William White, formerly Chief Naval Constructor of the British navy, contained every fundamental principle of " buoyancy, stability, and control of depth " which are found in the modern submarine ; " it cannot be claimed," he said in 1905, " that any new principle of design has been discovered or applied since Bushnell. . . . He showed the way to all his successors. . . . Although alternative methods of fulfilling essentials have been introduced and practically tested, in the end Bushnell's plans in substance have been found the best." The chief inspiration of Bushnell's work was a natural hostility to Great Britain, which was at that time engaged in war with his own country ; his submarine, invented in 1777, was intended to sink the British warships which were then anchored

16

off the American coast, break the communications of
Great Britain with her revolting colonies, and in this way
win our liberty. Bushnell did not succeed in this ambitious enterprise for reasons which it is hardly necessary
to set forth in this place ; the fact which I wish to emphasize is that he regarded his submarine as an agency which
would make it possible for the young United States, a
weak naval power, to deprive Great Britain, the dominant
sea power, of its supremacy. His successor, Robert
Fulton, was· inspired by a similar ambition. In 1801
Fulton took his *Nautilus* into the harbour of Brest, and
blew a merchant vessel into a thousand pieces ; this
dramatic experiment was intended to convince Napoleon
that there was one way in which he could destroy the
British fleet and thus deprive England of her sea control.
Dramatic as this demonstration was, it did not convince
Napoleon of the value of the submarine ; Fulton therefore took his ship to England and exhibited it to William
Pitt, who was then Prime Minister. The great statesman
was much impressed, but he did not regard the submarine
as an innovation that should arouse much enthusiasm in
England. " If we adopt this kind of fighting," he said,
" it will be the end of all navies."

Despite his own forebodings, Pitt sent Fulton to St.
Vincent, who was then the First Lord of the Admiralty.

" Pitt is the biggest fool in the world," remarked the
head of the victorious British navy. " Why does he
encourage a kind of warfare which is useless to those who
are the masters of the sea, and which, if it succeeds, will
deprive them of this supremacy ? "

The reason for St. Vincent's opposition is apparent.
He formed the conception of the submarine which has
prevailed almost up to the present time. In his opinion,
a submarine was a vessel which could constantly remain
under the surface, approach great warships unseen and
blow them to pieces at will. This being the case, a nation
which possessed two or three successfully working engines
of this kind could apparently wipe out the entire British
fleet. It therefore needed no argument to show that this
was a weapon which was hardly likely to prove useful
to the British navy. If the submarine could fulfil its
appointed mission, it would give the control of the sea
to that nation which used it successfully ; but since Great

Britain already controlled the sea, the new type of war craft was superfluous to her. In the hands of a weak naval power, however, which had everything to gain and nothing to lose, if might supply the means of overthrowing the British Empire. Could one submarine destroy another, it would present no particular menace, for then, in order to control the sea, it would merely be necessary to build a larger under-water fleet than that of any prospective enemy : but how could vessels which spent all their time under the water, in the dark, ever get a chance to come to blows ? From these considerations it seemed apparent to St. Vincent and other British experts of his time that the best interests of the British Empire would be served, not by developing the submarine, but by suppressing it. Fulton's biographer intimates that the British Government offered Fulton a considerable amount of money to take his submarine back to America and forget about it ; and there is a letter of Fulton's to Lord Granville, saying that " not for £20,000 a year would I do what you suggest." But there seemed to be no market for his invention, and Fulton therefore returned to America and subsequently gave all his time to exploiting the steamboat. On the defensive powers of the under-water vessel he also expressed the prevailing idea. " Submarine," he said, " cannot fight submarine."

The man who designed the type of submarine which has become the standard in all modern navies, John P. Holland, similarly advocated it as the only means of destroying the British navy. Holland was an American of Irish origin ; he was a member of the Fenian brotherhood, and it was his idea that his vessel could be used to destroy the British navy, blockade the British coast, and, as an inevitable consequence, secure freedom for Ireland. This is the reason why his first successful boat was known as the *Fenian Ram*, despite the fact that it was not a " ram " at all. And the point on which Holland always insisted was that the submarine vessel was a unique vessel in naval warfare, because there was no " answer " to it. " There is nothing that you can send against it," he gleefully exclaimed, " not even itself."

Parliamentary debates in the late nineties indicated that British naval leaders entertained this same idea. In **1900,** Viscount Goschen, who was then the First Lord of the Admiralty, dismissed the submarine as unworthy of consideration. " The idea of submarine navigation," he said, " is a morbid one. We need pay no attention to the submarine in naval warfare. The submarine is the arm of weaker powers." But Mr. Arnold-Forster, who was himself soon to become a member of the Admiralty, took exception to these remarks. " If the First Lord," he said, " had suggested that we should not build submarines because the problems which control them are not yet solved, I should have hesitated to combat his argument. But the First Lord has not said so : he has said that the Admiralty did not care to undertake any project for submarines because this type of boat could never be anything but the arm of the feeble. However, if this boat is made practical, the nation which possesses it will cease to be feeble and become in reality powerful. More than any other nation do we have reason to fear the submarine. It is, therefore, not wise to wait with indifference while other nations work at the solution of this problem without trying to solve it ourselves." " The question of the best way of meeting submarine attack," said Viscount Goschen at another time, " is receiving much consideration. It is in this direction that practical suggestions would be valuable. It seems certain that the reply to this weapon must be looked for in other directions than in building submarine boats ourselves, for it is clear that one submarine cannot fight another."

This prepossession dominated all professional naval minds in all countries, until the outbreak of the Great War. Yet the war had lasted only a few months when the idea was shown to be absurd. Practical hostilities soon demonstrated, as already said, that not only was the submarine able to fight another boat of the same type, but that it was the most effective anti-submarine agency which we possessed—so effective that the British Admiralty at once began the design of a special type of hunting submarine having a high under-water speed.

The fact is that the popular mind, in its attitude toward this new type of craft, is still too much under the spell of Jules Verne. There is still the disposition to look upon the submarine as an insidious vessel which spends practically all of its time under the water, stealthily slinks along, never once betraying its presence, creeps up at will to its enemy and discharges its torpedo. Yet the description which these pages have already given of its operations shows the falsity of this idea. It is important that we should keep constantly in mind the fact that the submarine is only occasionally a submarine; and that for the greater part of its career it is a surface boat. In the long journeys which the German U-boats made from the Heligoland Bight around Scotland and Ireland to those great hunting grounds which lay in the Atlantic trade routes, they travelled practically all the time on the surface of the water. The weary weeks during which they cruised around, looking for their victims, they also spent almost entirely on the surface. There were virtually only two circumstances which compelled them to disappear beneath the waves. The first of these was the occasion on which the submarine detected a merchant ship; in this case it submerged, for the success of its attempt to torpedo depended entirely upon its operating unseen. The second occasion which made it necessary to submerge was when it spied a destroyer or other dangerous patrolling craft; the submarine, as has been said, could not fight a vessel of this type with much chance of success. Thus the ability to submerge was merely a quality that was utilized only in those crises when the submarine either had to escape a vessel which was stronger than itself or planned to attack one which was weaker.

The time taken up by these disappearances amounted to only a fraction of the total period consumed in a cruise. Yet the fact that the submarine had to keep itself momentarily ready to make these disappearances is precisely the reason why it was obliged to spend the larger part of its time on the surface. The submarine has two sets of engines, one for surface travel and the other for subsurface travel. An oil-engine propels it on the top of the water, but this consumes a large amount of air, and, for this reason, it cannot be used when travelling under the surface. As soon as the vessel dives, therefore, it changes its motive power to an electric motor, which makes no inroads on the oxygen needed for sustaining the life of its crew. But the physical limitation of size prevents the submarine from carrying large storage batteries, which is only another way of saying that its cruising radius under the water is extremely small, not more than fifty or sixty miles. In order to recharge these batteries and gain motive power for subsurface travel, the submarine has to come to the surface. Yet the simple fact that the submarine can accomplish its destructive work only when submerged, and that it can avoid its enemy only by diving, makes it plain that it must always hold itself in readiness to submerge on a moment's notice and remain under water the longest possible time. That is, its storage batteries must always be kept at their highest efficiency ; they must not be wasted by unnecessary travelling under the water ; the submarine, in other words, must spend all its time on the surface, except those brief periods when it is attempting to attack a merchant ship or escape an enemy. Almost the greatest tragedy in the life of a submarine is to meet a surface enemy, such as a destroyer, when its electric batteries are exhausted. It cannot submerge, for it can stay submerged only when it is in motion, unless it is in water shallow enough to permit it to rest on the bottom. Even though it may have a little electricity, and succeed in getting under water, it cannot stay there long, for its electric power will soon be used up, and therefore it is soon faced with the alternative of coming to the surface and surrendering, or of being destroyed. The success of the submarine, indeed its very existence, depends upon the vessel spending the largest possible part of its time upon the surface, keeping its full supply of electric power constantly in reserve, so that it may be able to dive at a moment's notice and to remain under the water for the maximum period.

This purely mechanical limitation explains why the German submarine was not a submarine in the popularly accepted meaning of that term. Yet the fact that this vessel remained for the greater part of its existence on the surface was no particular disadvantage, so long as it was called upon to contend only with surface vessels. Even with the larger part of its decks exposed the U-boat was a comparatively small object on the vast expanse of the sea. I have already made clear the great disadvantage under which destroyers and other patrolling vessels laboured in their attempts to "hunt" this type of enemy. A destroyer, small as it is, was an immensely larger object than the under-water boat, and the consequence was that the lookout on a submarine, proceeding along on the surface, could detect the patrolling vessel long before it could be observed itself. All the submarine had to do, therefore, whenever the destroyer appeared on the horizon, was to seek safety under water, remain there until its pursuer had passed out of sight, and then rise again and resume its operations. Before the adoption of the convoy system, when the Allied navies were depending chiefly upon the patrol—that is, sending destroyers and other surface craft out upon the high seas to hunt for the enemy —the enemy submarines frequently operated in the same areas as the patrol vessels, and were only occasionally inconvenienced by having to keep under the water to conceal their presence. But let us imagine that the destroyer, in addition to its depth charges, its torpedoes, its guns, and its ability to ram, had still another quality. Suppose, for a moment, that, like the submarine, it could steam submerged, put up a periscope which would reveal everything within the radius of a wide horizon, and that, when it had picked up an enemy submarine, it could approach rapidly under the water, and discharge a torpedo. It is evident that such a manœuvre as this would have deprived the German of the only advantage which it possessed over all other war craft—its ability to make itself unseen.

No destroyer can accomplish any such magical feat as this : indeed, there is only one kind of vessel that can do so, and that is another submarine. This illustration immediately makes it clear why the Allied submarine itself was the most destructive enemy of the German submarine. When Robert Fulton, John P. Holland, and other authorities declared that the under-water vessel could not fight its own kind, it is evident that they had not themselves foreseen the ways in which their inventions were to be used. They regarded their craft as ships that would sail the larger part of the time under the waves, coming up only occasionally to get their bearings and to take in a fresh supply of air. It was plain to these pioneers that vessels which spent practically all their time submerged could not fight each other, for the sufficient reason that they could not see each other ; a combat under these conditions would resemble a prize-fight between two blindfolded pugilists. Neither would such vessels fight upon the surface, for, even though they were supplied with guns

—things which did not figure in the early designs of submarines—one boat could decline the combat simply by
submerging. In the minds of Fulton and Holland an
engagement between such craft would reduce itself to
mutual attempts to ram each other under the water, and
many fanciful pictures of the early days portrayed exciting
deep-sea battles of this kind, in which submarines, looking
like mighty sea monsters, provided with huge glaring
headlights, made terrific lunges at each other. None of
the inventors foresaw that, in such battles as would
actually take place, the torpedo would be used, and that
the submarine which was defeated would succumb to one
of those same stealthy attacks which it was constantly
meditating against surface craft.

Another point of the highest importance is that in a
conflict of submarine against submarine the Allied boats
had one great advantage over the German. Hans Rose
and Valentiner and Moraht and other U-boat commanders,
as already explained, had to spend most of their time on
the surface in order to keep their batteries fully supplied
with electricity, in readiness for the dives that would be
necessary when the Allied destroyers approached. But
the Allied submarine commander did not have to maintain this constant readiness ; the reason, it is hardly
necessary to say, is that the Allied submarine had no
surface enemies, for there were no German surface craft
operating on the high seas ; the Grand Fleet at Scapa
Flow was carefully attending to that very essential detail.
Occasionally, indeed, our submarines were attacked by
our own destroyers, but accidents of this kind, though
uncomfortably frequent, were not numerous enough to
interfere with the operation I have in mind. The statement seems almost like a contradiction in terms, yet it is
entirely true, that, simply because the Allied submarines
did not have to hold themselves constantly ready to submerge, they could in fact spend a considerable part of
their time under the water, for they were not compelled
to economize electric power so strictly. This gave them
a great advantage in hunting the U-boats. British and
American submarines could fully charge their batteries,
drop under water and cruise around with enough speed
to maintain a horizontal position at " periscope depth,"
that is, a depth just sufficient to enable them to project

the periscope above the water whenever desired. This speed was so very slow—about one mile an hour—that it could be kept up an entire day without exhausting the electric batteries.

The net result was this : The German submarine necessarily sailed most of the time on the surface with its conning-tower and deck exposed, whereas the Allied submarine when on its hunting grounds, spent all of the daylight hours under water, with only the periscope visible from time to time for a few seconds. Just as the German U-boat could " spot " an Allied destroyer at a great distance without being itself seen, so could the periscope invariably see the German submarine on the surface long before this tiny object came within the view of a U-boat conning-tower. Our submarine commander could remain submerged, sweep the ocean with his periscope until he had picked up the German enemy ; then, still under water, and almost invariably unseen, he could steal up to a position within range, and discharge a torpedo into its fragile side. The German submarine received that same treatment which it was itself administering to harmless merchantmen ; it was torpedoed without warning ; inasmuch, however, as it was itself a belligerent vessel, the proceeding violated no principle of international law.

II

The Allied submarines, like many other patrol craft, spent much of their time in those restricted waters which formed the entrances to the British Isles. Their favourite places were the English Channel, St. George's Channel, which forms the southern entrance to the Irish Sea, and the northern passage-way between Scotland and Ireland. At these points, it may be remembered, the cargo ships could usually be found sailing singly, either entirely unescorted, or escorted inadequately, while on their way to join a convoy or to their destinations after the dispersal of a convoy ; these areas were thus almost the only places where the German submarines had much chance of attacking single vessels. The territory was divided into squares, each one of which was indicated by a letter : and the section assigned to each submarine was known as its

" billet." Under ordinary circumstances, the Allied submarine spent all its time, while patrolling, on its own particular " billet " ; only in case the pursuit of an enemy led it outside the " square " was it permissible to leave. Allied submarines also hunted the U-boats in the North Sea on the routes which the latter had to take in coming out or returning through the passages in the German mine-fields of the Heligoland Bight, or through the Skager Rack.

As previously explained, in the daytime the Allied submarine remained under the water, its periscope exposed for a short time every fifteen minutes or so, sweeping the sea for a distance of many miles. As soon as darkness set in, the boat usually emerged, began taking in new air and recharging its batteries, the crew seizing the opportunity to stretch their legs and catch a welcome glimpse of the external world. The simple fact that the Allied submarines spent the larger part of their time under water, while the German spent the larger part of their time on the surface, gave our boats a great military advantage over the foe, but it likewise made existence in our submarine service more arduous. Even on the coldest winter days there could be no artificial heat, for the precious electricity could not be spared for that purpose, and the temperature inside the submarine was the temperature of the water in which it sailed. The close atmosphere, heavily laden also with the smell of oil from the engines and the odours of cooking, and the necessity of going for days at a time without a bath or even a wash, added to the discomfort. The stability of a submerged submarine is by no means perfect ; the vessel is constantly rolling, and a certain number of the crew, even the experienced men, are frequently seasick. This movement sometimes made it almost impossible to stay in a bunk and sleep for any reasonable period ; the poor seaman would perhaps doze off, but a lurch of the vessel would send him sprawling on the deck. One could hardly write, for it was too cold, or read, for there was little light ; and because of the motion of the vessel, it was difficult to focus one's eyes on the page. A limited amount of smoking was permitted, but the air was sometimes so vitiated that only the most vigorous and incessant puffing could keep a cigarette alight. One of the most annoying things

about the submarine existence is the fact that the air
condenses on the sides as the coldness increases, so that
practically everyth ng becomes wet ; as the sailor lies in
his bunk this moisture is precipitated upon him like rain-
drops. This combination of discomforts usually produced,
after spending a few hours under the surface, that mental
state commonly known as " dopey."

The usual duration of a " cruise " was eight days, and
by the end of that time many of the crew were nearly
" all in," and some of them entirely so. But the physical
sufferings were the least discomfiting. Any moment the
boat was likely to hit one of the mines the Germans were
always planting. A danger which was particularly vexa-
tious was that a British or an American submarine was
just about as likely to be attacked by Allied surface craft
as the Germans themselves. At the beginning, recognition signals were arranged by which it was expected
that an Allied under-water craft, coming to the surface,
could make its identity known to a friendly warship ;
sometimes these signals succeeded, but more frequently
they failed, and the attacks which British and American
destroyers made upon their own submarines demonstrated
that there was no certainty that such signals would offer
any protection. A rather grim order directed all destroyers
and other patrol craft to sink any submarine on sight,
unless there was positive information that a friendly
submarine was operating in the neighbourhood. To a
large extent, therefore, the life of our submarine sailors
was the same as that of the Germans. Our men know
how it feels to have a dozen depth charges explode around
them, for not infrequently they have had to endure this
sort of thing from their own comrades. Mistakes of this
sort, even though not very numerous, were so likely to
happen at any time that whenever an Allied submarine
saw an Allied destroyer at a distance, it usually behaved
just as a German would have behaved under the same
conditions : it dived precipitately to the safety of deep
water. Our men, that is, did not care to take the risk of
a discussion with the surface craft ; it was more prudent
to play the part of an enemy. One day one of the American submarines, lying on the surface, saw an American
destroyer, and, cheered in their loneliness by the sight of
such a friendly vessel, waited for it to approach, making

twenty rounds of projectiles began falling about the L-boat, which as hastily as possible dropped to sixty feet under the surface. In a few minutes depth charges began exploding around him in profusion, the plates of the vessel shook violently, the lights went out, and the end seemed near. Making a last effort, the American submarine rose to the surface, sent up all the recognition signals the officers could think of, and this time with success. The destroyer approached, the commander shouting from the bridge :

"Who are you ? "

"American submarine *A L*-10."

"Good luck, old man," came a now familiar voice from the bridge. "This is Bill."

The commander of the destroyer and the commander of the submarine had been room-mates at Annapolis !

In other ways our submarine force passed through the same experiences as the Germans. Its adventures shed the utmost light upon this campaign against merchant-men which the Germans had depended upon to win the war. The observer at the periscope was constantly spotting huge Allied merchantmen making their way into port. The great ships sailed on, entirely oblivious of the periscope and the eye of the British or American watcher fixed upon them.

"How easy to sink her ! " the observer would say to himself. This game in which the Germans were engaged was a dangerous one, because of Allied anti-submarine craft ; but, when it came to attacking merchant ships, it was the easiest thing in the world. After a few weeks in a submarine, it grew upon our men that the wonder was not that the Germans had sunk so many merchant ships, but that they had sunk so few. Such an experience emphasized the conviction, which was prevalent in both the British and American navies, that the Germans were not particularly skilful at the occupation which seemed to be so congenial to them. Indeed, there are few things in the world that appear so absolutely helpless as a great merchant ship when observed through the periscope of an under-water boat.

Whenever an Allied submarine met its enemy the contest was usually a short one. The issue, one way or the other, was determined in a few minutes. On rare occasions there were attempts to ram; almost invariably, however, it was the torpedo which settled the conflict. If our boat happened to be on the surface when it sighted the German, which, however, was very seldom the case, the first manœuvre was to dive as quickly and as unostentatiously as possible. If it succeeded in getting under before the U-boat discovered its presence, it then crept up, guided only by the periscope, until it had reached a spot that was within range. The combat, as was the case so frequently in this war, was one-sided. The enemy submarine seldom knew its assailant was anywhere in the neighbourhood; a merchant ship, from its relatively high bridge, could sometimes see the torpedo approach and turn out of its way; but it was almost impossible to see a wake from the low conning-tower or periscope of a submarine, and no one except the observer had a glimpse of the surface. The small size of the submarine was in itself a great protection; we launched many torpedoes, but only occasionally scored a hit. The missile would usually pass a few feet ahead or astern, or would glide over or under the submerged hulk, perhaps a few inches only saving it from destruction. Once an American torpedo hit its enemy squarely on the side but failed to explode! If the torpedo once struck and functioned, however, it was all over in a few seconds. A huge geyser of water would leap into the air; and the submarine would sometimes rise at the same time, or parts of it would fly in a dozen directions; then the waters would gradually subside, leaving a mammoth oil patch, in which two or three members of the crew might be discovered struggling in the waves. Most of the men in the doomed vessel never knew what had struck them.

Thus, early one evening in May, 1918, the *E*-35, a British submarine, was patrolling its billet in the Atlantic, about two hundred miles west of Gibraltar. About two or three miles on the port beam a long, low-lying object was distinguished on the surface; the appearance was nondescript, but, to the practised eye at the periscope, it quickly took shape as an enemy submarine. As the sea was rather rough, the *E*-35 dived to forty feet; after a little while it ascended to twenty-six, put up the periscope,

and immediately saw, not far away, a huge enemy submarine proceeding north at a leisurely pace, never once
suspecting that one of its own kind was on its trail. In
order to get within range and cut the German off, the
Britisher dived again to forty feet, went ahead for twenty
minutes with all the speed it could muster, and again came
near enough to the surface to put up its periscope. Now
it was directly astern ; still the British submarine was not
near enough for a sure shot, so again it plunged beyond
periscope depth, coming up at intervals during the next
hour, each time observing with satisfaction that it was
lessening the distance between itself and its prey. When
the range had been decreased to two hundred and fifty
yards, and when the E-35 had succeeded in getting in
such a position that it could fire its torpedo, the missile
was launched in the direction of the foe. But this was
only another of the numerous occasions when the shot
missed. Had the German submarine been a surface
ship, it would have seen the wake and probably escaped
by flight ; but still it sailed nonchalantly on its way,
never suspecting for a moment that a torpedo had missed
its vitals by only a few feet. Soon the E-35 crept still
closer, and fired two torpedoes simultaneously from its
bow tubes. Both hit at the same time. Not a glimpse of
the German submarine was seen from that moment. A
terrific explosion was heard, a mountain of water rose in
the air, then in a few seconds everything was still. A
small patch of oil appeared on the surface ; this gradually
expanded in size until it covered a great area ; and then
a few German sailors came up and started swimming
toward the British vessel.

We Americans had seven submarines based on Berehaven, Ireland, whose " billets " were located in the
approaches to the Irish Sea. The most spectacular
achievement of any one of our boats was a curious mix-up
with a German submarine, the details of which have never
been accurately ascertained, but the practical outcome of
which was indisputably the sinking of the German boat.
After a week's hard work on patrol, the A L-2 was running
back to her base on the surface when the lookout sighted
a periscope. The A L-2 at once changed her course, the
torpedo was made ready to fire, when the quiet of the
summer afternoon was rent by a terrific roar and explosion.

It was quite apparent that something exceedingly distressing had happened to the German submarine; the American turned, and made a steep dive, in an attempt to ram the enemy, but failed. Listening with the hydrophone, the *A L-2* could hear now the whirring of propellers, which indicated that the submarine was attempting to gain surface and having difficulty in doing so, and now and then the call letters of the German under-water signal set, which seemed to show that the vessel was in distress and was sending appeals for aid. According to the Admiralty records, a German submarine operating in that area never returned to port; so it seems clear enough that this German was lost. Commander R. C. Grady, who commanded the American submarine division, believes that the German spotted the American boat before it was itself seen, that it launched a torpedo, that this torpedo made an erratic course (a not infrequent trick of a torpedo) around our ship, returned and hit the vessel from which it started. There are others who think that there were two German submarines in the neighbourhood, that one fired at our boat, missed it, and that its torpedo sped on and struck its mate. Probably the real facts about the happening will never be explained.

Besides the actual sinkings to their credit, the Allied submarines accomplished strategic results of the utmost importance. We had reason to believe that the Germans feared them almost more than any other agency, unless it was the mine. " We got used to your depth charges," said the commander of a captured submarine, " and did not fear them; but we lived in constant dread of your submarines. We never knew what moment a torpedo was going to hit us." So greatly did the Germans fear this attack that they carefully avoided the areas in which the Allied under-water boats were operating. We soon learned that we could keep any section free of the Germans which we were able to patrol with our own submarines. It also soon appeared that the German U-boats would not fight our subsurface vessels. At first this may seem rather strange; certainly a combat between two ships of the same kind, size, and armament would seem to be an equal one; the disinclination of the German to give battle under such conditions would probably strike the layman as sheer cowardice. But in this attitude the Germans were undoubtedly right.

The business of their submarines was not to fight warships; it was exclusively to destroy merchantmen. The demand made upon the U-boat commanders was to get "tonnage! tonnage!" Germany could win the war in only one way: that was by destroying Allied shipping to such an extent that the Allied sea communications would be cut, and the supplies of men and munitions and food from the United States shut off. For this tremendous task Germany had an inadequate number of submarines and torpedoes. Only by economizing to the utmost extent on these vessels and these weapons could she entertain any hope of success. Had Germany possessed an unlimited quantity of submarines and torpedoes, she might perhaps have profitably expended some of them in warfare on British " H-boats " and American " L-boats "; or, had there been a certainty of " getting " an Allied submarine with each torpedo fired, it would have been justifiable to use these weapons, small as was the supply. The fact was, however, that the Allies expended many torpedoes for every submarine sunk; and this was clearly a game which Germany could not afford to play. Evidently the U-boats had orders to slip under the water whenever an Allied submarine was seen; at least this was the almost invariable procedure. Thus the Allied submarines compelled their German enemies to do the one thing which worked most to their disadvantage: that is, to keep submerged when in the same area with our submarines; this not only prevented them from attacking merchantmen, but forced them to consume their electric power, which, as I have already explained, greatly diminished their efficiency as attacking ships.

The operations of Allied submarines also greatly diminished the value of the " cruiser " submarines which Germany began to construct in 1917. These great subsurface vessels were introduced as an " answer " to the convoy system. The adoption of the convoy, as I have already explained, made it ineffective for the Germans to hunt far out at sea. Until the Allies had put this plan into operation, the relatively small German U-boats could go two or three hundred miles into the Atlantic and pick off almost at will the merchant ships, which were then proceeding alone and unescorted. But now the destroyers went out to a point two or three hundred miles from the British coast, formed a protecting screen around the convoy, and escorted the grouped ships into restricted waters. The result of this was to drive the submarines into these coastal waters ; here again, however, they had their difficulties with destroyers, subchasers, submarines, and other patrol craft. It will be recalled that no destroyer escort was provided for the merchant convoys on their way across the Atlantic ; the Allies simply did not have the destroyers for this purpose. The Germans could not send surface raiders to attack these convoys in mid-ocean, first, because their surface warships could not escape from their ports in sufficient numbers to accomplish any decisive results, and, secondly, because Allied surface warships accompanied every convoy to protect them against any such attack. There was only one way in which the Germans could attack the convoys in mid-ocean. A fleet of great ocean-going submarines, which could keep the sea for two or three months, might conceivably destroy the whole convoy system at a blow. The scheme was so obvious that Germany in the summer of 1917 began building ships of this type. They were about 300 feet long, displaced about 3,000 tons, carried fuel and supplies enough to maintain themselves for three or four months from their base, and, besides torpedoes, had six-inch guns that could outrange a destroyer. By the time the armistice was signed Germany had built about twenty of these ships. But they possessed little offensive value against merchantmen. The Allied submarines and destroyers kept them from operating in the submarine zone. They are so difficult to manœuvre that not only could they not afford to remain in the neighbourhood of our anti-submarine craft, but they were not successful in attacking merchant vessels. They never risked torpedoing a convoy, and rarely even a single vessel, but captured a number by means of their superior gunfire. These huge " cruiser submarines," which aroused such fear in the civilian mind when the news of their existence first found its way into print, proved to be the least harmful of any of the German types.

The Allied submarines accomplished another result of the utmost importance. They prevented the German

17

U-boats from hunting in groups or flotillas. All during 1917 and 1918 the popular mind conjured up frightful pictures of U-boat squadrons, ten or fifteen together, lying in wait for our merchantmen or troopships. Hardly a passenger crossed the ocean without seeing a dozen German submarines constantly pursuing his ship. In a speech which I made to a group of American editors who visited England in September, 1918, I touched upon this point. " I do not know," I told these journalists, " how many submarines you gentlemen saw on the way over here, but if you had the usual experience, you saw a great many. I have seen many accounts in our papers on this subject. If you were to believe these accounts, you could only conclude that many vessels have crossed the ocean with difficulty because submarines were so thick that they scraped all the paint off the vessels' sides. All of these accounts are, of course, unofficial. They get into the American papers in various ways. It is to be regretted that they should be published and thereby give a false impression. Some time ago I saw a letter from one of our men who came over here on a ship bound into the English Channel. This letter was written to his girl. He said that he intended to take the letter on shore and slip it into a post box so that the censor should not see it. The censor did see it and it eventually came to me. This man was evidently intent on impressing on his girl the dangers through which he had passed. It related that the vessel on which he had made the voyage had met two or three submarines a day ; that two spies were found on board and hanged ; and it said, ' When we arrived off our port there were no less than eighteen submarines waiting for us. Can you beat it ? ' "

Perhaps in the early days of the war the German U-boats did hunt in flotillas ; if so, however, they were compelled to abandon the practice as soon as the Allied submarines began to operate effectively. I have already indicated the circumstances which reduced their submarine operations to a lonely enterprise. In the open sea it was impossible to tell whether a submarine was a friend or an enemy. We never knew whether a submarine on the surface was one of our own or a German ; as a result, as already said, we gave orders to attack any under-water boat, unless we had absolute knowledge that it was a friend. Unquestionably the Germans had the same instructions. It would therefore be dangerous for them to attempt to operate in groups, for they would have no way of knowing that their supposed associate was not an Allied or an American submarine. Possibly, even after our submarines had become exceedingly active, the Germans may have attempted to cruise in pairs; one explanation of the strange adventure of the *A L-2*, as said above, was that there were two U-boats in the neighbourhood; yet the fact remains that there is no well-established case on record in which they did so. This circumstance that they had to operate singly was a strategic point greatly to our advantage, especially, as I shall describe, when we began transporting American troops.

CHAPTER IX

I

WAS there no more satisfactory way of destroying sub-marines than by pursuing them with destroyers, sloops, chasers, and other craft in the open seas ? It is hardly surprising that our methods impressed certain of our critics as tedious and ill-conceived, and that a mere glance at a small map of the North Sea suggested a far more reasonable solution of the problem. The bases from which the German submarines found their way to the great centres of shipping were Ostend and Zeebrugge on the Belgian coast, Wilhelmshaven and Cuxhaven on the German coast, and the harbour of Kiel in the Baltic Sea. From all these points the voyage to the waters that lay west and south of Ireland was a long and difficult one ; in order to reach these hunting grounds the German craft had either to pass through the Straits of Dover to the south, or through the wide passage-way of the North Sea that stretched between the Shetland Islands and Norway, and thence sail around the northern coast of Ireland. We necessarily had little success in attempting to interfere with the U-boats while they were making these lengthy open-sea voyages, but concentrated our efforts on trying to oppose them after they had reached the critical areas.

But a casual glance at the map convinced many people that our procedure was a mistake. And most newspaper readers in those days were giving much attention to this map. Many periodicals, published in Great Britain and the United States, were fond of exhibiting to their readers diagrams of the North Sea ; these diagrams contained one heavy black bar drawn across the Straits of Dover and another drawn across the northern passage from Scotland to Norway. The accompanying printed matter informed

244

the public that these pictures illustrated the one effective
" answer " to the submarine. The black bars of printer's
ink represented barrages of mines and nets, which, if
they were once laid between the indicated spots, would
blow to pieces any submarine which attempted to force
a way across. Not a single German U-boat could therefore succeed in getting out of the North Sea. All the
trans-Atlantic ships which contained the food supplies
and war materials so essential to Allied success would thus
be able to land on the west coast of England and France ;
the submarine menace would automatically disappear

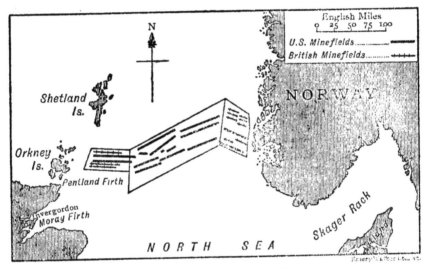

THE NORTH SEA BARRAGE

Just how many German submarines were sunk in attempting to get by this barrage will never
be known, for it did its work silently without any observers. It was probably a contributory
cause of the mutiny which demoralized the German fleet in the autumn of 1918.

and the war on the sea would be won. Unfortunately, it
was not only the pictorial artists employed on newspapers
and magazines who insisted that this was the royal road
to success. Plenty of naval men, in the United States and
in Europe, were constantly advancing the contention,
and statesmen in our own country and in Allied countries
were similarly fascinated by this programme. When I
arrived in London, in April, 1917, the great plan of con-
fining the submarines to their bases was everywhere a
lively topic of discussion. There was not a London club
in which the Admiralty was not denounced for its stupidity
in not adopting such a perfectly obvious plan. The way

to destroy a swarm of hornets—such was the favourite simile—was to annihilate them in their nests, and not to hunt and attack them, one by one, after they had escaped into the open. What the situation needed was not a long and wearisome campaign, involving unlimited new construction to offset the increasing losses of life and shipping, and altogether too probable defeat in the end, but a swift and terrible blow which would end the submarine menace overnight.

The naval officers who expressed fears that, under the shipping conditions prevailing in 1917, such a brilliant performance could not possibly be carried out in time to avoid defeat, merely gained a reputation for timidity and lack of resourcefulness. When the First Lord of the Admiralty, Winston Churchill, in 1915 declared that the British fleet would "dig the Germans out of their holes like rats," his remarks did not greatly impress naval strategists, but they certainly sounded a note which was popular in England. One fact, not generally known at that time, demonstrated the futility of the whole idea. Most newspaper critics assumed that the barrage from Dover to Calais was keeping the submarines out of the Channel. That the destroyers, aircraft, and other patrols were safely escorting troopships and other vessels across the Channel was a fact of which the British public was justly proud. Yet it did not necessarily follow that the submarines could not use the Channel as a passage-way from their German bases to their operating areas in the focus of Allied shipping routes. The mines and nets in the Channel, of which so much was printed in the first three years of the war, did not offer an effective barrier to the submarines. This was due to various reasons too complicated for description in a book of this untechnical nature. The unusually strong tides and rough weather experienced in the vicinity of the Straits of Dover are well known. As one British officer expressed it at the time, " our experience in attempting to close the Strait has involved both blood and tears "—blood because of the men who were lost in laying the mines and nets, and tears because the arduous work of weeks would be swept away in a storm of a single night. In addition, at this stage of the war the British were still experimenting with mines ; they had discovered gradually that the design which they had used up to that time—the same design which was used in the American navy—was defective. But the process of developing new mines in war-time had proved slow and difficult ; and the demands of the army on the munition factories had prevented the Admiralty from obtaining a sufficient number. The work of the Dover patrols was a glorious one, as will appear when all of the facts come to public knowledge. But in 1917 this patrol was not preventing the U-boats from slipping through the Channel. The Straits of Dover, at the point where this so-called barrage was supposed to have existed, is about twenty miles wide. The passage-way between Scotland and Norway is 250 miles wide. The water in the Channel has an average depth of a few fathoms ; in the northern expanse of the North Sea it reaches an average depth of 600 feet. Mining in such deep waters had never been undertaken or even considered before by any nation. The English Channel is celebrated for its strong tides and stormy weather, but it is not the scene of the tempestuous gales which rage so frequently in the winter months in these northern waters. If the British navy had not succeeded in constructing an effective mine barrier across the English Channel, what was the likelihood that success would crown an effort to build a much greater obstruction in the far more difficult waters to the north ?

The one point which few understood at that time was that the mere building of the barrage would not in itself prevent the escape of submarines from the North Sea. Besides building such a barrage, it would be necessary to protect it with surface vessels. Otherwise German minesweepers could visit the scene, and sweep up enough of the obstruction to make a hole through which their submarines could pass. It is evident that, in a barrage extending 250 miles, it would not be difficult to find some place in which to conduct such sweeping operations ; it is also clear that it would take a considerable number of patrolling vessels to watch such an extensive barrier and to interfere with such operations. Moreover, we could not send our mine-layers into the North Sea without destroyer escort ; that is, it would be necessary to detach a considerable part of our forces to protect these ships while they were laying their mines. Those responsible for anti-submarine operations believed that in the spring and summer of 1917 it would have been unwise to detach these anti-submarine vessels from the area in which they were performing such indispensable service. The overwhelming fact was that we needed all the surface craft we could assemble for the convoy system. The destroyers which we had available for this purpose were entirely inadequate ; to have diverted any of them for other duties would at that time have meant destruction to the Allied cause. The object of placing the barrage so far north was to increase the enemy's difficulty in attempting to sweep a passage through it and facilitate its defencé by our forces. The impossibility of defending a mine barrier placed too far south was shown by experience in that area of the North Sea which was known as the " wet triangle." By April, 1917, the British had laid more than 30,000 mines in the Bight of Heligoland, and were then increasing these obstructions at the rate of 3,000 mines a month. Yet this vast explosive field did not prevent the Germans from sending their submarines to sea. The enemy sweepers were dragging out channels through the minefields almost as rapidly as the British were putting new fields down ; we could not prevent this, because protecting vessels could not remain so near the German bases without losses from submarine attacks. Moreover, the Germans also laid mines in the same area in order to trap the British mine-layers ; and these operations resulted in very considerable losses on each side. These impediments made the egress of a submarine a difficult and nerve-racking process ; it sometimes required two or three days and the assistance of a dozen or so surface vessels to get a few submarines through the Heligoland Bight into open waters. Several were unquestionably destroyed in the operation, yet the activity of submarines in the Atlantic showed that these mine-fields had by no means succeeded in proving more than a harassing measure. It was estimated that the North Sea barrage would require about 400,000 mines, far more than existed in the world at that time, and far more than all our manufacturing resources could then produce within a reasonable period. I have already made the point, and I cannot make it too frequently, that time is often the essential element in war—and in this case it was of vital importance. Whether a programme is a wise one or not depends not only upon the feasibility of the plan itself, but upon the time and the circumstances in which it is proposed. In the spring of 1917 the situation which we were facing was that the German submarines were destroying Allied shipping at the rate of nearly 800,000 tons a month. The one thing which was certain was that, if this destruction should continue for four or five months, the Allies would be obliged to surrender unconditionally. The pressing problem was to find methods that would check these depredations and that would check them in time. The convoy system was the one naval plan—the point cannot be made too emphatically —which in April and May of 1917 held forth the certainty of immediately accomplishing this result. Other methods of opposing the submarines were developed which magnificently supplemented the convoy; but the convoy, at least in the spring and summer of 1917, was the one sure method of salvation for the Allied cause. To have started the North Sea barrage in the spring and summer of 1917 would have meant abandoning the convoy system; and this would have been sheer madness.

Thus in 1917 the North Sea barrage was not an answer to the popular proposal " to dig the Germans out of their holes like rats." We did not have a mine which could be laid in such deep waters in sufficient numbers to have formed any barrier at all; and even if we had possessed one, the construction of the barrage would have demanded such an enormous number that they could not have been manufactured in time to finish the barrage until late in the year 1918. Presently the situation began to change. The principal fact which made possible this great enterprise was the invention of an entirely new type of mine. The old mine consisted of a huge steel globe, filled with high explosive, which could be fired only by contact. That is, it was necessary for the surface of a ship, such as a submarine, to strike against the surface of the mine, and in this way start the mechanism which ignited the explosive charge. The fact that this immediate contact was essential enormously increased the difficulty of successfully mining waters that range in depth from 400 to 900 feet. If the mines were laid anywhere near the surface, the submarine, merely by diving beneath them, could avoid all danger; if they were laid any considerable depth, it could sail with complete safety above them. Thus, if such a mine were to be used at all, we should have had to plant several layers, one under the other, down to a depth of about 250 feet, so that the submarine, at number of mines as to render the whole project impossible. We Americans may take pride in the fact that it was an American who invented an entirely new type of mine and therefore solved this difficulty. In the summer of 1917 Mr. Ralph C. Browne, an electrical engineer of Salem, Mass., offered a submarine gun for the consideration of Commander S. P. Fullinwider, U.S.N., who was then in charge of the mining section of the Bureau of Ordnance. As a submarine gun this invention did not seem to offer many chances of success, but Commander Fullinwider realized that it comprised a firing device of excellent promise. The Bureau of Ordnance, assisted by Mr. Browne, spent the summer and autumn experimenting with this contrivance and perfecting it ; the English mining officers who had been sent to America to co-operate with our navy expressed great enthusiasm over it ; and some time about the beginning of August, 1917, the Bureau of Ordnance came to the conclusion that it was a demonstrated success. The details of Mr. Browne's invention are too intricate for description in this place, but its main point is comprehensible enough. Its great advantage was that it was not necessary for the submarine to strike the mine in order to produce the desired explosion. The mine could be located at any depth and from it a long " antenna," a thin copper cable, reached up to within a few feet of the surface, where it was supported in that position by a small metal buoy. Any metallic substance, such as the hull of a submarine, simply by striking this antenna at any point, would produce an electric current, which, instantaneously transmitted to the mine, would cause this mine to explode. The great advantage of this device is at once apparent. Only about one fourth the number of mines required under the old conditions would now be necessary. The Mining Section estimated that 100,000 mines would form a barrier that would be extremely dangerous to submarines passing over it or through it, whereas, under the old conditions, about 400,000 would have been required. This implies more than a mere saving in manufacturing resources ; it meant that we should need a proportionately smaller number of mine-laying ships, crews, officers, bases, and supplies—all those things which are seldom considered by the amateur in warfare, but which are as essential to its prosecution as the more spectacular details.

I wish to emphasize the fact that, in laying such a barrage, it was not our object to make an absolute barrier to the passage of submarines. 'To have done this we should have needed such a great number of mines that the operation would have been impossible. Nor would such an absolute barrier have been necessary to success ; a field that could be depended upon to destroy one-fourth or one-fifth of the submarines that attempted the passage would have represented complete success. No enemy could stand such losses as these ; and the *moral* of no crew could have lasted long under such conditions.

Another circumstance which made the barrage a feasible enterprise was that by the last of the year 1917 it was realized that the submarine had ceased to be a decisive factor in the war. It still remained a serious embarrassment, and every measure which could possibly thwart it should be adopted. But the writings of German officers which have been published since the war make it apparent that they themselves realized early in 1918 that they would have to place their hopes of victory on something else besides the submarine. The convoy system and the other methods of fighting under-water craft which I have already described had caused a great decrease in sinkings. In April of 1917 the losses were nearly 900,000 tons ; in November of the same year they were less than 300,000 tons.[1] Meanwhile, the construction of merchant shipping, largely a result of the tremendous expansion of American shipbuilding facilities, was increasing at a tremendous rate. A diagram of these, the two essential factors in the submarine campaign, disclosed such a rapidly rising curve of new shipping, and such a rapidly falling curve of sinkings, that the time could be easily foreseen when the net amount of Allied shipping, after the submarines had done their worst, would show a promising increase. But, as stated above, the submarines were still a distinct menace ; they were still causing serious losses ; and it was therefore very important that we should leave no stone unturned toward demonstrating beyond a shadow of doubt that warfare as conducted by these craft could be entirely put down. The more successfully we

---

[1] Complete statistics of shipping losses, new ship construction for 1917 and 1918, will be found in Appendices VIII and IX.

demonstrated this fact and the more energetically we prosecuted every form of opposition, the earlier would the enemy's general *moral* break down and victory be assured. In war, where human lives as well as national interests are at stake, no thought whatever can be given to expense. It is impossible to place a value on human life. Therefore, on November 2, 1917, the so-called " Northern Barrage " project was officially adopted by both the American and the British Governments. When I say that the proposed mine-field was as long as the distance from Washington to New York, some idea of its magnitude may be obtained. Nothing like it had ever been attempted before. The combined operations involved a mass of detail which the lay mind can hardly comprehend. The cost—$40,000,000—is perhaps not an astonishing figure in the statistics of this war, but it gives some conception of the size of the undertaking.

II

During the two years preceding the war Captain Reginald R. Belknap commanded the mine-laying squadron of the Atlantic fleet. Although his force was small, consisting principally of two antiquated warships, the *Baltimore* and the *San Francisco*, Captain Belknap had performed his duties conscientiously and ably, and his little squadron therefore gave us an excellent foundation on which to build. Before the European War the business of mine-laying had been unpopular in the American navy as well as in the British ; such an occupation, as Sir Eric Geddes once said, had been regarded as something like that of " rat catching " ; as hostilities went on, however, and the mine developed great value as an anti-submarine weapon, this branch of the service began to receive more respectful attention. Captain Belknap's work not only provided the nucleus out of which the great American mine force was developed, but he was chiefly responsible for organizing this force. The " active front " of our mine-laying squadron was found in the North Sea ; but the sources of supply lay in a dozen shipyards and several hundred manufacturing plants in the United States.

We began this work with practically nothing ; we had to obtain ships and transform them into mine-layers ; to enlist and to train their crews ; to manufacture at least 100,000 mines ; to create bases both in the United States and Scotland ; to transport all of our supplies more than 3,000 miles of wintry sea, part of the course lying in the submarine zone ; and we had to do all this before the real business of planting could begin.   The fact that the Navy made contracts for 100,000 of these new mines before it had had the opportunity of thoroughly testing the design under service conditions shows the great faith of the Navy Department in this new invention.   More than 500 contractors and sub-contractors, located in places as far west as the Mississippi River, undertook the work of filling this huge order.   Wire-rope mills, steel factories, foundries, machine shops, electrical works, and even candy makers, engaged in this great operation ; all had their troubles with labour unions, with the railroads, and with the weather —that was the terrible winter of 1917–18 ; but in a few months trainloads of mine cases—great globes of steel— and other essential parts began to arrive at Norfolk, Virginia.   This port was the place where the mine parts were loaded on ships and sent abroad.   The plant which was ultimately constructed at this point was able to handle 1,000 mines a day ; the industry was not a popular one in the neighbourhood, particularly after the Halifax explosion had proved the destructive powers of the materials in which it dealt.   In a few months this establishment had handled 25,000,000 pounds of TNT.   The explosive was melted in steel kettles until it reached about the density of hasty pudding ; with the aid of automatic devices it was then poured into the mine cases, 300 pounds to a case, and thence moved on a mechanical conveyor to the end of the pier.   Twenty-four cargo vessels, for the most part taken from the Great Lakes, carried these cargoes to the western coast of Scotland.   Beginning in February, 1918, two or three of these ships sailed every eight days from Norfolk, armed against submarines and manned by naval crews.   The fact that these vessels were slow made them an easy prey for the under-water enemy ; one indeed was sunk, with the loss of forty-one men ; regrettable as was this mishap, it represented the only serious loss of the whole expedition.

The other vital points were Newport, Rhode Island, where the six mine-layers were assembled ; and Fort William and Kyle of Lochalsh on the western coast of Scotland, which were the disembarking points for the ships transporting the explosives. Captain Belknap's men were very proud of their mine-layers, and in many details they represented an improvement over anything which had been hitherto employed in such a service. At this point I wish to express my very great appreciation of the loyal and devoted services rendered by Captain Belknap. An organizer of rare ability, this officer deserves well of the nation for the conspicuous part which he played in the development of the North Sea Mine Barrage from start to finish. Originally, these mine-layers had been coastwise vessels ; two of them were the *Bunker Hill* and the *Massachusetts*, which for years had been " outside line " boats, running from New York to Boston ; all had dropped the names which had served them in civil life and were rechristened for the most part with names which eloquently testified to their American origin—*Canonicus, Shawmut, Quinnebaug, Housatonic, Saranac, Roanoke, Aroostook,* and *Canandaigua.* These changes in names were entirely suitable, for by the time our forces had completed their alterations the ships bore few resemblances to their former state. The cabins and saloons had been gutted, leaving the hulls little more than empty shells ; three decks for carrying mines had been installed ; on all these decks little railroad tracks had been built on which the mines could be rolled along the lower decks to the elevators and along the upper mine deck to the stern and dropped into the sea. Particularly novel details, something entirely new in mine-layers, were the elevators, the purpose of which was to bring the mines rapidly from the lower decks to the launching track. So rapidly did the work progress, and so well were the crews trained, that in May, 1918, the first of these ten ships weighed anchor and started for their destination in Scotland. Already our navy had selected as bases the ports of Inverness and Invergordon, on Moray Firth, harbours which were reasonably near the waters in which the mines were to be laid. From Invergordon the Highland Railway crosses Scotland to Lochalsh, and from Inverness the Caledonian Canal runs to Fort William. These two transportation lines—the Highland Railway and the Caledonian Canal—served as connecting links in our communications. If we wish a complete picture of our operation, we must call to mind first the hundreds of factories in all parts of our country, working day and night, making the numerous parts of these instruments of destruction and their attendant mechanisms ; then hundreds of freight cars carrying them to the assembling plant at Norfolk, Virginia ; then another small army of workmen at this point mixing their pasty explosive, heating it to a boiling point, and pouring the concoction into the spherical steel cases ; then other groups of men moving the partially prepared mines to the docks and loading them on the cargo ships ; then these ships quietly putting to sea, and, after a voyage of ten days or two weeks, as quietly slipping into the Scottish towns of Fort William and Kyle ; then trains of freight cars and canal boats taking the cargoes across Scotland to Inverness and Invergordon, where the mines were completed and placed in the immense storehouses at the bases and loaded on the mine-layers as the necessity arose. Thus, when the whole organization was once established on a working basis, we had uninterrupted communications and a continuous flow of mines from the American factories to the stormy waters of the North Sea.

The towns in which our officers and men found themselves in late May, 1918, are among the most famous in Scottish history and legend. Almost every foot of land is associated with memories of Macbeth, Mary Queen of Scots, Cromwell, and the Pretender. " The national anthem woke me," says Captain Belknap, describing his first morning at his new Scottish base. " I arose and looked out. What a glorious sight ! Green slopes in all freshness, radiant with broom and yellow gorse ; the rocky shore mirrored in the Firth, which stretched, smooth and cool, wide away to the east and south ; and, in the distance, snow-capped Ben Wyvis. Lying off the entrance to Munlochy Bay, we had a view along the sloping shores into the interior of Black Isle, of noted fertility. Farther out were Avoch, a whitewashed fishing village, and the ancient town of Fortrose, with its ruined twelfth-century cathedral. Across the Firth lay Culloden House, where Bonnie Prince Charlie slept before the battle. Substantial, but softened in outline by the morning haze, the Royal Burgh of Inverness covered the banks and heights along the Ness River, gleaming in the bright sunshine. And how peaceful everywhere ! The *Canandaigua* and the *Sonoma* lay near by, the *Canonicus* farther out, but no movement, no signal, no beat of the engine, no throbbing pumps." The reception which the natives gave our men was as delightful as the natural beauty of the location. For miles around the Scots turned out to make things pleasant for their Yankee guests. The American naval forces stationed at the mining bases in those two towns numbered about 3,000 officers and men, and the task of providing relaxations, in the heart of the Highlands, far removed from theatres and moving-picture houses, would have been a serious one had it not been for the cordial co-operation of the people. The spirit manifested during our entire stay was evidenced on the Fourth of July, when all the shops and business places closed in honour of American Independence Day and the whole community for miles around joined our sailors in the celebration. The officers spent such periods of relaxation as were permitted them on the excellent golf links and tennis courts in the adjoining country ; dances were provided for the men, almost every evening, the Scottish lassies showing great adaptability in learning the American steps. Amateur theatricals, in which both the men from the warships and the Scottish girls took part, cheered many a crew after its return from the mine-fields. Baseball was introduced for the first time into the country of William Wallace and Robert Burns. Great crowds gathered to witness the matches between the several ships ; the Scots quickly learned the fine points and really developed into " fans," while the small boys of Inverness and Invergordon were soon playing the game with as much enthusiasm and cleverness as our own youngsters at home. In general, the behaviour of our men was excellent and made the most favourable impression.

These two mine-assembly bases at Inverness and Invergordon will ever remain a monumental tribute to the loyal and energetic devotion to duty of Captain Orin G. Murfin, U.S. Navy, who designed and built them ; originally the bases were intended to handle 12,000 mines, but in reality Captain Murfin successfully handled as many as 20,000 at

one time. It was here also that each secret firing device
was assembled and installed, very largely by reserve personnel. As many as **1,200** mines were assembled in one
day, which speaks very eloquently for the foresight with
which Captain Murfin planned his bases.

III

But of course baseball and dancing were not the serious
business in hand ; these Americans had come this long
distance to do their part in laying the mighty barrage which
was to add one more serious obstacle to the illegal German
submarine campaign. Though the operation was a joint
one of the American and British navies, our part was
much the larger. The proposal was to construct this
explosive impediment from the Orkney Islands to the
coast of Norway, in the vicinity of Udsire Light, a distance
of about 230 nautical miles. Of this great area about 150
miles, extending from the Orkneys to 3 degrees east longitude, was the American field, and the eastern section,
which extended fifty nautical miles to Norway, was taken
over by the British. Since an operation of this magnitude required the supervision of an officer of high rank,
Rear-Admiral Joseph Strauss, who had extended experience in the ordnance field of the navy, came over in March,
1918, and took command. The British commander was
Rear-Admiral Clinton-Baker, R.N.

The mines were laid in a series of thirteen expeditions, or
" excursions," as our men somewhat cheerfully called them.
The ten mine-layers participated in each " excursion," all
ten together laying about 5,400 mines at every trip. Each
trip to the field of action was practically a duplicate of the
others ; a description of one will, therefore, serve for all.
After days, and sometimes after weeks of preparation the
squadron, usually on a dark and misty night, showing no
lights or signals, would weigh anchor, slip by the rocky
palisades of Moray Firth, and stealthily creep out to sea.
As the ships passed through the nets and other obstructions
and reached open waters, the speed increased, the gunners
took their stations at their batteries, and suddenly from a
dark horizon came a glow of low, rapidly moving vessels ;

18

these were the British destroyers from the Grand Fleet which had been sent to escort the expedition and protect it from submarines. The absolute silence of the whole proceeding was impressive ; not one of the destroyers showed a signal or a light; not one of the mine-layers gave the slightest sign of recognition ; all these details had been arranged in advance, and everything now worked with complete precision. The swishing of the water on the sides and the slow churning of the propellers were the only sounds that could possibly betray the ships to their hidden enemies. After the ships had steamed a few more miles the dawn began to break ; and now a still more inspiring sight met our men. A squadron of battleships, with scout cruisers and destroyers, suddenly appeared over the horizon. This fine force likewise swept on, apparently paying not the slightest attention to our vessels. They steamed steadily southward, and in an hour or so had entirely disappeared. The observer would hardly have guessed that this squadron from Admiral Beatty's fleet at Scapa Flow had anything to do with the American and British mine-layers. Its business, however, was to establish a wall of steel and shotted guns between these forces and the German battle fleet at Kiel. At one time it was believed that the mine forces on the northern barrage would prove a tempting bait to the German dreadnoughts ; and that, indeed, it might induce the enemy to risk a second general engagement on the high seas. At any rate, a fleet of converted excursion steamers, laying mines in the North Sea, could hardly be left exposed to the attacks of German raiders ; our men had the satisfaction of knowing that while engaged in their engrossing if unenviable task a squadron of British or American battleships—for Admiral Rodman's forces took their regular turn in acting as a " screen " in these excursions— was standing a considerable distance to the south, prepared to make things lively for any German surface vessels which attempted to interfere with the operation.

Now in the open seas the ten mine-layers formed in two columns, abreast of each other and five hundred yards apart, and started for the waters of the barrage. Twelve destroyers surrounded them, on the lookout for submarines, for the ships were now in the track of the U-boats bound for their hunting ground or returning to their home ports. At a flash from the flagship all slackened speed, and put out

their paravanes—those under-water outrigger affairs which
protected the ships from mines ; for it was not at all
unlikely that the Germans would place some of their own
mines in this field, for the benefit of the barrage builders.
This operation took only a few minutes ; then another
flash, and the squadron again increased its speed. It
steamed the distance across the North Sea to Udsire Light,
then turned west again and headed for that mathematical
spot on the ocean which was known as the " start point "—
the place, that is, where the mine-laying was to begin.   In
carrying out all these manœuvres—sighting the light on
the Norwegian coast—the commander was thinking,
not only of the present, but of the future ; for the time
would come, after the war had ended, when it would
be necessary to remove all these mines, and it was therefore wise to " fix " them as accurately as possible in
reference to landmarks, so as to know where to look for
them.   All this time the men were at their stations,
examining the mines to see that everything was ready,
testing the laying mechanisms, and mentally rehearsing
their duties.   At about four o'clock an important signal
came from the flagship :

" Have everything ready, for the squadron will reach
' start point ' in an hour and mine-laying will begin."

Up to this time the ships were sailing in two columns ;
when they came within seven miles of " start point,"
another signal was broken out ; the ships all wheeled like a
company of soldiers, each turning sharply to the right, so
that in a few minutes, instead of two columns, we had eight
ships in line abreast, with the remaining two, also in line
abreast, sailing ahead of them.   This splendid array,
keeping perfect position, approached the starting point like
a line of racehorses passing under the wire.   Not a ship was
off this line by so much as a quarter length ; the whole
atmosphere was one of eagerness ; the officers all had their
eyes fixed upon the stern of the flagship, for the glimpse of
the red flag which would be the signal to begin.   Suddenly
the flag was hauled down, indicating :

" First mine over."

If you had been following one of these ships, you would
probably have been surprised at the apparent simplicity of
the task.   The vessel was going at its full speed ; at
intervals of a few seconds a huge black object, about five

feet high, would be observed gliding toward the stern ; at this point it would pause for a second or two, as though suspended in air ; it would then give a mighty lurch, fall head first into the water, sending up a great splash, and then sink beneath the waves.   By the time the disturbance was over the ship would have advanced a considerable distance ; then, in a few seconds, another black object would roll toward the stern, make a similar plunge, and disappear. You might have followed the same ship for two or three hours, watching these mines fall overboard at intervals of about fifteen seconds.   There were four planters, each of which could and did on several trips lay about 860 mines in three hours and thirty-five minutes, in a single line about forty-four miles long.   These were the *Canandaigua*, the *Canonicus*, the *Housatonic*, and the *Roanoke.*   Occasionally the monotony of this procedure would be enlivened by a terrible explosion, a great geyser of water rising where a mine had only recently disappeared ; this meant that the " egg," as the sailors called it, had gone off spontaneously, without the assistance of any external contact ; such accidents were part of the game, the records showing that about 4 per cent. of all the mines indulged in such initial premature explosions.   For the most part, however, nothing happened to disturb the steady mechanical routine.   The mines went over with such regularity that, to an observer, the whole proceeding seemed hardly the work of human agency.   Yet every detail had been arranged months before in the United States ; the mines fell into the sea in accordance with a time-table which had been prepared in Newport before the vessels started for Scotland.   Every man on the ship had a particular duty to perform and each performed it in the way in which he had been schooled under the direction of Captain Belknap.

The spherical mine case, which contains the explosive charge and the mechanism for igniting it, is only a part of the contrivance.   While at rest on board the ship this case stands upon a box-like affair, about two feet square, known as the anchor ; this anchor sinks to the bottom after launching and it contains an elaborate arrangement for maintaining the mine at any desired depth beneath the surface. The bottom of the " anchor " has four wheels, on which it runs along the little railroad track on the launching deck to the jumping-off place at the stern.   All along these railroad tracks the mines were stationed **one** back **of** another ; as one went overboard, they would **all** advance a peg, a mine coming up from below on an elevator to fill up the vacant space at the end of the procession. It took a crew of hard-working, begrimed, and sweaty men **to** keep these mines moving and going over the stern at the regularly appointed intervals. After three **or** four hours had been spent in this way and the ships had started back to their base, the decks would sometimes be covered with the sleeping figures of these exhausted men. It would be impossible to speak too appreciatively of the spirit they displayed ; in the whole summer there was not a single mishap of any importance. The men all felt that they were engaged in a task which had never been accomplished before, and their exhilaration increased with almost every mine that was laid. " Nails in the coffin of the Kaiser," the men called these grim instruments of vengeance.

IV

I have described one of these thirteen summer excursions, and the description given could be applied to all the rest. Once or twice the periscope of a submarine was sighted—without any disastrous results—but in the main this business of mine-laying was uneventful. Just what was accomplished the chart makes clear. In the summer and autumn months of 1918 the American forces laid 56,571 mines and the British 13,546. The operation was to have been a continuous one ; had the war gone on for two years we should probably have laid several hundred thousand ; Admiral Strauss's forces kept at the thing steadily up to the time of the armistice ; they had become so expert and the barrage was producing such excellent results that we had plans nearly completed for building another at the Strait of Otranto, which would have completely closed the Adriatic Sea. Besides this undertaking the American mine-layer *Baltimore* laid a mine-field in the North Irish Channel, the narrow waters which separate Scotland and Ireland ; two German submarines which soon afterward attempted this passage were blown to pieces, and after this the mine-field **was** given a wide berth.

Just what the North Sea barrage accomplished, in the actual destruction of submarines, will never be definitely known. We have information that four certainly were destroyed, and in all probability six and possibly eight ; yet these results doubtless measure only a small part of the German losses. In the majority of cases the Germans had little or no evidence of sunken submarines. The destroyers, subchasers, and other patrol boats were usually able to obtain some evidences of injury inflicted ; they could often see their quarry, or the disturbances which it made on the surface ; they could pursue and attack it, and the resultant oil patches, wreckage, and German prisoners—and sometimes the recovered submarine itself or its location on the bottom—would tell the story either of damage or destruction. But the disconcerting thing about the North Sea barrage, from the viewpoint of the Germans, was that it could do its work so secretly that no one, friend or enemy, would necessarily know a thing about it. A German submarine simply left its home port ; attempting to cross the barrage, perhaps at night, it would strike one of these mines, or its antenna ; an explosion would crumple it up like so much paper ; with its crew it would sink to the bottom ; and not a soul, perhaps not even the crew itself, would ever know what had happened to it. It would in truth be a case of " sinking without a trace "—though an entirely legitimate one under the rules of warfare. The German records disclosed anywhere from forty to fifty submarines sunk which did not appear in the records of the Allies ; how these were destroyed not a soul knows, or ever will know. They simply left their German ports and were never heard of again. That many of them fell victims to mines, and some of them to the mines of our barrage, is an entirely justifiable assumption. That probably even a larger number of U-boats were injured is also true. A German submarine captain, after the surrender at Scapa Flow, said that he personally knew of three submarines, including his own, which had been so badly injured at the barrage that they had been compelled to limp back to their German ports.

The results other than the sinking of submarines were exceedingly important in bringing the war to an end. It was the failure of the submarine campaign which defeated the German hopes and forced their surrender ; and in this

defeat the barrage was an important element. That submarines frequently crossed it is true ; there was no expectation, when the enterprise was started, that it would absolutely shut the U-boats in the North Sea ; but its influence
in breaking down the German *moral* must have been great.
To understand this, just place yourself for a moment in the
position of a submarine crew. The width of this barrage
ranged from fifteen to thirty-five miles ; it took from one to
three hours for a submarine to cross this area on the surface
and from two to six hours under the surface. Not every
square foot, it is true, had been mined ; there were certain
gaps caused by the spontaneous explosions to which I have
referred ; but nobody knew where these openings were, or
where a single mine was located. The officers and crews
knew only that at any moment an explosion might send
them to eternity. A strain of this sort is serious enough
if it lasts only a few minutes ; imagine being kept in this
state of mind anywhere from one to six hours ! Submarine
prisoners constantly told us how they dreaded the mines ;
going through such a field, I suppose, was about the most
disagreeable experience in this nerve-racking service. Our
North Sea barrage began to show results almost immediately
after our first planting. The German officers evidently
kept informed of our progress and had a general idea of the
territory which had been covered. For a considerable time
a passage-way, sixty miles wide, was kept open for the Grand
Fleet just east of the Orkney Islands ; the result was that
the submarines, which had hitherto usually skirted the
Norwegian coast, now changed their route, and attempted
to slip through the western passage-way—a course that
enabled them to avoid the mine-field. When the entire
distance from the Orkneys to Norway had been mined,
however, it became impossible to " run around the end."
The Germans were now obliged to sail boldly into this
explosive field, taking their chances of hitting a mine.
Stories of this barrage were circulated all over Germany ;
sailors who had been in contact with it related their experiences to their fellows ; and the result was extremely
demoralizing to the German submarine flotilla. The North
Sea barrage was probably a contributory cause of the
mutiny which demoralized the German fleet in the autumn
of 1918.

I think I am therefore justified in saying that this enterprise was a strong factor in overcoming the submarine menace, though the success of the convoy system had already brought the end in sight, and had thus made it practicable to assign, without danger of defeat, the tonnage necessary to lay the barrage and maintain and augment it as long as might be necessary. The Germans saw the barrage not only as it was in the autumn of 1918, but as it would be a few months or a year hence. We had started a steady stream of mines from hundreds of factories in the United States to our Scottish bases ; these establishments were constantly increasing production, and there was practically no limit to their possible output. We had developed a mine-laying organization which was admittedly better than any that had been hitherto known ; and this branch of the service we could now enlarge indefinitely. In time we could have planted this area so densely with explosives that it would have been madness for any submarines even to attempt a passage. To be sure, the Pentland Firth, between the Orkneys and Scotland, was always open, and could not be mined on account of its : wift tides, but besides being a dangerous passage at best it was constantly patrolled to make it still more dangerous.

The loyal devotion to duty and the skilful seamanship which our officers displayed in this great enterprise were not only thoroughly in keeping with the highest traditions of the navy, but really established new standards to guide and inspire those who will follow us. These gallant officers who actually laid the mines are entitled to the nation's gratitude, and I take great pleasure in commending the work of Captain H. V. Butler, commanding the flagship *San Francisco* ; Captain J. Harvey Tomb, commanding the *Aroostook* ; Captain A. W. Marshall, commanding the *Baltimore* ; Commander W. H. Reynolds, commanding the *Canandaigua* ; Captain T. L. Johnson, commanding the *Canonicus*; Captain J. W. Greenslade, commanding the *Housatonic*; Commander D. Pratt Mannix, commanding the *Quinnebaug*; Captain C. D. Stearns, commanding the *Roanoke* ; Captain Sinclair Gannon, commanding the *Saranac*; and Captain W. T. Cluverius, commanding the *Shawmut.*

This splendid squadron, of which the flagship was the *San Francisco,* was organized by Captain R. R. Belknap and, by order of the Secretary of the Navy, was placed under his direct command ; and he was therefore responsible for all preparations, tactics, general instructions, special instructions for each mine-laying " excursion," the intricate navigation required, and in fact all arrangements necessary for the successful planting of the mines in their assigned positions.

CHAPTER X

IT was in the summer of 1918 that the Germans made their only attempt at what might be called an offensive against their American enemies. Between the beginning of May and the end of October, 1918, five German submarines crossed the Atlantic and torpedoed a few ships on our coast. That submarines could make this long journey had long been known. Singularly enough, however, the impression still prevails in this country that the German U-boats were the first to accomplish the feat. In the early autumn of 1916 the *U-53*—commanded by that submarine officer, Hans Rose, who has been previously mentioned in these pages—crossed the Atlantic, dropped in for a call at Newport, R.I., and, on the way back, sank a few merchant vessels off Nantucket. A few months previous the so-called merchant submarine *Deutschland* had made its trip to Newport News. The Teutonic press, and even some Germanophiles in this country, hailed these achievements as marking a glorious page in the record of the German navy. Doubtless the real purpose was to show the American people how easily these destructive vessels could cross the Atlantic ; and to impress upon their minds the fate which awaited them in case they maintained their rights against the Prussian bully. As a matter of fact, it had been proved, long before the *Deutschland* or the *U-53* had made their voyages, that submarines could cross the Atlantic. In 1915, not one but ten submarines had gone from North America to Europe under their own power. Admiral Sir John Fisher tells about this expedition in his recently published memoirs. In 1914, the British Admiralty had contracted for submarines with Charles M. Schwab, president of the Bethlehem Steel Company. As international law prohibited the construction of war vessels by a nation in wartime for the use of a belligerent with which it was at peace, the parts of ten submarines were sent to Canada, where they were put together. These submarines then crossed the Atlantic under their own power, and were sent from British ports to the Dardanelles, where they succeeded in driving Turkish and German shipping out of the Sea of Marmora.   Thus a crossing of the Atlantic by American-built submarines manned by British crews had been accomplished before the Germans made their voyages.   It was therefore not necessary for the two German submarines to cross the Atlantic to prove that the thing could be done ; but the Germans doubtless believed that this demonstration of their ability to operate on the American coast would serve as a warning to the American people.

We were never at all deceived as to what would be the purpose of such a visit after our entrance into the war.   In the early part of 1917 the Allies believed that a few German U-boats might assail our coast, and I so informed the Navy Department at Washington.   My cables and letters of 1917 explained fully the reasons why Germany might indulge in such a gesture.   Strategically, as these despatches make clear, such attacks would have no great military value.   To have sent a sufficient number of submarines to do any considerable damage on the American coast would have been a great mistake.   Germany's one chance of winning the war with the submarine weapon was to destroy shipping to such an extent that the communications of the Allies with the outside world, and especially with the United States, would be cut.   The only places where the submarine warfare could be conducted with some chance of success were the ocean passage routes which lead to European ports, especially in that area south and south-west of Ireland in which were focussed the trade routes for ships sailing from all parts of the world and destined for British and French ports.   With the number of submarines available, the Germans could keep enough of their U-boats at work in these areas to destroy a large number of merchant ships.   Germany thus needed to concentrate all of her available submarines at these points ; she had an inadequate number for her purpose ; to send any considerable force three thousand miles across the Atlantic would simply weaken her efforts in the real scene of warfare and would make her submarine campaign a failure.   The cruises of submarines on the

American coast would have been very much longer and would have been a much more serious strain on the submarines than were the shorter cruises in the inshore waters of Europe. As has already been explained, the submarine did not differ from other craft in its need for constant repairs and careful upkeep, except that perhaps it was a more delicate instrument of warfare than any other naval craft, and that it would require longer and more frequent periods of overhaul. Any operations carried out three thousand miles from their bases, where alone supplies, spare parts, and repair facilities were available, would have soon reduced the submarine campaign to comparative uselessness ; each voyage would have resulted in sinking a relatively small amount of shipping ; a great number of submarines would be out of commission at all times for repairs, or would be lost through accidents. The Germans had no submarine bases in American waters and could establish none. Possibly, as the newspaper writer has pointed out, they might have seized a deserted island off the coast of Maine or in the Caribbean, and cached there a reservoir of fuel and food ; unless, however, they could also have created at these places adequate facilities for repairing submarines or supplying them with torpedoes and ammunition, such a place would not have served the purpose of a base at all. Comparatively few of the German submarines could have made the cruise to the American coast and operated successfully there so far away from their bases for any considerable time. In the time spent in such an enterprise, the same submarine could make three or four trips in the waters about the British Isles, or off the coast of France, and could sink four or five times the tonnage which could be destroyed in the cruise on the Atlantic coast. In the eastern Atlantic, the submarine could seek its victims in an area comprising a comparatively few square miles, at points where shipping was so dense that a submarine had only to take a station and lie in wait, and be certain, within a short time, of encountering valuable ships which it could attack successfully with its torpedoes. If the U-boats should be sent to America, on the other hand, they would have to patrol up and down three thousand miles of coast, looking for victims ; and even when they found them the ships that they could sink would usually be those engaged in the coastwise traffic, which were of infinitely less military importance than the transports which were carrying food, munitions, and supplies to the Allies and which were being sunk in the eastern Atlantic.

Anything resembling an attack in force on American harbours was therefore improbable. Yet it seemed likely from the first that the Germans would send an occasional submarine into our waters, as a measure of propaganda rather than for the direct military result that would be achieved. American destroyers and other vessels were essential to the success of the whole anti-submarine campaign of the Allies. The sooner they could all be sent into the critical European waters the sooner the German campaign of terrorism would end. If these destroyers, or any considerable part of them, could be kept indefinitely in American waters, the Germans might win the war. Any manœuvre which would have as its result the keeping of these American vessels, so indispensable to the Allies, out of the field of active warfare, would thus be more than justified and, indeed, would indicate the highest wisdom on the part of the German navy. The Napoleonic principle of dividing your enemy's forces is just as valuable in naval as in land warfare. For many years Admiral Mahan had been instructing American naval officers that the first rule in warfare is not to divide your fighting forces, but always to keep them together, so as to bring the whole weight at a given moment against your adversary. Two of the fundamental principles of the science of warfare, on land and sea alike, are contained in the maxims : Keep your own forces concentrated, and always endeavour to divide those of the enemy. Undoubtedly, the best method which Germany could use to keep our destroyers in our own waters would be to make the American people believe that their lives and property were in danger ; they might accomplish this by sending a submarine to attack our shipping off New York and Boston and other Atlantic seaports, and possibly even to bombard our harbours. The Germans doubtless believed that they might create such alarm and arouse such public clamour in the United States that our destroyers and other anti-submarine craft would be kept over here by the Navy Department, in response to the popular agitation to protect our own coast. This is the reason why American headquarters in London, and the Allied admiralties, expected such a visitation. The Germans obviously endeavoured to create the impression that such an attack was likely to occur at any time. This was part of their war propaganda. The press was full of reports that such attacks were about to be made. German agents were continually circulating these reports.

Of course it was clear from the first, to the heads of the Allied navies and to all naval authorities who were informed about the actual conditions, that these attacks by German submarines on the American coast would be in the nature of raids for moral effect only. It was also quite clear from the first, as I pointed out in my despatches to the Navy Department, that the best place to defend our coast was in the critical submarine areas in the European Atlantic, through which the submarines had to pass in setting out for our coast, and in which alone they could have any hope of succeeding in the military object of the undersea campaign. It was not necessary to keep our destroyers in American waters, patrolling the vast expanse of our three thousand miles of coastline, in a futile effort to find and destroy such enemy submarines as might operate on the American coast. So long as these attacks were only sporadic—and carried out by the type of submarine which used its guns almost exclusively in sinking ships, and which selected for its victims unarmed and unprotected ships—destroyers and other anti-submarine craft would be of no possible use on the Atlantic coast. The submarine could see these craft from a much greater distance than it could itself be seen by them ; and by diving and sailing submerged it could easily avoid them and sink its victims without ever being sighted or attacked by our own patrols, however numerous they might have been. Even in the narrow waters of the English Channel, up to the very end of the war, submarines were successfully attacking small merchant craft by gunfire, although the density of patrol craft in this area was naturally a thousand times greater than we could ever have provided for the vast expanse of our own coast. Consequently, so long as the submarine attacks on the American coast were only sporadic, it was absolutely futile to maintain patrol craft in those waters, as this could not provide any adequate defence against such scattered demonstrations. If, on the other hand, the Germans had ever decided to commit the military mistake of concentrating a considerable number of submarines off our Atlantic ports, we could always have countered such a step by sending back from the war zone an adequate number of craft to protect convoys in and out of the Atlantic ports, in the same manner that convoys were protected in the submarine danger zone in European waters.   This is a fact which even many naval men did not seem to grasp.   Yet I have already explained that we knew practically where every German submarine was at any given time.   We knew whenever one left a German port ;   and we kept track of it day by day until it returned home.   No U-boat ever made a voyage across the Atlantic without our knowledge.   The submarine was a slow traveller, and required a minimum of thirty days for such a trip ;   normally, the time would be much longer, for a submarine on such a long voyage had to economize oil fuel for the return trip and therefore seldom cruised at more than five knots an hour. Our destroyers and anti-submarine craft, on the other hand, could easily cross the Atlantic in ten days and refuel in their home ports.   It is therefore apparent that a flotilla of destroyers stationed in European waters could protect the American coast from submarines almost as successfully as if it were stationed at Hampton Roads or Newport.   Such a flotilla would be of no use at these American stations unless there were submarines attacking shipping off the coast ;   but as soon as the Germans started for America—a fact of which we could always be informed, and of which, as I shall explain, we always were informed—we could send our destroyers in advance of them.   These agile vessels would reach home waters about three weeks before the submarines arrived ;   they would thus have plenty of time to refit and to welcome the uninvited guests.   From any conceivable point of view, therefore, there was no excuse for keeping destroyers on the American side of the Atlantic for " home defence."   Moreover, the fact that we could keep this close track of submarines in itself formed a great protection against them.   I have already explained how we routed convoys entering European waters in such ways that they could sail around the U-boat and thus escape contact.   I think that this simple procedure saved more shipping than any other method.   In the same way we could keep these vessels sailing frm American ports outside of the area in which the submarines were known to be operating in our own waters.

Yet the enemy sent no submarines to our coast in 1917 ;

why they did not do so may seem difficult to understand, for that was just the period when a campaign of this kind might have served their purpose. During this time, however, we had repeated indications that the Germans did not take the American entrance into the war very seriously; moreover, looking forward to conditions after the peace, they perhaps hoped that they might soon be able once again to establish friendly relations. In 1917 they therefore refrained from any acts which might arouse popular hatred against them. We had more than one indication of this attitude. Early in the summer of 1917 we obtained from one of the captured German submarines a set of the orders issued to it by the German Admiralty Staff. Among these was one dated May 8, 1917, in which the submarine commanders were informed that Germany had not declared war upon the United States, and that, until further instructions were received, the submarines were to continue to look upon America and American shipping as neutral. The submarine commanders were especially warned against attacking or committing any overt act against such American war vessels as might be encountered in European waters. The orders explained that no official confirmation had been received by the German Government of the news which had been published in the press that America had declared war, and that, therefore, the Germans, officially, were ignoring our belligerence. From their own standpoint such a policy of endeavouring not to offend America, even after she became an enemy, may have seemed politically wise; from a military point of view, their failure to attempt the submarine demonstration off our coast in 1917 was a great mistake; for when they finally started warfare on our coast, the United States was deeply involved in hostilities, and had already begun the transportation of the great army which produced such decisive results on the Western Front. The time had passed, as experience soon showed, when any demonstration on our coast would disturb the calm of the American people or affect their will to victory.

In late April, 1918, I learned through secret-service channels that one of the large submarines of the *Deutschland* class had left its German base on the 19th of April for a long cruise. On the 1st of May, 1918, I therefore cabled to the Department that there were indications that this sub-

marine was bound for our own coast.   A few days afterward I received more specific information, through the
interception of radio despatches between Germany and the
submarine ; and therefore I cabled the Department, this
time informing them that the submarine was the *U*-151,
that it was now well on its way across the Atlantic, and that
it could be expected to begin operations off the American
coast any time after May 20th.   I gave a complete description of the vessel, the probable nature of her cruise, and
her essential military characteristics.   She carried a supply
of mines, and I therefore invited the attention of the Department to the fact that the favourite areas for laying
mines were those places where the ships stopped to pick
up pilots.   Since at Delaware Bay pilots for large ships
were taken on just south of the Five Fathom Bank Light,
I suggested that it was not unlikely that the *U*-151 would
attempt to lay mines in that vicinity.   Now the fact is
that we knew that the *U*-151 intended to lay mines at this
very place.   We had obtained this piece of information
from the radio which we had intercepted ; as there was a
possibility that our own cable might fall into German hands,
we did not care to give the news in the precise form in which
we had received it, as we did not intend that they should
know that we had means of keeping so accurately informed.
As had been predicted, the *U*-151 proceeded directly to the
vicinity of this Five Fathom Bank off Delaware Bay, laid
her mines, and then, cruising northward up the coast, began
her demonstration on the 25th of May by sinking two small
wooden schooners.   These had no radio apparatus, and it
was not until June 2nd that the Navy Department and the
country received the news that the first submarine was
operating.   On June 29th I informed Washington that
another U-boat was then coming down the west coast of
Ireland, bound for the United States, and that it would
arrive some time after July 15th.   Complete reports of
this vessel were sent from day to day, as it made its slow
progress across the ocean.   On July 6th I cabled that still
another U-boat had started for our coast ; and the progress
of this adventurer, with all details as to its character and
probable area of operations, were also forwarded regularly.
From the end of May until October there was nearly always
one submarine operating off our coast.   The largest number
active at any one time was in August, when for a week or

19

ten days three were more or less active in attacking coastwise vessels. These three operated all the way from Cape Hatteras to Newfoundland, attempting by these tactics to create the impression that dozens of hostile U-boats were preying upon our commerce and threatening our shores. These submarines, however, attacked almost exclusively sailing vessels and small coastwise steamers, rarely, if ever, using torpedoes. A number of mines were laid at different points off our ports, on what the Germans believed to be the traffic routes ; but the information which we had concerning them made it possible to counter successfully their efforts and, from a military point of view, the whole of the submarine operations off our coast can be dismissed as one of the minor incidents of the war, as the Secretary of the Navy described it in his Annual Report. The five submarines sunk in all approximately 110,000 tons of shipping, but the vessels were, for the most part, small and of no great military importance. The only real victory was the destruction of the cruiser *San Diego*, which was sunk by a mine which had been laid by the *U-156* off Fire Island.

CHAPTER XI

THE Allied navies were harrowing the submarines not only under the water and on the surface, but from the air. In the anti-submarine campaign the several forms of aircraft—airplane, seaplane, dirigible, and kite balloon—developed great offensive power. Nor did the fact that our fighters in the heavens made few direct attacks which were successful diminish the importance of their work. The records of the British Admiralty attribute the destruction of five submarines to the British air service ; the French Admiralty gives the American forces credit for destroying one on the French coast. These achievements, compared with the tremendous efforts involved in equipping air stations, may at first look like an inconsiderable return ; yet the fact remains that aircraft were an important element in defeating the German campaign against merchant shipping.

Like the subchaser and the submarine, the seaplane operated most successfully in coastal waters. I have already indicated that one advantage of the convoy system was that it forced the U-boats to seek their victims closer to the shore. In our several forms of aircraft we had still another method of interfering with their operation in such quarters. In order to use these agencies effectively we constructed aircraft stations in large numbers along the coast of France and the British Isles, assigned a certain stretch of coastline to each one of these stations, and kept the indicated area constantly patrolled. The advantages which were possessed by a fleet of aircraft operating at a considerable height above the water are at once apparent. The great speed of seaplanes in itself transformed them into formidable foes. The submarine on the surface could make a maximum of only 16 knots an hour, whereas an airplane made anywhere from 60 to 100 ; it therefore had little difficulty, once it had sighted the under-water boat, in catching up with it and starting hostilities. Its great speed also made it possible for an airplane or dirigible to patrol a much greater area of water than a surface or a sub-surface vessel. An observer located several hundred feet in the heavens could see the submarine much more easily than could his comrades on other craft. If the water were clear he could at once detect it, even though it were submerged ; in any event, merely lifting a man in the air greatly extended his horizon, and made it possible for him to pick up hostile vessels at a much greater distance. Moreover, the airplane had that same advantage upon which I have laid such emphasis in describing the anti-submarine powers of the submarine itself : that is, it was almost invisible to its under-water foe. If the U-boat were lying on the surface, a seaplane or a dirigible was readily seen ; but if it were submerged entirely, or even sailing at periscope depth, the most conspicuous enemy in the heavens was invisible. After our submarines and our aircraft had settled down to their business of extermination, existence for those Germans who were operating in coastal waters became extremely hazardous and nerve-racking ; their chief anxiety was no longer the depth bomb of a destroyer ; they lived every moment in the face of hidden terrors ; they never knew when a torpedo would explode into their vitals, or when an unseen bomb, dropped from the heavens, would fall upon their fragile decks.

I have said that the destructive achievements of aircraft figure only moderately in the statistics of the war ; this was because the greater part of their most valuable work was done in co-operation with war vessels. Aircraft in the Navy performed a service not unlike that which it performed in the Army. We are all familiar with the picture of airplanes sailing over the field of battle, obtaining information which was wirelessed back to their own forces, " spotting " artillery positions, and giving ranges. The seaplanes and dirigibles of the Allied navies performed a similar service on the ocean. To a considerable extent they became the " eyes " of the destroyers and other surface craft, just as the airplanes on the land became the " eyes " of the army. As part of their equipment all the dirigibles had wireless telegraph and wireless telephone ; **as soon as** a submarine was " spotted," the news was immediately flashed broadcast, and every offensive warship which was anywhere in the neighbourhood, as well as the airplane itself, started for the indicated scene. There are several cases in which the sinking of submarines by destroyers was attributed to information wirelessed in this fashion by American aircraft ; and since the air service of the British navy was many times greater than our own, there are many more such " indirect sinkings " credited to the British effort.

The following citation, which I submitted to the Navy Department in recommending Lieutenant John J. Schieffelin for the Distinguished Service Medal, illustrates this co-operation between air and surface craft :

This officer performed many hazardous reconnaissance flights, and on July 9th, 1918, he attacked an enemy submarine with bombs and then directed the British destroyers to the spot, which were successful in seriously damaging the submarine. Again, on July 19th, 1918, Lieutenant Schieffelin dropped bombs on another enemy submarine, and then signalled trawlers to the spot, which delivered a determined attack against the submarine, which attack was considered highly successful and the submarine seriously damaged, if not destroyed. This officer was at all times an example of courageous loyalty.

Besides scouting and " spotting " and bombing, the aerial hunters of the submarine developed great value in escorting convoys. A few dirigibles, located on the flanks of a convoy, protected them almost as effectively as the destroyers themselves ; and even a single airship not infrequently brought a group of merchantmen and troop-ships safely into port. Sometimes the airships operated in this way as auxiliaries to destroyers, while sometimes they operated alone. In applying this mechanism of protection to merchant convoys, we were simply adopting the method which Great Britain had been using for three years in the narrow passages of the English Channel. Much has been said of the skill with which the British navy transported about 20,000,000 souls back and forth between England and France in four years ; and in this great movement seaplanes, dirigibles, and other forms of aircraft played an important part. In the same way this scheme of protection was found valuable with the coastal convoys, particularly with the convoys which sailed from one French port to another, and from British ports to places in Ireland, Holland, or Scandinavia. I have described the dangers in which these ships were involved owing to the fact that the groups were obliged to break up after entering the Channel and the Irish Sea, and thus to proceed singly to their destinations. Aircraft improved this situation to a considerable extent, for they could often go to sea, pick up the ships, and bring them safely home. The circumstance that our seaplanes, perched high in the air, could see the submarine long before they had reached torpedoing distance, and could, if necessary, signal to a destroyer for assistance, made them exceedingly valuable for this kind of work.

Early in 1918, at the request of the British Government, we took over a large seaplane base which had been established by the British at Killingholme, England, a little seacoast town at the mouth of the Humber River. According to the original plan we intended to co-operate from this point with the British in a joint expedition against enemy naval bases, employing for this purpose especially constructed towing lighters, upon which seaplanes were to be towed by destroyers to within a short flying distance of their objectives. Although this project was never carried out, Killingholme, because of its geographical location, became a very important base for seaplanes used in escorting mercantile convoys to and from Scandinavian ports, patrolling mine-fields while on the lookout for enemy submarines and making those all-important reconnaissance flights over the North Sea which were intended to give advanced warning of any activity of the German High Seas Fleet. These flights lasted usually from six to eight hours ; the record was made by Ensign S. C. Kennedy and C. H. Weatherhead, U.S.N., who flew for nine hours continuously on convoy escort duty. For a routine patrol, this compares very favourably indeed with the flight of the now famous trans-Atlantic *NC*-4.

I can no better describe the splendid work of these enthusiastic and courageous young Americans than by quoting a few extracts from a report which was submitted to me by Ensign K. B. Kéyes, of a reconnaissance flight in which he took part, while attached temporarily to a British seaplane station under post-graduate instruction. The picture given by Ensign Keyes is typical of the flights which **our** boys were constantly making :

On June 4, 1918, we received orders to carry out a reconnaissance and hostile aircraft patrol over the North Sea and along the coast of Holland. It was a perfect day for such work, for the visibility was extremely good, with a light wind of fifteen knots and clouds at the high altitude of about eight or ten thousand feet.

Our three machines from Felixstowe rose from the water at twelve o'clock, circled into patrol formation, and proceeded north-east by north along the coast to Yarmouth. Here we were joined by two more planes, but not without some trouble and slight delay because of a broken petrol pipe which was subsequently repaired in the air. We again circled into formation, Capt. Leckie, D.S.O., of Yarmouth, taking his position as leader of the squadron.

At one o'clock the squadron proceeded east, our machine, being in the first division, flew at 1,500 feet and at about half a mile in the rear of Capt. Leckie's machine, but keeping him on our starboard quarter.

We sighted nothing at all until about half-past two, when the Haaks Light Vessel slowly rose on the horizon, but near this mark and considerably more to the south we discovered a large fleet of Dutch fishing smacks. This fleet consisted of more than a hundred smacks.

Ten minutes later we sighted the Dutch coast, where we changed our course more to the north-east. We followed the sandy beaches of the islands of Texel and Vlieland until we came to Terschelling. In following the coast of Vlieland we were close enough to distinguish houses on the inside of the island and even to make out breakers rolling up on the sandy beach.

At Terschelling we proceeded west in accordance with our orders, but soon had to turn back because of Capt. Leckie's machine which had fallen out of formation and come to the water. This machine landed at three fifteen and we continued to circle around it, finding that the trouble was with a badly broken petrol pipe, until about fifteen minutes later, when we sighted five German planes steering west, a direction which would soon bring them upon us.

At this time Capt. Barker had the wheel, Lt. Galvayne was seated beside him, but if we met the opposing forces he was to kneel on the seat with his eyes above the cowl, where he could see all the enemy planes and direct the pilot in which direction to proceed.   I was in the front cockpit with one gun and four hundred rounds of ammunition.   In the stern cockpit the engineer and wireless ratings were to handle three guns.

We at once took battle formation and went forward to meet the enemy, but here we were considerably surprised to find that when we were nearly within range they had turned and were running away from us.   At once we gave chase, but soon found that they were much too fast for us. Our machine had broken out of the formation and, with nose down, had crept slightly ahead of Capt. Leckie, and we being the nearest machine to the enemy, I had the satisfaction of trying out my gun for a number of rounds.   It was quite impossible to tell whether I had registered any hits or not.

Our purpose in chasing these planes was to keep them away from the machine on the water which, if we had not been there, would have been shot to pieces.   Finding that it was useless to follow them, as they could easily keep out of our range, we turned back and very shortly we were again circling around our machine on the water.

It was not long before the enemy again came very close, so we gave chase the second time.   This time, instead of five machines as before, there were only four, and one small scout could be seen flying in the direction of Borkum.

It was the fourth time that we went off in pursuit of the enemy that we suddenly discovered that a large number of hostile planes were proceeding towards us, not in the air with the other four planes but very close to the water. There were ten planes in this first group, but they were joined a few minutes later by five more.

We swung into battle formation and steered for the middle of the group.   When we were nearly within range four planes on the port side and five planes on the starboard side rose to our level of fifteen hundred feet.   Two planes passed directly beneath us firing upward.   Firing was incessant from the beginning and the air seemed blue with tracer smoke.   I gave most of my time to the four planes on our port side, because they were exactly on the same level with us and seemed to be within good range, that is about two hundred yards.   When we had passed each other

I looked around and noticed that Lt. Galvayne was in a stooping position, with head and one arm on his seat, the other arm hanging down as if reaching for something. I had seen him in this position earlier in the day so thought nothing of it. All this I had seen in the fraction of a second, for I had to continue firing. A few minutes later I turned around again and found with a shock that Lt. Galvayne was in the same position. It was then that the first inkling of the truth dawned upon me. By bending lower I discovered that his head was lying in a pool of blood.

From this time on I have no clear idea of just what our manœuvring was, but evidently we put up a running fight steering east, then circled until suddenly I found our machine had been cut off from the formation and we were surrounded by seven enemy seaplanes.

This time we were steering west or more to the south-west. We carried on a running fight for ten miles or so until we drove the seven planes off. During the last few minutes of the fight our engine had been popping altogether too frequently and soon the engineer came forward to tell us that the port engine petrol pipe had broken.

By this time I had laid out Lt. Galvayne in the wireless cockpit, cleaned up the second pilot's seat, and taken it myself.

The engagement had lasted about half an hour, and the closest range was one hundred yards while the average range was two hundred. The boat with Ensign Eaton in it landed between the Islands of Texel and Vlieland, while the other boat, which had not taken any part in the fight, was last seen two miles off Vlieland and still taxiing in toward the beach.

We descended to the water at five forty-five, ten miles north-west of Vlieland. During the ten minutes we were on the water I loosened Lt. Galvayne's clothing, made his position somewhat easier, and felt for his heart which at that time I was quite sure was beating feebly.

When we rose from the water and ascended to fifteen hundred feet, we sighted two planes which later proved to be the two Yarmouth boats. We picked them up, swung into formation, and laid our course for Yarmouth.

At ten minutes to seven we sighted land and twenty minutes after we were resting on the water in front of Yarmouth slipway.

We at once summoned medical aid but found that nothing could be done. The shot had gone through his head, striking the mouth and coming out behind his ear,. tearing a gash of about two inches in diameter.

The boat had been more or less riddled, a number of shots tearing up the top between the front cockpit and the beginning of the cowl.

The total duration of the flight was seven hours and ten minutes.

American naval aviation had a romantic beginning ; indeed, the development of our air service from almost nothing to a force which, in European waters, comprised 2,500 officers and 22,000 men, is one of the great accomplishments of the war. It was very largely the outcome of civilian enterprise and civilian public spirit. In describing our subchasers I have already paid tribute to the splendid qualities of reserve officers ; and our indebtedness to this type of citizen was equally great in the aviation service. I can pay no further tribute to American youth than to say that the great aircraft force which was ultimately assembled in Europe had its beginnings in a small group of undergraduates at Yale University. In recommending Mr. Trubee Davison for a Distinguished Service Medal, the commander of our aviation forces wrote : " This officer was responsible for the organization of the first Yale aviation unit of twenty-nine aviators who were later enrolled in the Naval Reserve Flying Corps. . . . This group of aviators formed the nucleus of the first Naval Reserve Flying Corps, and, in fact, may be considered as the nucleus from which the United States Aviation Forces, Foreign Service, later grew." This group of college boys acted entirely on their own initiative. While the United States was still at peace, encouraged only by their own parents and a few friends, they took up the study of aviation. It was their conviction that the United States would certainly get into the war, and they selected this branch as the one in which they could render greatest service to their country. These young men worked all through the summer of 1916 at Port Washington, Long Island, learning how to fly : at this time they were an entirely unofficial body, paying their own expenses. Ultimately the unit comprised about twenty men ; they kept constantly at work, even after college opened in the fall of

1916, and when war broke out they were prepared—for they had actually learned to fly. When the submarine scares disturbed the Atlantic seaboard in the early months of the war these Yale undergraduates were sent by the department scouting over Long Island Sound and other places looking for the imaginary Germans. In February, 1917, Secretary Daniels recognized their work by making Davison a member of the Committee on Aeronautics ; in March practically every member of the unit was enrolled in the aviation service ; and their names appear among the first one hundred aviators enrolled in the Navy—a list that ultimately included several thousand. So proficient had these undergraduates become that they were used as a nucleus to train our aircraft forces ; they were impressed as instructors at Buffalo, Bayshore, Hampton Roads, the Massachusetts Institute of Technology, Key West and Moorhead City. They began to go abroad in the summer of 1917, and they were employed as instructors in schools in France and England. These young men not only rendered great material service, but they manifested an enthusiasm, an earnestness, and a tireless vigilance which exerted a wonderful influence in strengthening the *moral* of the whole aviation department. " I knew that whenever we had a member of the Yale unit," says Lieutenant-Commander Edwards, who was aide for aviation at the London headquarters in the latter part of the war, " everything was all right. Whenever the French and English asked us to send a couple of our crack men to reinforce a squadron, I would say, ' Let's get some of the Yale gang.' We never made a mistake when we did this."

There were many men in the regular navy to whom the nation is likewise indebted. Captain T. T. Craven served with very marked distinction as aide for aviation on the staff of Admiral Wilson, and afterward, after the armistice was signed, as the senior member of the Board which had been appointed to settle all claims with the French Government. Lieutenant (now Commander) Kenneth Whiting was another officer who rendered great service in aviation. Commander Whiting arrived in St. Nazaire, France, on the 5th of June, 1917, in command of the first aeronautic detachment, which consisted of 7 officers and 122 men.

Such were the modest beginnings of American aviation in France. In a short time Commander Whiting was assigned to the command of the large station which was taken over at Killingholme, England, and in October, 1917, Captain Hutch I. Cone came from the United States to take charge of the great aviation programme which had now been planned. Captain Cone had for many years enjoyed the reputation of being one of the Navy's most efficient administrators ; while still a lieutenant-commander, he had held for a considerable time the rank of rear-admiral, as chief of the Bureau of Steam Engineering ; and in 1917 he was commanding naval officer of the Panama Canal, a position which required organizing ability of the highest order. It was at my request that he was ordered abroad to organize our European air forces. Captain Cone now came to Paris and plunged into the work of organizing naval aviation with all his usual vigour.

It subsequently became apparent, however, that London would be a better place for his work than Paris, and Captain Cone therefore took up his headquarters in Grosvenor Gardens. Under his administration naval aviation foreign service grew to the proportions I have indicated and included in France six seaplane stations, three dirigible stations, two kite balloon stations, one school of aerial gunnery, one assembly and repair base, and the United States Naval Northern Bombing Group. In the British Isles there were established four seaplane stations and one kite balloon station in Ireland ; one seaplane station and one assembly and repair base in England ; and in Italy we occupied, at the request of the Italian Government, two seaplane stations at Pescara and Porto Corsini on the Adriatic. From these stations we bombed to good effect Austrian naval bases in that area. To Lieutenant-Commander J. L. Callan, U.S.N.R.F., is due much of the credit for the cordial relations which existed between the Italians and ourselves, as well as for the efficient conduct of our aviation forces in Italy under his command.

Probably the most completely equipped aviation centre which we constructed was that at Pauillac, France, under the command of Captain F. T. Evans, U.S.N. ; here we built accommodation for 20,000 men ; we had here what would have eventually been a great airplane factory ; had the war continued six months longer, we would have been turning out planes in this place on a scale almost large enough to supply our needs. The far-sighted judgment and

the really extraordinary professional ability of civil engineers D. G. Copeland and A. W. K. Billings made such work
possible, but only, I might add, with the hearty co-operation
of Lieutenant-Commander Benjamin Briscoe and his small
band of loyal and devoted co-workers.   Another great
adventure was the establishment of our Northern Bombing
Group, under the command of Captain David C. Hanrahan,
U.S.N. ; here we had 112 planes, 305 officers, and more than
2,000 enlisted personnel, who devoted all of their attention
to bombing German submarine bases at Zeebrugge and
Ostend.   This enterprise was a joint one with the marines
under the command of Major A. A. Cunningham, an experienced pilot and an able administrator, who performed
all of his various duties not only to my entire satisfaction
but in a manner which reflected the greatest credit to himself as well as to the Marine Corps of which he was a worthy
representative.   Due to the fact that the rapidity of our
construction work had exceeded that with which airplanes
were being built at home, we entered into an agreement with
the Italian Government whereby we obtained a number of
Caproni planes in exchange for raw materials.   Several of
these large bombing airplanes were successfully flown over
the Alps to the fields of Flanders, under the direction of
Lieutenant-Commander E. O. MacDonnell, who deserves
the greatest credit for the energetic and resourceful manner
in which he executed this difficult task.

In September, 1918, Captain Cone's duties took him to
Ireland ; the ship on which he sailed, the *Leinster*, was torpedoed in the Irish Sea ; Captain Cone was picked up
unconscious in the water, and, when taken to the hospital,
it was discovered that both his legs were broken.   It was
therefore necessary to appoint another officer in his stead,
and I selected Lieutenant W. A. Edwards, who had served
with credit on the destroyer *Cushing*, and who, for some
time, had been second in command to Captain Cone in the
aviation section.   It was almost unprecedented to put at
the head of such an important branch a young lieutenant
who had only been out of the naval academy for a few
years ; ordinarily the duties would have required a man of
Admiral's rank.   Lieutenant Edwards, however, was not
only extremely capable, but he had the gift of getting along
splendidly with our Allies, particularly the British, with
whom our intercourse was necessarily extensive, and with

whom he was very popular. He remained in charge of the department for the rest of the war, winning golden opinions from his superiors and his subordinates, and the Distinguished Service Order from King George.

The armistice was signed before our aviation work had got completely into running order. Yet its accomplishments were highly creditable ; and had the war lasted a little longer they would have reached great proportions. Of the thirty-nine direct attacks made on submarines, ten were, in varying degrees, " successful." Perhaps the most amazing hit made by any seaplane in the war was that scored by Ensign Paul F. Ives ; he dropped a bomb upon a submarine, striking it directly on its deck ; the result was partly tragical, partly ludicrous, for the bomb proved to be a " dud " and did not explode ! In commenting upon this and another creditable attack, the British Admiralty wrote as follows :

I beg to enclose for your information reports of attacks made on two enemy submarines on the 25th March by Pilot Ensign J. F. McNamara, U.S.N., and Pilot Ensign P. F. Ives, U.S.N.

The Admiralty are of opinion that the submarine attacked by Pilot Ensign McNamara was damaged and that the attack of Pilot Ensign Ives might also have been successful had not his bombs failed to explode, which was due to no fault of his own.

I should add that Wing Commander, Portsmouth Group has expressed his appreciation of the valuable assistance rendered by the United States Pilots.

At the cessation of hostilities we had a total of more than 500 planes of various descriptions actually in commission, a large number of which were in actual operation over the North Sea, the Irish Sea, the Bay of Biscay, and the Adriatic ; our bombing planes were making frequent flights over enemy submarine bases, and 2,500 officers and 22,000 enlisted men were making raids, doing patrols, bombing submarines, bombing enemy bases, taking photographs, making reconnaissance over enemy waters, and engaging enemy aircraft. There can be no doubt but that this great force was a factor in persuading the enemy to acknowledge defeat when he did.

A few simple comparisons will illustrate the gigantic task which confronted us and the difficulties which were successfully overcome in the establishment of our naval aviation force on foreign service. If all the buildings constructed and used for barracks for officers and men were joined end to end, they would stretch for a distance of twelve miles. The total cubic contents of all structures erected and used could be represented by a box 245 ft. wide, 300 ft. long, and 1,500 ft. high. In such a box more than ten Woolworth buildings could be easily placed. Twenty-nine telephone exchanges were installed, and in addition connections were made to existing long-distance lines in England and France, and approximately 800 miles of long-distance lines were constructed in Ireland, so that every station could be communicated with from London headquarters. The lumber used for construction work would provide a board-walk one foot wide, extending from New York City to the Isle of Malta—a distance of more than 4,000 miles.

When we consider the fact that during the war naval aviation abroad grew in personnel to be more than one-half the size of the entire pre-war American navy, it is not at all astonishing that all of those regular officers who had been trained in this service were employed almost exclusively in an administrative capacity, which naturally excluded them from taking part in the more exciting work of bombing submarines and fighting aircraft. To their credit be it said that they chafed considerably under this enforced restraint, but they were so few in number that we had to employ them not in command of seaplanes, but of air stations where they rendered the most valuable service.

For the reserves I entertain the very highest regard and even personal affection. Collectively they were magnificent and they reflected the greatest credit upon the country they served so gallantly and with such brilliant success. I know of no finer individual exploit in the war than that of Ensign C. H. Hammon who, while attached to our Air Station at Porto Corsini, took part in a bombing raid on Pola, in which he engaged two enemy airplanes and as a result had his plane hit in several places. During this engagement a colleague, Ensign G. H. Ludlow, was shot down. Ensign Hammon went to his rescue, landed his boat on the water just outside of Pola harbour, picked up the stricken aviator, **and** flew back to Porto Corsini, a distance **of** seventy-five devotion to duty I recommended Ensign Hammon for the Congressional Medal of Honour.

The mention of this officer calls to my mind the exploits of Lieutenant-Commander A. L. Gates, who was the second of only three officers attached to the Naval Forces in Europe whom I recommended for the Congressional Medal of Honour. The citation in the case of Gates reads as follows and needs no elaboration to prove the calibre of the man : " This officer commanded the U.S. Naval Air Station, Dunkirk, France, with very marked efficiency and under almost constant shell and bomb fire from the enemy. Alone and unescorted he rescued the crew of a British airplane wrecked in the sea off Ostend, for which he was awarded the Distinguished Flying Cross by the British Government. This act of bravery was actually over and above the duties required of this officer and in itself demonstrates the highest type of courage. Lieutenant-Commander Gates took part in a number of flights over the enemy lines and was shot down in combat and taken prisoner by the enemy. He made several heroic and determined attempts to escape. During all of his service this officer was a magnificent example of courage, modesty, and energetic devotion to duty. He at all times upheld the very highest traditions of the Naval Service."

Volumes could well be written about the work of these splendid young Americans—of how Ensign Stephen Potter shot down in flames an enemy seaplane from a position over Heligoland Bight ; unfortunately he made the supreme sacrifice only a month later when he in turn was shot down in flames and fell to his resting-place in the North Sea ; and of De Cernea and Wilcox and Ludlow. Theirs was the spirit which dominated the entire Force and which made it possible to accomplish what seemed at times to be almost the impossible. It was the superior " will to victory " which proved to be invincible.

CHAPTER XII

BESIDES transporting American troops, the Navy, in one detail of its work, actually participated in warfare on the Western Front. Though this feature of our effort has nothing to do with the main subject, the defeat of the submarine, yet any account of the American navy in the war which overlooks the achievements of our naval batteries on land would certainly be incomplete. The use of naval guns in war operations was not unprecedented ; the British used such guns in the Boer War, particularly at Ladysmith and Spion Kop ; and there were occasions in which such armament rendered excellent service in the Boxer Rebellion. All through the Great War, British, French, and Germans frequently reinforced their army artillery with naval batteries. But, compared with the American naval guns which under the command of Rear-Admiral Charles P. Plunkett performed such telling deeds against the retreating Germans in the final phases of the conflict, all previous equipment of naval guns on shore had been less efficient in one highly important respect.

For the larger part of the war, the Germans had had a great gun stationed in Belgium bombarding Dunkirk. The original purpose in sending American naval batteries to France was to silence this gun. The proposal was made in November, 1917 ; but, rapidly as the preparations progressed, the situation had entirely changed before our five fourteen-inch guns were ready to leave for France. In the spring of 1918 the Germans began the great drive which nearly took them to the Channel ports ; and under the conditions which prevailed in that area it was impossible to send our guns to the Belgian coast. Meanwhile, the enemy had stationed a gun, having a range of nearly seventy-five miles, in the forest of Compiégne ; the shells from this weapon, con-

stantly falling upon Paris, were having a more demoralizing
effect upon the French populace than was officially admitted.
The demand for the silencing of this gun came from all sides;
and it was a happy coincidence that, at just about the time
when this new peril appeared, the American naval guns
were nearly ready to be transported to France. Encouraged
by the success of this long-range gun on Paris, the Germans
were preparing long-range bombardments on several sections
of the front. They had taken huge guns from the new
battle-cruiser *Hindenburg* and mounted them at convenient
points for bombarding Dunkirk, Chalons-sur-Marne, and
Nancy. In all, the Allied intelligence departments reported
that sixteen guns of great calibre had left Kiel in May, 1918,
and that they would soon be trained upon important
objectives in France. For this reason it was welcome news
to the Allies, who were deficient in this type of artillery,
that five naval fourteen-inch guns, with mountings and
ammunition and supply trains, were ready to embark for
the European field. The Navy received an urgent request
from General Pershing that these guns should be landed at
St. Nazaire; it was to be their main mission to destroy the
" Big Bertha " which was raining shells on Paris, and to
attack specific points, especially railroad communications
and the bridges across the Rhine.

The initiative in the design of these mobile railway
batteries was taken by the Bureau of Ordnance of the Navy
Department, under Rear-Admiral Ralph Earle, and the
details of the design were worked out by the officers of that
bureau and Admiral Plunkett. The actual construction
of the great gun mounts on the cars from which the guns
were to be fired, and of the specially designed cars of the
supply trains for each gun, was an engineering feat which
reflects great credit upon the Baldwin Locomotive Works
and particularly upon its president, Mr. Samuel M. Vauclain,
who undertook the task with the greatest enthusiasm. The
reason why our naval guns represented a greater achievement than anything of a similar nature accomplished by the
Germans was that they were mobile. Careful observations
taken of the bombardment of Dunkirk revealed the fact
that the gun with which it was being done was steadily
losing range. This indicated that the weapon was not a
movable one, but that it was firmly implanted in a fixed
position. The seventy-five mile gun which was bombard-

ing Paris was similarly emplaced. The answering weapon which our ordnance department now proposed to build was to have the ability to travel from place to place—to go to any position to which the railroad system of France could take it. To do this it would be necessary to build a mounting on a railroad car and to supply cars which could carry the crews, their sleeping quarters, their food and ammunition ; to construct, indeed, a whole train for each separate gun. This equipment must be built in the United States, shipped over three thousand miles of ocean, landed at a French port, assembled there, and started on French railroads to the several destinations at the front. The Baldwin Locomotive Works accepted the contract for constructing these mountings and attendant cars; it began work February 13, 1918 ; two months afterward the first mount had been finished and the gun was being proved at Sandy Hook, New Jersey ; and by July all five guns had arrived at St. Nazaire and were being prepared to be sent forward to the scene of hostilities. The rapidity with which this work was completed furnished an illustration of American manufacturing genius at its best. Meanwhile, Admiral Plunkett had collected and trained his crews ; it speaks well for the *moral* of the Navy that, when news of this great operation was first noised about, more than 20,000 officers and men volunteered for the service.

At first the French, great as was their admiration for these guns and the astonishingly accurate marksmanship which they had displayed on their trials, believed that their railroad beds and their bridges could not sustain such a weight ; the French engineers, indeed, declined at the beginning to approve our request for the use of their rails. The constant rain of German shells on Paris, however, modified this attitude ; the situation was so urgent that such assistance as these American guns promised was welcome. One August morning, therefore, the first train started for Helles Mouchy, the point from which it was expected to silence the "Big Bertha." The progress of this train through France was a triumphant march. Our own confidence in the French road bed and bridges was not much greater than that of the French themselves ; the train therefore went along slowly, climbed the grades at a snail's pace, and took the curves with the utmost caution. As they crossed certain of the bridges, the crews held their breath and sat tight, expecting almost every moment to crash through. All along the route the French populace greeted the great battery train with one long cheer, and at the towns and villages the girls decorated the long muzzle of the gun with flowers. But there were other spectators than the French. Expertly as this unusual train had been camouflaged, the German airplane observers had detected its approach. As it neared the objective the shells that had been falling on Paris ceased ; before the Americans could get to work, the Germans had removed their mighty weapon, leaving nothing but an emplacement as a target for our shells. Though our men were therefore deprived of the privilege of destroying this famous long-range gun, it is apparent that their arrival saved Paris from further bombardment, for nothing was heard of the gun for the rest of the war.

The guns proved exceedingly effective in attacking German railroad centres, bridges, and other essential positions ; and as they could be fired from any point of the railroad tracks behind the Western Front, and as they could be shifted from one position to another, with all their personnel and equipment, as fast as the locomotives could haul them, it was apparent that the more guns of this design that could be supplied the better. These qualities were at once recognized by the Army, which called upon the Navy for assistance in building a large number of railway batteries ; and if the war had continued these great guns would soon have been thundering all along the Western Front.

From the time the naval guns were mounted until the armistice Admiral Plunkett's men were busy on several points of the Allied lines. In this time the five naval guns fired 782 shells at distances ranging from 18 to 23 miles. They played great havoc in the railroad yards at Laon, destroying large stretches of track that were indispensable to the Germans, and in general making this place practically useless as a railroad centre. Probably the greatest service which they rendered to the cause of the Allies was in the region north of Verdun. In late October three naval batteries were brought up to Charny and Thierville and began bombarding the railroad which ran through Montmédy, Longuyon, and Conflans. This was the most important line of communication on the Western Front ; it was the road over which the German army in the east was supplied, and there was practically no other line by which the great German armies engaging the Americans could escape. From October 23rd to the hour when the armistice was signed our fourteen-inch guns were raining shells upon this road. So successful was this bombardment that the German traffic was stopped, not only while the firing was taking place, but for several hours each day after it had ceased. What this meant to the success of the Allied armies the world now knows. The result is perfectly summed up in General Pershing's report :

" Our large calibre guns," he says, " had advanced and were skilfully brought into position to fire upon the important lines at Montmédy, Longuyon, and Conflans ; the strategical goal which was our highest hope was gained. We had cut the enemy's main line of communications and nothing but surrender or an armistice could save his army from complete disaster."

These guns were, of course, only one of many contributing factors, but that the Navy had its part in this great achievement is another example of the success with which our two services co-operated with each other throughout the war— a co-operation which, for efficient and harmonious devotion to a common cause, has seldom, if ever, been equalled.

CHAPTER XIII

TRANSPORTING TWO MILLION AMERICAN SOLDIERS TO FRANCE

I

In March, 1918, it became apparent that the German submarine campaign had failed. The prospect that confronted the Allied forces at that time, when compared with the conditions which had faced them in April, 1917, forms one of the most impressive contrasts in history. In the first part of the earlier year the cause of the Allied Powers, and consequently the cause of liberty throughout the world, had reached the point almost of desperation. On both land and sea the Germans seemed to hold the future in their hands. In Europe the armies of the Central Powers were everywhere in the ascendant. The French and British were holding their own in France, and in the Somme campaign they had apparently inflicted great damage upon the German forces, yet the disintegration of the Russian army, the unmistakable signs of which had already appeared, was bringing nearer the day when they would have to meet the undivided strength of their enemy. At the time in question, Rumania, Serbia, and Montenegro were conquered countries, and Italy seemed unable to make any progress against the Austrians. Bulgaria and Turkey had become practically German provinces, and the dream of a great Germanic eastern empire was rapidly approaching realization. So strong was Germany in a military sense, so little did she apprehend that the United States could ever assemble her resources and her men in time to make them a decisive element in the struggle, that the German war lords, in their effort to bring the European conflict to a quick conclusion, did not hesitate to take the step which was destined to make our country their enemy.   Probably no nation ever adopted a war measure with more confidence in its success.   The results which the German submarines could accomplish seemed at that time to be simply a matter of mathematical calculation.   The Germans estimated that they could sink at least 1,000,000 tons a month, completely cut off Great Britain's supplies of food and war materials, and thus end the war by October or November of 1917.   Even though the United States should declare war, what could an unprepared nation like our own accomplish in such a brief period ?   Millions of troops we might indeed raise, but we could not train them in three or four months, and, even though we could perform such a miracle, it was ridiculous to suppose that we could transport them to Europe through the submarine danger zone.   I have already shown that the Germans were not alone in thus predicting the course of events.   In the month of April, 1917, I had found the Allied officials just about as distressed as the Germans were jubilant.   Already the latter, in sinking merchant ships, had had successes which almost equalled their own predictions ;   no adequate means of defence against the submarine had been devised ;   and the chiefs of the British navy made no attempts to disguise their apprehension for the future.

Such was the atmosphere of gloom which prevailed in Allied councils in April, 1917 ;   yet one year later the naval situation had completely changed.   The reasons for that change have been set forth in the preceding pages.   In that brief twelve months the relative position of the submarine had undergone a marked transformation.   Instead of being usually the pursuer it was now often the pursued.   Instead of sailing jauntily upon the high seas, sinking helpless merchantmen almost at will, it was half-heartedly lying in wait along the coasts, seeking its victims in the vessels of dispersed convoys.   If it attempted to push out to sea, and attack a convoy, escorting destroyers were likely to deliver one of their dangerous attacks ;   if it sought the shallower coastal waters, a fleet of yachts, sloops, and subchasers was constantly ready to assail it with dozens of depth charges.   An attempt to pass through the Straits of Dover meant almost inevitable destruction by mines ;   an attempt to escape into the ocean by the northern passage involved the momentary dread of a similar end or the hazard of navigating the difficult Pentland Firth. In most of the narrow passages Allied submarines lay constantly in wait with their torpedoes ; a great fleet of airplanes and dirigibles was always circling above ready to rain a shower of bombs upon the under-water foe. Already the ocean floor about the British Isles held not far from 200 sunken submarines, with most of their crews, amounting to at least 4,000 men, whose deaths involved perhaps the most hideous tragedies of the war. Bad as was this situation, it was nothing compared with what it would become a few months or a year later. American and British shipyards were turning out anti-submarine craft with great rapidity ; the industries of America, with their enormous output of steel, had been enlisted in the anti-submarine campaign. The American and British shipbuilding facilities were neutralizing the German campaign in two ways : they were not only constructing war vessels on a scale which would soon drive all the German submarines from the sea, but they were building merchant tonnage so rapidly that, in March, 1918, more new tonnage was launched than was being destroyed. Thus by this time the Teutonic hopes of ending the war by the submarine had utterly collapsed ; if the Germans were to win the war at all, or even to obtain a peace which would not be disastrous, some other programme must be adopted and adopted quickly.

Disheartened by their failure at sea, the enemy therefore turned their eyes once more toward the land. The destruction of Russian military power had given the German armies a great numerical superiority over those of the Allies. There seemed little likelihood that the French or the British, after three years of frightfully gruelling war, could add materially to their forces. Thus, with the grouping of the Powers, such as existed in 1917, the Germans had a tremendous advantage on their side, for Russia, which German statesmen for fifty years had feared as a source of inexhaustible man-supply to her enemies, had disappeared as a military power. But a new element in the situation now counterbalanced this temporary gain ; that was the daily increasing importance of the United States in the war. The Germans, who in 1917 had despised us as an enemy, immediate or prospective, now despised us no longer. The army which they declared could never be raised and trainedwas actually being raised and trained by the millions.

The nation which their publicists had denounced as lacking cohesion and public spirit had adopted conscription simultaneously with their declaration of war, and the people whom the Germans had affected to regard as devoted only to the pursuit of gain and pleasure had manifested a unity of purpose which they had never before displayed, and had offered their lives, their labours, and their wealth without limit to the cause of the Allies. Up to March, 1918, only a comparatively small part of this American army had reached Europe, but the Germans had already tested its fighting quality and had learned to respect it. Yet all these manifestations would not have disturbed the Germanic calculations except for one depressing fact. Even a nation of 100,000,000 brave and energetic people, fully trained and equipped for war, is not a formidable foe so long as an impassable watery gulf of three thousand miles separates them from the field of battle.

For the greater part of 1917 the German people believed that their submarines could bar the progress of the American armies. By March, 1918, they had awakened from this delusion. Not only was an American army millions strong in process of formation, but the alarming truth now dawned upon the Germans that it could be transported to Europe. The great industries of America could provide munitions and food to supply any number of soldiers indefinitely, and these, too, could be brought to the Western Front. Outwardly, the German chiefs might still affect to despise this new foe, but in their hearts they knew that it spelt their doom. They were not now dealing with a corrupt Czardom and hordes of ignorant and passionless Slavs, who could be eliminated by propaganda and sedition ; they were dealing with millions of intelligent and energetic freemen, all animated by a mighty and almost religious purpose. Yet the situation, desperate as it seemed, held forth one more hope. If the German armies, which still greatly outnumbered the French and British, could strike and win a decisive victory before the Americans could arrive, then they might still force a satisfactory peace. " It is a race between Ludendorff and Wilson " is the terse and accurate way in which Lloyd George summed up the situation. The great blow fell on March 21, 1918 ; the British and the French met it with heroism, but it was quite evident that they were fighting against terrible odds. At this time the American army in France numbered about 300,000 men ; it now became the business of the American navy, assisted by the British, to transport the American troops who could increase these forces sufficiently to turn the balance in the Allies' favour.

The supreme hour, to which all the anti-submarine labours of the preceding year were merely preliminary, had now arrived. Since the close of the war there has been much discussion of the part which the American navy played in bringing it to a successful end. Even during the war there was some criticism on this point. There were two more or less definite opinions in the public mind upon this question. One was that the main business of our war vessels was to convoy the American soldiers to France ; the other emphasized the anti-submarine warfare as its most important duty. Anyone would suppose, from the detached way in which these two subjects have been discussed, that the anti-submarine warfare and the successful transportation of troops were separate matters. An impression apparently prevails that, at the beginning of the war, the American navy could have quietly decided whether it would devote its energies to making warfare on the submarine or to convoying American armies ; yet the absurdity of such a conception must be apparent to anyone who has read the foregoing pages. The several operations in which the Allied navies engaged were all part of a comprehensive programme ; they were all interdependent. According to my idea, the business of the American navy was to join its forces whole-heartedly with those of the Allies in the effort *to win the war*. Anything which helped to accomplish this great purpose became automatically our duty. Germany was basing her chances of success upon the submarine ; our business was therefore to assist in defeating the submarine. The cause of the Allies was our cause ; our cause was the cause of the Allies ; anything which benefited the Allies benefited the United States ; and anything which benefited the United States benefited the Allies. Neither we nor France nor England were conducting a separate campaign ; we were separate units of an harmonious whole. At the beginning the one pressing duty was to put an end to the sinking of merchantmen, not because these merchantmen were for the larger part British, but because the failure to do so would have meant the elimination of Great Britain from the war, with results which would have meant defeat for the other Allies. Let us imagine, for a moment, what the sequence of events would have been had the submarine campaign against merchant shipping succeeded ; in that case Britain and France would have been compelled to surrender unconditionally and the United States would therefore have been forced to fight the Central Empires alone. Germany's terms of peace would have included the surrender of all the Allied fleets ; this would eventually have left the United States navy to fight the German navy reinforced by the ships of Great Britain, Austria, France, and Italy. In such a contest we should have been outnumbered about three or four to one. I have such confidence in the power and purpose of America as to believe that, even in a single-handed conflict with Germany, we should have won in the end ; but it is evident that the problem would have been quite a different one from that of fighting in co-operation with the Allies against the Germanic foe.

Simply as a matter of self-interest and strategy it was certainly wisdom to throw the last ounce of our strength into the scale of the Allied navies ; and it was therefore inevitable that we should first of all use our anti-submarine craft to protect all shipping sailing to Europe and to clear the sea of submarines. In doing this we were protecting the food supply not only of Great Britain, but of France and our other Allies, for most of the materials which we sent to our European friends were transported first to England and thence were shipped across the Channel. Moreover, our twelve months' campaign against the submarine was an invaluable preliminary to transporting the troops. Does any sane person believe that we could have put two million Americans into France had the German submarines maintained until the spring and summer of 1918 the striking power which had been theirs in the spring of 1917 ? Merely to state the question is to answer it. In that same twelve months we had gained much experience which was exceedingly valuable when we began transporting troops in great numbers. The most efficacious protection to merchant shipping, the convoy, was similarly the greatest safeguard to our military transports. Those methods which had been so successfully used in shipping food, munitions, and materials were now used in shipping soldiers. The section of the great headquarters which we had developed in London for routing convoys was used for routing transports, and the American naval officer, Captain Byron A. Long, who had demonstrated such great ability in this respect, was likewise the master mind in directing the course of the American soldiers to France.

In other ways we had laid the foundations for this, the greatest troop movement in history. In the preceding twelve months we had increased the oil tankage at Brest more than fourfold, sent over repair ships, and augmented its repair facilities. This port and all of our naval activities in France were under the command first of Rear-Admiral Wm. B. Fletcher, and later Rear-Admiral Henry B. Wilson. It was a matter of regret that we could not earlier have made Brest the main naval base for the American naval forces in France, for it was in some respects strategically better located for that purpose than was any other port in Europe. Even for escorting certain merchant convoys into the Channel Brest would have provided a better base than either Plymouth or Queenstown. A glance at the map explains why. To send destroyers from Queenstown to pick up convoys and escort them into the Channel or to French ports and thence return to their base involved a long triangular trip ; to send such destroyers from Brest to escort these involved a smaller amount of steaming and a direct east and west voyage. Similarly, Queenstown was a much better location for destroyers sent to meet convoys bound for ports in the Irish Sea over the northern " trunk line." But unfortunately it was utterly impossible to use the great natural advantages of Brest in the early days of war ; the mere fact that this French harbour possessed most inadequate tankage facilities put it out of the question, and it was also very deficient in docks, repair facilities, and other indispensable features of a naval base. At this time Brest was hardly more than able to provide for the requirements of the French, and it would have embarrassed our French allies greatly had we attempted to establish a large American force there, before we had supplied the essential oil fuel and repair facilities. The ships which we did send in the first part of the war were mostly yachts, of the " dollar-a-year " variety, which their owners had generously given to the national service ; their crews were largely of that type of young business man and college undergraduate to whose skill and devotion I have already paid tribute. This little flotilla acquitted itself splendidly up and down the coast of France. Meanwhile, we were constructing fuel-oil tanks ; and as soon as these were ready and repair ships were available, we began building up a large force at Brest—a force which was ultimately larger than the one we maintained at Queenstown ; at the height of the troop movements it comprised about 36 destroyers, 12 yachts, 3 tenders, and several mine-sweepers and tugs. The fine work which this detachment accomplished in escorting troop and supply convoys is sufficient evidence of the skill acquired by the destroyers and other vessels in carrying out their duties in this peculiar warfare.

Meanwhile, on the other side of the Atlantic, a great organization had been created under the able direction of Rear-Admiral Albert Gleaves for maintaining and administering the fleet of transports and their ocean escorts. Also, as soon as war was declared the work was begun of converting into transports those German merchant ships which had been interned in American ports. The successful completion of this work was, in itself, a great triumph for the American navy. Of the vessels which the Germans had left in our hands, seventeen at New York, Boston, Norfolk, and Philadelphia, seemed to be adapted for transport purposes, but the Germans had not intended that we should make any such use of them. The condition of these ships, after their German custodians had left, was something indescribable ; they reflected great discredit upon German seamanship, for it would have been impossible for any people which really loved ships to permit them to deteriorate as had these vessels and to become such cesspools of filth. For three years the Germans had evidently made no attempt to clean them ; the sanitary conditions were so bad that our workmen could not sleep on board, but had to have sleeping quarters near the docks ; they spent weeks scrubbing, scraping, and disinfecting, in a finally successful effort to make the ships suitable habitations for human beings. Not only had the Germans permitted such liners as the *Vaterland* and the *Kronprinzessin Cecilie* to go neglected, but, on their departure, they had attempted to injure them in all conceivable ways. The cylinders had been broken, engines had been smashed, vital parts of the machinery had been removed and thrown into the sea, ground glass had been placed in the oil cups, gunpowder had been placed in the coal—evidently in the hope of causing explosions when the vessels were at sea—and other damage of a more subtle nature had been done, it evidently being the expectation that the ships would break down when on the ocean and beyond the possibility of repair. Although our navy yards had no copies of the plans of these vessels or their machinery —the Germans having destroyed them all—and although the missing parts were of peculiarly German design, they succeeded, in an incredibly short time, in making them even better and speedier vessels than they had ever been before.

The national sense of humour did not fail the transport service when it came to rechristening these ships ; the *Princess Irene* became the *Pocahontas*, the *Rhein* the *Susquehanna* ; and there was also an ironic justice in the fact that the *Vaterland*, which had been built by the Germans partly for the purpose of transporting troops in war, actually fulfilled this mission, though not quite in the way which the Germans had anticipated. Meanwhile, both the American and the British mercantile marines were supplementing this German tonnage. The first troops which we sent to France, in June, 1917, were transported in ships of the United Fruit Company ; and when the German blow was struck, in March, 1918, both the United States and Great Britain began collecting from all parts of the world vessels which could be used as troop transports. We called in all available vessels from the Atlantic and Pacific coasts and the Great Lakes ; England stripped her trade routes to South America, Australia, and the East, and France and Italy also made their contributions. Of all the American troops sent to France from the beginning of the war, the United States provided transports for 46·25 per cent., Great Britain for 51·25, the remainder being provided by France and Italy. Of those sent between March, 1918, and the armistice, American vessels carried 42·15 per cent., British 55·40 per cent.[1]

Yet there was one element in the safe transportation of troops which was even more fundamental than those which I have named. The basis of all our naval operations was the dreadnoughts and the battle-cruisers of the Grand Fleet. It was this aggregation, as I have already indicated,

[1] These figures are taken from the Annual Report of the Secretary of the Navy for 1919, page 207.

which made possible the operation of all the surface ships that destroyed the effectiveness of the submarines. Had the Grand Fleet suddenly disappeared beneath the waves, all these offensive craft would have been driven from the seas, the Allies' sea lines of communication would have been cut, and the war would have ended in Germany's favour. From the time the transportation of troops began the United States had a squadron of five dreadnought battleships constantly with the Grand Fleet. The following vessels performed this important duty : the *New York*, Captain C. F. Hughes, afterward Captain E. L. Beach ; the *Wyoming*, Captain H. A. Wiley, afterward Captain H. H. Christy ; the *Florida*, Captain Thomas Washington, afterward Captain M. M. Taylor ; the *Delaware*, Captain A. H. Scales ; the *Arkansas*, Captain W. H. G. Bullard, afterward Captain L. R. de Steiguer ; and the *Texas*, Captain Victor Blue. These vessels gave this great force an unquestioned preponderance, and made it practically certain that Germany would not attempt another general sea battle. Under Rear-Admiral Hugh Rodman, the American squadron performed excellent service and made the most favourable impression upon the chiefs of the Allied navies. Under the general policy of co-operation established throughout our European naval forces these vessels were quickly made a part of the Grand Fleet in so far as concerned their military operations. This was, of course, wholly essential to efficiency—a point the layman does not always understand—so essential, in fact, that it may be said that, if the Grand Fleet had gone into battle the day after our vessels joined, the latter might have decreased rather than increased the fighting efficiency of the whole ; for, though our people and the British spoke the same language, the languages of the ships, that is, their methods of communication by signals, were wholly different. It was therefore our duty to stow our signal flags and books down below, and learn the British signal language. This they did so well that four days after their arrival they went out and manœuvred successfully with the Grand Fleet. In the same way they adopted the British systems of tactics and fire control, and in every other way conformed to the established practices of the British. Too great praise cannot be given the officers and men of our squadron, not only for their efficiency and the cordiality of their co-operation, but for the patience with which they bore the almost continuous restriction to their ships, and the long vigil without the opportunity of a contact with the enemy forces.   Just how well our ships succeeded in this essential co-operation was expressed by Admiral Sir David Beatty in the farewell speech which he made to them upon the day of their departure for home.   He said in part :

" I want, first of all, to thank you, Admiral Rodman, the captains, officers, and ships' companies of the magnifi- cent squadron, for the wonderful co-operation and the loyalty you have given to me and to my admirals ; and the assistance that you have given us in every duty you had to undertake.   The support which you have shown is that of true comradeship ; and in time of stress, that is worth a very great deal.

" You will return to your own shores ; and I hope in the sunshine, which Admiral Rodman tells me always shines there, you won't forget your ' comrades of the mist ' and your pleasant associations of the North Sea. . . .

" I thank you again and again for the great part the Sixth Battle Squadron played in bringing about the greatest naval victory in history.   I hope you will give this message to your comrades : ' Come back soon.   Good-bye and good luck ! ' "

But these were not the only large battleships which the United States had sent to European waters.   Despite all the precautions which I have described, there was still one danger which constantly confronted American troop transports.   By June and July, 1918, our troops were crossing the Atlantic in enormous numbers, about 300,000 a month, and were accomplishing most decisive results upon the battlefield.   A successful attack upon a convoy, involving the sinking of one or more transports, would have had no important effect upon the war, but it would probably have improved German *moral* and possibly have injured that of the Americans.   There was practically only one way in which such an attack could be made ; one or more German battle-cruisers might slip out to sea and assail one of our troop convoys.   In order to prepare for such a possibility, the Department sent three of our most powerful dreadnoughts to Berehaven, Ireland—the *Nevada,* Captain

A. T. Long, afterward Captain W. C. Cole ; the *Oklahoma,*
Captain M. L. Bristol, afterward Captain C. B. McVay ;
and the *Utah,* Captain F. B. Bassett, the whole division
under the command of Rear-Admiral Thomas S. Rodgers.
This port is located in Bantry Bay, on the extreme south-
western coast. For several months our dreadnoughts lay
here, momentarily awaiting the news that a German raider
had escaped, ready to start to sea and give battle. But the
expected did not happen. The fact that this powerful
squadron was ready for the emergency is perhaps the reason
why the Germans never attempted the adventure.

II

A reference to the map which accompanies this chapter
will help the reader to understand why our transports were
able to carry American troops to France so successfully
that not a single ingoing ship was ever struck by a torpedo.
This diagram makes it evident that there were two areas of
the Atlantic through which American shipping could reach
its European destination. The line of division was about
the forty-ninth parallel of latitude, the French city of Brest
representing its most familiar landmark. From this point
extending southward, as far as the forty-fifth parallel, which
corresponds to the location of the city of Bordeaux, is a
great stretch of ocean, about 200 miles wide. It includes
the larger part of the Bay of Biscay, which forms that huge
indentation with which our school geographies have made
us Americans so familiar, and which has always enjoyed
a particular fame for its storms, the dangers of its coast,
and the sturdy and independent character of the people on
its shores. The other distinct area to which the map calls
attention extends northerly from the forty-ninth parallel
to the fifty-second; it comprises the English Channel,
and includes both the French channel ports, the British
ports, the southern coast of Ireland, and the entrance to the
Irish Sea. The width of this second section is very nearly
the same as that of the one to the south, or about 200 miles.
Up to the present moment this narrative has been concerned chiefly with the northernmost of these two great sea
pathways. Through this one to the north passed practically
all the merchant shipping which was destined for the Allies.

21

Consequently, as I have described, it was the great hunting ground of the German submarines.   I have thus far had little to say of the Bay of Biscay section because, until 1918, there was comparatively little activity in that part of the ocean.   For every ship which sailed through this bay I

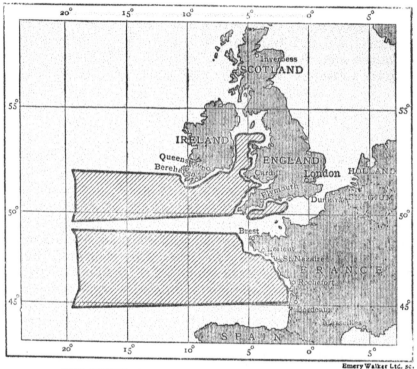

THE OPTION OFFERED TO THE GERMAN SUBMARINES

This diagram explains why the American navy succeeded in transporting more than 2,000,000 American soldiers to France without loss because of submarines. The Atlantic was divided into two broad areas—shown by the shaded parts of the diagram. Through the northern area were sent practically all the merchant ships with supplies of food and materials for Europe. The southern area, extending roughly from the forty-fifth to the forty-ninth parallel, was used almost exclusively for troopships. The Germans could keep only eight or ten U-boats at the same time in the eastern Atlantic ; they thus were forced to choose whether they should devote these boats to attacking mercantile or troop convoys. The text explains why, under these circumstances, they were compelled to use nearly all their forces against merchant ships and leave troop transports practically alone.

suppose that there were at least 100 which came through the Irish Sea and the English Channel.   In my first report to the Department I described the principal scene of submarine activity as the area of the Atlantic reaching from the French island of Ushant—which lies just westward of Brest—to the tip of Scotland, and that remained the chief scene of hostilities to the end.   Along much of the coastline

south of Brest the waters were so shallow that the submarines could operate only with difficulty; it was a long
distance from the German bases; the shipping consisted
largely of coastal convoys; much of this was the coal trade
from England; it is therefore not surprising that the
Germans contented themselves with now and then planting
mines off the most important harbours. Since our enemy
was able to maintain only eight or ten U-boats in the
Atlantic at one time it would have been sheer waste of
energy to have stationed them off the western coast of
France. They would have put in their time to little
purpose, and meanwhile the ships and cargoes which they
were above all ambitious to destroy would have been safely
finding their way into British ports.

The fact that we had these two separate areas and that
these areas were so different in character was what made it
possible to send our 2,000,000 soldiers to France without
losing a single man. From March, 1918, to the conclusion
of the war, the American and British navies were engaged in
two distinct transportation operations. The shipment of
food and munitions continued in 1918 as in 1917, and on
an even larger scale. With the passing of time the mechanism of these mercantile convoys increased in efficiency, and
by March, 1918, the management of this great transportation system had become almost automatic. Shipping from
America came into British ports, it will be remembered, in
two great "trunk lines," one of which ran through the
English Channel and the other up the Irish Sea. But when
the time came to bring over the American troops, we
naturally selected the area to the south, both because it was
necessary to send the troops to France and because we had
here a great expanse of ocean which was relatively free of
submarines. Our earliest troop shipments disembarked at
St. Nazaire; later, when the great trans-Atlantic liners,
both German and British, were pressed into service, we
landed many tens of thousands at Brest; and all the largest
French ports from Brest to Bordeaux took a share. A
smaller number we sent to England, from which country
they were transported across the Channel into France;
when the demands became pressing, indeed, hardly a ship
of any kind was sent to Europe without its quota of American soldiers; but, on the whole, the business of transportation in 1918 followed simple and well-defined lines. **We**

sent mercantile convoys in what I may call the northern
" lane " and troop convoys in the southern " lane." We
kept both lines of traffic for the most part distinct ; and
this simple procedure offered to our German enemies a
pretty problem.

For, I must repeat, the German navy could maintain in
the open Atlantic an average of only about eight or ten of her
efficient U-boats at one time. The German Admiralty thus
had to answer this difficult question : Shall we use these
submarines to attack mercantile convoys or to attack troop
convoys ? The submarine flotilla which was actively
engaged was so small that it was absurd to think of sending
half into each lane ; the Germans must send most of their
submarines against cargo ships or most of them against
troopships. Which should it be ? If it were decided to
concentrate on mercantile vessels then the American armies,
which the German chiefs had declared to their people could
never get to the Western Front, would reach France and
furnish General Foch the reserves with which he might crush
the German armies before winter. If, on the other hand,
the Germans should decide to concentrate on troopships,
then the food and supplies which were essential to the Allied
cause would flow at an even greater rate into Great Britain
and thence to the European nations. Whether it were more
important, in a military sense, to cut the Allies' commercial
lines of communication or to sink troop transports is an
interesting question. It is almost impossible for the Anglo-
Saxon mind to consider this as a purely military matter,
apart from the human factors involved. The sinking of a
great transport, with 4,000 or 5,000 American boys on
board, would have been a dreadful calamity and would have
struck horror to the American people ; it was something
which the Navy was determined to prevent, and which we
did prevent. Considered as a strictly military question,
however—and that was the only consideration which
influenced the Germans—it is hard to see how the loss of one
transport, or even the loss of several, would have materially
affected the course of the war. In judging the purely
military results of such a tragedy, we must remember that
the Allied armies were losing from 3,000 to 5,000 men a day ;
thus the sinking of an American transport once a week
would not have particularly affected the course of the war.
The destruction of merchant shipping in large quantities,

however, represented the one way in which the Germans could win. There were at least a hundred merchant ships to every one of our troopships ; if a considerable number of the former could be sunk, Germany would have scored a decisive advantage. From the declaration of submarine warfare, the objective of the German Admiralty had been for " tonnage " ; by March, 1918, as already said, the chances of destroying sufficient tonnage to win had become extremely slight ; yet it still represented the one logical mission of the submarine.

The two alternatives, however, that of attacking mercantile convoys or troop convoys, hardly existed in fact. Let us suppose for a moment that the Germans had changed their programme, had taken their group of operating submarines from the northern trade routes, and had stationed them to the south, in the track of the troop transports. What would the results have been ? " Lane," though a convenient word for descriptive purposes, is hardly an accurate one ; for this ocean passage-way was really about 200 miles wide. Imagine eight or ten submarines, stretched across that expanse and hunting for troopships. At this rate the Germans would have had about one submarine for every twenty miles. Instead of finding themselves sailing amid a swarm of surface ships, as they were when they were stationed in the busy trade routes of the Irish Sea or the English Channel, the submarines would have found themselves drifting on a great waste of waters. Our troop convoys averaged not more than three a week even in the busiest period ; in all probability the submarines would therefore have hung around for a month without catching a glimpse of one. Even if by some chance the patient vigil should finally have been rewarded, it is extremely unlikely that the submarine would ever have found a favourable opportunity to attack. We must keep in mind that the convoy room at the Admiralty knew, within certain limits, the location of submarines from day to day ; any time one was located in the track of a troop convoy, therefore, a wireless to the convoy would have conveyed this information and directed it to reach the coast of France by another route.

At the beginning the speediest vessels only were used for transporting troops. Ships which made less than twelve knots an hour were not deemed safe for such precious cargoes; when the need for troops became more and more pressing and when our transport service had demonstrated great skill in the work, a few slower vessels were used; but the great majority of our troop transports were those which made twelve knots or more. Now one of the greatest protections which a ship possesses against submarine attack is unquestionably high speed. A submarine makes only eight knots when submerged—and it must submerge immediately if its attack is to be successful. It must be within at least a mile of its quarry when it discharges its torpedo ; and most successful attacks were made within three hundred yards. Now take a pencil and a piece of paper and figure out what must be the location of a submarine, having a speed of eight knots, when it sights a convoy, which makes twelve knots and more, if it hopes to approach near enough to launch a torpedo. A little diagramming will prove that the U-boat must be almost directly in line of its hoped-for victim if it is to score a hit. But even though the god of Chance should favour the enemy in this way, the likelihood of sinking its prey would still be very remote. Like all convoys, the troopships began zigzagging as soon as they entered the danger zone ; and this in itself made it almost impossible for a submarine to get its bearings and take good aim. I believe that these circumstances in themselves —the comparative scarcity of troop transports, the width of the " lane " in which they travelled, the high speed which they maintained, and their constant zigzagging, would have defeated most of the attempts which the Germans could have made to torpedo them. Though I think that most of them would have reached their destinations unharmed without any other protection, still this risk, small as it was, could not be taken ; and we therefore gave them one other protection greater than any of those which I have yet mentioned—the destroyer escort. A convoy of four or five large troopships would be surrounded by as many as ten or a dozen destroyers. Very properly, since they were carrying human cargoes, we gave them an escort at least three times as large per vessel as that given to large mercantile convoys of twenty or more vessels ; and this fact made them very uninviting baits for the most venturesome U-boat commanders.

When the engineers build a Brooklyn bridge they introduce an element which they call the factor of safety. It is their usual procedure to estimate the greatest weight which their structure may be called upon to bear under any conceivable circumstances and then they make it strong enough to stand a number of times that weight. This additional strength is the "factor of safety"; it is never called into use, of course, but the consciousness that it exists gives the public a sense of security which it could obtain in no other way. We adopted a similar policy in transporting these millions of American boys to Europe. We also had a large margin of safety. We did not depend upon one precaution to assure the lives of our soldiers; we heaped one precautionary measure on another. From the embarking of the troops at New York or at Hampton Roads to the disembarkation at Brest, St. Nazaire, La Pallice, Bordeaux, or at one of their other destinations, not the minutest safeguard was omitted. We necessarily thus somewhat diminished the protection of some of the mercantile convoys—and properly so. This was done whenever the arrival of a troop convoy conflicted with the arrival of a merchant convoy. Also, until they reached the submarine zone, they were attended by a cruiser or a battleship whose business it was to protect them against a German raider which might possibly have made its escape into the ocean; the work performed by these ocean escorts, practically all of which were American, was for the most part unobtrusive and unspectacular, but it constitutes a particularly fine example of efficiency and seamanlike devotion. At Berehaven, Ireland, as described above, we had stationed three powerful American dreadnoughts, momentarily prepared to rush to the scene in case one of the great German battle-cruisers succeeded in breaking into the open sea. Even the most minute precautions were taken by the transports.

The soldiers and crews were not permitted to throw anything overboard which might betray the course of a convoy; the cook's refuse was dropped at a particular time and in a way that would furnish no clue to a lurking submarine; even a tin can, if thrown into the sea, was first pierced with holes to make sure that it would sink. Anyone who struck a match at night in the danger zone committed a punishable offence. It is thus apparent why the Germans never "landed" a single one of our transports. The records show only three or four cases in which even attempts were made to do this; and those few efforts were feeble and ineffectual.   Of course, the boys all had exciting experiences with phantom submarines ; indeed I don't suppose that there is a single one of our more than 2,000,000 troops who has not entertained his friends and relatives with accounts of torpedo streaks and schools of U-boats.

But the Germans made no concerted campaign against our transports ; fundamental conditions, already described, rendered such an offensive hopeless ; and the skill with which our transport service was organized and conducted likewise dissuaded them.   I have always believed that the German Admiralty ordered their U-boat captains to let the American transports alone ; or at least not to attack except under very favourable circumstances, and this belief is rather confirmed by a passage in General Ludendorff's memoirs.   " From our previous experience of the submarine war," General Ludendorff writes, " I expected strong forces of Americans to come, but the rapidity with which they actually did arrive proved surprising.   General von Cramon, the German military representative at the Austro-Hungarian Headquarters, often called me up and asked me to insist on the sinking of American troopships ; public opinion in Austria-Hungary demanded it.   Admiral von Holtzendorff could only reply that everything was being done to reduce enemy tonnage and to sink troopships.   It was not possible to direct the submarines against troopships exclusively.   They could approach the coasts of Europe anywhere between the north of England and Gibraltar, a front of some fourteen hundred nautical miles. It was impossible effectively to close this area by means of submarines.   One could have concentrated them only on certain routes ; but whether the troopships would choose the same routes at the same time was the question.   As soon as the enemy heard of submarines anywhere he could always send the ships new orders by wireless and unload at another port.   It was, therefore, not certain that by this method we should meet with a sufficient number of troopships.   The destruction of the enemy's freight tonnage would then have been undertaken only spasmodically, and would have been set back in an undesirable manner ; and in that way the submarine war would have become diverted from its original object.   The submarine war against commerce was therefore continued with all the vigour possible."

Apparently it became the policy of the German Admiralty,

as I have said, to concentrate their U-boats on merchant shipping and leave the American troopships practically alone—at least those bound to Europe. Unfortunately, however, at no time did we have enough destroyers to provide escorts for all of these transports as fast as they were unloaded and ready to return to America, but as time in the " turn around " was the all-important consideration in getting the troops over, the transports were sent back through the submarine zone under the escort of armed yachts, and occasionally not escorted at all. Under these conditions the transports could be attacked with much less risk, as was shown by the fact that five were torpedoed, though of these happily only three were sunk.

III

The position of the German naval chiefs, as is shown by the quotation from General Ludendorff's book, was an extremely unhappy one. They had blatantly promised the German people that their submarines would prevent the transportation of American troops to Europe. At first they had ridiculed the idea that undisciplined, unmilitary America could ever organize an army ; after we adopted conscription and began to train our young men by the millions, they just as vehemently proclaimed that this army could never be landed in Europe. In this opinion the German military chieftains were not alone. No such army movement had ever before been attempted. The discouraging forecast made by a brilliant British naval authority in July, 1917, reflected the ideas of too many military people on both sides of the ocean. " I am distressed," he said, " at the fact that it appears to me to be impossible to provide enough shipping to bring the American army over in hundreds of thousands to France, and, after they are brought over, to supply the enormous amount of shipping which will be required to keep them full up with munitions, food, and equipment."

It is thus not surprising that the German people accepted as gospel the promises of their Admiralty ; therefore their anger was unbounded when American troops began to arrive. The German newspapers began to ask the most embarrassing questions. What had become of their sub-

marines ?   Had the German people not been promised that
their U-boats would sink any American troopships that
attempted to cross the ocean ?   As the shipments increased,
and as the effect of these vigorous fresh young troops began
to be manifest upon the Western Front, the outcries in
Germany waxed even more fierce and abusive.   Von
Capelle and other German naval chiefs made rambling
speeches in the Reichstag, once more promising their people
that the submarines would certainly win the war—speeches
that were followed by ever-increasing arrivals of American
soldiers in France.   The success of our transports led
directly to the fall of Von Capelle as Minister of Marine ;
his successor, Admiral von Mann, who was evidently
driven to desperation by the popular outburst, decided to
make one frantic attempt to attack our men.   The new
minister, of course, knew that he could accomplish no
definite results ; but the sinking of even one transport with
several thousand troops on board would have had a tremendous effect upon German *moral.*   When the great
British liner *Justicia* was torpedoed, the German Admiralty
officially announced that it was the *Leviathan,* filled with
American soldiers ; and the jubilation which followed in
the German press, and the subsequent dejection when it
was learned that this was a practically empty transport,
sailing westward, showed that an actual achievement of
this kind would have raised their drooping spirits.   Admiral
von Mann, therefore, took several submarines away from
the trade routes and sent them into the transport zone.
But they did not succeed even in attacking a single east-
bound troopship.   The only result accomplished was the
one which, from what I have already said, would have been
expected ; the removal of the submarines from the commercial lane caused a great fall in the sinking of merchant
ships.   In August, 1918, these sinkings amounted to
280,000 tons ; in September and October, when this futile
drive was made at American transports, the sinkings fell
to 190,000 and 110,000 tons.

Too much praise cannot be given to the commanders of
our troop convoys and the commanding officers of the troop
transports, as well as the commanders of the cruisers and
battleships that escorted them from America to the western
edge of the submarine zone.   The success of their valuable
services is evidence of a high degree not only of nautical

skill, judgment, and experience, but of the admirable seamanship displayed under the very unusual conditions of steaming without lights while continuously manœuvring in close formation. Moreover, their cordial co-operation with the escorts sent to meet them was everything that could be desired. In this invaluable service these commanding officers had the loyal and enthusiastic support of the admirable petty officers and men whose initiative, energy, and devotion throughout the war enabled us to accomplish results which were not only beyond our expectations but which demonstrated that they are second to none in the world in the qualities which make for success in war on the sea.

On the whole, the safeguarding of American soldiers on the ocean was an achievement of the American navy. Great Britain provided a slightly larger amount of tonnage for this purpose than the United States ; but about 82 per cent. of the escorting was done by our own forces. The cruiser escorts across the ocean to France were almost entirely American ; and the destroyer escorts through the danger zone were likewise nearly all our own work. And in performing this great feat the American navy fulfilled its ultimate duty in the war. The transportation of these American troops brought the great struggle to an end. On the battlefield they acquitted themselves in a way that aroused the admiration of their brothers in the naval service. When we were reading, day by day, the story of their achievements, when we saw the German battle lines draw nearer and nearer to the Rhine, and, finally, when the German Government raised its hands in abject surrender, the eighteen months' warfare against the German submarines, in which the American navy had been privileged to play its part, appeared in its true light—as one of the greatest victories against the organized forces of evil in all history.

THE END

APPENDIX I

OFFICIAL AUTHORIZATION TO PUBLISH "THE VICTORY AT SEA"

U.S. NAVAL WAR COLLEGE,
NEWPORT, RHODE ISLAND

14 June 1919.

From : Rear-Admiral Wm. S. Sims, U.S. Navy.
To : The Secretary of the Navy.
Subject : Requests Permission to Publish a Book on the Activities of the U.S. Navy during The Great War.
Reference (a) : Paragraph 1534 of the Articles for the Government of the Navy of the United States.

1. In accordance with the provisions of reference (a) I request authority to publish in my name a book descriptive of the activities of the U.S. Naval Forces operating in European waters during The Great War.

2. My object in preparing this book is to familiarize the American people with the great work accomplished by the Navy during the war. It will be a popular presentation written in a non-technical style, illustrated with photographs taken in Europe and various diagrams indicating the nature of our activities.

[s] WM. S. SIMS.

9 July 1919.
APPROVED.
[s] Josephus Daniels.

HWS-MEF   2nd Indorsement.
OFFICE OF NAVAL INTELLIGENCE,
Washington, D.C.

From : Director of Naval Intelligence.   11 July 1919.
To : President Naval War College.
    1. Forwarded.

[s] A. P. NIBLACK.

THE SECRETARY OF THE NAVY,
WASHINGTON

June 26, 1919.

MY DEAR ADMIRAL :
    I am sending you in the regular official course my approval of

your plan to print and publish a book relative to the operations of the naval forces under your command during the great war. I am happy that you are going to undertake this, because I am sure it will be of great value to the Navy and of interest to the world.

With sentiments of esteem and high regard,

Sincerely yours,

[s] JOSEPHUS DANIELS.

P.S.

Of course any facilities or assistance that the Navy Department can render you will be at your disposal.

Rear-Admiral W. S. Sims, U.S.N.,
President Naval War College,
Newport, Rhode Island.

Extract from Navy Regulations, 1913, Article 1534

" (2) No person belonging to the Navy or employed under the Navy Department shall publish or cause or permit to be published, directly or indirectly, or communicate by interviews, private letters, or otherwise, except as required by his official duties, any information in regard to the foreign policy of the United States, or concerning the acts or measures of any department of the Government or of any officer acting thereunder, or any comments or criticisms thereon ; or the text of any official instructions, reports, or letters upon any subject whatever, or furnish copies thereof to any person, without the express permission of the Navy Department.

" (4) Nothing in this article shall be construed as prohibiting officers from forwarding to the department, through official channels, well-considered comment and suggestions with a view to promoting the efficiency of the service and the public interests ; on the contrary, such suggestions are invited, but they should be in regard to things or methods and not a criticism of persons, and should in all cases be accompanied by a well-digested plan for improvement. Such suggestions, if approved by the department, will be entered on the officer's record and he will be duly notified to that effect."

FIRST CABLE MESSAGE TO WASHINGTON

To : Secretary of the Navy.

Sent April 14, 1917.

Through : State Department.

File No. 25-9-2.

The situation is as follows :

The submarine issue is very much more serious than the people realize in America. The recent success of operations and the rapidity of construction constitute the real crisis of the war. The *moral* of the enemy submarines is not broken, only about fifty-four are known to have been captured or sunk and no voluntary surrenders have been recorded. The reports of our press are greatly in error. Recent reports circulated concerning surrenders are simply to depreciate enemy *moral* and results are [not] very satisfactory.

Supplies and communications of forces all fronts, including the Russians, are threatened and control of the sea actually imperilled.

German submarines are constantly extending their operations into the Atlantic, increasing areas and the difficulty of patrolling. Russian situation critical. Baltic fleet mutiny, eighty-five admirals, captains, and commanders murdered, and in some armies there is insubordination.

The amount of British, neutral and Allied shipping lost in February was 536,000 tons, in March, 517,000 tons, and in the first ten days of April 205,000 tons. With short nights and better weather these losses are increasing.

The British forces could not effectively prevent the escape of some raiders during the long nights, but the chances are better now.

The Allies were notified that hospital ships will continue to be sunk, this in order to draw destroyers away from operations against submarines to convoy hospital ships ; in this way causing a large demand for large convoy forces in all areas not before necessary, and also partially immobilizing the main fleet.

On account of the immense theatre and the length and

number of lines of communication, and the material deterioration resulting from three years' continuous operation in distant fields with inadequate base facilities, the strength of the naval forces is dangerously strained. This applies to all of the sea forces outside of the Grand Fleet. The enemy has six large and sixty-four small submarine mine-layers; the latter carry eighteen mines and the former thirty-four, also torpedoes and guns. All classes submarines for actual commission completed at a rate approaching three per week. To accelerate and insure defeat of the submarine campaign immediate active co-operation absolutely necessary.

The issue is and must inevitably be decided at the focus of all lines of communications in the Eastern Atlantic, therefore I very urgently recommend the following immediate naval co-operation.

Maximum number of destroyers to be sent, accompanied by small anti-submarine craft; the former to patrol designated high seas area westward to Ireland, based on Queenstown, with an advance base at Bantry Bay, latter to be an inshore patrol for destroyers: small craft should be of light draft with as high speed as possible but low speed also useful. Also repair ships and staff for base. Oil and docks are available but I advise sending continuous supply of fuel. German main fleet must be contained, demanding maximum conservation of the British main fleet.   South of Scotland no base is so far available for this force.

At present our battleships can serve no useful purpose in this area, except that two divisions of dreadnoughts might be based on Brest for moral effect against anticipated raids by heavy enemy ships in the channel out of reach of the British main fleet.

The chief other and urgent practical co-operation is merchant tonnage and a continuous augmentation of anti-submarine craft to reinforce our advanced forces. There is a serious shortage of the latter craft. For towing the present large amount of sailing tonnage through dangerous areas sea-going tugs would be of great use.

The co-operation outlined above should be expedited with the utmost despatch in order to break the enemy submarine *moral* and accelerate the accomplishment of the chief American objective.

It is very likely the enemy will make submarine mine-laying raids on our coast or in the Caribbean to divert attention and to keep our forces from the critical areas in the Eastern Atlantic through effect upon public opinion. The difficulty of maintaining submarine bases and the focussing of shipping on this side will restrict such operations to minor importance, although they should be effectively opposed, principally by keeping the Channel swept on soundings. Enemy submarine mines have been anchored as deep as ninety fathoms but majority at not more than fifty fathoms. Mines do not rise from the bottom to set depth until from twenty-four to forty-eight hours after they have been laid.

So far all experience shows that submarines never lay mines out of sight of landmarks or lights on account of danger to themselves if location is not known. Maximum augmentation merchant tonnage and anti-submarine work where most effective constitute the paramount immediate necessity.

Mr. Hoover informs that there is only sufficient grain supply in this country for three weeks. This does not include the supply in retail stores. In a few days Mr. Hoover will sail for the United States.

SIMS.

APPENDIX III

FIRST DETAILED REPORT ON THE ALLIED
NAVAL SITUATION

LONDON, ENGLAND.
April 19, 1917.

From : Rear-Admiral Wm. S. Sims, U.S.N.
To : Secretary of the Navy.
Subject : Confirmation and elaboration of recent cablegrams
concerning War situation and recommendations for U.S.
Naval co-operation.

1. *Reception :*
My reception in this country has been exceptionally cordial
and significant of the seriousness of present situation and the
importance to be attached to the United States' entry into the
war.
I was met at Liverpool by Rear-Admiral Hope, R.N., a
member of Admiral Jellicoe's staff, and the Admiral of the Port,
the former having been sent by the Admiralty to escort me to
London. A special train was provided which made a record
run, and within a few hours after arrival in London I was
received by the First Sea Lord and his principal assistants in
a special conference.

2. *Conferences :*
More or less hesitancy was noted at first in presenting a full
statement of the true situation, particularly (as it developed
later) on account of its seriousness, combined with a natural
reluctance against appearing to seek assistance, and a hesitancy
in taking chances of allowing information indirectly to reach
the enemy, and thereby improve enemy *moral.*
I therefore positively took the position that I must be considered a part of the Admiralty organization, and that it was
essential to safe and efficient co-operation that I be trusted
with a full knowledge of the exact situation.
They finally consented, only after reference to the Imperial
War Council, to my exposing the true state of affairs both as

regards the military situation and rate of destruction of merchant shipping.

I have had daily conferences with the First Sea Lord, both at his office and residence, and also have been given entire freedom of the Admiralty and access to all Government Officials. I have freely consulted with such officials as the following :

Prime Minister.

First Lord of Admiralty (Sir Edward Carson).

Ministers of Munitions, Shipping, Trade, and other Cabinet officials.

First Sea Lord, and his assistants.

Chief of Naval Staff.

Directors (corresponding to our Chiefs of Bureaus) of Intelligence, Anti-submarine operations, Torpedoes, Mines, Mining, etc.

3. *General Statement of the Situation :*

Since the last declaration of the enemy Government, which from intelligence information was anticipated, the submarine campaign against merchant shipping of all Nations has resolved itself into the real issue of the war and, stated briefly, the Allied Governments have not been able to, and are not now, effectively meeting the situation presented.

4. As stated in my first despatch, the communications and supplies to all forces on all fronts, including Russian, are threatened, and the " Command of the Sea " is actually at stake.

5. My own views of the seriousness of the situation and the submarine menace have been greatly altered. My convictions and opinions, as probably those of the Department also, had been largely based upon Press reports and reports of our Attachés and other professional Americans who have been abroad during the War. All of this information has been either rigidly censored or else has been given out in such form that it would be of minimum assistance to enemy *moral.*

6. The necessity for secrecy, which the British Government has experienced, and which I repeatedly encounter in London, and even in the Admiralty itself, is impressive. There have been remarkable and unexpected leakages of information throughout the war. Certain neutral legations of smaller countries are now under strong suspicion.

7. The extent to which the submarine campaign is being waged is in itself excellent evidence of the importance attached to it by the enemy, and of the degree to which they counted, and still are counting, upon it.

The Intelligence Department has reliable information (as reliable as can be) that the enemy really reckoned that the Allies would be defeated in *two* months through shortage of supplies.

8. With improved weather and the shorter nights now coming on we may expect even more enemy submarine success.

9. The Commander-in-Chief of the Grand Fleet was yesterday in conference in the Admiralty as to what greater extent destroyers and auxiliaries of the Fleet may be utilized without endangering its power in the remote possibility of another fleet engagement.

The consensus of opinion seems to be that the latter will not occur, but there is not complete unanimity in this belief, and of course, in any case, the possibility must be adequately and continuously provided against.

General discussion of situation :

10. I delayed [four days] forwarding my first report of the situation with a view of obtaining the maximum information consistent with the importance of the time element. I was also somewhat deterred by a natural reluctance to alter so radically my preconceived views and opinions as to the situation.

11. The evidence is conclusive that, regardless of any enemy diversions such as raids on our coasts or elsewhere, the critical area in which the war's decision will be made is in the eastern Atlantic at the focus of all lines of communications.

The known number of enemy submarines and their rate of construction, allowing liberal factors for errors of information, renders it inevitable that the main submarine effort must continue to be concentrated in the above critical area.

12. Even in this critical area, it is manifest that the field is relatively large for the maximum number of submarines which the enemy can maintain in it. For example, with the present Admiralty policy (explained below) they are forced to cover all the possible trade routes of approach between the north of Scotland and Ushant.

13. From consideration of the above and all other essential information available, it is apparent that the enemy could not disperse his main submarine campaign into other quarters of the Globe without diminishing results in this and all areas to a degree which would mean failure to accomplish the Mission of the submarine campaign, which can be nothing else than a final decision of the war.

14. Considerable criticism has been, and still is, concentrated upon the Admiralty for not taking more effective steps and for failing to produce more substantial and visible results. One of the principal demands is for convoys of merchant shipping, and more definite and real protection within the war zone.

The answer, which manifestly is not publicly known, is simply that the necessary vessels are not available, and further that those which are available are suffering from the effects of three years of arduous service.

15. It is insistently asked (was asked by myself) why shipping is not directed to and concentrated at various rendezvous and from these convoyed through the dangerous areas. The answer is the same—the area is too large; the necessary vessels are not available.

16. However, I am now consulting with the Director of Shipping as to the practicability and advisability of attempting some approach to such a plan in case the United States is able to put in operation sufficient tonnage to warrant it.

17. After trying various methods of controlling shipping, the Admiralty now believes the best policy to be one of dispersion. They use about six relatively large avenues or arcs of approach to the United Kingdom and Channel, changing their limits or area periodically if necessity demands.

Generally speaking, one is to the north of Scotland, another to the north of Ireland, and three or four others covering the Irish Sea and Channel. Individual ships coming into any of these areas of approach are instructed, generally before sailing, to cross the twentieth meridian at certain and different latitudes and thence steer certain courses to port.

At times in the past they have found one of these avenues of approach free of submarines under such conditions as to lead them to concentrate shipping therein, but invariably the enemy has become aware of the course pursued.

18. The great difficulty in any method of shipping control is communication with the shipping itself and full co-operation by the merchant personnel. The moment a ship is captured the code either becomes dangerous or useless. The merchant code is being continually changed, and at all times it cannot be counted upon for more than a fortnight. The immense difficulty of changing the code and keeping shipping all over the world in touch with changes is apparent.

19. Continual trouble is experienced with some merchant Captains taking the law into their own hands and exhibiting contempt, or at least indifference, for Admiralty instructions. The American Liner *New York* upon which I took passage furnishes a typical example. She was instructed to make Fastnet Light at daylight but she passed it about nine P.M., thus passing in daylight through the most dangerous area.

20. The Admiralty has had frequent conferences with Merchant masters and sought their advice. Their most unanimous demand is " Give us a gun and let us look out for ourselves." They are also insistent that it is impracticable for merchant vessels to proceed in formation, at least in any considerable numbers, due principally to difficulty in controlling their speed and to the inexperience of their subordinate officers.

With this view I do not personally agree but believe that with a little experience merchant vessels could safely and sufficiently well steam in open formations.

21. The best protection against the submarine menace for all classes of ships, merchant as well as Naval, is **SPEED** and **ZIGZAGGING**, not more than fifteen minutes on a course. Upon this point no one disagrees, but on the contrary there is absolutely unanimity of opinion.

22. In the absence of adequate patrol craft, *particularly destroyers*, and until the enemy submarine *moral* is broken, there is but one sure method of meeting the submarine issue upon which there is also complete unanimity—increased number of merchant bottoms, preferably small.

" More Ships! More Ships! More Ships!" is heard on every hand.

23. It is also significant that until very recently the Admiralty have been unable completely to convince some members of the Cabinet that the submarine issue is the deciding factor in the War. The civilian mind, here as at home, is loath to believe in unseen dangers, particularly until the pinch is felt in real physical ways.

24. The Prime Minister only two days ago expressed to me the opinion that it ought to be possible to find physical means of absolutely sealing up all escape for submarines from their own ports. The fact that all such methods (nets, mines, obstructions, etc.) inherently involve the added necessity of continuous protection and maintenance by our own Naval forces is seldom understood and appreciated. I finally convinced the Prime Minister of the fallacy of such propositions by describing the situations into which we would be led : namely, that in order to maintain our obstructions we would have to match the forces the enemy brought against them, until finally the majority if not all of our forces would be forced into dangerous areas where they would be subject to continual torpedo and other attack, in fact in a position most favourable to the enemy.

25. Entirely outside of the fact that the enemy does, and always can, force exits, and thereby nullify the close blockade, the weather is a serious added difficulty. The heaviest anchors obtainable have been used for nets, mines, and obstructions, only to have the arduous work of weeks swept away in a few hours of heavy weather. Moorings will not hold. They chafe through. In this respect we could be of great assistance, i.e. in supply of moorings and buoys.

26. The Channel is not now, and never has been, completely sealed against submarine egress, let alone the vaster areas of escape to the north. Submarines have gone under mine-fields,

and have succeeded in unknown ways in evading and cutting through nets and obstructions.

27. In addition to submarines, heavy forces are free to raid, and in fact escape through, the Channel at any time when the enemy decides that the necessity or return will justify the risk. Hence the suggestion that two divisions of our fast Dreadnoughts might be based upon Brest, primarily for the resulting moral effect against such possible raids.

I was told yesterday by an important Admiralty official that while he thought the chances of raids in, or escape through, the Channel by heavy enemy forces out of reach of the Grand Fleet (North of Scotland) were very remote, nevertheless the possibility existed and was principally thwarted on moral grounds, that is, the uncertainty in his mind of the opposition which would be encountered. He agreed with others, including the First Sea Lord, that the addition of some of our heavy forces to those maintained in southern Channel approaches by the French and British would undoubtedly entirely preclude the possibility of such raids.

28. *Submarine Losses:*

It has been found necessary to accept *no* reports of submarine losses as authentic and certain unless survivors are captured or the submarine itself is definitely located by dragging. No dependence even is placed upon evidence of oil on the surface after a submarine has been attacked and forced down, as there is reason to believe that when an enemy submarine dives to escape gunfire she is fitted to expel oil for the particular purpose of conveying the impression that she has been sunk and thereby avoid further pursuit. It has been shown that the amount of damage a submarine can stand is surprising and much more than was anticipated before the experience of the war. Upon a recent occasion a British submarine was mistaken for an enemy and though struck by several shells, dived and escaped to port.

The submarine losses which are certain since outbreak of war are as given in attached cablegram.

It is estimated that between thirty and forty submarines operate at a time in the waters surrounding the British Islands and French Coast. At least one is now known to be on White Sea trade lanes.

29. *Best anti-submarine weapons:*

One of the most efficient weapons now used by all destroyers and patrol craft against submarines is the so-called " Depth Charge," sample and drawings of which have been forwarded by our Naval Attaché. These are merely explosive charges designed to explode at a certain depth, formerly eighty feet, now about one hundred feet. They are dropped overboard where a submarine that has submerged is assumed to be and are counted upon to badly shake up and demoralize if they do not actually cause serious damage.

Howitzers and Bomb-throwers of large calibre are under construction, designed to throw similar depth charges to distances of about 2,000 yards. Details will be forwarded.

30. *Torpedo Protection:*

This subject may be summed up by the statement of the Captain of a British Dreadnought who said in effect that after a year's experience he did not fear being sunk by a torpedo. Unless struck by several the worst to be anticipated is damage to shafts or rudder, thus necessitating towing. Cruisers have often been struck and been able to reach port. Vital watertight doors are kept continuously closed at sea.

Destroyer officers have been heard to express the curious opinion that the enemy ships were more or less unsinkable. This is probably to be explained by the fact that they carry very few supplies ; that they have their storage spaces compartmented or filled with wood or other water-excluding material ; and that when in port, they quarter their crews in barracks, and when leaving for a cruise carry the minimum amount of berthing and supply facilities. These points, however, are not positively known.

On the contrary, all vessels of the British Fleet must be kept fully supplied and fuelled at all times for extended cruising. This is particularly true of Battle-cruisers and Cruisers.

31. All officers of rank and actual experience consulted are convinced that the enemy have no unusual methods of protection, or in fact any " surprises " in ordnance or other fighting equipment.

32. All are agreed that the best protection against torpedoes is **SPEED** and **ZIGZAGGING**.

33. It is a common experience of the Naval as well as Merchant service that torpedo wakes are reported where none exist. Many reports are received of torpedoes barely missing ships. This was true in the Jutland Battle. The Captain on one Battleship said that he received numerous reports of torpedoes passing just ahead and just astern, nearly all of which he had reason to believe did not exist.

Streaks of suds, slicks, etc., are very deceiving and are easily mistaken for torpedo wakes, particularly when the danger of torpedoes is present. This accounts for many reports by passengers on liners and other merchant craft of seeing many torpedoes just miss their mark.

34. *Submarine versus Submarine:*

There has always been opposition to using submarines against submarines, principally on the grounds that the possibilities of their accomplishments would not be sufficiently great to justify the risk involved of mistaken identity and resulting damage to friends.

The Director of Anti-Submarine Warfare believes, however, that such operations promise well, and the experiment is now being tried with as many submarines as can be spared from the Grand Fleet. Some enemy submarines have been destroyed by this method, usually torpedoed. One valuable feature of this method lies in the fact that as long as our submarines are not so used, the enemy submarine is always perfectly safe in assuming that all submarines sighted are friends. If this certainty is removed the enemy will be forced to keep down more, and to take much greater precautions against detection. This is an advantage of no small account.

In addition to the possible offensive work that may be accomplished by our submarines on such duty, the plan furnishes us with more reliable information as to the limitations and capabilities of enemy vessels under the actual conditions existing in the areas in which they operate. Without this knowledge based on actual experience too much is left to conjecture which is liable to lead to a great deal of misdirected effort.

(Signed) WM. S. SIMS.

THE QUESTION OF ARMING MERCHANT SHIPS

To : Secretary of the Navy.
Through Admiralty.   From Queenstown.
Sent : June 28, 1917.
Admiralty for Secretary Navy Washington, providing it meets
  Admiralty's full approval.
From Admiral Sims.

Referring to Department's opinion, reported in last two
cables, to the effect that adequate armament and trained crews
constitute one of the most effective defensive anti-submarine
measures, I again submit with all possible stress the following
based on extended [Allied] war experience.   The measures
demanded, if enemy defeat in time is to be assured, are not
defensive but offensive defensive.   The merchantman's inherent
weakness is lack of speed and protection.   Guns are no defence
against torpedo attack without warning, which is necessarily
the enemy method of attack against armed ships.   In this area
alone during the last six weeks thirty armed ships were sunk
by torpedoes without submarine being seen, although three of
these were escorted each by a single destroyer.   The result
would of course have been the same no matter how many guns
these ships carried or what their calibre.   Three mystery ships,
heavily manned by expert naval crews with much previous
experience with submarine attack, have recently been torpedoed
without warning.   Another case within the month of mystery
ship engaging submarine with gunfire at six thousand yards
but submarine submerged and approached unseen and torpedoed ship at close range.   The ineffectiveness of heaviest
batteries against submarine attack is conclusively shown by
Admiralty's practice always sending destroyers to escort their
men-of-war.   The comparative immunity of the relatively
small number American ships, especially liners, is believed here
to be due to the enemy's hopes that the pacifist movement will
succeed.   Cases are on record of submarines making successful
gun attacks from advantageous sun position against armed

ships without ship being able to see submarine. I submit that if submarine campaign is to be defeated it must be by offensive measures. The enemy submarine mission must be destruction of shipping and avoidance of anti-submarine craft. Enemy submarines are now using for their final approach an auxiliary periscope less than two inches in diameter. This information just acquired. All of the experience in this submarine campaign to date demonstrates that it would be a seriously dangerous misapprehension to base our action on the assumption that any armament on merchantmen is any protection against submarines which are willing to use their torpedoes. The British have now definitely decided the adoption, to the maximum practicable extent, convoys from sixteen to twenty ships. This is an offensive measure against submarines, as the latter will be subject to the attack of our anti-submarine craft whenever they come within torpedoing distance of convoyed merchantmen. Moreover it permits of concentrated attack by our forces and obliges the enemy to disperse his forces to cover the various routes of approach.

Concerning Department's reference to a scheme for protection of merchant shipping which will not interfere with present escort duties, I submit that the time element alone prevents utilization of any new anti-submarine invention. The campaign may easily be lost before any such schemes can come into effective operation. The enemy is certainly counting on maximum effort being exerted before long nights and bad weather of autumn, that is, in next three months. Heaviest effort may be anticipated in July and August. I again submit that protection of our coastlines and of Allied shipping must necessarily be carried out in field of enemy activity if it is to be effective. The mission of the Allies must be to force submarines to give battle. Hence no operations in home waters should take precedence over, or be allowed to diminish, the maximum effort we can exert in area in which enemy is operating, and must continue to operate in order to succeed.

SIMS.

THE ADVANTAGES OF THE CONVOY SYSTEM

LONDON,
June 29, 1917.

From : Commander U.S. Naval Forces operating in European
  Waters.
To : Secretary of the Navy (Operations).
Subject : General report concerning military situation.

1. I feel that there is little to add to my recent cable despatches which, in view of the importance of the time element,
have been made full and detailed.

2. To sum up my despatches briefly, I would repeat that I
consider that the military situation is very grave indeed on
account of the success of the enemy submarine campaign.

If the shipping losses continue as they have during the past
four months, it is submitted that the Allies will be forced to
dire straits indeed, if they will not actually be forced into an
unsatisfactory peace.

The present rate of destruction is very much greater than the
rate of building, and the shortage of tonnage is already so great
that the efficiency of the naval forces is already reduced by
lack of oil. Orders have just been given to use three-fifths
speed, except in cases of emergency. This simply means that
the enemy is winning the war.

3. My reasons for being so insistent in my cable despatches
have been because of my conviction that measures of co-
operation which we may take will be inefficient if they are not
put into operation immediately, that is, within a month.

There is every reason to believe that the maximum enemy
submarine effort will occur between now and the first of
November, reaching its height probably during the latter part
of July, if not earlier.

4. There is certainly no sovereign solution for the submarine
menace except through well-established methods of warfare
based upon fundamental military principles.

5. It is submitted that the cardinal military principle of

concentration of effort is at present being pursued by the enemy and not by the Allies.

6. We are dispersing our forces while the enemy is concentrating his. The enemy's submarine mission is and must continue to be the destruction of merchant shipping. The limitations of submarines and the distances over which they must operate prevent them from attacking our naval forces, that is, anti-submarine craft. They cannot afford to engage anti-submarine craft with guns ; they must use torpedoes. If they should do so to any considerable extent their limited supply would greatly reduce their period of operation away from base, and the number of merchantmen they could destroy. Their object is to avoid contact with anti-submarine craft. This they can almost always do, as the submarine can see the surface craft at many times the distance the surface craft can see a periscope, particularly one less than two inches in diameter.

Moreover, the submarine greatly fears the anti-submarine craft because of the great danger of the depth charges. Our tactics should therefore be such as to force the submarine to incur this danger in order to get within range of merchantmen.

7. It therefore seems to go without question that the only course for us to pursue is to revert to the ancient practice of convoy. This will be purely an offensive measure, because if we concentrate our shipping into convoys and protect it with our naval forces we will thereby force the enemy, in order to carry out his mission, to encounter naval forces which are not embarrassed with valuable cargoes, and which are a great danger to the submarine. At present our naval forces are wearing down their personnel and material in an attempted combination of escorting single ships, when they can be picked up, and also of attempting to seek and offensively engage an enemy whose object is to avoid such encounters. With the convoy system the conditions will be reversed. Although the enemy may easily know when our convoys sail, he can never know the course they will pursue or the route of approach to their destinations. Our escorting forces will thus be able to work on a deliberate prearranged plan, preserving their oil supplies and energy, while the enemy will be forced to disperse his forces and seek us. In a word, the handicap we now labour under will be shifted to the enemy ; we will have adopted the essential principal of concentration while the enemy will lose it.

8. The most careful and thorough study of the convoy system made by the British Admiralty shows clearly that while we may have some losses under this system, owing to lack of adequate number of anti-submarine craft, they nevertheless will not be critical as they are at present.

9. I again submit that if the Allied campaign is to be viewed

as a whole, there is no necessity for any high sea protection on our own coast. The submarine as a type of war vessel possesses no unusual characteristics different from those of other naval craft, with the single exception of its ability to submerge for a limited time. The difficulty of maintaining distant bases is the same for the submarine as it is for other craft. As long as we maintain control of the sea as far as surface craft are concerned, there can be no fear of the enemy establishing submarine bases in the Western Hemisphere.

10. To take an extreme illustration, if the enemy could be led or forced into diverting part of his submarine effort to the United States coast, or to any other area distant from the critical area surrounding the coast of France and the United Kingdom, the anti-submarine campaign would at once be won. The enemy labours under severe difficulties in carrying out his campaign, even in this restricted area, owing to the material limitations and the distances they must operate from their bases, through extremely dangerous localities. The extent of the United States coastline and the distances between its principal commercial ports preclude the possibility of any submarine effort in that part of the world except limited operations of diversion designed to affect public opinion, and thereby hold our forces from the vital field of action.

11. The difficulties confronting the convoy system are, of course, considerable. They are primarily involved in the widely dispersed ports of origin of merchant shipping; the difficulty of communication by cable; the time involved by communications by mail; and the difficulties of obtaining a co-operation and co-ordination between Allied Governments.

As reported by cable despatch, the British Government has definitely reached the decision to put the convoy system into operation as far as its ability goes. Convoys from Hampton Roads, Canada, Mediterranean, and Scandinavian countries are already in operation. Convoys from New York will be put in operation as soon as ships are available. The British navy is already strained beyond its capacity, and I therefore urgently recommend that we co-operate, at least to the extent of handling convoys from New York.

12. The dangers to convoys from high sea raiders is remote, but, of course, must be provided against, and hence the necessity for escorting cruisers or reserve battleships. The necessity is even greater, however, for anti-submarine craft in the submarine war zone.

13. As stated in my despatches, the arming of merchantmen is not a solution of the submarine menace, it serves the single purpose of forcing the submarine to use torpedoes instead of guns and bombs. The facts that men-of-war cannot proceed

safely at sea without escort, and that in the Queenstown avenue of approach alone in the past six weeks there have been thirty armed merchantmen sunk, without having seen the submarine at all before the attack, seem to be conclusive evidence. A great mass of other evidence and war experience could be collected in support of the above.

14. The week ending June 19th has been one of great submarine activity. Evidence indicates that fifteen to nineteen of the largest and latest submarines have been operating, of which ten to thirteen were operating in the critical area to the west and south-west of the British Isles. The above numbers are exclusive of the smaller and earlier type of submarines, and submarines carrying mines alone. Two submarines are working to the westward of the Straits of Gibraltar. A feature of the week was the sinking of ships as far west as nineteen degrees. Three merchant ship convoys are en route from Hampton Roads, the last one, consisting of eighteen ships, having sailed on the 19th of June. One hundred and sixteen moored mines have been swept up during the week.

Twenty-two reports of encounters with enemy submarines in waters surrounding the United Kingdom have been reported during the week—three by destroyers, two by cruisers, two by mystery ships, one by French gunboat, three by submarines, nine by auxiliary patrol vessels, one by seaplane, and one by merchant vessel.

There is attached copy of report of operations by anti-submarine craft based on Queenstown.

(Signed) WM. S. SIMS.

THE NAVY DEPARTMENT'S POLICY

From : Secretary of Navy.
To : Vice-Admiral Sims, U.S.S. *Melville*.
Received : July 10, 1917.

The following letter from the Secretary to the Secretary of State is quoted for your information and guidance as an index of the policy of the Department in relation to the co-operation of our naval forces with those of our Allies. Quote : After careful consideration of the present naval situation taken in connection with possible future situations which might arise, the Department is preparing to announce as its policy, in so far as it relates to the Allies. First, the most hearty co-operation with the Allies to meet the present submarine situation in European or other waters compatible with an adequate defence of our own home waters. Second, the most hearty co-operation with the Allies to meet any future situation arising during the present war period. Third, the realization that while a successful termination of the present war must always be the first Allied aim, and will probably result in diminished tension throughout the world, the future position of the United States must in no way be jeopardized by any disintegration of our main fighting fleet. Fourth, the conception that the present main military rôle of the United States naval force lies in its safeguarding the line of communications of the Allies. In pursuing this aim there will be generally speaking two classes of vessels engaged : minor craft and major craft, and two rôles of action, first, offensive and, second, defensive. Fifth, in pursuing the rôle set forth in paragraph four, the Department cannot too strongly insist on its opinion that the offensive must always be the dominant note in any general plans of strategy prepared. But as the primary rôle in all offensive preparations must perforce belong to the Allied powers, the Navy Department announces as its policy that in general it is willing to accept any joint plan of action of the Allies deemed necessary to meet immediate need. Sixth, pursuant to the above general policy, the Navy Department announces as its general plan of action the following : One, its willingness to send its minor fighting forces, composed of destroyers, cruisers, submarine chasers, auxiliaries in any number not incompatible with home needs, and to any field of action deemed expedient by the joint Allied Admiralties which would not involve a violation of our present state policy. Two, its unwillingness as a matter of policy to separate any division from the main fleet for service abroad, although it is willing to send the entire battleship fleet abroad to act as a united but co-operating unit when, after joint consultations of all Admiralties concerned, the emergency is deemed to warrant it and the extra tension imposed upon the line of communications due to the increase of fighting ships in European waters will stand the strain imposed upon it. Three, its willingness to discuss more fully plans for joint operations. End of Quote 11009.

(Sd) JOSEPHUS DANIELS.

APPENDIX VII

COMMENTS UPON NAVY DEPARTMENT'S POLICY

Office Vice-Admiral, Commanding
U.S. Destroyer Forces
European Waters.

LONDON,
July 16, 1917.

From : Vice-Admiral Sims.
To : Secretary of the Navy.
Subject : Concerning Policy of U.S. Naval co-operation in war, and allied subjects.

1. The Department's cablegram of July 10, 1917, quoting a letter which had been addressed to the Secretary of State concerning naval policy in relation to the present war, was received on July 10th.

In view of the nature of certain parts of the policy set forth therein, I wish to indicate the general policy which has heretofore governed my recommendation.

2. I have assumed that our mission was to promote the maximum co-operation with the Allies in defeating a common enemy.

All of my despatches and recommendations have been based on the firm conviction that the above mission could and would be accomplished, and that hence such questions as the possibility of post war situations, or of all or part of the Allies being defeated and America being left alone, were not given consideration—in fact, I cannot see how we could enter into this war whole-heartedly if such considerations were allowed to diminish in any way the chances of Allied success.

3. The first course open to us which naturally occurs to mind is that we should look upon our service as part of the combined Allied service, of which the British Grand Fleet is the main body, and all other Allied naval forces disposed throughout the world, as necessary branches thereof.

This conception views our battleship fleet as a support or reserve of the Allied main body (the British Grand Fleet) and would lead to utilizing our other forces to fill in weak spots and to strengthen Allied lines, both offensively and defensively, wherever necessary.

Such a course might be considered as a disintegration of our fleet, and it is only natural, therefore, that hesitation and caution should be felt in its adoption.

4. I have felt, however, that it was possible to accomplish our mission without in any way involving the so-called disintegration of our fleet as a whole.

In the first instance I have assumed that our aim would be to project, or prepare to project, our maximum force against the enemy offensively.

5. An estimate of the situation shows clearly that the enemy is depending for success upon breaking down the Allies' lines of communications by virtue of the submarine campaign.

A necessary part of such a plan is to divert strength from the main fleet and from anti-submarine operations by such means as coastal raids, threats of landing operations, air raids, and attacks on hospital ships, which last necessitates destroyer escort for such vessels.

The submarine campaign itself, while it is of necessity concentrated primarily on the most vital lines of communications, is nevertheless carried out in such a manner as to lead the Allies to disperse, and not concentrate, their inadequate anti-submarine Forces.

The Allies are, of course, forced to contemplate at all times, and hence provide against, the possibility of another main fleet action.

6. A study of the submarine situation, the number of submarines available to the enemy, and the necessary lines of the Allies' communications, for both Army and Navy as well as civil needs, shows clearly that the enemy must direct his main effort in certain restricted areas.

These areas, as has repeatedly been reported, are included approximately in a circle drawn from about Ushant to the north of Scotland. The most effective field for enemy activity is, of course, close into the Irish Sea and Channel approaches, where all lines must focus.

But, as stated above, the enemy also attacks occasionally well out to sea and in other dispersed areas with a view of scattering the limited anti-submarine forces available.

It therefore seems manifest that the war not only is, but must remain, in European waters, in so far as success or failure is concerned.

7. Speaking generally, but disregarding for the moment the question of logistics, our course of action, in order to throw our main strength against the enemy, would be to move all our forces, including the battleship fleet, into the war area.

8. In view of the nature of the present sea warfare as effected by the submarine, such a movement by the battleships would necessitate a large force of light craft—much larger than our peace establishment provided. In addition to all destroyers, adequate protection of the fleet would require all other available light craft in the service, or which could be commandeered and put into service—that is, submarines, armed tugs, trawlers, yachts, torpedo boats, revenue cutters, mine-layers and mine-sweepers, and in fact any type of small craft which could be used as protective or offensive screens.

9. In view of the shipping situation, as affected by the submarine campaign, it has been impossible to date to see in what way our battleships could be supplied in case they were sent into the war area. This refers particularly to oil-burning vessels. It would therefore seem unwise to recommend such a movement until we could see clearly far enough ahead to ensure the safety of the lines of communication which such a force would require.

10. It is to be observed, however, that even in case the decision were made to move the battleships into the war area, it would unavoidably be greatly delayed both in getting together the necessary screening forces and also in getting such craft across the Atlantic.

In the meantime, and while awaiting a decision as to the movements of the battleship fleet, the submarine campaign has become so intensive, and the available anti-submarine craft have been so inadequate to meet it, that the necessity for increasing the anti-submarine forces in the war area to the maximum possible extent has become imperative.

11. As long, therefore, as the enemy fleet is contained by the stronger British fleet in a position of readiness, it would not seem a disintegration of our fleet to advance into the war area all the light craft of every description which would necessarily have to accompany the fleet in case it should be needed in this area.

Such movements of the light craft would not in any way separate them strategically from the battleships, as they would be operating between the enemy and our own main body and based in a position to fall back as the main body approached, or to meet it at an appointed place. This advance of light forces, strategically, would mean no delay whatever to our heavy forces, should the time come for their entry into the active war zone.

12. Another very important consideration is the fact that, pending the movement of the battleships themselves, all of the light forces would be gaining valuable war experience and would be the better prepared for operations of any nature in

the future, either in connection with the fleet itself or independently.

It is also considered that it would not constitute a disintegration of our fleet to advance into the war zone, in co-operation with the British Grand Fleet or for other duty, certain units of our battleship fleet. These would merely constitute units advanced for purpose of enemy defeat, and which would always be in a position to fall back on the main part of our Fleet, or to join it as it approached the war zone.

It is for this reason that I recommended, on July 7, 1917, that all coal-burning dreadnoughts be kept in readiness for distant service in case their juncture with the Grand Fleet might be deemed advisable in connection with unexpected enemy developments.

It would, of course, be preferable to advance the entire fleet providing adequate lines of communications could be established to ensure their efficient operation. At the present time there is a sufficient coal supply in England to supply our coal-burning dreadnoughts, but the oil would be a very difficult problem as it must be brought in through the submarine zone.

When notified that the *Chester, Birmingham,* and *Salem* were available for duty in the war area, I recommended, after consultation with the Admiralty, that they join the British Light Cruiser Squadrons in the North Sea, where there is always a constant demand for more ships, especially to oppose enemy raiding and other operations aimed at dispersing the Allied sea forces.

In view of the Department's reference to the Gibraltar situation, and also in consideration of the sea-keeping qualities of the seven gunboats of the *Sacramento* class, it was recommended that they be based on Gibraltar for duty in assisting to escort convoys clear of the Straits, and particularly as this would release some British destroyers which are urgently needed in critical areas to the northward.

13. The Department's policy, as contained in its letter to the Secretary of State, refers in the first statement to an adequate defence of our own home waters. It would seem to be sound reasoning that the most effective defence which can be afforded to our home waters is an offensive campaign against the enemy which threatens those waters. Or in other words, that the place for protection of home waters is the place in which protection is necessary—that is, where the enemy is operating and must continue to operate in force.

As has been stated in numerous despatches, it is considered that home waters are threatened solely in the submarine zone—in fact are being attacked solely in that zone, and must continue to be attacked therein if the enemy is to succeed against us as well as against the European Entente.

The number of available enemy submarines is not unlimited, and the difficulties of obtaining and maintaining bases are fully as difficult for submarine as for surface craft.

The difficulties experienced by enemy submarines en route and in operating as far from their bases as they now do are prodigious.

Operations on our coast without a base are impracticable, except by very limited numbers for brief periods, purely as diversions.

In view of our distance from enemy home bases, the extent of our coastline, and the distances between our principal ports, it is a safe assumption that if we could induce the enemy to shift the submarine war area to our coasts his defeat would be assured, and his present success would be diminished more than in proportion to the number of submarines he diverted from the more accessible area where commerce necessarily focuses.

14. The Department's policy refers to willingness to extend hearty co-operation to the Allies, and to discuss plans for joint operations, and also to its readiness to consider any plans which may be submitted by the joint Allied Admiralties.

15. I submit that it is impossible to carry out this co-operation, to discuss plans with the various Admiralties, except in one way—and that is, to establish what might be termed an advance headquarters in the war zone composed of Department representatives upon whose recommendations the Department can depend.

I refer to exactly the same procedure as is now carried out in the army—that is, the General Headquarters in the field being the advance headquarters of the War Department at home, and the advance headquarters must of necessity be left a certain area of discretion and freedom of action as concerns the details of the measures necessitated by the military situations as they arise.

16. The time element is one of the most vital of all elements which enter into military warfare, and hence delays in communications by written reports, together with the necessity for secrecy, render it very difficult to discuss plans at long range. The enemy secret service has proved itself to be of extraordinary efficiency.

Moreover, I believe it to be very unsafe to depend upon discussion of military plans by cable, as well as by letter. The necessary inadequacy of written or cable communications needs no discussion. The opportunities for misunderstandings are great. It is difficult to be sure that one has expressed clearly one's meaning in writing, and hence phrases in a letter are very liable to misinterpretation. They cannot explain themselves.

17. One of the greatest military difficulties of this war, and perhaps of all Allied wars, has been the difficulty of co-ordination and co-operation in military effort. I am aware of a great mass of information in this connection which it is practically impossible to impart except by personal discussion.

It is unquestionable that efficiency would be greatly improved if *any one* of the Allies—Italy, France, England, or the United States—were selected to direct all operations, the others merely keeping the one selected fully informed of their resources available, and submitting to complete control and direction in regard to the utilization of these resources.

18. If the above considerations are granted, it then becomes necessary to decide as to the best location in which to establish such advanced headquarters, or what might be called an advance branch war council at the front—that is, an advanced branch upon whose advice and decisions the War Council itself largely depends.

I fully realize the pressure and the influences which must have been brought to bear upon the Department from all of the Allies, and from various and perhaps conflicting sources.

I also realize that my position here in England renders me open to suspicion that I may be unduly influenced by the British viewpoint of the war. It should be unnecessary to state that I have done everything within my ability to maintain a broad viewpoint with the above stated mission constantly in mind.

19. From the *naval* point of view it would seem evident that London is the best and most central location in the war area for what I have termed above the Advance Branch of our Naval War Council.

The British navy, on account of its size alone, is bearing the brunt of the naval war, and hence all naval information concerning the war therefore reaches and centres in London.

It will be quite possible for all of our advanced headquarters staff, or parts or divisions thereof, to visit Paris and other Allied Admiralties at any time.

I wish to make it quite clear that up to date it has been wholly impossible for me, with one military Aide, to perform all of the functions of such an advanced branch of the Department.

As stated in my despatches, it has been evident for some time that I have been approaching a state in which it would be physically impossible to handle the work without an increase of staff.

The present state of affairs is such that it is quite within range of possibility for serious errors to occur which may involve disaster to our ships, due to the physical impossibility of handling the administrative and other work with the thoroughness which is essential to safety.

20. I consider that a very minimum staff which would be required is approximately as follows. More officers could be well employed with resulting increase of efficiency :

(1) One Chief of Staff, who should be free to carry on a continuous estimate of the situation, based upon all necessary information. He would be given the freedom of the Operations Department of the British and French Admiralties.

(2) An officer, preferably of the rank of commander, for duties in connection with shipping and convoy to handle all the numerous communications in relation to the movements of American shipping, particularly military shipping, and also other shipping carrying American troops.

(3) An officer, at least a lieutenant-commander, for duties in connection with Anti-Submarine Division operations in order to insure perfect co-operation in that field of work between our service and other Allied Services.

(4) An officer of all-round ability and discretion for duties in connection with general military intelligence. He should be in constant touch with the Secret Service Departments of the Admiralties to insure that all military intelligence, which in any way affects the Navy Department or our Forces, is properly and promptly acted upon.

(5) At least two lieutenants or lieutenant-commanders of the line in my own office in connection with general administrative questions in addition to the one now available. The necessity for these additional officers is imperative.

(6) One communication officer to take general charge of codes and communications both with the Department at home, the Allied Admiralties, and with the various bases of our Forces in the war area. (At present Queenstown, Brest, Bordeaux, St. Nazaire, London, and Paris.)

(7) A paymaster to have complete charge of all financial matters connected with our naval organization abroad. This officer should be in addition to Paymaster Tobey, who is performing necessary and invaluable service on my staff in connection with all logistic questions.

(Signed) WM. S. SIMS.

APPENDIX VIII

MONTHLY LOSSES SINCE FEBRUARY, 1917, FROM ENEMY ACTION

During the twenty-one months of unrestricted submarine warfare from February, 1917, to October, 1918, inclusive, 3,843 merchant vessels (British fishing vessels included) of a total gross tonnage of 8,478,947 have been sunk by enemy action, a monthly average of 183 vessels totalling 403,760 gross tons. The October tonnage losses show a decrease from this average of 291,333 gross tons, or 72 per cent.

The following gives the tonnage losses by months from February, 1917, to October, 1918, inclusive :

Period.	British Merchant Vessels.	Other Allied Merchant Vessels.	Neutral Merchant Vessels.	British Fishing Vessels.	Total.
1917					
February	313,486	84,820	135,090	3,478	536,334
March	353,478	81,151	165,225	3,586	603,440
April	545,282	134,448	189,373	5,920	875,023
May	352,289	102,960	137,957	1,448	594,654
June	417,925	126,171	139,229	1,342	684,667
July	364,858	111,683	70,370	2,736	549,647
August	329,810	128,489	53,018	242	511,559
September	196,212	119,086	29,941	245	345,484
October	276,132	127,932	54,432	227	458,723
November	173,560	87,646	31,476	87	292,769
December	253,087	86,981	54,047	413	394,528

Period.	British Merchant Vessels.	Other Allied Merchant Vessels.	Neutral Merchant Vessels.	British Fishing Vessels.	Total.
1918					
January	179,973	87,078	35,037	375	302,463
February	226,896	54,904	36,374	686	318,860
March	199,458	94,321	51,035	293	345,107
April	215,453	50,879	11,361	241	277,934
May	192,436	80,826	20,757	504	294,523
June	162,990	51,173	38,474	639	253,276
July	165,449	70,900	23,552	555	260,456
August	145,721	91,209	41,946	1,455	280,331
September	136,864	39,343	10,393	142	186,742
October	57,607	41,308	13,512	—	112,427

APPENDIX IX

TONNAGE CONSTRUCTED BY ALLIED AND NEUTRAL NATIONS SINCE AUGUST, 1914

Construction of merchant shipping is shown in the following table, which gives tonnage completed since the beginning of the war for the United Kingdom, United States, and for other Allied and Neutral Nations.

Period.	United Kingdom. Gross tons.	United States. Gross tons.	Other Allied and Neutral. Gross tons.	World Total. Gross tons.
1914 . . .	675,610	120,000[1]	217,310	1,012,920
1915 . . .	650,919	225,122	325,959	1,202,000
1916 . . .	541,552	325,413	821,036	1,688,000
1917 . . .	1,163,474	1,034,296	505,585	2,703,355
1918 1st quarter .	320,280	328,541	220,496	869,317
2nd ,, .	442,966	559,939	240,369	1,243,274
3rd ,, .	411,395	834,250	232,127	1,477,772
October . .	136,100	357,532[1]	50,000	543,632
1918 (10 months) .	1,310,741	2,080,262	742,992	4,133,995

[1] Estimated.

INDEX

MacDonnell, Lt. - Commr. E. O., in charge of flying Caproni bombers from Italy to Flanders, 285

MacDougall, Capt. W. D., at London headquarters, 204

McBride, Capt. L. B., at London headquarters, 212, 214

McCalla, Capt., meets Adm. Jellicoe in China, 44

McCormick, E. H., volunteers services at London headquarters, 206

McCullough, Commr. Richard P., recommended for decoration, 136

McDougal, in first American destroyer contingent, 42; highly commended, 139

McDowell, Commr. Clyde S., work on listening devices, 178

McGrann, Commr. W. H., at London headquarters, 212

McNamee, Capt. L., at London headquarters, 215

McVay, Capt. C. B., commanding the *Oklahoma*, 305

Magruder, Rear-Adm. T. P., good work in convoying subchasers, 178

Mannix, Commr. D. Pratt, with mine-laying squadron, 264

Marshall, Capt. A. W., with mine-laying squadron, 264

Mary Rose, welcomes American destroyers at Queenstown, 41

Massachusetts, converted as mine-layer, 254

Melville, "Mother Ship" of the destroyers at Queenstown, 58, 62

Millard, H., volunteers services at London headquarters, 206

Milner, Lord, on convoy system, 95

Mine barrage, at first not effective against submarines, 20, 24

Mine barrage in North Sea, American, 245; immensity of, 252; how laid, 257

Mine laying by German submarines, 51, 273, 274

Mines, Americans perfect new type, 250; immense organization of supply and transport, 252

Moewe, commerce raider, 95

Murfin, Capt. Orin G., designer and builder of mine-assembly bases in Scotland, 256

Mystery ships, greatly aid in combating the submarine, 103; accompanying convoy, 118; method of operating, 118; operations of, 142; technique, 148; difficulty of identifying, 151; number in operation, 152; heroic fight of the *Dunraven*, 157; exploit of *Prize*, 165; American ship *Santee*, 166; *Stockforce* destroys submarine, 183

Nautilus, submarine of Robert Fulton, 226

Naval guns, German, bombarding Dunkirk and Paris, 290

Naval guns, U.S., used on the Western Front, 289

Nelson, Capt. C. P., good work in convoying subchasers, 178; commanding subchaser squadrons at Corfu, 194; in bombardment of Durazzo, 199, 200

Neptune attacked by *U-29*, 84, 85

Nevada, guarding transports, 304

New York, on duty with Grand Fleet, 303

Niblack, Rear-Adm. Albert P., commanding forces at Gibraltar, 134; asks that subchasers be sent to Gibraltar, 195

Nicholson, in submarine chase, 123; on convoy duty, 129; assists *Fanning* in capture of submarine and crew, 130; highly commended, 139

Noma, goes to relief of sinking mystery ship *Dunraven*, 163

Northern Bombing Group, established, 284, 285

O'Brien, highly commended, 163

Oil, scarcity of, for Great Britain's fleet, 34

Oklahoma, guarding transports, 305

Orama, torpedoed, 125

Ostend, bombing of submarine base at, 285

Otranto barrage, the, 181, 195

Page, Ambassador Walter Hines, asks that high naval representative be sent to England, 1; states that England faces defeat by submarines, 8; on critical submarine situation, 38; advised of submarine peril, 52; a tower of strength, 207

Pargust, "mystery ship," destroys submarine, 147

Parker, in hunt for submarine, 119; highly commended, 139; supporting ship for subchasers at Plymouth, 182; seriously damages the *U-53*, 189

Pauillac, France, U.S. aviation centre at, 284

Pennsylvania, transmits mobilization orders to destroyer division, 42

Pershing, Gen., request for naval guns at St. Nazaire, 290; report of their skilful use, 293

Pescara, Italy, U.S. seaplane station at, 284

Pisa, in attack on Durazzo, 199

Pitt, William, early opinion of the submarine, 226

Planning Section at London headquarters, 215

Pleadwell, Capt. F. L., at London headquarters, 212

Plunkett, Adm. Charles P., commanding naval guns on Western Front, 289; aids in designing mobile railway batteries, 290

Plymouth, subchaser base at, 182

Pocahontas, converted from German liner to transport, 302

Porter, in first American destroyer contingent, 42

Porto Corsini, Italy, U.S. seaplane station at, 284

Poteet, Lt.-Commr. Fred H., with first American destroyer contingent, 42

Potter, Ensign Stephen, fight with enemy seaplane, 288

Powell, Lt.-Commr. Halsey, of destroyer *Parker*, 119; highly commended, 139

Princess Irene, converted into transport, 302

Pringle, Capt. J. R. P., at Queenstown, 58; commended by Adm. Bayly, 139

Prize, mystery ship, damages submarine and captures captain and two of crew, 165

Q-ships, *see* Mystery ships